This classic study of the ethics of Jean-P
Sartre, written in 1947, remains one of the
best introductions to Sartre's philosophy a
to French existentialism, as it developed in
the post-World War II era. It is the only
commentary on his thought that Sartre himself ever fully recommended. Jeanson focuses on the doctrine of existentialist
morality, which he believes to be inherent,
although not articulated, in the works of
Sartre. He presents a perceptive explication
of the relationship between freedom, action,
and morality in Sartre's major writings, particularly *Being and Nothingness.* In his 1965
postface, "Somebody Called Sartre," Jeanson offers the fruits of eighteen years of
close work and association with Sartre.
Robert V. Stone's introduction provides vital
insights into this relationship and also into
Sartre's more recent thinking on ethics. In
view of the continuing strong interest in this
subject among modern philosophers, *Sartre
and the Problem of Morality,* long esteemed by
students of Sartre's thought, will be a timely

addition to philosophy collections. Stone's
precise and fluid translation makes Jeanson's work accessible to students as well as to
readers generally interested in the problems
of existentialism.

Sartre and the Problem of Morality

Studies in Phenomenology and
Existential Philosophy

SARTRE

and the

Problem of Morality

FRANCIS JEANSON

Translated from the French and with an Introduction by
Robert V. Stone

Indiana University Press • Bloomington

To C. C.

Published in French as *Le problème moral et la pensée de Sartre*,
© Editions du Seuil, 1965

Manufactured in the United States of America

Library of Congress Cataloging in Publication Data

Jeanson, Francis, 1922–
    Sartre and the problem of morality.

    (Studies in phenomenology and existential
philosophy)
    Translation of Le problème moral et la pensée de
Sartre.
    Includes bibliographical references.
    1. Sartre, Jean Paul, 1905–   —Ethics.
2. Existential ethics. I. Stone, Robert V.,
1938–   II. Title.
B2430.S34J413 1980   194   80–7807
ISBN 0–253–16603–9   1 2 3 4 5 84 83 82 81 80

Tranquility is a dishonesty of the soul.

TOLSTOY

CONTENTS

TRANSLATOR'S INTRODUCTION

FRANCIS JEANSON's *Le Problème moral et la pensée de Sartre* was published in Paris by Editions du Seuil in 1965. The text was preceded by a letter-foreword by Jean-Paul Sartre and was followed by Jeanson's "Postface 1965: Un Quidam nommé Sartre" ("Somebody called Sartre"). Except for the added postface, this book, here translated, was an unchanged reissue of the original *Le Problème moral*, published by the now defunct Editions du Myrte in 1947.

World War II was then not three years over. Existentialism had surfaced as Marxism's competitor among French youth for philosophical articulation of the Nazi occupation experience. During these years traditional authorities had provided no guidance (that is, until the Communist party committed itself to the Resistance one year into the occupation). Yet existentialism's faith in the liberating potential in individual freedom had been confirmed by Resistance militants who maintained solidarity with their comrades under isolated torture as "communists." "A republic of silence" Sartre had called it.[1] This travail accelerated France's history. After the Liberation Camus's newspaper, *Combat*, emerged with the hopeful masthead slogan "From Resistance to Revolution" and de Beauvoir, Merleau-Ponty, Sartre, and others founded *Les Temps modernes*, a review devoted to a literature of free commitment. These writers were lumped together by existentialist faddists, who saved themselves some study by assuming that existentialism held individual freedom was already complete and forever absurd. Borrowing criticisms from the right, Communists condemned the movement as petty bourgeois decadence. Neither Christian nor Communist writers wanted existentialist converts to the working class's side: compared with Thomism, existentialism simply couldn't be called a philosophy, Luc-J. Lefèvre had argued,[2] and compared with Stalinism, Henri Lefebvre found, it was locked in prewar narcissism.[3]

Faced with this "complete mental jumble," Jeanson, a twenty-five-year-old veteran forced by tuberculosis to abandon philosophical studies after the *diplôme d'études supérieures*, wrote *Sartre and the Problem of Morality* in four months beginning in January 1947, with no personal contact with Sartre. It was the first careful study of French existentialism and remains one of the best introductions to Sartre's philosophy. This book is the only detailed interpretation of his work that Sartre has ever fully recommended to readers. Immediately successful because of its merits and Sartre's strong letter-foreword—written after reading the completed manuscript[4]—the work launched Jeanson's writing career. Sartre has written similar letter-forewords but not to any other independent "totalizations" of his works around a central theme like Jeanson's around existentialist morality, a subject on which Sartre was himself then intending to publish a major work. Told in 1951 that the American public was interested more in his moral thinking than in his dialectics, Sartre again recommended Jeanson's book "as interpreting my views to my complete satisfaction."[5] Focussing on ostensively nonethical works in which Sartre gave bleak descriptions of emotions, imagination, and the human condition (but overlooking *The Transcendence of the Ego*,[6] which until recently was better known in the United States than in France), Jeanson discerned the underlying possibility of a positive "moral conversion" scarcely outlined by Sartre. Jeanson insisted Sartre must be saying that human liberty *is* absurd but only so long as it fails to commit itself to concrete tasks of "liberation." Sartre's letter-foreword confirmed Jeanson's adventurous reading and a working collaboration between the two men ensued.

After eighteen years of work (and disagreement) with Sartre and *Les Temps modernes* on the concrete tasks in question, Jeanson wrote "Somebody called Sartre" in 1965. Like the 1947 work, to which it was written as a postface in the later reissue, this 1965 study synthesizes Sartre's more recent works around their author's evolving moral life-project; unlike the 1947 work, it is informed by close and regular contact with Sartre himself. As Sartre's collaborator in a common enterprise rather than his "disciple," Jeanson changed his focus from the philosophy to the philosopher, explaining, in the process, his own relationship to Sartre as a reader. As this book now finally appears in English translation, Sartre's attitude has cooled toward Jeanson's later works on him. In 1976 he contrasted them with André Gorz's *The Traitor*: "If [Gorz's] book interested me—and that is why I wrote the preface—it was not because I found some of my own ideas in it, a way of trying to understand a man in his entirety. It was because I learned things from it. . . . [Jeanson] has written books about me, which is different. The most recent ones were less interesting."[7] Sartre here overlooks or undervalues Jeanson's *Sartre by Himself*[8] and the 1965 postface, both of which perceptively apply Sartre's existential psychoanalysis to its author.

Together, Jeanson's 1965 postface and his original *Sartre and the Problem of Morality* can help in understanding a philosophy and a philosopher that are still "too well known for being badly misunderstood." They bring out a theme and a problem from which Sartre has never wandered far and to which he has recently returned, as I shall explain. But perhaps more important, Jeanson's two works, and the political action he undertook during the period between them, illuminate, from within, the struggles of a group of men and women who have lived as a personal dilemma our shared twentieth-century situation.

Jeanson announces his philosophical focus early in his 1947 text as "a single systematic attitude which consists in always giving precedence to the 'moral' point of view or, if you wish, to the governance of self."[9] How, then, could Sartre's early works satisfy him, being phenomenological descriptions of evasions of such governance through emotion, imagination, and bad faith?

Jeanson holds *both* that Sartre's philosophy cannot be understood outside the moral perspective *and* that Sartre offers no principles of right conduct or characterizations of the good, confining himself to ontological description of what is.

Jeanson is not confused. Traditional ethical theory supposes that *there is* a living morality to be described, even if only as a requirement of reason or as an ideal entity, whereas Sartre believes there are only abstract, alienated moralisms and declines to add on a new one. Yet Jeanson shows that Sartre's descriptions are really tests of the hypothesis that a potentially liberating freedom, the ground of any possible morality, lurks even in the deepest degradations of our time. If such failures can be understood best not as expressions of a flawed "human nature," but as free alienations of freedom, then determinism is bad faith and freedom may be recovered and made an end. Those who choose to enjoy a mere inner freedom in the midst of oppression, rationalizing their own "half-century of egoistic enterprises," will find this philosophy spiritually dangerous, Jeanson admits.[10] However the danger flows, not from its atheism or its alleged pessimism or even from its depiction of human relations as permeated by conflict, but rather from its comprehension of such conflicts as expressions of freedoms that *could be* directed to building community.

Husserl's reflective "reduction" of the "natural attitude" of one's consciousness is given a moral turn in the Sartre/Jeanson version of phenomenology.[11] They contend that my initial natural attitude of belief in the world's objectivity also contains my inauthentic wish to "be," that is, an act of *moral* valorization of being, that imbues with value what is, merely because it is. Such valorizing conceals itself because it is ashamed of itself qua valorizing act. I thereby allow myself to uncritically recapitulate my given social conditions. Reduction of, or "purifying reflection" on, the natural attitude, by uncovering this wish as merely one choice, allows me to "radically convert" my attitude, to turn from being to human existence, and to positively rather than negatively valorize my own inescapable authorship of values by choosing freedom as my value. Jeanson concludes Sartre means morality *is not*, but *might be* or, rather, morality is lived as a possibility, a "moral demand" [*une exigence morale*] to invent with others concrete terms of free self-governance, a demand we are also free to ignore.

What, then, are human reality and the human condition such that morality is possible? Jeanson holds that for Sartre human reality is ambiguous—neither mind nor matter but action that determines itself on the basis of conditions that are given but that are never determinative. Jeanson's rebuttals to charges of dualism, materialism, and idealism merit study by Sartre's recent critics. The distinctions he draws between the views of Sartre and those of Merleau-Ponty clarify their later debate. One of Merleau-Ponty's early criticisms was that Sartre conferred on individuals a "ready-made freedom" that renders social liberation superfluous.[12] Similar criticisms from different premises were later made by Lukács[13] and Marcuse.[14] Jeanson contends that Merleau-Ponty had overlooked Sartre's distinction between a "natural" or unreflective freedom evinced in our alienations—which is the object of ontological description—and a "freedom-as-valued" in which freedom is recovered and practiced as the explicit objective of a reflective moral attitude. True, the former is never absent, but the latter is never "ready-made." Freedom-as-valued arises when alienated freedom and its conditions are freely assumed in a transcendence of them toward an individual liberation that is also, necessarily, a collective liberation.[15]

Why "necessarily"? Why can't I consistently choose to value one freedom— my own—at the cost of others' enslavement? Can fascism be proven to be inconsistent with existentialism? An existentialist morality evidently depends on proof of the indivisibility of freedom. Jeanson proposed such a proof in 1948, summing up his discussion of Being-for-others the previous year in *Sartre and the Problem of Morality*: "I may try to abolish another through violence or seduction, and I may try to abolish myself, but I cannot reach the limit in either case since we both remain there to expose my attitude as an absolute failure. In other words, I cannot make myself free *against*, I must make myself free *with*. I am compelled to assume the very meaning that another gives to my own existence. And clearly I cannot fully consent to that meaning without desiring that the look on which I consent to depend be the look of a consciousness that is free, since only then can the consciousness of another attribute to my existence the value of freedom that I myself try to confer upon it. . . . The subject must make himself responsible not only for himself but for this aspect of himself that he presents to another. And if he then wishes not to be treated as an object, he must treat the other as a free subject— and this means aiding him to be one, attempting with him to bring about conditions favorable to the recapture of freedom."[16] My slave can "recognize" me, but only as his master, that is, as a being devoid of subjectivity. Thus, even choosing my freedom alone, as does bourgeois individualism, is inconsistent with subordination of another's. And since collectively we could alter our relationship according to values we choose together, it will not do to appeal to a priori values in "the spirit of seriousness" or to argue that oppression is due to our mutual victimization by circumstances. I am constrained to choose freedom itself, that is, my own freedom along with that of all others, because, however small a local pocket of oppressed persons may be, their glance is sufficient to transform my presumably independent freedom into sheer performance.

Clearly, then, so long as there are people who are oppressed, the choice of freedom for all will be directed to their liberation. To make this choice in a capitalist world, Sartre argued in "Materialism and Revolution" in 1946, entails commitment to a nonmaterialist form of revolutionary socialism.[17] Noting that under capitalism workers are inveigled into subordination to the goals and profit of others in place of their own, he called for a revolutionary philosophy of concrete freedom that would unmask the bourgeois ideology of abstract freedom, without, however, falling into a materialism that denies with its metaphysics the transcendence it calls for in its revolutionism. *Being and Nothingness* had not provided this philosophy. As "an eidetic of bad faith"[18] it had advanced a *reductio ad absurdum* argument against bourgeois individualism analogous to Marx's demonstrations of the self-defeating character of capitalism in the previous century. But it had not provided a way out; its practical terminus had been an existentialist psychoanalysis. Although it is ambiguous on whether to diagnose bad faith's "self-negation" as an *internalization* of negations originating in social reality (for example, in caretakers, overseers, gaolers) or as a spontaneous inner choice that *calls forth* these repressive social roles, its cure of "radical conversion," being based on Husserl's reduction to pure consciousness, implicitly opted for the latter model of self-negation inasmuch as its first step would not be social change but radical reformulation of each person's "original project" *ad seriatim*.[19] Clearly this contains an element of faith that social change will by implication take care of itself.

Jeanson took a further step, arguing that while radical conversion must *start with* reflection on the individual's own natural bad faith, its only chance of moving away from this attitude lay in a "realism" which requires simultaneous engagement in a project of social liberation.[20] In a warning pertinent to our own era of narcissistic stock-taking, he foresaw "a dangerous crossing" for existentialism if it culminates in "a subjective conversion" *simpliciter*: Such an existentialism "is tempted to capitulate either in the direction of a transcendental philosophy ignorant of individual historical situations or in the direction of exclusive preoccupation with historicity, where the risk is great that one will give up all concern for authenticity." If existentialism is to *maintain* the ambiguity of human existence, as Jeanson counsels it should, then, he urged, it must move on to "some synthesis between radical conversion and historical development or, if you will, between the realism of authenticity in Husserl, or even in Heidegger, and the realism of history in Marx."[21] An abstractly universal self-transcendence that rests content with a historical situation that denies freedom cannot be authentic, Jeanson had concluded; liberating *action* is necessary in such a situation.

Jeanson's warning struck home: "you have so perfectly followed the development of my thought" Sartre responded, "that you have come to pass beyond the position I had taken in my books at the moment I was passing beyond it myself and to raise with regard to the relations between morality and history, the universal and the concrete transcendence, the very questions I was asking myself at that time." Now throughout this period (1943–1950), and particularly from 1947 on, Sartre was working hard on a "Treatise of Morality" ("Traité de morale")[22] that would be the promised moral sequel to *Being and Nothingness*. But it would also provide at least some of the philosophy of revolution solicited by "Materialism and Revolution," for, in 1947, a month after writing his letter to Jeanson, Sartre told a group of French philosophers "I am not thinking of a morality of progress, but a morality of revolution, in the sense that there is a revolution in Descartes or Kant, and an evolution in Leibniz."[23] But while individual radical conversion in an oppressive world requires revolutionary action, because of the indivisibility of freedom, revolutionary action presents its own moral problem in the context of Sartre's early thought. In an important interview given in 1949 Sartre disclosed that the topic of his "Treatise" would be "the problem of morality" (the very terms Jeanson had used), which he characterized as follows: "If I take another's freedom objectively as my goal [*but*], I do him violence. But if I take my own freedom as my goal, it entails the calling forth of all others as freedoms [*elle entraîne l'exigence de toutes les autres commes des libertés*]. In the choice I make of my freedom, that of others is also demanded; but when I move to the plane of action, I have to take the other person as means and not as end. Here we are obviously faced with an antinomy. I shall examine this antinomy in my 'Morality.' . . ."[24]

Sartre was evidently unable to treat this antinomy to his satisfaction, for he abandoned the "Treatise" soon after raising "the problem of morality" in this form.[25] The phrase "when I move to the plane of action" implies the "I" here is not already *on* that plane, even that moving to it is an option for such an "I." This ahistorical "I"—inherited from Husserl's conception of a transcendental consciousness that is throughout transparent and ultimate—may elect to retain moral purity by inaction or by pursuit of bourgeois virtues, which are the same.[26] This brings out a tension in Sartre's early thinking between freedom as action and freedom as consciousness. On the one hand, he holds freedom to be a structure of worldly actions and denies idealism's claim that consciousness contains intentions or emanates from an ego that would make its "inner life" a substance in its own right.[27] At the same time, liberating and tethering actions are themselves equal options for a purified and free consciousness; having thus freely reflected, though, it tends to choose liberating action as consistent with this freedom.[28] Unable to then sacrifice this freedom in the collective action enjoined by it, Sartre locked himself in a variant of the "unhappy consciousness" he presumed merely to describe. He would later redefine human reality as historical *praxis* and absorb consciousness—including its innermost intentions—as a "moment" of *praxis*, limiting his conception of freedom correspondingly. But meanwhile, just as Baudrillard argues that Marx internalized too much of the productivist image of man undergirding capitalism to point radically beyond the latter, so Sartre's *reductio ad absurdum* of bourgeois individualism accepted too many of the latter's premises to point radically beyond it.[29] Concurrently, Sartre's efforts in electoral politics also reached an impasse. The *Rassemblement Démocratique Révolutionnaire* (Revolutionary Democratic Assembly), an internationally neutral socialist grouping of which Sartre was a cofounder, collapsed after turning decisively pro-American.[30] The postwar era was over. Peacetime habits of subordination to capitalism, whose violence is invisible because normal, make liberation from it more difficult than the populist uprising of Parisians against their occupiers that had so moved Sartre in 1944.[31] By 1950 it was clear there would be no move "From Resistance to Revolution."

The next year Jeanson, later describing himself as having felt "more Marxist than the Marxists,"[32] set out on his own to avoid the danger he had warned against in 1947 in a 1951 essay "Definition of the Proletariat?" [*Définition du prolétariat?*]. This is a significant early attempt at synthesizing the existential-ist doctrine of freedom with a Marxist analysis of class struggle. Though dis-tantly indebted to Lukács's characterization of the proletariat as the object and subject of history,[33] it remained independent of the French Communist party's variations on the theme of historical determinism. The features of ambiguity and self-transcendence which Jeanson had earlier found in human reality generally he now finds in the working class, which is a project, not an object of knowledge. And what he had earlier said of individual conversion he now says of historical conversion through proletarian revolution: ". . . the pro-letariat *is* the meaninglessness of history. And the meaning of history is pre-cisely that it must be *converted*, seized by the living and purged of that evil spell by which human energies always develop at the expense of humanity."[34]

Determinism is a mistaken theory which nevertheless acquires historical force, according to Jeanson, as a license for the oppressors' claims to be mere unwilling transmitters of oppression. But he argues that this alibi is inherently flimsy, since, on determinism's own terms, it is right only so long as its might is unquestioned. Both the bourgeoisie and party ideologues *succeed* in dominat-ing the working class and thus in creating a bourgeois or Bolshevik world (that is, one in which it is natural for workers to be powerless) precisely to the extent that workers and their allies fail to challenge the reigning de-terminist rationalization, whether it be to "merely obey economic determinism" or to perceive history's necessary outcome. Conversely, individual workers are defined not by the sum of " 'proletarian' conditions" (that is, poverty, property-lessness, exploitation) but by their response to them. More precisely, workers *define themselves* as the proletariat "to the extent that individual proletarians express through a collective behavior their becoming conscious of a common destiny. . . ." Individual liberation is an absurdity of history as well as of nature (a total absurdity, as envisioned by Camus), but only so long as it does not consciously challenge capitalism as the epoch's instrument of oppression. The collective nature of the working class, its character as a *class*, arises from its members' self-transcendence. Workers constitute themselves as the prole-tariat or working class in the moment of the latter's triumph and death as such: ". . . *the proletariat will be revolutionary or it will not be at all.*"[35]

Thus Jeanson transposes individual transcendence, without change, into historical transcendence. This transposition is consistent with Jeanson's premises and again represents an advance over Sartre's published writings at this time in the direction of concretizing the notion of "radical conversion." But because intersubjective reciprocity is to be constructed out of whole cloth, Jeanson purchases the solidarity of free revolutionaries at the price of making revolution a collocation of externally related decisions, hence supererogatory. "The task of the proletariat is not in history," Jeanson is compelled to say, "it is to effect the conversion of history."[36] The proletariat as a whole, and not just individual purifying reflection, is thereby placed outside of history, and we reenter Sartre's antinomy—now in collectivist form. Yet the article helped open new space for the discourse of revolution outside the Communist party, and it prefigured the optimism of the French student-worker uprising of May 1968. Precisely because Camus had also begun to see in revolutionism an attempt to moralize an immoral history, withdrawing from this task to an ahistorical perspective just as Jeanson approached it from the same perspective, the article set Jeanson on course for a collision with Camus the following year.

Camus's *The Rebel* appeared in the fall of 1951 and embarrassed several people associated with *Les Temps modernes*. It appeared that an old friend had gone over to the right. Jeanson's unfavorable review in the May 1952 issue was, as Jeanson later put it, the "occasional cause" of the split between Sartre and Camus.[37] Jeanson had never agreed philosophically with Camus: one of his first published pieces criticized the author of *The Myth of Sisyphus* for an immoderate faith in reason, which faith, when confronted with a disappointing real world, inevitably fell into a dark "absurdism," a caricature of the existential fad.[38] *Sartre and the Problem of Morality* had distinguished Camus's view of absurdity, as permeating human behavior *per se*, from Sartre's, where it is primarily characteristic of the existence of things, penetrating into the human domain only when the latter attempts to forsake meaning-giving in order to imitate and acquire the solidity of things.[39]

In *The Rebel* Camus had turned from the question of suicide to the question of murder, in particular to the requirements of *justification* for the "logical crimes" characteristic of Hitler and Stalin. Believing with such criminals that it is permissible to sacrifice a single life for a future generation entails believing what cannot be proved, namely, that history has a *sens*, a vector and meaning apart from the individual acts that constitute it. Such belief "deifies" man and history and overlooks nearby correctable ills. However, Camus thinks we can "diminish" such ills only "arithmetically," since "the injustice and suffering of the world will remain and, no matter how limited they are, they will not cease to be an outrage."[40] Thus revolt, not revolution, emerges as the only attitude from which to combat these ills rather than multiply them.

Jeanson defends the revolutionary outlook, and, detecting a religious resignation behind Camus's atheism, he turns the charge of cryptotheology against Camus. To gain plausibility for his attempt to retrospectively blame Marx for

Stalin, Camus had resorted to first reducing revolution to the slogan "the divinization of man" and then substituting the ideology of revolution for its reality. But "this odd conception of history comes down to a suppression of it as such. It eliminates every concrete situation in order to obtain a pure dialogue among ideas."[41] Having condemned history to *metaphysical* absurdity from an impossible extrahistorical perspective, Camus cannot take human, infrahistorical injustices seriously. Camus's disengaged perspective inherently overlooks the meaning and direction that history *does* have for those locked in concrete, if partial, struggles—which might not be undertaken at all if one could honestly foresee provoking greater injustice, as Camus claims to do. Camus is not an atheist but "a passive anti-theist": "since [the rebel] doesn't really try to accomplish anything, he at least succeeds in depriving God of the pleasure of contemplating his failures."[42]

Jeanson evades the central issue, Camus rebutted: "To legitimate the position he takes toward my book your reviewer should demonstrate . . . that history has a necessary meaning and an end; that the frightful and disordered face of contemporary history is only an illusion; and that, on the contrary, it inevitably progresses, although with ups and downs, toward that moment of reconciliation when we can jump into ultimate freedom."[43]

In the same issue of *Les Temps modernes* Sartre defended his journal against Camus's charge that it had overlooked Stalin's labor camps and replied: "The question is not whether History has direction, and whether we should condescend to participate in it, but, since we are in it up to here, whether we should try to *give* history the direction we believe salutary and not refuse our assistance, however small it may be, to any concrete action that requires it."[44] Also in the same issue, Jeanson moderated his tone and offered a critical defense of the French Communist party during a period of intense anti-Communism: "we don't consider the Stalinist movement around the world to be authentically revolutionary, but it is the only movement that pretends to be so and that appears, particularly in France, able to rally a proletarian majority."[45] Criticizing the strategies of the workers' movement, he insisted, was the right only of those who shared the workers' deepest hopes, and, since the working class alone can move history toward freedom, opposing workers in the person of their elected (if defective) leaders would primarily defeat workers and only secondarily defeat Stalinism.

The debate must be counted something of a standoff. To be sure, Camus had erected an impossible demand: the end of history cannot be an object of *knowledge* except perhaps for God. But it would not have been unfair to ask for revolution to base itself on some proof that we are already in a violent history "up to here." Sartre had only the theoretical tools of *Being and Nothingness* with its individual conversion and Jeanson had provided only an abstract schema for a moral conversion of history. Neither was in a position to answer Camus, to account for the political passivity of French workers, or to

separate a positive conception of revolutionary democracy from the static electoral model accepted by both the bourgeoisie and the Communists.[46] In
focussing on certain issues my account of the debate has ignored some of its
personal antipathy. Although this antipathy developed further than any of the
participants wished, affecting Camus particularly adversely, it is unlikely that
Jeanson ever wished to "apologize" for anything to Camus, despite such claims
by Camus's biographer.[47] Yet these two men had more in common than either
had with Sartre: a lifelong struggle with tuberculosis, an unbroken moral outlook on life, and a need for domestic tenderness.

How to maintain the ambiguity between individual authenticity and revolutionary liberation was for Jeanson as much a practical as it was a theoretical
problem. His most noteworthy effort was not in his philosophical works, nor
in his role in the Camus/Sartre split, but in his political action during the
Algerian War of 1954–1962. Two years after the first uprisings Jeanson initiated the "Jeanson network," thirty or so French artists, academicians, workers,
and actors who gave illegal clandestine support to Algerian independence
leaders in France. Pursued by the police out of the public's sight, the group
suddenly came to international attention at the war's height in February 1960—
as good a marker of the onset of that decade as any—when six key Algerians
and eighteen of their French supporters were arrested. Jeanson and several
others were still at large when the trial began in September. Foreign journalists watched as National Liberation Front (FLN) "rebels" and their "accomplices" were reunited in court with their suitcases full of francs destined
for Tunis. My own first knowledge of Jeanson came at this time through Joe
Barry's first-hand reports of the trial to the *New York Post*. The defendants
were charged (and so was Jeanson, *in absentia*) with treason and incitement
to military disobedience. But their novel lack of contrition in explaining their
actions, combined with timely support from scores of major French intellectuals in the famous Manifesto of the 121,[48] quickly turned the trial into an
indictment of the war itself, as similar trials were to do in the later Vietnam
era. Meanwhile, massed supporters of a "French Algeria" abroad and a tough
government at home marched in protest down the Champs-Elysées. This dem-
onstration helped reawaken the left to its anti-imperialist principles. One
observer remarked just after the trial: "Dominating the whole 'homecoming'
[of the left to its basic principles] with its tumultuous sessions, the trial will
perhaps have marked a turning point in French politics."[49] No great resurgence
of the left ensued, but within a year, by March 1962, the government had reversed its policy and Algeria was independent. Examining this action may help
us understand the political implications of *Sartre and the Problem of Morality*.

Like his confrontation with Camus, Jeanson's commitment to Algerian liberation was rooted in solitary choices which later influenced his personal relationships and his nation's history. During World War II Jeanson had been
captured while crossing into Spain to join the Free French and had been put

in a concentration camp; released months later, after a recurrence of tuberculosis, he served with the Free French in Algeria, where he made many Moslem friends. Back in Paris, he warned that France was "sitting on a volcano"
and sided with those who demanded justice against a historically sordid
French policy.[50]

Then, in 1952, Jeanson met Frantz Fanon. It was on a non-Algerian matter.
Jeanson had read the manuscript of *Black Skin, White Masks*, a meditation by
the Martinican doctor on the fact of having black skin, which everyone con-
trived to ignore, including many who had it. Four years after Fanon's death
Jeanson described this encounter as follows (and drew criticisms from Algerians): "In 1952, we almost broke off our relations, he and I, the very day
of our first meeting. Having found his manuscript exceptionally interesting, I
committed the error of telling him so, which made him suspect me of having
thought, 'for a Negro, that wasn't so bad.' As a result of which, I showed him
the door and expressed my own reaction in the liveliest terms—which he had
the good sense to take well."[51]

Sartre had earlier characterized the Negritude movement among black poets
as a necessary but "negative moment," an antithesis to white racism that was
a "means" or "transition" on the road to "a society without races."[52] In *Black
Skin* Fanon had replied: "For once that born Hegelian had forgotten that
consciousness has to lose itself in the night of the absolute, the only condition
to attain to consciousness of self. In opposition to rationalism, he summoned
up the negative side, but he forgot that this negativity draws its worth from
an almost substantive absoluteness."[53] Jeanson mediated between them in his
preface to the first edition of *Black Skin*. Fanon, he pointed out, had said he
did not want to be "the victim of the Ruse of a black world. My life must not
be consecrated to drawing up the balance sheet of black values."[54] And Sartre,
he noted, had not forgotten that "of the man of color and of him alone can it
be asked to renounce pride in his color."[55] Fanon, Jeanson remarks, had been
"tempted to make love with his race" but "he immediately saw that this love
itself is nothing if not militant love that wishes to realize itself in the world,
a love that could only be incarnated by making itself ever more conscious of
its own resources and actual conditions of struggle."[56]

Events soon tested Sartre, de Beauvoir, Fanon, Jeanson and Camus. In November 1954 the first Algerian uprising compelled France to face the demand
for independence and the terror this demand stimulated in Algerian colonials
after a century of colonization. Premier Mendès-France promised a quick
suppression. The Communists declared for peace rather than independence,
suspicious of the FLN which, unlike the earlier Indo-Chinese rebels under Ho
Chi Minh, required its Communists to leave the party. As the cycle of FLN
attacks and French Army repressions speeded up, Camus, a native of Algeria,
intervened to advocate a civil truce and negotiation. He was unaware until the
last moment (and was then delighted to learn) that the Moslem "liberals"

sharing the podium with him in a hall next to the casbah in Algiers were in fact FLN leaders supporting his efforts, though with more moderate hopes for reversing French policy. Fanon had been in Algeria for two years and was in the audience but was disappointed by Camus's equivocations.[57] Without having fortified Algerian resistance, Camus's peace appeal was rejected by an immense crowd of anti-independence "ultras" massed outside the hall, screaming "Camus to the wall!" "Mendès to the wall!" "Down with the Jews!" and "French Algeria!" Camus returned to Paris.

That was in January of 1956. Both Jeanson's lonely action and Fanon's final *coupure* with Europe were provoked that March when the Communist deputies in parliament, weakened and willing to give Guy Mollet's social democratic regime the rope with which to hang itself, joined in voting the government special repressive powers to be used in Algeria as it wished. Whatever their motives, the Communists thereby exploited the gap between Algerian and French workers, relying on the latter's image of the former as strikebreakers in order to retain its electoral position. French Army "pacification," as it was called, already involved massive retaliations reminiscent of the Nazi occupation. Like Vietnam before and after it, it was a dirty war on both sides. But for Jeanson one either chose sides personally or, feigning indifference, allowed the French government, clearly bent on repression, to count that indifference as endorsement and thereby to choose repression in one's name. The issue of Islamic nationalism was not yet settled within the FLN. Fanon would later side with secularist forces internally. Jeanson argued in France that the issue was secondary; the primary concern of Europeans was to liberate both the colony and the metropole from the colonial syndrome. Metropolitan workers were held in thrall by the meager but real increases in purchasing power conferred on them by French capitalists at the expense of colonized colored peoples. In 1955 Jeanson and his first wife, Colette, had published *Outlaw Algeria*, in which they unraveled the history of this syndrome and argued that continued suppression of Algerian independence would cost French citizens their civil liberties and French workers their remaining bargaining power.[58] Through Jeanson and his Algerian associates, Fanon arranged to join the FLN, leaving his hospital directorship at Blida-Joinville in January 1957 for full-time medical and journalistic work at FLN headquarters in Tunis. He went via Paris, where he met again with Jeanson.[59]

The network had just begun its illegal work. It found lodging, escape routes, and names (loaned by sympathetic persons) for the "federal committee" of the FLN. But its main job was to funnel money to Tunis from tithing Algerian workers in France.[60] Arms themselves were not transported, though not out of principle, since the money was to be taken abroad to buy arms. Within France the police had long pursued a racist policy of arbitrarily stopping and searching Algerians on sight, including FLN militants, who, as a result, could not themselves transport the money. The network provided some of the white-skinned, straight-haired French people needed for that job, earning criticism by some as "traitorous" and by others as "individualistic." The weighty and anonymous fact of color that seems to have burdened Jeanson's meetings with Fanon was thereby neatly turned against itself and transformed into a means of liberation. This sudden "conversion" of inertia into transcendence, of negative into positive, this disarming and reversal of a socially divisive force through complete personal openness, constituted the novelty and potency of the FLN/network conspiracy. Having heeded his own call to action, Jeanson, and the conspiracy-in-liberation he served, constructed at least for a short time what he had described in *Sartre and the Problem of Morality* as a "community" of lucid equals[61] around which French and Algerian workers could rally in order to dismantle the colonial system.

Unity of purpose between Jeanson and Fanon was now complete despite, or perhaps because of, the physical distance between them. Both had undertaken direct, illegal action without consulting either "public opinion" or the impotent French left. Sartre was in Paris, hence physically nearer to Jeanson than Fanon; but he was morally more distant because of his legality. Sartre and Jeanson had not spoken since 1956 owing to the latter's objection to Sartre's use of the anti-Communist media to protest the Soviet suppression of the Budapest uprising.[62] Jeanson's name had been quietly removed from the masthead of *Les Temps modernes*. But de Beauvoir acknowledges she and Sartre mistakenly hesitated to support Jeanson and his network: "we still believed that it was possible to work for [Algerian] independence by legal means. Knowing Jeanson, we were sure he had not committed himself without careful consideration; there was no doubt that he must have had very good reasons. I shied away from the idea all the same." Unimpressed by two flippant network members she had met (they soon left it), she had explained their action to herself as personal resentment. Later she castigated herself for this "psychologism," which she had always detested in others, and admitted: "Even if I had appraised his action more lucidly, the fact remained that participation, in the eyes of the country generally, would have meant going over to the traitors' camp and something in me—timidity, vestiges of mistaken beliefs—still prevented me from contemplating such a thing."[63] The mutual sympathy between Jeanson and de Beauvoir, which this account betokens, bore fruit in 1966 in Jeanson's *Simone de Beauvoir ou l'entreprise de vivre*,[64] in which, mainly through analyses of her autobiographical works and in two penetrating interviews, he evokes de Beauvoir's "optimistic" presence.

In 1950 Sartre's thinking had entered what he would later call a "realist" period, extending up to 1968.[65] Instead of working "down" to political action from a clarified morality, Sartre would now work "up" from such action, since ". . . true politics contains within it implicitly, its own moral appraisal."[66] Though he began this period with greater proximity to the Communists,[67] he did not abandon the problem of morality but instead attacked it from a new, empirical angle.[68] This resulted in a more satisfactory (but still unpublished) "second morality" which we shall presently examine in outline. But during the climactic period of the Algerian War (1958–1959), much of Sartre's time was devoted to his second major philosophical synthesis, the *Critique of Dialectical Reason*.[69] De Beauvoir reports that "Sartre *protected himself* by working furiously on the *Critique*."[70] But the description seems inexact. Horrified by their compatriots' indifference to the massive torturing they saw as integral to war policy, feeling the same revulsion to the French uniform that they had felt to the Nazi uniform, Sartre and de Beauvoir constantly demanded Algerian independence and offered a concrete program of extrication in *Les Temps modernes*. And the *Critique* itself, started in 1954, like the Algerian War, may be read as encircling this war as its absent and haunting center, just as *Being and Nothingness*, written in part during the occupation, had been read by Jeanson as haunted by the morality of radical conversion as its absent center.

This work, a profound but sometimes turgid revision and expansion of Marx's theory of history, is still relatively unused by the new-left activists to whom it was offered as a tool. We shall only touch on a few themes here. The *Critique* understands *praxis* rather than consciousness as the mediation through which all human reality can become comprehensible to itself. However, it saw even revolutionary *praxis*—within what Sartre called "the group-in-fusion"— as inevitably diverted into oppressive "counter-finalities" and its fusion reabsorbed into individualism so long as the specific problem of human history— scarcity—is attacked only locally and not globally. It offered the mechanism of colonial "superexploitation" of Algerians as a paradigm of imperialism's circle of frustration[71] and uncovered the source of the left's impotence against it in the central phenomenon of "seriality."[72] The immediate condition for capitalism's peacetime violence, seriality is the being-alone-together of individuals within families, nations, and classes, a negative reciprocity that is masked by the overt conformism of their members. Though born of an original encounter with scarcity, seriality acquires a "pratico-inert" momentum sustained by serializing mechanisms of the market, bourgeois electoral politics, the media, and production techniques. Seriality is the *social* content of "the Other" of *Being and Nothingness*, who may be either a life-partner or a stranger on the sidewalk. The sadomasochistic conflicts between such "others" which this work described can now be seen as internalizations of decisions by previous generations to live scarcity within serial structures such as racism, sexism and imperialism, structures through which society anonymously "selects its victims" in advance. So long as scarcity prevails on a global scale seriality will be abolished only temporarily. Even in socialist countries its inertial weight may undercut the positive reciprocity necessary to coordinate individuals' needs through class consciousness, workers' parties, and unions.[73] A "single history" in which man is directly rather than indirectly his own product is possible, but only after group *praxis* masters production in such a way as to allow a margin of freedom to all men.

While Sartre wrote, Jeanson's "action group" acted, at its height sending $1,000,000 per month in 1980 dollars to Tunis. In May 1959 Jeanson contacted Sartre, who finally joined in the illegalism of Fanon and Jeanson by giving Jeanson a clandestine interview for his banned bulletin, thereby inculpating himself before French law.[74] Was Jeanson's action successful? The accounting books in Tunis would help to answer, but only in part. Like Sartre's group-in-fusion, the network had revealed the potency of collective *praxis* in combatting superexploitation and seriality. But if straightforward repression had only strengthened its secondary aim of appealing from without to France's conscience on the war, it was thereby rendered all the more vulnerable to cooptation from within the political structure. As with Vietnam later, to undercut the network's political effects, it was sufficient to reverse policy, which de Gaulle finally did when civil war threatened. Jeanson "surfaced" immediately after the cease fire in March 1962. His *in absentia* conviction would hold only if a new trial convicted him in his presence; were a prosecutor to pursue this course, opposing the consensus for Algerian independence, Jeanson was ready for a showdown—wishing not to spend his life underground. In 1965 he was arrested and then immediately released three times in one month. One arrest was cleared up when the commissaire learned from Paris that "The measures to be taken upon encountering M. Jeanson are still in effect [*exécutoires*] but must not be effectuated [*exécutées*]." The commissaire grumbled about his job and Jeanson had a good laugh. Finally granted amnesty in July 1966, Jeanson's commitment to a free Algeria has not weakened: since 1975 he has periodically assisted the Ministry of Education in Algiers in setting up university programs in the social sciences.[75]

The network's action replicated the Resistance movement's struggle for liberation inside a "legal" order that was itself criminal. However, open civil disobedience—rather than the efficient, clandestine illegalism of the network—was the likely form of political expression that had been projected for Jeanson's "moral conversion" by André Gorz, a Sartre collaborator two years Jeanson's junior, if I interpret correctly Gorz's remarkable *Foundations for a Morality*.[76] This lengthy work, written between 1946 and 1955— but published recently with a retrospective preface—goes beyond Jeanson's book of the same era in attempting to systematically found a Sartrean morality parallel to the ontology of *Being and Nothingness*. This morality turns on an "*existential* conversion" based on the For-itself's "diasporic" and unrecoverable existence in the past, present, and future. Freedom and choice themselves "cannot be the objects of a choice"; what is chosen in "my existential choice" is not a new form of self-coincidence and being, but my very "consciousness-existence" qua "power of liberation."[77] I am thereby referred directly to the transformation of my actual situation without necessarily having to begin from zero in an initial

self-reform. In his 1976 preface Gorz finds in Jeanson's "moral conversion" a
"'valorization of value' ["*valoriser la valeur*"] in place of being possessed or
haunted by it"; but, without having mentioned Jeanson by name, he had connected this procedure in the antecedently written text with "saintliness," an
essentially inauthentic attitude.[78] It would seem, therefore, that in 1976 Gorz
is willing to let his earlier criticism of saintliness "cover" Jeanson. For Gorz,
moral conversion includes but must not terminate with a valorization of
value, which is the act of imbuing with value the act of valuing itself. The
saintly attitude rests inauthentically at this stage and is expressed in an ascetic
ethic of "good intentions" like Luther's and, typically, a politics of nonviolence
like Gandhi's. Because the saint would oppose both oppression and colonial
revolt in favor of an immediate relation of abstract love, his vision is com-
patible with an actual order of class divisions and exploitation, so long as it is
purged of evil by pervasive acts of individual goodwill.[79] The saintly attitude
aims not at transcendent ends but at its own manner of being toward the
world and others, unmindful of its efficacy or objective meaning. Because of
its concern with the immediate and the present at the expense of the mediated
and the future, this essentially *aesthetic* impulse may overlook or even exploit
the many evils that are beyond reach of its (solely internal) processes of purification. Do we recognize Jeanson in this incisive analysis?

Though Gorz's work is indispensable for anyone who would continue
Sartre's reflections on the problem of morality, his category of saintliness is inappropriate for the Jeanson of 1960 and unhelpful also for the Jeanson of 1947.
Jeanson's "Christian formation"[80] and frequent convergence with contemporary
Christian thought are undeniable,[81] as is his opposition of the "revolutionary"
and "moral" attitudes in his 1947 text.[82] Yet we recognize the Jeanson of the
network in the following 1947 passage: "I cannot be said to choose liberty
without engaging myself in a liberating enterprise. The approach of a consciousness to authenticity would itself be inauthentic if this consciousness—in
order to reach authenticity more quickly—were to forget that it is situated.
Freedom cannot be immediately salvaged by abstracting itself from a situation;
rather, it is the situation that must be progressively penetrated by freedom."[83]
Though Jeanson frequently reflects tensions in Sartre's own thinking, it is
clear here that for Jeanson concrete freedom, rather than the quality of one's
own motive, is what is "valorized" in moral conversion. Camus and others had
opposed France's Algerian policy by legal if unpopular appeals based on charity
and tolerance. Jeanson had begun his career by diverging from Camus's
"absurdism"—later expressed in Camus's "saintliness." Consistent with his
1947 work, Jeanson believed freedom was better "salvaged" by acting directly
on the situation in giving support to the Algerians' own liberation struggle,
even if it meant doing so without the protection of the law or the media.[84]
Later, in his dialogue with religion, *The Faith of a Non-believer*, Jeanson explains: "I believe that nonviolence 'through love' is angelism [*angélisme*] and

vanity, that there is more true love in indignity than in acceptance, in generous anger that rouses men against injustice than in the charity of the victim who pardons his executioner, and that one must feel quite solitary, isolated, and alien from one's kind to wind up behaving toward them as God alone might do—were he among us without being anyone in particular."[85] To avoid both the danger of supposing that technical alteration of production arrangements will automatically create new interpersonal relationships and the opposite "saintly" mistake of supposing that individual conversion *ad seriatim* will abolish structural injustices is the aim of Jeanson's activist morality.

The final status, as well as the intermediate stages, of Sartre's own thinking on the "morality" he has been "founding," abandoning, and refounding since his first published work in philosophy in 1937[86] are at present still largely matters of speculation. While Jeanson's 1947 study exposes the moral core of Sartre's early nonmoral works and projects the outlines of the morality Sartre had promised, staying close to the few explicit statements about it in *Being and Nothingness*, it does not attempt to work out the details of that morality or to posit a morality *based on* Sartre's thought.[87] He left this project in one respect to our singular choice and, in another respect, to Sartre, who quietly dropped one approach to it in 1950 and announced in 1964 that he had evolved beyond the project altogether.[88] Jeanson refused to take Sartre at his word and insisted in his 1965 postface that, given the moral *nisus* of Sartre's philosophical enterprise, he "still thinks of" doing a major work on morality.[89] Jeanson's expectation may at last be fulfilled: Sartre recently told an interviewer "I have not ceased to be a moral philosopher" and announced that the main point of his present efforts—a taped dialogue with Pierre Victor to be titled *Power and Freedom*—is to finally produce "that morality which I announced in *Being and Nothingness*—I will finish my life with it, which is valid since it's at the end of my life that I've seen all the difficulties of morality, and what it can be."[90] Thus at present *there is no* published work fully presenting Sartre's own views on morality, but—if the experiment in "writing" a book *à deux* with Victor is successful—*there might be* such a work in the near future.

Sartre values only his published works.[91] The fact that he has not published some of his writings on morality means that he considers them unrepresentative or incomplete. He has made it clear that this material may be published only after his death, that is, only when there is no chance of perfecting his thought.[92] This caveat applies to the "first morality" discussed above but must also be borne in mind when considering the nature of the two remaining unpublished "moralities" which external evidence indicates exist, and which I shall discuss in their chronological order.

The "second morality:" "Studies for a Morality," also known as the "dialectical morality," corresponds to Sartre's "realist" period, starting in 1950 with the discouraging failure of his political efforts, and ending with the encouraging resistance of the Vietnamese to the world's premier military power and the French student-worker uprising of May, 1968.[93] Sartre moves from declaring in 1952 that "the problem of morality" is that *all* moralities are "impossible today" to uncovering in 1965 (albeit in an unpublished work) "the unconditioned possibility of MAKING MAN."[94]

Asked in early 1964 to give some lectures at Cornell University, Sartre accepted, drafting 600 pages of notes in the following year under the announced title: "Studies for a Morality."[95] Some of what he was planning to say was conveyed in a paper on "Determinism and Freedom" given in Italy in May 1964.[96] Sartre here answers structuralist theories of norms by developing the *Critique of Dialectical Reason*'s account of values as free individual interiorizations of social tethers, a valuable treatment of aspects of the problem of facts and values in Marxism. More interesting is the glimpse Jeanson affords of the 200 pages of notes drafted "on the occasion of" this paper, themselves part of the 600-page "dialectical morality." Remembering Jeanson's interest in "the relations between morality and history," Sartre showed Jeanson these notes and allowed him to publish extracts in a volume underway for a religious publisher; the following passage from these extracts conveys some of their Promethean optimism:

> *Man is the future of man.* Which is to say that history is real only through man's unconditioned possibility of realizing himself in his full autonomy: as *praxis*, which dissolves the pratico-inert in its bosom in proportion as it produces itself. As *praxis* of all men joined together.
>
> *Man is to be made.* Man is the end—unknowable but graspable as an orientation—for a being that defines itself by *praxis*, that is, for the incomplete and alienated men that we are.
>
> *History and ethics are bound up together.* . . . genuine ethics [*la veritable éthique*] grounds and dissolves alienated moralities [*les morales aliénées*], inasmuch as it is the direction of history: that is, the rejection of all historical repetition in the name of the unconditioned possibility of MAKING MAN.[97]

Sartre continued work on the Cornell lectures, scheduled for April 1965, and has since declared himself pleased with the results, but he cancelled the lectures in March 1965 and also dropped the dialectical morality project, after President Johnson started bombing North Vietnam.[98]

The "third morality": The French uprising of May 1968 was as close as an advanced capitalist state has come to insurrection in recent decades, but, along with the government and big proprietors, the French Communist party firmly opposed it, trying to restate the workers' and students' demands for self-management as mere wage pleas. Sartre broke immediately and cleanly with the Communists, concluding they wanted a comfortable spot in the electoral status quo more than the abolition of exploitation. Rejecting the bourgeois humanism of work, family, and country would no longer lead Sartre into a political realism concerned first with efficacy; it would now mean understanding and supporting in *moral* terms workers' spontaneous, direct resistance to "the supreme immorality, which is precisely the exploitation of man by man."[99] Morality becomes an outcome, even a feature, of such mass action. But in 1973 Sartre's health deteriorated dramatically, leaving him blind, and he developed his new synthesis of morality and politics in taped discussions with Pierre Victor and Philippe Gavi: "living morality"—as opposed to "moral systems"— is not part of the cultural "superstructure," as the Communists would have it, an epiphenomenon to be automatically replaced by a new morality after a Machiavellian revolution; rather, living morality already exists at the level of production itself, in a worker's use of a particular tool, and in the struggle waged daily over the control of this tool-use and its product.[100] But does this new synthesis have a basis in Sartre's major philosophical statements? *Power and Freedom*, a philosophical dialogue with the young Maoist activist Pierre Victor, will evidently address this question.

This work-in-progress, Sartre reported to Michel Sicard in 1977–1978, will "consider ethical problems at their ontological sources." Already, though, Sartre considers that "the ontology that I developed up to now is incomplete and false." Indeed the new philosophical work "will of necessity leave standing unquestioned nothing in *Being and Nothingness* and the *Critique of Dialectical Reason*." Sartre told Sicard that it will differ from the first, "individualist," morality and from the second, "realist," morality in holding that "ontologically, consciousnesses are not isolated, there are planes in which they enter into one another: there are planes common to two or to *n* different consciousnesses." But, Sicard asks, how does this differ from the second morality? "It's different in that men have relations: their perceptions or their thoughts are in relation one with the others, not only because they are exposed to the other, but because there are penetrations among consciousnesses. Consequently, original morality [*la morale originelle*] is one where the word "bifid" has a meaning: these are not double moralities but simple ones, grasped by two or more consciousnesses who bind themselves one to the others. My previous works never left the *I* [*le JE*], if you will, and this one is a morality of the *WE* [*une morale du NOUS*]." This departs from the Marxist dialectic "because men are [for Marxism] integrated as *men*, as individuals belonging to a community, and not as *consciousness* having common points with another consciousness. For Marx, the liaison between agents is made outside. For us, it is first made within. But it's very complicated. I would have to explain at length. . . "[101]

If Jeanson's 1947 work belongs to the first ("moralistic") stage of an Hegelian triad, it will perhaps be useful in interpreting the ("much enriched") morality as the final synthesis of the triad. In 1966, as Sartre's intermediate period of realism was ending, Jeanette Colombel took Jeanson to task for not accepting Sartre at his word when he said in 1964 that he was "no longer thinking of" writing a morality. Colombel held that Sartre, having entered a Marxist problematic, would be "prevented" from treating morality as anything but "the study of ideologies" and "all slipping into the normative plane would be excluded."[102] There is some truth to Colombel's point. Sartre's evolution reflects an earnest attempt to move beyond all traces of moral absolutism. Jeanson diverged from this route in 1965 when he asked, rhetorically, "And why should one want to exchange worlds if everything is relative, if there is nothing absolute in our 'condition' except its inescapable ending, which is imposed on it from without?"[103] The *Critique*, by contrast, had attempted a totalization of history from inside "without a totalizer," that is, without any extrahistorical principle (be it divine or natural) that would serve as midwife at the birth of new epochs. Hence the equivalence of Sartre's third stage with Jeanson's first-stage Sartre is probably illusory, inasmuch as the negation of the negation restates the original thesis only formally, whereas, meanwhile, Sartre passed through a stage of existential Marxist realism, which Jeanson had partly anticipated in 1947 but which, Colombel correctly notes, he did not fully absorb or follow.[104] But in the end neither has Sartre, as attested to by his passage to a third stage. Thus Jeanson's "error" in 1965 appears indirectly vindicated in 1980 as Sartre resumes the effort to produce an existentialist normative moral theory. Jeanson's 1947 work is essential for regaining a correct reading of *Being and Nothingness*. And, as subsequent events show, his profound understanding of Sartre's philosophy emanates, in part, from what Jeanson calls the "incarnation" of that philosophy in history and in Jeanson's own acts (often the same). If only because among Sartre's collaborators only Jeanson seems to have pushed practice as far as theory—which always illuminate each other—this book will likely be as valuable in interpreting Sartre's future efforts as it is in grasping his past accomplishments. Whatever Sartre's vicissitudes have been I would be surprised if he did not retain his distinctive revolutionism expressed in 1946: "if man is not originally free, but determined once and for all, we cannot even conceive what his liberation might be."[105] And so long as our historical situation diverts this original freedom to the service of ends alien to it—be it profit or faceless bureaucracy—he will continue to speak to us.

Faithfulness and readability are thought to be necessary but incompatible values of translations. I have nevertheless aimed at a faithful, readable rendering of an important text that stands on its own, preferring to err, if error be necessary, on the side of faithfulness. Gallicisms have been purged, but expunging all flavor of the author's French would not have increased accuracy. I have used "morality" rather than "ethics," where appropriate, to reflect both the lower degree of interchangeability between their French cognates and the philosophical focus of Jeanson and the early Sartre, who derive their problematic from a practical urgency ["*morale*"] rather than from a theoretical tradition ["*éthique*"]. The title of the present translation is easily recognized by those familiar with the French title of the original and is handier than its literal translation, *The Problem of Morality and Sartre's Philosophy.* Translations of quotations from French sources are my own. Jeanson's pagetop section headings have been incorporated into the text; his paragraphing has almost always been respected.

In order to facilitate the use of this translation as a commentary on many of Sartre's works, I have added documentation and annotation. I have been more concerned with citing readily available (and inexpensive) texts than with providing detailed information about dates of first publication, since those dates are usually indicated by Jeanson. To the sources Jeanson cites I have undertaken to append, without brackets, references to English translations, where these are available. All other translator's interventions are within brackets, including many added citations in the same French/English form. These dual references will help those who do not read French to follow Jeanson's interpretations in translations of the cited texts and to gain a sense of context. They will also allow those who read French to consult alternative renderings.

In the case of both bracketed and unbracketed footnotes, I have used abbreviated titles for several frequently cited works according to the following key:

ABBREVIATED TITLES

Le Diable/The Devil   J.-P. Sartre, *Le Diable et le bon Dieu* (Paris: Gallimard, 1951); *The Devil and the Good Lord*, translated by Kitty Black, in *The Devil and the Good Lord and Two Other Plays* (New York: Knopf, 1960).

EN/BN   J.-P. Sartre, *L'Etre et le néant: essai d'ontologie phénoménologique* (Paris: Gallimard, 1943); *Being and Nothingness: An Essay in Phenomenological Ontology*, translated by Hazel E. Barnes (New York: Washington Square Press, 1966).

Esquisse/Emotions   J.-P. Sartre, *Esquisse d'une théorie des émotions* (Paris: Hermann, 1939); *The Emotions: Outline of a Theory*, translated by Bernard Frechtman (New York: Philosophical Library, 1948).

L'Imaginaire/Psychology of Imagination   J.-P. Sartre, *L'Imaginaire: psychologie phénoménologique de l'imagination* (Paris: Gallimard, 1940; reprinted, 1966); *The Psychology of Imagination*, translator anonymous (New York: Philosophical Library, 1948).

Ideen I/Ideas   Edmund Husserl, *Ideen zu einer reinen Phänomenologie und phänomenologischen Philosophie*, Vol. I (Halle: Max Niemeyer, 1922); *Ideas: General Introduction to Pure Phenomenology*, translated by W. R. Boyce Gibson (London: Allen and Unwin, 1931).

For assistance in this project I should like to thank John Fremstad, Douglas Browning, Edward Casey, William McBride, William Cobb, Norman Rudich, and, especially, Rosine Lambiotte Donhauser for checking renderings; William Cobb and J. N. Jordan for editing suggestions; Max C. Marx for finding many "unfindable" sources and for extensive help in organizing the footnotes; the C. W. Post College Research Committee for supporting the undertaking with grants and released time; Irene Yarrow and Lorraine M. Walla for their craftsmanship in preparing a beautiful typescript; Marjorie B. Neumann for exemplary editing of the final manuscript; William Cobb for first suggesting this project; and Francis and Christiane Jeanson for their hospitality on visits in 1970 and 1973, when, on top of detailed assistance with footnote and translation problems, our discussions gave me materials and perspective for this introduction. Finally, Patricia Amyett Stone has shared in this work, as in my life generally, through her unfailing encouragement of me since I first started this project.

If any translation errors remain, though, the fault is mine alone.

Robert V. Stone

New York, February 1980

I note with sorrow the death of Jean-Paul Sartre on April 15, 1980.—RVS

NOTES

1. Jean-Paul Sartre, "La République du silence," in *Situations, III* (Paris: Gallimard, 1949); "The Republic of Silence," translated by Lincoln Kirstein, *Atlantic Monthly* 174 (December 1944): 39–40.

2. See below, pp. 12 and 21–22.

3. See below, p. 9.

4. The manuscript was not changed as a result of this consultation with Sartre, Jeanson has explained to me. For Jeanson's amusing description of these first encounters with Sartre, see below, pp. 227–228. Sartre's letter-foreword might be compared to Husserl's foreword to Eugen Fink's "Die phänomenologische Philosophie Edmund Husserls in der gegenwärtigen Kritik," *Kant-Studien* 38 (1933): 319–320; "The Phenomenological Philosophy of Edmund Husserl and Contemporary Criticism," *The Phenomenology of Husserl: Selected Critical Readings*, edited, translated, and introduced by R. O. Elveton (Chicago: Quadrangle, 1970), pp. 73–74.

5. Jacques Salvan, *The Scandalous Ghost* (Detroit: Wayne State University Press, 1967), p. 14.

6. J.-P. Sartre, *La Transcendance de l'Ego: esquisse d'une description phénoménologique*, notes by Sylvie Le Bon (Paris: J. Vrin, 1978); *The Transcendence of the Ego: An Existentialist Theory of Consciousness*, translated by Forrest Williams and Robert Kirkpatrick (New York: Noonday, 1957).

7. "Autoportrait à soixante-dix ans," interview with Michel Contat, in *Situations, X* (Paris: Gallimard, 1976), p. 210; "Self-Portrait at Seventy," in *Life/Situations: Essays Written and Spoken*, translated by Paul Auster and Lydia Davis (New York: Pantheon, 1977), pp. 76–77. Sartre may have had in mind particularly Jeanson's *Sartre dans sa vie* (Paris: Seuil, 1974), an intellectual biography that reviews the stages of Sartre's evolution. While it does not attempt analytical interpretation like *Sartre and the Problem of Morality*, it is informative and useful. Note (below, p.

269) that Jeanson considers Sartre's preface to Gorz's book—*Le Traître* (Paris: Seuil, 1958); *The Traitor* translated by Richard Howard (New York: Simon and Schuster, 1960)—reveals Sartre's own thinking on morality, as of 1965.

8. Francis Jeanson, *Sartre par lui-même*, Ecrivains de toujours (Paris: Seuil, 1955). A revised edition with a newly written second half appeared in 1971. This is the most popular book on Sartre in France. It is not to be confused with a recent work whose early impressions had the same title. See below, note 25.

9. P. 11 below.

10. P. 225 below.

11. See below, p. 183 et seq. and Jeanson's *La Phénoménologie* (Paris: Téqui, 1952), esp. p. 85 et seq.

12. Maurice Merleau-Ponty, *Phénoménologie de la perception* (Paris: Gallimard, 1945), pp. 501, 509; *Phenomenology of Perception*, translated by Colin Smith (New York: Humanities Press, 1962), pp. 439, 446.

13. Georg Lukács, "Zwei europaische Philosophien (Marxismus und Existentialismus)," *Die Umschau* 2 (January 1947); translated as "Existentialism" by Henry F. Mins, in *Marxism and Human Liberation*, edited by E. San Juan, Jr. (New York: Delta, 1973).

14. Herbert Marcuse, "Existentialism: Remarks on J.-P. Sartre's *Being and Nothingness*," *Philosophy and Phenomenological Research* 8, no. 3 (March 1948): 309–336. For related debates see Mark Poster's *Existential Marxism in Postwar France: From Sartre to Althusser* (Princeton: Princeton University Press, 1975), chap. 4.

15. P. 219 below.

16. Francis Jeanson, "L'Existentialisme: philosophie du sujet humain," in *Pour et contre existentialisme*, by J.-B. Pontalis, J. Pouillon, F. Jeanson, Julien Benda, Emmanuel Mounier and R. Vaillard (Paris: Editions Atlas, 1948), p. 46.

17. J.-P. Sartre, "Matérialisme et révolution," in *Situations, III* (Paris: Gallimard, 1949); "Materialism and Revolution," in *Literary and Philosophical Essays*, translated by Annette Michelson (New York: Criterion Books, 1955).

18. J.-P. Sartre, "Merleau-Ponty," in *Situations, IV* (Paris: Gallimard, 1964), p. 196n; "Merleau-Ponty," in *Situations*, translated by Benita Eisler (New York: George Braziller, 1965), p. 234n. Cf. Simone de Beauvoir's remark that *"Being and Nothingness* is in large part a description of the serious man and his universe." *Pour une morale de l'ambiguité* (Paris: Gallimard, 1947), p. 67; *The Ethics of Ambiguity*, translated by Bernard Frechtman (New York: Philosophical Library, 1948), p. 46.

19. J.-P. Sartre, *L'Etre et le néant: essai d'ontologie phénoménologique* (Paris: Gallimard, 1943), pp. 85–86; *Being and Nothingness: An Essay in Phenomenological Ontology*, translated by Hazel E. Barnes (New York: Washington Square Press, 1966), pp. 86–87. For a fuller discussion of this ambiguity see my "Sartre on Bad Faith," in *The Philosophy of Jean-Paul Sartre*, edited by Paul Arthur Schilpp (LaSalle, Ill.: Open Court, forthcoming). In Sartre's later, massive study on Gustave Flaubert this ambiguity is resolved in favor of an internalization model of bad faith. See J.-P. Sartre, *L'Idiot de la famille: Gustave Flaubert de 1821 à 1857*, 3 vols. (Paris: Gallimard: 1971–1973).

20. See below, p. 219.

21. See below, p. 220.

22. This title was used by Sartre in a 1949 interview by François Erval, "Pour Lukács la terre ne tourne pas," *Combat*, 3 February 1949. Extracts from this interview appear in Michel Contat and Michel Rybalka, *Les Ecrits de Sartre: chronologie, bibliographie commentée* (Paris: Gallimard, 1970), pp. 210–211; *The Writings of Jean-Paul Sartre*, translated by Richard C. McCleary, 2 vols. (Evanston: North-

western University Press, 1974), vol. 1, *A Bibliographical Life*, pp. 222–223. Sartre filled ten fat notebooks, but only one, most likely the first, or "one-tenth" of the massive effort (apparently about 800 pages), is extant. See Contat and Rybalka, *The Writings of Jean-Paul Sartre*, 1: 229–230. Various extracts from this first volume of notes for the "Treatise" have appeared in three places: "Le Noir et le Blanc aux Etats-Unis," in Contat and Rybalka, *The Writings of Jean-Paul Sartre*; "'Sur la bêtise'—fragment des 'Notes pour une Morale' (1947)," *Magazine Littéraire*, no. 103–104 (September 1975), pp. 28–34; "La Grande Morale: extraits d'un 'Cahier de notes' (1947)," *Obliques*, special number on Sartre edited by Michel Sicard, no. 18–19 (1979), pp. 249–262. Michel Contat has shown me a typescript of around 800 pages, a transcription of the whole of the "one-tenth" that remains from the lost notebooks. This typescript will be published posthumously. See above p. xxv. Sartre's famous lecture on existential morality—*L'Existentialisme est un humanisme* (Paris: Nagel, 1970); "Existentialism is a Humanism," translated by Philip Mairet, in *Existentialism from Dostoevsky to Sartre*, edited by Walter Kaufmann (Cleveland: Meridian, 1956)—is probably an accurate if compressed presentation of some of the main themes of the "Treatise" as of 1945. As late as 1949, in the interview cited above, Sartre defended this lecture, at least as a "transitional work" consistent with *Being and Nothingness*. On the issue of whether Sartre considers this lecture an "error," and if so, what kind, see below p. 22, n. 4.

23. J.-P. Sartre, "Conscience de soi et connaissance de soi," read 2 June 1947 to the Société française de philosophie, *Bulletin de la Société française de philosophie*, no. 3 (April–June 1948), pp. 90–91; "Consciousness of Self and Knowledge of Self," translated by Mary Ellen Lawrence and Nathaniel M. Lawrence, in *Readings in Existential Phenomenology*, edited by Nathaniel M. Lawrence and D. J. O'Connor (Englewood Cliffs: Prentice-Hall, 1967), p. 142.

24. Interview in *Combat*, 3 February 1949, extracts in Contat and Rybalka, *Les Ecrits de Sartre*, p. 210; *The Writings of Jean-Paul Sartre*, 1: 222–223.

25. This "first morality" (of three) corresponds to what Sartre called in 1972 his period of "moralism," a politically naïve voluntarism that started in his adolescence and ended in 1950, with abandonment of the work begun in 1943. "I talk about [the class struggle] in my 'Morality,' but on the level of a concept; so long as it was not felt as a concrete reality, there could be no morality in it. Therefore I stopped, because I was lacking something. . . . In that period I still wanted to show—I never succeeded, though I wrote masses of pages trying, which I never published—that whatever one does one makes reference to some morality or other." See *Sartre,* transcript of a film directed by Alexandre Astruc and Michel Contat (Paris: Gallimard, 1977), pp. 98–103; *Sartre by Himself*, translated by Richard Seaver (New York: Urizen, 1978), pp. 78–81. (Early impressions of this work carried the title *Sartre par lui-même*.) On the question of why Sartre abandoned this work, see also Simone de Beauvoir, *La Force des choses* (Paris: Gallimard, 1963), p. 218; *Force of Circumstance*, translated by Richard Howard (New York: G. P. Putnam's Sons, 1964), p. 199; and, below, p. 13, n. 4.

26. Cf. an earlier version of the antinomy in "Qu'est-ce que la littérature?" in *Situations, II* (Paris: Gallimard, 1948), pp. 296–297; *What is Literature?* translated by Bernard Frechtman (London: Methuen, 1950), pp. 203–204.

27. Motive, act, and end constitute a single "temporalizing nihilation of the in-itself [that] is one with freedom," Sartre tells us in *Being and Nothingness*. Though this work investigates only "the technical and philosophical concept of freedom"—that is, freedom qua "autonomy of choice" and not freedom qua "obtaining what one wishes"—to choose is always to *act*, Sartre insists, for otherwise choosing would

be conflated with merely dreaming and wishing. *L'Etre et le néant*, pp. 513, 563; *Being and Nothingness*, pp. 565, 621–622. See also Sartre, *La Transcendance de l'Ego*, p. 86; *Transcendence of the Ego*, p. 105.

28. For example: "a society in which one would practice pure reflection . . . would be a city of Kantian ends. . . . There is nothing but freedom [in such a city]. In other words, it depends on man that he should build the city of ends or the immediate society of ants. It depends on him and no one else. There is no a priori law which determines it." And how is this to be consistently attained in action? Sartre at first says "there's no necessity for transition" and then later "by some miracle"—which I take to indicate he has no solution to this problem at this stage (1947). "Conscience de soi et connaissance de soi," *Bulletin de la Société française de philosophie*, no. 3 (April-June 1948), pp. 86–87; "Consciousness of Self and Knowledge of Self," in *Readings in Existential Phenomenology*, pp. 136–137.

29. Cf. Jean Baudrillard, *Le Miroir de la production* (Paris: Casterman, 1973); *The Mirror of Production*, translated by Mark Poster (St. Louis: Telos Press, 1975). Full analysis of the rich antinomy of 1949—not greatly helped by extracts from the "Treatise" published so far—should probably await publication of the remainder of the extant portion of the notes for it. Such an analysis would also need to take into account the fictional—and apparently, in Sartre's eyes, also the merely "conceptual" —solution of the antinomy represented by Goetz, the hero of Sartre's *Le Diable et le bon Dieu* (Paris: Gallimard, 1951); translated by Kitty Black, in *The Devil and the Good Lord and Two Other Plays* (New York: Knopf, 1960). Goetz accepts the solidarity of revolutionaries without renouncing his subjectivity. " 'I made Goetz do what I was unable to do,' " de Beauvoir, quotes Sartre's unpublished notes, " 'The contradiction was not one of ideas. It was in my own being. For my liberty implied also the liberty of all men. And all men were not free. I could not submit to the discipline of solidarity with all men without breaking beneath the strain. And I could not be free alone.' " *La Force des choses*, pp. 261–262; *Force of Circumstance*, p. 243. See Jeanson's excellent analysis of this play in *Sartre par lui-même* (Paris: Seuil, 1955), pp. 48–67. See also Thomas C. Anderson's (I believe successful) attempt to resolve a *related* Sartrean antinomy that applies to others not as goals of our action but as objects of our knowledge, in "Is a Sartrean Ethics Possible?" *Philosophy Today* 14 (Summer 1970): 116–141, esp. pp. 126, 133.

30. De Beauvoir, *La Force des choses*, pp. 189–190, 193–194; *Force of Circumstance*, pp. 171–172, 176. Also see below, p. 229, n. 5.

31. See Simone de Beauvoir, *La Force de l'âge* (Paris: Gallimard, 1960), pp. 606–613; *The Prime of Life*, translated by Peter Green (Cleveland: World, 1962), pp. 470–472; and *Les Ecrits de Sartre*, pp. 103–106; *The Writings of Jean-Paul Sartre*, I: 100–104. By 1952 Sartre had come to believe that his theoretical antinomy was reflected in a historical impasse: "The abstract separation of these two concepts [Good and Evil] simply expresses man's alienation. The fact remains that, in the present historical situation, this synthesis cannot be achieved. Thus any Morality which does not explicitly present itself as *impossible today* contributes to the mystification and alienation of men. The 'problem' of morality is born of the fact that Morality is *for us* at the same time both inevitable and impossible. Action must give itself ethical norms in this climate of unsurpassable impossibility." *Saint Genet: comédien et martyr* (Paris: Gallimard, 1952), p. 177n; *Saint Genet: Actor and Martyr*, translated by Bernard Frechtman (New York: George Braziller, 1963), p. 186n. Also see below, p. 265, n. 95.

32. P. 235 below.

33. Cf. esp. Georg Lukács, "Geschichte und Klassenbewusstsein: Studien über

Marxistische Dialektik (1923)," in *Fruschriften*, vol. 2 (Berlin and Neuwied: Luchterhand, 1968), pp. 240, 246–247, 349–350, 355–356, 393–394; *History and Class Consciousness: Studies in Marxist Dialectics*, translated by Rodney Livingstone (Cambridge: MIT Press, 1971), pp. 65–66, 71–72, 165–166, 171–172, 205. Lukács later renounced this work and still later claimed for it only a "documentary" value.

34. Francis Jeanson, "Définition du prolétariat?" *Lignes de départ* (Paris: Seuil, 1963), p. 139. This essay, reprinted in the collection of Jeanson's essays, appeared first in *Esprit*, July-August 1951. See also Jeanson's existential criticisms of official Marxism in "La Morale de l'histoire," *Esprit*, May-June 1948, pp. 904–917.

35. "Définition du prolétariat?", p. 134. Jeanson's emphasis.

36. Ibid., p. 139.

37. *Sartre dans sa vie*, p. 183. Contat and Rybalka remark, without explanation, on Jeanson's part in the Camus/Sartre break: "It is intriguing [*piquant*] to note that a similar perplexity, albeit of lesser consequence, seems to have been generated several years later at the *Temps modernes* precisely by a book of Francis Jeanson's, *A Letter to Women* (*Lettre aux femmes*) (Seuil, 1965)." *Les Ecrits de Sartre*, p. 250n; *The Writings of Jean-Paul Sartre*, 1: 269n.

38. Francis Jeanson, "Le Mythe de l'absurde," *La France intérieure*, no. 53 (February 1947), pp. 27–30. See also Jeanson's "Albert Camus ou le mensonge de l'absurde," *Revue Dominicaine*, no. 53 (February 1947), pp. 104–107.

39. P. 65 and 243–244 below.

40. Albert Camus, *L'Homme révolté* (Paris: Gallimard, 1951), p. 374; *The Rebel*, translated by Anthony Bower (New York: Vintage Books, 1957), p. 303.

41. Francis Jeanson, "Albert Camus ou l'âme révoltée, *Les Temps modernes*, no. 79 (May 1952), p. 2077.

42. Ibid., p. 2085.

43. Albert Camus, "Lettre au directeur des *Temps modernes*," *Les Temps modernes*, no. 82 (August 1952), p. 329.

44. J.-P. Sartre, "Réponse à Albert Camus," *Les Temps modernes*, no. 82 (August 1952), p. 353; "Reply to Albert Camus," in *Situations*, translated by Benita Eisler (New York: George Braziller, 1965), p. 104. Sartre's emphasis.

45. Francis Jeanson, "Pour tout vous dire . . .," *Les Temps modernes*, no. 82 (August 1952), p. 378.

46. See below, pp. 230, 234 et seq., for Jeanson's account of his evolution beyond the position he took in the early 1950's.

47. Herbert R. Lottman, *Albert Camus: A Biography* (New York: Doubleday, 1979), p. 511.

48. Despite efforts at a party boycott of the Manifesto, it was signed by Henri Lefebvre, Sartre's early Communist critic. Lefebvre had opposed suppression of the Hungarian Revolt in 1956, like Sartre, and was expelled from the party in 1958. In the postwar confluence of existentialism and Marxism, Mark Poster demonstrates, movement was at least as much from Marxism toward existentialism as it was the reverse. *Existential Marxism*, chap. 6.

49. Marcel Péju, *Le Procès du réseau Jeanson* (Paris: Maspero, 1961), p. 8.

50. Francis Jeanson, "Le Tournant Algérien," *Esprit*, October 1951, p. 528.

51. From "Reconnaissance de Fanon," Jeanson's postface added to the 1965 reissue of Fanon's *Peau noir, masques blancs* (Paris: Seuil, 1952), p. 213. See also Irene L. Gendzier, *Frantz Fanon: A Critical Study* (New York: Vintage, 1974), pp. 28, 29n.

52. J.-P. Sartre, "Orphée noir," in *Situations, III* (Paris: Gallimard, 1949), p. 280; *Black Orpheus*, translated by S. W. Allen (Paris: Présence Africaine, ND), pp. 59–60.

53. Frantz Fanon, *Peau noir, masques blancs* (Paris: Seuil, 1952), p. 128; *Black

Skin, White Masks, translated by Charles Lam Markman (New York: Grove Press, 1967), pp. 133–134.

54. Quoted in Jeanson's preface to *Peau noir,* p. 17; *Peau noir,* p. 206; *Black Skin,* p. 229.

55. Quoted in Jeanson's preface to *Peau noir,* p. 19; "Orphée noir," p. 283; *Black Orpheus,* p. 62.

56. Preface to *Peau noir,* p. 19.

57. "He insisted at length that the civilian population be protected, but he categorically opposed fund raising for the innocent families of political prisoners." Frantz Fanon, "La Minorité européenne d'Algérie en l'an V de la révolution," *Les Temps modernes,* no. 159–160 (May–June 1959), p. 1863; "Algeria's European Minority," *A Dying Colonialism,* translated by Haakon Chevalier (New York: Grove Press, 1967), pp. 172–173. See also Lottman, *Albert Camus,* p. 572 et seq.

58. Francis Jeanson and Colette Jeanson, *L'Algérie hors la loi* (Paris: Seuil, 1955).

59. Gendzier, *Frantz Fanon,* pp. 98–99, 141–142. Jeanson reported that "in the process of recounting with complete openness the terror which weighed daily on him in that 'hospitable' hell at Blida . . . Fanon showed utter disdain for what was happening in France, for what we were trying to do there, and for the very organization that had taken him in charge in order to facilitate his passage." The two men were never true friends, Jeanson writes, "a fact of which I am not proud; but it at least allows me today to give him, quite freely, the most sincere homage—of the head and of the heart." "Reconnaissance de Fanon," *Peau noir,* pp. 214–215.

60. Jeanson, *Sartre dans sa vie,* p. 213.

61. See below, pp. 212, 220. Of course to fully understand the internal workings of the network we would need reports on it from Jeanson or other participants, but unfortunately there are none to date.

62. See below, pp. 229–231.

63. Simone de Beauvoir, *La Force des choses,* pp. 392–393; *Force of Circumstance,* pp. 370–371. Cf. pp. 231–232 below.

64. Francis Jeanson, *Simone de Beauvoir où l'entreprise de vivre* (Paris: Seuil, 1966).

65. *Sartre,* transcript of a film by Alexandre Astruc and Michel Contat, pp. 99–101; *Sartre by Himself,* pp. 78–81.

66. J.-P. Sartre, "Le Fantôme de Staline," in *Situations, VII* (Paris: Gallimard, 1965), pp. 147–148; *The Ghost of Stalin,* translated by Martha H. Fletcher with the assistance of John R. Kleinschmidt (New York: George Braziller, 1968), p. 4.

67. J.-P. Sartre, "Les Communistes et la paix," originally serialized in *Les Temps modernes,* nos. 81 (July 1952), 84–85 (October–November 1952), 101 (April 1954); *Situations, VI* (Paris: Gallimard, 1964); *The Communists and Peace,* translated by Martha H. Fletcher with the assistance of John R. Kleinschmidt (New York: George Braziller, 1968). See also Michel-Antoine Burnier, *Les Existentialistes et la politique* (Paris: Gallimard, 1966), chap. 6; *Choice of Action: The French Existentialists on the Political Front Line,* translated by Bernard Murchland (New York: Random House, 1968), chap. 6.

68. C. A. Van Peursen, reporting in a Dutch journal his interview in French with Sartre in 1954: "He believes that his work in relation to questions of ontology in *Being and Nothingness* has been terminated and concluded, for the time being. His present reflections are completely concentrated on and move in the direction of philosophical ethics. He had planned this work earlier, though in a different way, which was to deal with ethics as a generalized system that would be parallel to his work on ontology in *Being and Nothingness.* Today his work is instead developing

in a direction in which he prefers to start from concrete social questions, avoiding abstract discourse, in order to draw from them a few more general guidelines or directives [*richtlijnen*] for moral conduct. . . . On a social level constraints on individual freedom are strongest: For example, what can somebody individually do about his being born in a capitalist society? What can freedom mean in that case?" *Wending* (The Hague) 9 (March 1954): 18. Translation from the Dutch by Leo Alting von Geusau.

69. J.–P. Sartre, *Critique de la raison dialectique*, vol. 1, *Théorie des ensembles pratiques* (Paris: Gallimard, 1960); *Critique of Dialectical Reason*, vol. 1, *Theory of Practical Ensembles*, translated by Alan Sheridan-Smith, edited by Jonathan Rée (London: New Left Books, 1976).

70. De Beauvoir, *La Force des choses*, p. 407; *Force of Circumstance*, p. 385. My emphasis.

71. Sartre, *Critique de la raison dialectique*, pp. 671–688; *Critique of Dialectical Reason*, pp. 714–734.

72. *Critique de la raison dialectique*, pp. 153, 308–319, and esp. pp. 346–358; *Critique of Dialectical Reason*, pp. 65, 256–269, and esp. 306–318.

73. See the extract from the projected but never published second volume of the *Critique*, "Socialism in One Country," *New Left Review*, no. 100 (November 1976–January 1977), pp. 143–163. The 500-page manuscript from which the extract is taken will be published posthumously.

74. "Entretien de Sartre avec Francis Jeanson," *Les Ecrits de Sartre*, pp. 723–729; "Francis Jeanson interviews Sartre," *The Writings of Jean-Paul Sartre*, vol. 2, *Selected Prose*, pp. 229–235. See also Jeanson's description of this clandestine encounter, below, pp. 231–232. Sartre's apartment was bombed in July 1961 and January 1962. But Jeanson had no apartment and rarely slept twice in the same place. He told me in 1973: "I had too much in my head." Did he expect torture? "Exactly. If they'd wanted to, I don't know what I would have done, so I preferred not to be caught."

75. On the question of whether independent Algeria reflected the plan of action outlined by Fanon—in *Les Damnés de la terre* (Paris: Maspero, 1961); *The Wretched of the Earth*, translated by Constance Farrington (New York: Grove Press, 1966)—Jeanson wrote in 1965, "I do not believe we should now hasten to stigmatize Fanonian 'chimeras' in the name of the Benbella-ist reality [Ahmed Ben Bella, Algeria's first president] or that we should draw from them an argument for condemning the regime that the Algerian people have given themselves up to now." Jeanson called for an unprejudiced effort to comprehend developments from both viewpoints, an effort Algerian revolutionaries themselves are best placed to carry out. "Reconnaissance de Fanon," *Peau noir*, pp. 230, 232. See also Gendzier, *Frantz Fanon*, pp. 238–260.

76. André Gorz, *Fondements pour une morale* (Paris: Galilée, 1977).

77. Ibid., pp. 98–99. Merleau-Ponty refers to "a conversion of our existence" in *Phénoménologie de la perception*, p. 501; *Phenomenology of Perception,* p. 439; and de Beauvoir refers to an "existential conversion" in *Pour une morale de l'ambiguité*, p. 19; *The Ethics of Ambiguity*, p. 14. See also de Beauvoir's later reservations about this book in *La Force des choses*, pp. 79–80; *Force of Circumstance*, p. 67.

78. Gorz, *Fondements pour une morale*, pp. 16n, 423.

79. Ibid., pp. 418–419.

80. Francis Jeanson, "Les Caractères existentialistes de la conduite humaine selon Jean-Paul Sartre," *Lignes de départ* (Paris: Seuil, 1963), p. 153.

81. See, for example, his distinction between belief and faith, p. 206 below.

82. See p. 219–220 below.

83. See below, p. 219. Among Jeanson's uses of "valorize" (see below, pp. 17, 202, 206, 208, 209, 212, 218) I do not find any corresponding to the phrase Gorz attributes to Jeanson, "*valoriser la valeur*," and Jeanson rejects such procedures, if understood as valorization of value *simpliciter*, or of all values as such, since this would involve taking an ideal presence as irreducible. See, for example, p. 199. Jeanson does speak of a reflexive valorization of "value," but he places the latter in square quotes and explains that he is referring to "the self-surpassing constitutive of human reality." See below, p. 208. Moreover, Jeanson's 1947 criticism of the "modest" or "resigned" attitude toward the possibility of achieving sincerity (see below, pp. 134–135) seems to run parallel to Gorz's critique of the saintly attitude.

84. Once it was exposed, Jeanson defended the network from underground against the charge of treason in his remarkable *Notre guerre* (Paris: Editions de Minuit, 1960).

85. Francis Jeanson, *La Foi d'un incroyant* (Paris: Seuil, 1963), p. 182.

86. Sartre, *La Transcendance de l'Ego*, p. 87; *The Transcendence of the Ego*, p. 106.

87. For such attempts see, in addition to the works on morality by de Beauvoir and Gorz cited above: Hazel E. Barnes, *An Existentialist Ethics* (New York: Knopf, 1967), and Thomas C. Anderson, *The Foundations and Structure of Sartrean Ethics* (Lawrence: Regents' Press of Kansas, 1979).

88. "Jean-Paul Sartre s'explique sur *Les Mots*," interview by Jacqueline Piatier, *Le Monde*, 18 April 1964; "A Long, Bitter, Sweet Madness," translated by Anthony Hartley, in *Encounter*, 22, no. 6 (June 1964): 62.

89. P. 269 below.

90. "J.–P. Sartre et M. Sicard: Entretien," interview dated "1977–1978" by Michel Sicard, *Obliques*, no. 18–19 (1979), p. 14.

91. Ibid., pp. 17–18.

92. "Autoportrait à soixante-dix ans," in *Situations, X*, pp. 207–209; "Self-Portrait at Seventy," in *Life/Situations*, pp. 74–76. There are at least three known unpublished manuscripts treating morality, in addition to *Power and Freedom*. They are in the hands of de Beauvoir, Contat, and Gorz.

93. "The element which unified the struggle [in May 1968] was something which, in my opinion, came from afar; it was an idea which came to us from Vietnam and which the students expressed in the formula: 'L'imagination au pouvoir.' [Imagination to power]." Sartre, "Masses, spontanéité, parti," in *Situations, VIII* (Paris: Gallimard, 1972), p. 273; "France: Masses, Spontaneity, Party," *Between Existentialism and Marxism*, translated by John Mathews (New York: Pantheon, 1974), p. 125.

94. J.–P. Sartre, "Notes sur les rapports entre la morale et l'histoire," in Jeanson, *Sartre*, Les Ecrivains devant Dieu (Paris: Desclée de Brouwer, 1966), p. 137.

95. In French: "Recherches pour une morale." See "J.–P. Sartre et M. Sicard: Entretien," *Obliques*, p. 14. See also Contat and Rybalka's bibliographical entry titled "Notes sur la Morale" in their "Manuscrits inédits," *Obliques*, no. 18–19 (1979), p. 347.

96. J.–P. Sartre, "Détermination et liberté," *Les Ecrits de Sartre*, pp. 735–745; *The Writings of Jean-Paul Sartre*, 2:241–252.

97. J.–P. Sartre, "Notes sur les rapports entre la morale et l'histoire," in Jeanson's *Sartre*, p. 137.

98. He would have felt at home among the students and professors who had invited him, Sartre explained, but his third-world comrades would have considered it a visit to the enemy's homeland in wartime; and besides, he contended, had Faulkner lectured in France during the bombing of Sakiet in Algeria, his protests

would have been defused by his presence, which would have been a *de facto* acceptance in principle of the system through which French policy was imposed on Algeria. See "Il n'y a plus de dialogue possible," in *Situations, VIII* (Paris: Gallimard, 1972), pp. 13–14.

99. Foreword by Sartre to Michèle Manceaux, *Les Maos en France* (Paris: Gallimard, 1972), p. 13; "The Maoists in France," in *Life/Situations*, p. 170.

100. Jean-Paul Sartre, Philippe Gavi and Pierre Victor, *On a raison de se révolter* (Paris: Gallimard, 1974), pp. 45, 76, 118. The major study overshadowing this period (roughly 1965–1973) is Sartre's work on Flaubert, *L'Idiot de la famille*.

101. "J.–P. Sartre et M. Sicard: Entretien," *Obliques*, p. 15. Sartrean doctrines that *appear* to be questioned here include: the mutually refractory and nonreciprocal intersubjectivity of Being-for-Others and the evanescent and merely psychological status of the "We-subject," both in *Being and Nothingness*, and, in the *Critique of Dialectical Reason*, the *external* source of the initial totalization of the group-in-fusion. But, since Sartre's report must be placed in the context of unseen work still in progress, this interpretation is only speculative.

102. Jeanette Colombel, "Sartre et Simone de Beauvour vus par Francis Jeanson," *La Pensée*, n.s. no. 129 (October 1966), pp. 98–99.

103. See below, p. 267.

104. Another example: Jeanson's failure fully to absorb or follow Sartre's existential realism was his post-Algerian political work as a director of a regional *maison de culture*, work that involved organizing popular discussion of contemporary issues and popular creation of plays under the aegis of government attempts to decentralize Parisian culture. Sartre has said that such work "inside the structures" may "accompany a properly revolutionary effort" and says he is glad Jeanson is doing it, but that it would have too many frustrations for him. See Jeanson, *Sartre dans sa vie*, p. 296. Part of Sartre's attitude may have been due to the fact that Jeanson got the job under a Ministry of Culture run by André Malraux, who had kicked *Les Temps modernes* out of Gallimard in 1950 for Sartre's anti–de Gaulle statements. See below, p. 227, n. 2. But in 1960 Sartre had criticized attempts to develop "workers' culture" apart from revolutionary *praxis*. *Critique de la raison dialectique*, pp. 50, 57; *Search for a Method*, translated by Hazel E. Barnes (New York: Knopf, 1963), pp. 67, 80. In any case, in his *L'Action culturelle dans la cité* (Paris: Seuil, 1973), Jeanson recounts how, with community support, he successfully resisted politicians' efforts to unseat him for his pro-FLN activities, only to run aground on government bureaucracy, abandoning this work in November 1971. His more recent endeavors include work toward a *doctorat d'état* in political science at the University of Dijon and a teaching post as a layperson in the psychiatry department at the University of Lyons. His most recent book is *Eloge de la psychiatrie* (In Praise of Psychiatry) (Paris: Seuil, 1979).

105. Sartre, "Matérialisme et révolution," in *Situations, III*, p. 207; "Materialism and Revolution," in *Literary and Philosophical Essays*, p. 228.

LETTER-FOREWORD

My dear Jeanson,

An author of good will always expects criticisms, even the most hostile ones, to reveal to him something about himself, if only by reflecting to him "from without" what he has thought and lived from within. However, when it came to existentialism, passion was unfortunately so mixed with philosophy and so many ignoramuses believed they could take up the pen to combat or defend this doctrine, that until now I could never recognize my intentions or thought in the articles and books claiming to speak of me. They all seemed to concern someone else. This is why I appreciate your book so much. You are the first to give me an image of myself which is sufficiently close for me to recognize myself, yet sufficiently alien for me to be able to assess myself. You have not committed the error of judging the work of a living author as if he were dead and his work forever arrested. On the contrary, you have elected to study it from the most difficult but also the most fruitful viewpoint: you have considered it as an unfinished philosophy that is still in motion and you have tried to sketch its future perspectives. Consequently, you did not hesitate to take existentialist morality as your guiding theme, which was all the more worthy since that part of the doctrine has not yet been really treated—at least not in its totality—and since most of the critics, choosing to refute theses which I have not yet advanced and which they do not know, have introduced the deepest confusion into this matter. At the same time, you could not have chosen a better standpoint from which to project the direction and orientation of my philosophy. Since for me the existent individual is in fact a being "who must exist his being," it follows that ontology cannot be separated from ethics, and I make no distinction between the moral attitude a man has chosen and what the Germans call his Weltanschauung. Were it necessary to demonstrate the excellence of your method, as well as your rigorous honesty, I would give this proof: you have so perfectly followed the development of my thought that you have come to pass beyond the position I had taken in my books at the moment I was passing beyond it myself and to raise with regard to the relations between morality and history, the universal and the concrete transcendence, the very questions I was asking myself at that same time.

Thus I have no hesitation in recommending your work to the public; it is something much more and much better than an introduction to existentialism.

Your exposition is related to the other works on the same subject that I have
been able to read as genetic definitions in geometry are to purely descriptive
definitions.

   With my best wishes, my dear Jeanson,

J.–P. Sartre

[1947]

Sartre and the Problem of Morality

AUTHOR'S PREFACE

A PHILOSOPHY that is proposed to us is at first a shock that we feel. One must pity philosophers contaminated by their profession in whom the capacity for response has become a mania for exegesis. Their work is uninspired, their minds not having lived what they insist on dissecting.

We admit—and the admission costs us little—to having responded violently to each of our contacts with Sartre's thought. Approaching it through its literary aspect, we first felt something like disgust; in particular, we could not get past the thirtieth page of *The Roads to Freedom*.[1] Pushed by a quasi-professional necessity, we later turned to the philosophical works and encountered the magic of a method of expression perfectly adapted to theoretical perspectives and capable of remedying lacks we had found in other, already classical, orientations. Our discovery was decisively deepened when we returned to the stories and novels and attended much-discussed theatrical presentations. Finally, this philosophy gave itself to us in its very movement, in its veritable dynamism, and we felt capable of putting it to practical use.

It was then that the critics' reactions and those of our best friends began to disturb us. Trying to understand the former and to answer the latter by displaying our personal understanding of a body of work, we became conscious of a certain error on our part, namely, believing we had read in those works what was still only a potentiality in the movement of the author's thinking. The moral perspective through which this movement had reached us was there only as a sketch and was apparently capable of alternative and unexpected completions.

We also became conscious of the correlative error of those who based their condemnations on the work completed to that point, while we based our judgment on certain implications of its movement. Their error, frankly, seemed the more serious one. A body of thought has value only in its move-

1. [A three-volume novel about World War II titled *Les Chemins de la liberté*: vol. 1, *L'Age de raison* (Paris: Gallimard, 1945); vol. 2 *Le Sursis* (Paris: Gallimard, 1945); vol. 3, *La Mort dans l'âme* (Paris: Gallimard, 1949). English translations are, respectively: *The Age of Reason*, translated by Eric Sutton (New York: Knopf, 1947); *The Reprieve*, translated by Eric Sutton (New York: Knopf, 1947); *Troubled Sleep*, translated by Gerard Hopkins (New York: Knopf, 1951). A draft for a fourth volume—which was to have been titled *La Dernière Chance (The Last Chance)*—was written but never published. Sartre abandoned this project in late 1949 or early 1950 for reasons discussed below, Introduction to the Criticism of Sartre, n. 4. However, excerpts from this final volume appeared in *Les Temps modernes*, no. 49 (November 1949) and no. 50 (December 1949) under the title "Drôle d'amitié" ("Strange Friendship").]

ment, and we hold that it is better to err in wrongly interpreting the direction of this movement than it is to suppress it altogether in favor of positions thereby deprived of all meaning. In the one case, one's thinking at least follows the author's, even if it does not do so exactly. In the other, however, one exerts oneself against him fruitlessly. And if our own delineation of the as yet non-existent Sartrean morality turns out to be premature, we shall be greatly surprised if we see condemnations of this morality based on its letter rather than its spirit. Too frequently, such criticisms are in fact based, not on the literal totality of the work, but on certain of its aspects, selected to suit what is to be "proven."

We have sought to sift out the *movement*—which had first appeared to us in its own right—from close study of the *positions* and from the contradictions they engender when viewed only as positions.

We have not compromised in the face of the difficulties of the subject, preferring silence to indulgence in "popularization" and being convinced, moreover, that every intelligent person can grasp philosophical questions, since they ultimately concern the way one lives one's life and one's vocation as human being. The real danger is complicating these questions by enclosing them in the kind of intellectualism that is ignorant of life.

Choosing to proceed by rather short chapters, we have linked these questions in a development whose plan is perhaps not as rigorous as its initial formulation might lead one to suppose. We believed that a plan ought in practice to follow a "progressive" motion, regularly resuming the fundamental theme in order to illuminate the detailed analyses, while receiving from them a perpetual deepening. To find something, one must know what one is looking for; but this becomes even better known as the search brings in its first results. Repetitions are therefore apparent only, and the reader can reapprehend in each new point the basic aim of the investigation into which he has allowed himself to be drawn.

We became convinced, moreover, that *Being and Nothingness* occupies an absolutely central place in Sartre's work. It was therefore necessary both to indicate its significance and exact role and to retrace its principal stages, setting in relief the argument that Sartre develops—at least for the first third of his book.

Only in this way might our results help readers who wish to overcome the difficulty inherent in the most fundamental aspect of this philosophy.

However, we do not believe comprehension of this philosophy depends on such an effort, which many will not have time to pursue effectively. The first chapters of Part One and of Part Three convey the essential results of the more searching analyses that constitute the principal purpose of Part Two. The reader may therefore decide whether he prefers to pass rapidly through these analyses or to linger and further deepen them himself.

Let us repeat our deep conviction that every reader interested in Sartre's existentialism can and ought to make himself capable of understanding its spirit—even at the level of the themes which are reputed to be the most difficult. All that is needed, in our opinion, is that the reader not allow himself to be discouraged by difficulties in the language and that he be willing to admit from the start that these exist only to guarantee to some particularly important idea the more rigorous or striking formulation it requires.

We have sought to eliminate only the superfluous from our own text. At the same time we provide in the midst of each delicate passage those transitions, focusings, and returns to the concrete which enable thought to recover itself by refamiliarizing itself with the stage through which it is passing.

The reader alone will be able to say whether we have facilitated his penetration of a philosophy that is too well known for being badly misunderstood. Our failure would not necessarily mean that this enterprise is impossible or vain; rather, it would indicate only that we were not equal to it. At least others might come away from it with the desire to make it a success.

Introduction to the Criticism of Sartre

Within an uproar to an identical silence.

The Cemetery by the Sea
—P. Valéry

THIS BOOK WAS born of a profound astonishment. It is the fruit of a naïveté whose survival is odd, given the contemporary climate of "thought." It tries to retain the vigilance of this naïveté despite several disappointments and a few temptations to cynicism. The only merit it claims is an obstinate belief in the preeminent value of personal judgment.

Alienation is fashionable in our time. Opinions unionize. Slogans replace reflection, and striking a pose—whether conformist or eccentric—handles the rest. We are on a battlefield where confronting one another is all that matters. The battle is sometimes beautiful, but, in the intoxication of combat among the militants of thought, the "civilian's" fate may be forgotten. Dialectics collide, and the public—whether or not it imprudently comes to observe—always ends up bearing the cost. Once the fight has ended, the armies retreat—always temporarily—leaving only disorder and confusion.

Within this situation Jean-Paul Sartre's existentialism seems to deserve a special kind of attention. Existentialism is a monster. Monsters constitute dangers which are great in proportion as they are ill defined. Existentialism, insofar as it is such a monster, must be destroyed.

Some would add that this amounts to destroying it altogether and gladly offer their help. Two points must be made in reply:

Existentialism is in fact not so easily destroyed. The attacks it undergoes seem to sustain its vitality by constantly stimulating it. Thus the creator need not be overly concerned about his work: criticism, by its very hostility, guarantees him a sort of continued creation.

Secondly, if there are monsters in our organized society, it is because there are "monster-mongers," peddlers of thought who cling to deformities or, if necessary, fabricate them, in order to feed the industry of sensationalism and fakery which is their livelihood. If existentialism was born, it is not their fault. But, if it has become impossible to agree on the very meaning of the word,

7

assuredly they are not blameless. Their purpose was to destroy a doctrine they considered pernicious. However, by introducing into it a confusion not previously present, they have only made it stronger and more able to ridicule their own efforts.

We are in a complete mental jumble, and this is no cause for rejoicing. The impact of Sartre's work is immense: it can increase the disorder in our minds. The question is thus to know how we should accommodate ourselves to its existence. This work exists, it is not finished; a man undertook it and immediately set forth, in the most diverse forms, several essential themes. We cannot foresee subsequent development of these themes, but certain indications permit us to attempt an outline for ourselves. The human perspectives in Sartre are certainly original: he does have something to say. We are therefore as responsible as he for whatever use we make of his work.

A body of written work exists for us only in the present. Its present is *our* present—and this is whatever we make of the message the work carries or implies in that part of it which we know. If the work creates a scandal, it is we who make that scandal out of its message. All genuine messages are dangerous, but the author is never solely responsible for this danger. The only question is how to define what is for us the most useful attitude toward it.

Here we must enter into further detail. Critics too often judge an author as if they could condemn him or absolve him. In our study of "Sartrism," however, it is not Sartre who interests us; nor do we propose to constitute ourselves a tribunal in order to make him appear before us.

Some may reply that we are forcing doors that are already open, that one never judges the man but rather his work. The quarrel is in any case linguistic, they urge, since to be an author means to be responsible for the works, and therefore, everything considered, to judge the works is to judge the man. But for us that is precisely the problem. It is not the man who has in fact been judged by many critics in judging the works but rather the works *as one would judge a man.*

Such a process seems to us worthless. Moral propositions have scarcely any common meaning from one human being to another. The meaning we give another's acts—his work, for example—testifies more about us than about him. His essential attitude may remain unknown to us forever.

We do not wish to relieve Sartre of his responsibility. But to deem Sartre totally responsible is to totally annul our own responsibility. If some of Sartre's readers cannot bear the strain of his "message," then the available works of criticism—which are doubtless read as much as his works—may help. The situation will be aggravated instead of helped if this criticism turns out to be so external as, for example, one moment to accuse Sartre of favoring bourgeois ideologies and the next moment to charge him with being the servant of

Marxist doctrines, or, in another context, to accuse him either of pushing his realism too far or of remaining indefinitely in the realm of the imaginary.

But we are quite familiar with this practice. Imagine a national assembly whose most powerful party is considered a public menace by the others. Charging this party with all the country's ills would be in vain. The other parties would thereby confess their inability to reach anything except exclusively negative agreement. And even this kind of agreement could not occur if the parties consume their energy in hardening their respective positions, in opposing all others without trying to understand them. A certain harmony could appear only through a common effort in the national interest, aimed at comprehending the theses of the menacing party. If these theses were all unjustified, it would be odd. Even if they were, even if the popular opinion which voted for that party had allowed itself to be totally deluded, the best way to awaken that opinion would not be to attack the party from several incompatible vantage points, but to manifestly do one's utmost to discover some practical value in the position in question. As long as this is omitted, responsibility for the nation's ills falls not on that party alone but on the entire assembly.

Similarly, we do not believe criticism, especially philosophical criticism, should attack a work in the name of a preexisting, dogmatic position congealed in its own formulation. One might as well put on colored glasses to judge a painting. The work repels such approaches; they prove nothing against it, since it remains essentially a dynamism and a novelty. But neither do such attacks leave the work unmolested: rather, they progressively encircle it with a halo of ideologies, a fog in which all the emotional reactions of the partisan spirit are condensed. Blows directed against such a target become ever more uncertain as the previous attacks obscure it in an opaque cloud.

Finally, we must take into account any political biases; their preponderance in the heart of a criticism completely nullifies it. A personal philosophy cannot be judged by persons claiming to have given up all personal philosophy, and this applies especially to Sartre's work. These persons may not be wrong to prefer social action to individual thought, but then they should fight indiscriminately against all manifestations of the latter, not against this or that particular philosophy. In any case they gain nothing by placing the question in the field of philosophy, where their own weapons fail them and where they cannot use their adversary's. Henri Lefebvre's difficulties provide a touching and instructive example of this,[1] and the same points hold for religious biases.

One may still be partisan and, even more insidiously, quite outside politics or religion. At least true believers in politics and religion *act*: they have faith, and if they are constantly seeking to make conversions, that is itself a positive

1. Henri Lefebvre, *L'Existentialisme,* in the series Que sais-je? (Paris: Presses Universitaires de France, 1946).

witness of their faith's practical value. Those faithful who do nothing but polemicize behave negatively and may find their taste for action souring on them. However, the most hidden and thus the most powerful bias—creating in us distortions that render a work incomprehensible, opaque, and pernicious —is the kind that colors judgment in philosophers, men of thought whose principles include free examination and an authentic effort at penetration.

Insofar as philosophy is itself contradictory—being torn between profoundly personal demands and the desire to represent others—the philosopher's conscience is troubled by a dogmatism that is half-acknowledged and half-repressed. In solitude, the thinker reconstitutes his good faith and rediscovers the positive creative impulse. Faced with others, this good faith abandons him: he may see about him only raw dogmatism and feel bound to answer it with an equivalent dogmatism. It appears to him that he can define himself only by opposing others. His exasperated sense of individualism thus occasions disappointments analogous to those the political partisan experiences in trying to obey some party line. In short, he becomes a polemicist himself, attacking the thought of others before attempting to truly understand it. It is as if he were unwilling to let it seduce him for fear he might then be compelled to renounce his personal originality.

From the preceding remarks it appears the best defense against an attitude that is, a priori, suspect is to master it by means of an independent effort at comprehension pushed as far as possible. We remain enslaved to the unknown even in pretending—through tricks by which we ourselves are never fooled— to represent it as something known. When this picture is completed, the deeper essence of the matter remains, as does the discomfort of never having sought it out. To be liberated from a philosophy, one must at least have tried to make it his own. Only then will the risk of being dominated by it be altogether past; it may even become an instrument of mastery. It must in any case cease to be an opaque object, an undigested lump, against which our bellicose maneuvers remain, for ourselves at least, ineffective.

Once an alien philosophy assumes importance for us, our most urgent task must be to free ourselves from it. This is accomplished, not by smothering it magically through the remote control of words, but by mobilizing it in the fullest sense, activating it within ourselves and perhaps using it in a battle in which it is always only ourselves whom we oppose. If the instrument is useless, we may reject it. But to reject it before trying to get hold of it would not rid us of it at all: we thereby repress an enemy that will live on within us—and against us—precisely as a result of such repression.

We are often tempted to take the means for the end. We lose sight of the true goal, which is to put ourselves in harmony with ourselves, to arrive at a mastery of self devoid of tyranny. In this effort we may have to adopt certain landmarks and a system of reference. We will have to search out our own attitude by confronting it with that of others, by formulating positions and creating oppositions. Yet if we limit ourselves to this, we deny ourselves true movement; we regress to our starting point and become immobile, with a soul, as Plato says, like "several beasts living in discord," paralyzed in a negativity that renders it impotent against its own inner anarchy. Replacing the initial richness of our capacities, an unproductive hostility inhabits our heart. The mind has no outward enemies: those it makes it houses within.

In the name of an essential partiality, one must free oneself from such factitious biases. One must give up the spirit of system building, in the name of a single systematic attitude which consists in always giving precedence to the "moral" point of view or, if you wish, to the governance of self. If there is a psychic unconscious in us, it is we who create it. It then becomes the most dangerous part of ourselves; we must, therefore, struggle against its initial constitution. Divorce here is an easy but infinitely costly solution, since it is always from oneself that one is divorced.

A fundamental bias guides man; each of us must constantly return to it to come to grips with his own moral demands. The question of the possible meaning of life persists to our death. Since, in the end, life's meaning is never anything else but the one we give to it, the task is to enable ourselves to give it meaning. One is alone in this task, and formulas are valuable only if tested by living them.

This is why we are concerned neither to put "Sartrism" in formulas nor to pile up rhetorical precautions against other positions. As for one's own encounter with a philosophical movement, the only judgment is practice. The other person's freedom of judgment must equally be safeguarded: that which helps me construct myself may unbalance my neighbor. My responsibility begins when I express my own viewpoint; it becomes a culpability if I forget to specify that it is *only* my viewpoint.

Our central question seemed divisible between the personal perspective—"What use can I make of Sartrism?"—and the perspectives of others—"How much of it can I propose to my fellow men?" However, in light of the reservations made above, the issue boils down to the first of these two. Proposing a theme no longer involves the will to impose it on others in its particular formulation. It means only the offer to others of that comprehension of it that one has been able to put into effect in his own essential practical concerns.

And that is precisely our purpose: to determine what Sartre's thought can bring to the practical conception of the moral enterprise that one develops for oneself.

Understandably, we shall abstain as much as possible—that is, wherever it would be most tempting—from recourse to this philosophy's sources and from accumulation of philosophic erudition. Nor have we attempted detailed analyses of all Sartre's existing works. A complete enough exposition of these has been furnished in the rather short book by Robert Campbell.[2]

In a word, *objectivity*, in the historical sense, cannot be our concern. Genuine criticism, in our view, abjures this form of objectivity, which amounts only to neutrality. Again, the bias we avow is enveloped in a personal moral effort. As such, this bias takes in the whole philosophical attitude, whose only valid meaning has always been as a practical endeavor with two aspects—knowledge of self and control of self. And these aspects may be separated only at the price of abstraction, which is frequently useful but sometimes misleading.

However, those "philosophers" who deny Sartre the right to call himself a philosopher might consider vain any attempt to philosophically comprehend and employ Sartrism. We have Luc-J. Lefèvre's astonishing little book in mind.[3] We shall return to it, but we would like to indicate two basic faults in it from our present viewpoint:

There is the error, first of all, of transferring to Sartre's *positions* an importance too often denied the movement that animates them, that is, criticizing— mostly under its static aspect—a philosophy which has meaning only inasmuch as it opposes everything static. One could more justifiably and effectively turn such a philosophy against itself when it betrays itself than reject it *in toto* as useless and dangerous. Something may always be gained from a body of thought that exhibits some power of acting on our minds, even with evil results.

An error of different origin, though it is perhaps linked with the first, consists in forgetting that Socrates himself, to whom Lefèvre occasionally refers, was rather roughly treated by the "philosophers" of his time. Despite his lifelong struggle against sophism, he was himself condemned to death for being a sophist and an instigator of scandals. He made the mistake of reasoning about Athenian beliefs, applying to them the free judgment and access to truth of one who preferred in all things to consult his personal "demon." Since then, Socrates the frenzied, Socrates the possessed, Socrates the dissolute and impious has been transmuted into a perfect symbol of Wisdom. A man's death facilitates many things, particularly the effort at comprehension owed him during his life simply because he is a man. Without comparing this with Sartre's actual doctrines, it is worthwhile to ponder philosophical errors that follow upon the surprise or shocking effect of a philosophy. It is in any case pointless to deny that Socrates could have corrupted youths, as he was accused of doing; the very effectiveness granted his method also required that it not be inoffensive.

Once again, to sum up this question of method, one combats a spiritual

2. Robert Campbell, *Jean-Paul Sartre, ou une littérature philosophique* (Paris: Pierre Ardent, 1945).
3. Luc-Jean Lefèvre, *L'Existentialiste est-il un philosophe?* (Paris: Alsatia, 1946).

danger by first doing one's utmost to extract the very dynamism and effectiveness that make it a danger.

We should also defend ourselves against the charge of considering the moral aspects of Sartre's philosophy when he has not yet expressed himself specifically in this area. His "Morality," as well as the third and fourth volumes of *The Roads to Freedom*, have yet to be published.[4] These works may hold for certain commentators surprises which they might not acknowledge but which could singularly complicate their task.

Every critic of Sartrism could be accused of anticipation. This reproach is all the more unavoidable for us, since we maintain that there can be no Sartrean philosophy outside the moral perspective. It is generally agreed that this perspective must be implied in the part of the work already published. But we dissent from other "judgments" we have read up to now on the manner in which this perspective emerges.

Let us put forth our criterion and the ways we would apply it to Sartre's work.

We have said we favor a philosophy that is essentially a morality. To this extent the traditional opposition between fact and right, between what is and what ought to be, between nature and practical accomplishment, seems to us artificial. While we recognize their methodological primacy, we deny these distinctions the right to consolidate themselves by claiming to represent two philosophical pseudorealities, one that would be the object of a "metaphysics," the other the object of a "morality."

But once you allow your metaphysical perspectives to crystallize, their influence will crystallize your "moral" perspectives. Such so-called philosophizing

4. [The "Treatise of Morality" ("Traité de morale") has never been published. The third volume of *The Roads to Freedom*, titled *Troubled Sleep (La Mort dans l'âme)*, appeared in 1949, but only excerpts from the fourth volume were published later that year, as mentioned above, n. 1, Author's Foreword. *The Roads to Freedom* was written concurrently with and was abandoned about the same time as the "Treatise of Morality"—that is, late 1949–early 1950—and both the "internal" and the "external" reasons for both abandonments seem to have been related. Regarding internal reasons, Contat and Rybalka call "Strange Friendship" "the most rigid and aesthetically the least successful of the series. This failure . . . seems to correspond to the failure of the 'Morality' Sartre had projected . . . and marks the end of his moral period." Michel Contat and Michel Rybalka, *Les Ecrits de Sartre: chronologie, bibliographie commentée* (Paris: Gallimard, 1970), p. 221; *The Writings of Jean-Paul Sartre*, translated by Richard C. McCleary, 2 vols. (Evanston: Northwestern University Press, 1974), vol. 1, *A Bibliographical Life*, p. 234. In a 1959 interview quoted by Contat and Rybalka, Sartre spoke of having abandoned the last volume of *The Roads to Freedom* for external reasons, ones which might equally apply to the "Morality": "The fourth volume was supposed to deal with the Resistance. The choice then was easy—even though it took a lot of strength and courage to stick to it. You were either for or against the Germans. It was black or white. Today—and since '45—the situation has become more complicated. It takes less courage, perhaps, to choose, but the choices are much more difficult. I cannot express the ambiguities of our time in a novel situated in '43." Ibid.]

results in a purely theoretical vision of being and a conception of freedom devoid of meaning and efficacy.

You will end up with an absurdism, and this is quite often the light in which Sartrism appears.

In fact, and until the contrary is shown, a becoming is always the becoming of something that becomes. The practical impulse is only one aspect of Morality, and it acquires meaning by reference to the knowledge of being, which is its other aspect. Conversely, being is always for us only what it comes to be: theoretical knowledge of being has value only if engaged in the concrete perspective of a practical impulse. What we do is not in itself more *moral* than what we are; by itself, our action is not more valuable than our nature. Whatever else may be related to Morality, the truly and uniquely philosophical question bears on what we make out of what we are.

One must start either with the practical or with the theoretical, and it seems normal to seek to understand before acting. Thus one begins by trying to describe "the human condition." If one finds in that condition a type of freedom that is coextensive with the very existence of man, that too must be described. It will be said that this freedom is ineluctable, that by right nothing can limit it, and that there are no already realized values inscribed in the nature of things that might contribute to such a limitation. Nothing is amiss up to this point; a philosophical viewpoint on human reality has been sustained.

The danger is that from this point on one will hint to the reader that this freedom is itself a value, that it already has moral value, and that to create authentic values it is enough to abandon oneself to its impulse. Thus few new terms are needed to pass from a negative viewpoint—in which the human being merely escapes the fate of things, which are limited to themselves—to a positive viewpoint, in which preoccupation with the goal to be attained implicitly disposes one to imbue with value a freedom that is as yet only theoretical.

Such, we believe, is the basic drama between Sartre and his critics, be they detractors or advocates. Certain appearances aside, though, we hold that Sartre's "freedom" simply refers to human freedom as opposed to the determinism of the thing. However, this freedom to which we are "condemned" must be made *our own* or else it too will soon appear as yet another determinism. We *are* free, but this in no way relieves us from having to *make* ourselves free. First, ontology had only to tell us whether such an endeavor has a meaning. It does have a meaning, one that is wholly negative, since *essentially* we are not determined. It remains for us to give it a positive meaning in the practical attitude. We determine ourselves *existentially*, through the practical attitude, drawing support from the very difficulties inherent in our presence in the world.

It would be odd if an author who calls his doctrine "existentialism" had no intention of pursuing the above theme. But we have argued that one must not pass judgment on the moral perspective of Sartre's existentialism solely on the basis of those aspects of it presented and formulated to date. Since these aspects all depend on an "essentialist" methodology, they could not as such be reflected within a moral perspective. This methodology obviously prepares for and implies such a perspective, but it has not yet been explicitly approached in its own right.

Let us retain from these remarks the fundamental *ambiguity* of the human mode of being. To have meaning, a philosopher's efforts must be grounded in recognition of this ambiguity; without this ambiguity, such efforts would not even be conceivable. Man is that "existent" who lacks common measure with other existents. Though free, he must liberate himself; though human, he must humanize himself. Were a man fully human from birth, he would simply be an individual case of the human species. But he is a person, a being we have already seen defining itself as a perpetual escape from all a priori definition, continually having to be what it is, always capable of backing away from itself in order to write its own history, reflect on its existence, alter its way of being, or reaffirm fidelity to it.

The value of a philosophy resides primordially, then, in what it makes of this ambiguity. To philosophize entails that one exist ambiguously, but it does not entail that one recognize this. Thus the materialist, for example, cannot reduce consciousness to some material phenomenon without also exhibiting the ability of consciousness to think matter. Yet there always have been and there always will be materialists who derive support from their own ambiguity in order to reduce it artificially to the absolute and sterile unity of matter. Such solutions of the problem of human existence serve the cause of authentic philosophy no better than do traditional methods, which cut the Gordian knot by substituting an irreducible duality of terms for this ambiguity and by then reconstructing man with two autonomous principles that coexist in him like eternal strangers. Such methods fail to recognize that a man's abilities are engaged in transcending the species in the direction of personality; they establish only his simultaneous membership in two species whose essential characteristics are irreconcilable: the species of pure minds and pure mechanisms.

But perhaps the problem lies with the temptation which philosophers find hard to combat and to which they most frequently yield: that of *explaining* man, the being by whom all explanations come into the world. Philosophers often believe their explanations follow a rigorous scientific method. Yet they sometimes resolutely turn their backs on such rigor, since to explain scientifically is to give an account of the unknown in terms of the known, and such philosophers propose to do the opposite, that is, to give an account of the very knowing activity from which knowledge itself originates. This temptation is called metaphysics. The taste for risks assumes this form when it reaches the speculative domain. Thus one speaks of "audacious systems" and "rash constructions." When the collapse occurs, the engineer is usually far away. His fame will not be diminished by this event, since there will always be well-meaning specialists who celebrate him for the collapse itself by describing with profound subtlety the richness of the materials used—without mentioning their lack of cohesion.

It seems we are bound to acknowledge sooner or later that philosophy differs radically from the scientific disciplines. Physics, for example, studies natural phenomena; human physiology studies man from the viewpoint of his corporeal functions and considers his body from without, like an object. But philosophy's sole object is the very subject who philosophizes, the philosopher in person. Trickery is out of the question here. It would be especially vain to pretend that in doing the psychology of man in general one could ignore the obtrusive presence of this subjectivity. The following alternatives arise: either one decides to elude it, thereby losing the specifically human in man, the "I" who puts himself in question in his psychological research; or one sees the necessity to make a place for this subjectivity, a preponderant place. But if one elects the latter, a new method must be adopted.

Given an ambiguous reality, an ambiguous method is alone suitable. The problem will then be to reconcile the subjectivity that is a functional characteristic of the matter under study with the objectivity that is indispensable for any serious study.

The German phenomenological method elaborated by Husserl and transposed by Heidegger to a different level seemed to Sartre—as to other French thinkers, including at least Merleau-Ponty and Raymond Aron—capable of satisfying the requirements of ambiguity and thus deserving of preliminary clarification.

As a first approximation, and to tie down our ideas, let us note that the term "existentialism" itself conceals a formidable ambiguity: it implies one can elaborate a *system* of existence. Since metaphysical, explanatory solutions are excluded, and since the existence of consciousness is pure subjectivity, this system will have to articulate the natural, permanent grasp this subjectivity has of itself—without being constructive. Thus its method will be descriptive explication [*explication descriptive*] rather than scientific explanation. Although such a method must use whichever concepts, notions, and "essences" best allow examination of the various aspects of this self-comprehension of consciousness, it must use them without suppressing the fact that such "essences" have no reality of their own outside the existence that is made explicit through them.

In other words, human existence manifests itself indefinitely to itself in the form of phenomena. Understanding these "existential" phenomena requires connecting them to "essential" structures of consciousness, that is, to a certain number of fundamental attitudes that can be named and described but that are nothing outside their existential unfolding.

Phenomenology will therefore imply an essentialist movement that can furnish the basis of our knowledge of the human condition. Such knowledge would lack any interest if it did not permit us to envision subsequent action by the subject upon himself. It cannot by itself provide the principles for such moral action, but it must allow for the possibility of such action. This merely reasserts that the description of man must recognize him as a *moral being*, referring, however, to a morality of the act that must itself be grasped in an active and reflective moral effort if its values are to be understood.

If the fact of human existence must be able to be transcended in the direction of its valorization [*valorisation*], it is because that fact already contains its own perpetual self-transcendence. Underlying and conditioning all *moral transcendence of fact* must be *a fact of transcendence*. Any realization that includes valorizing [*réalization valorisante*] implies that the reality was already *more* than merely real. This "more" can be misinterpreted either by attributing to it a moral value it does not possess by itself or by ignoring the subsequent possibilities of value development that it contains. In the first case, one will take the description as a moral statement and accuse it of being immoral; in the second, one will take it as mere description and reproach it for its amorality. In the latter case one will have missed the movement already implied; in the former one will have taken this movement as something that it is not yet.

We shall try to show the extent to which the act of transcendence makes a moral conversion possible. The first two parts of this study—one devoted to the psychological starting points, the other to the general description of the human condition—outline a transition whose meaning lies in the equation established between human consciousness and freedom. Part Three will point out the insufficiency and failure of such freedom when it is left to itself in the natural attitude. It will also describe the factors involved in a liberating conversion—a passage to the moral attitude, in the course of which man takes hold of himself in order to orient his own humanization.

We have not attempted to define this orientation itself and its practical results. We must excuse ourselves, on the one hand, for not having made any definitive judgment on the as yet unknown continuations of the undertaking which we shall examine and, on the other, for suggesting only the essential lines of development of this orientation, since the moral choice of oneself is authentic only if singular. Men can choose to fight for their fellow men and with them, but such a choice is valid only if it is made in solitude, as the invention of a strictly personal mode of rapport with other persons. It is by starting with the world that man undertakes to understand his own existence, but it is only by starting with himself that he can attempt to endow his acts with value.

PART ONE

The Phenomenology of Ambiguity:
Human Reality

Chapter 1

A Practical Manifestation of Ambiguity

Existence precedes essence.

—J.–P. Sartre
"Existentialism is a Humanism"

Essences and facts are incommensurate, and he
who initiates his inquiry with facts never succeeds
in recovering essences.

—J.–P. Sartre
Outline of a Theory of the Emotions

IN AN ATTEMPT to refute Sartre's existentialism, one critic, Luc-J. Lefèvre (*Is the Existentialist a Philosopher?*),[1] has addressed himself exclusively to the text of the lecture entitled "Existentialism is a Humanism."[2] This procedure seems a bit hasty to us, but the results are rich in lessons.

The central theme of this attack is to assimilate the idea of phenomenology to the ideas of psychoanalysis and phenomenalism, even epiphenomenalism. We shall later return to these ideas. We are here concerned with the criticism that Sartre abandoned the concept of "human nature," of the human species as it were, in order to begin with subjectivity. The objection is that "to say that man is nothing other than *what he makes of himself* is to . . . see in him nothing but the future. At this point we rejoin Bergsonism, the system of pure movement."[3]

Thus, to pretend that existence precedes essence is to attribute to man a freedom proper only to freedom itself, since it is a *freedom prior to being*, which amounts to a *freedom without being*. Human freedom then becomes a spontaneity which strongly resembles determinism, a sort of "*élan vital*" from which one could derive an evolutionism, a morality of facts, an amorality.

This is a harsh conclusion and one can understand its basis. The only difficulty is that the text criticized puts forth a position that is the exact inverse

1. [Luc-Jean Lefèvre, *L'Existentialiste est-il un philosophe?* (Paris: Alsatia, 1946).]
2. [Jean-Paul Sartre, *L'Existentialisme est un humanisme* (Paris: Nagel, 1946); "Existentialism is a Humanism," translated by Philip Mairet, in *Existentialism from Dostoevsky to Sartre*, ed. Walter Kaufmann (Cleveland: Meridian, 1956).]
3. Lefèvre, *L'Existentialiste est-il un philosophe?* pp. 21–22.

of the methodological approach Sartre adopts in all of his other philosophical works. Thus, to focus on this work exclusively seems rather odd. Indeed, this very opposition within Sartre's works may be a problem regarding which Luc-J. Lefèvre could have made more pertinent observations, inasmuch as he is abreast of "Philosophy" (meaning Thomism, just as in medieval scholasticism one referred to Aristotle simply as "the Philosopher").

In this very short piece, Sartre set himself the sole task of answering criticisms of a moral kind. He was thus obliged to sharply accent an "existentialism" for which he had up to then concentrated upon and produced only the essentialist preparation. Those relying exclusively on this text will therefore naturally be inclined to reproach him for a quite empty pseudomorality. Sartre himself shares this view, considering the lecture in this respect an "error."[4] Actually the work limits itself to boldly abstracting the outlines of the most revolutionary side of what may ultimately be a Sartrean morality but which has not as yet been elaborated.

Again, being human is ambiguous; it is inseparably both *fact* and *value*. And we would like to show that viewing it from the perspective of facts leads one to incorporate values within facts and thus to construct a metaphysics of inefficacious values; inversely, viewing it according to value compels one to turn facts into values, which entails a morality without a foundation.

The former error is just what we find in the case of Lefèvre, who considers

4. [I have not found this statement by Sartre in Sartre's writings or interviews published between 28 October 1945, the date of the lecture, and the end of May 1947, when Jeanson finished writing his book. Perhaps I've overlooked the source. Sartre has criticized but never *renounced* any previous work to my knowledge, and, when Georg Lukács criticized him in 1949 for changing from "a Heideggerian attitude in *Being and Nothingness* to a Kantian morality in 'Existentialism is a Humanism,'" he responded heatedly: "But that [criticism] is entirely false. Lukács thereby demonstrates he's hardly read *Being and Nothingness*, because all the so-called noxious aspects of my philosophy that he thinks he's discovered in my lecture have already been laid out in *Being and Nothingness*. Criticizing a book of fifty pages—which in any case is only a transitional work [*une oeuvre de passage*]—will not result in the demolition of existentialism. But it's a quite special philosophical method consisting of criticizing a morality that for the time being has scarcely been outlined; Lukács knows quite well that I am now preparing a 'Treatise of Morality' ['*Traité de morale*']." Interview by François Erval, *Combat*, 20 January, 1949. In 1976, Sartre might have been referring to the same "error" Jeanson mentions when he explained that immediately after the lecture he had approved a limited publication of its text for those unable to attend and was surprised when "50,000 or 100,000 copies, and even more," were printed and sold worldwide: "And that bothered me, I have to admit.... That said, you will note that there's an element of insincerity in my attitude. If I found what I said meaningful for 500 or 1,000 people, why wouldn't I have found it equally meaningful for all the people who wanted to buy it? And yet that always struck me as a serious error. There were a lot of people who thought they understood what I meant by reading only *Existentialism* [the lecture]. Which meant they had only a vague idea of what existentialism was all about." *Sartre (Sartre par lui-même)*, transcript of a film by Alexandre Astruc and Michel Contat (Paris: Gallimard, 1977), pp. 94–95; *Sartre by Himself*, translated by Richard Seaver (New York: Urizen Books, 1978), pp. 74–75.]

human existence as a fact, "the human fact." The total value of "humanity" therefore resides essentially in each man *by nature* or by definition, which amount to the same thing. But then the moral attitude, the effort to progress, becomes mysterious, for one can no longer explain how there can be any motion. On the other hand, Sartre, in his lecture, considers "human reality" as a value, a freedom. It thereby becomes the unique fact, and there is nothing on which to base this perpetual project or motion. But then one cannot attribute moral significance to such motion, since one does not see what could confer on it the significance of progress. In the first case it seems that morality becomes useless, since the human has already been acquired; in the second, it seems morality could be anything whatever: the human remains completely to be invented.

Lefèvre dodges our remarks because, though he rejects Sartre's perspective in the lecture in favor of its inverse, he nevertheless remains in a mixed position which allows him to retain the benefits of both perspectives in a clever, perpetual juxtaposition. But this is *only* a juxtaposition; in its effect, Lefèvre's attitude would sacrifice morality to metaphysics, for otherwise he would not have refused to uncover the possibility of an authentic morality in Sartre's position. In reproaching Sartre for confusing the human fact with the "brute fact of matter" and for replacing morality with psychoanalysis, he is perhaps unaware that he himself risks confounding values with facts and replacing morality with a physics of values.

However, when Lefèvre declares that phenomenology makes consciousness a tributary of facts and that "all phenomena considered as such are amoral," he places us more clearly at the center of the debate. For he alone takes existential phenomena to be facts, while Sartre everywhere insists that the existential phenomenon is "human reality" in its ambiguity, simultaneously and indissolubly both value and fact, transcendence and nature.

A method should not be ambiguous in the same way its object may be. It can at most be allowed to be oriented toward ambiguity, but only at the cost of having already posited ambiguity as such, that is, of having isolated by abstraction the two aspects which it must then reunite. Thus, while never losing sight of the existential phenomenon itself, one may nevertheless be constrained to approach it either through an essentialism of facts that seems to deprive those facts of their value or, correlatively, through an essentialism of values that seems to reduce values to the realm of facts.

This helps us to pin down the terms in which the ambiguity of phenomenology will constitute a problem for us. We can now ask that one of Sartre's early works, *Outline of a Theory of the Emotions*, furnish us, not only an application whereby this method will define itself, but also the precise features of this problem, as they were conceived by their author at that time.

Chapter 2

The Psychology of the Emotions

FROM THE VIEWPOINT we have adopted, the study of the emotions is of cardinal interest.

This study pertains initially to psychology and, as such, it requires an account of how we can know ourselves. Emotion is also a phenomenon in which we appear to be reduced to the roles of spectator of ourselves and passive victim of events. Being a frequent phenomenon, emotion would seem to be the practical manifestation of a psychobiological determinism that is resistant to all moral interpretations.

Our inquiry will therefore encounter both a problem of method through which phenomenology can take form for us, and also, within the perspective of practical philosophy, the problem of self-mastery, without which any theory is self-defeating. We know only what we can know; every science requires a technique and can become established only through testing of that technique.

PSYCHOLOGY AND THE SCIENTIFIC ATTITUDE

Classical psychology seems to have been concerned to define itself at the level of pure theory, as opposed to that of "moral" behavior, and the latter is thereby made theoretical. Having made this start, it then explores "psychological consciousness," a consciousness which has been disengaged from the total being and from active consciousness. Of course this psychology can discover in such a consciousness only "psychic facts" before which the being in whom they appear finds himself ineffective. In this way classical psychology sets in relief the "fact" in order to ignore the "action," considering *what is* apart from its *realization.* It thereby limits itself to the analysis of a *matter* which one shall never thereafter be able to grasp as showing a *power* to form itself. By thus treating consciousness as another sector of being, classical psychology deprives consciousness of just those characteristics it exhibits in its active rapport with a world which it opposes to itself.

Under these conditions psychology becomes mental physics. Whether concerned with objects, movements, or powers within the "soul," such a psychology always naturalizes the soul, overlooking its character as a force affecting the world and itself. And even if there is evolution from this static psychology to the psychology of the mental future, and thence to the psychology of mental dynamism, the force attributed to consciousness remains that of a merely natural power with manifestations in consciousness. The true roles of consciousness in relation to this power are those of passive witness and register. On this view *there is* a power *in* consciousness, but it is not a power *of* consciousness. Always merely traversed and affected by it, consciousness never exercises that power. Always coming second with respect to what happens within itself, consciousness is reduced—even by some would-be antimaterialist psychologists—to the role of "epiphenomenon," of adjunct phenomenon, an effect that is never in turn a cause, a seeing which is produced but which produces nothing in turn.

As we have tried to show in another work,[1] this view is the product of excessive faith in Reason, which faith easily inverts itself into a total "absurdism." Applied incautiously to psychology, the scientific attitude leads to the antiscientific notion of the epiphenomenon. For having expected too much of its own rationality, consciousness is condemned indefinitely to play before its own eyes the irrational part of the stranger, so perfectly described in Albert Camus's novel.[2]

We know how elsewhere Camus systematizes the "absurdist" position of which *The Stranger* is only an individual illustration: the world is "irrational"; life has no meaning; the human individual is condemned without reprieve to the lot of Sisyphus, hopelessly rolling a stone that always falls back to its starting point.[3] Yet, from the perspective that now concerns us, it is interesting to note that Camus takes care to "maintain the absurd" at the cost of perpetual revolt. The fundamental absurdity that is supposed to be "established," that shows itself with "evidence," must nevertheless be consolidated by an attitude which, on this basis, could only be one of absurdification. But if Camus's stranger ultimately "liberates" himself—applying the Absurd to himself alone and thereby ceasing, according to Camus, to be its victim—he manages to do so only through violent anger at a chaplain who comes to his cell to console him. This anger typifies all emotion. It shows both the intentional character of these psychic phenomena and the voluntary self-degradation of consciousness when it chooses to immerse itself in what was at first only a vague urging, a feeling of strangeness regarding other persons.

These, then, are the two features we will encounter in our phenomenological study of the emotions.

1. Francis Jeanson, *La France intérieure*, 1947, particularly no. 53 (February), "Le Mythe de l'absurde."
2. [Albert Camus, *L'Etranger* (Paris: Gallimard, 1942); *The Stranger*, translated by Stuart Gilbert (New York: Vintage, 1954).]
3. [Jeanson alludes here to Camus's *Le Mythe de Sisyphe* (Paris: Gallimard, 1942); *The Myth of Sisyphus and Other Essays*, translated by Justin O'Brien (New York: Knopf, 1955).]

THE CLASSICAL THEORIES

Sartre begins his *Outline* by inviting us, in light of his critique of classical views, to raise consciousness to its proper rank as consciousness. Psychology cannot be the simple study of facts. Psychologists should not expect internal events either to organize themselves or to obey the norms of a transcendental, impersonal consciousness that is alien to our concrete consciousness. Each such internal event is also an advent, an appearance through which consciousness manifests both its situation in the world and its own attitude toward that situation. It is thus a "phenomenon" which, although it cannot be attributed to any being or "noumenon" closed off from psychological investigation, can at least be attributed to its author, thereby *indicating* the totality of a consciousness cast in a particular attitude. Such an event finds within the world not its cause but only a "motivation."[4] Its consistency is therefore due solely to its character as a human behavior in which an original form of presence-to-the-world is expressed.

Sartre's outlook seems paradoxical when compared with our intellectual habits, which tend to present "facts of consciousness" as assimilable to natural processes. And Sartre's position on emotion seems even more paradoxical, since in this case one typically experiences loss of self, or self-dispossession.

Now, classically, emotion can be considered under three aspects: physiological reactions, objective behavior, and the "state of consciousness" itself. All theories of emotion to date privilege one or another of these aspects by taking it as essential and reducing the remaining two to accessory accompaniments.

Thus for William James the whole of emotion consists of *physiological phenomena* followed by their projection into consciousness.[5] Anger is merely a disorder within the organism plus consciousness of this disorder. Yet it appears that, whatever may be its organic seat, an angry consciousness is an

---

4. [See also below, pp. 88–89. "Motivation" is Husserl's term for what has not been fully given, as indicated by what has been; for example, if I presently observe this side of the moon, the other side is given, not merely as a logical possibility, but as "motivated," that is, as having a certain undetermined but determinable configuration, etc. See Edmund Husserl, *Ideen zu einer reinen Phänomenologie und phänomenologischen Philosophie*, Vol. I (Halle: Max Niemeyer, 1922), pp. 88–90; *Ideas: General Introduction to Pure Phenomenology,* translated by W. R. Boyce Gibson (London: Allen and Unwin, 1931), pp. 148–149. Sartre modifies Husserl by holding that a "nothing" is perpetually inserted between human reality's present and its past. See *L'Etre et le néant: essai d'ontologie phénoménologique* (Paris: Gallimard, 1943), pp. 63–64; *Being and Nothingness: An Essay in Phenomenological Ontology,* translated by Hazel E. Barnes (New York: Washington Square Press, 1966), pp. 62–63. For a more sympathetic interpretation of Husserl's notion, see Maurice Merleau-Ponty, *Phénoménologie de la perception* (Paris: Gallimard, 1945), pp. 61–62; *Phenomenology of Perception,* translated by Colin Smith (New York: Humanities Press, 1962), pp. 49–50.]

5. [See William James, *The Principles of Psychology,* vol. 2 (New York: Henry Holt and Co., 1890), p. 449.]

oriented consciousness, one with a direction and a meaning. Physiology fails to distinguish those changes within the organism which are due to anger from those due to joy, except by their intensity; yet we persist in taking these two emotions as irreducible in that we never count as joyful the demeanor presented to us by a man in anger. Anger is itself capable of subtle shadings, apprehensible within the angry behavior, and this too seems to rule out any view of emotion as mere transposition into consciousness of an organic sensation.

It is precisely from the angle of *behavior* that Pierre Janet approaches the study of emotion. He hoped thereby to retain the distinctively psychic without leaving the field of scientific objectivity, since a behavior is an observable psychic phenomenon. Emotion consists of a transition from a superior behavior to an inferior one (that is, to a behavior of failure, of maladaption) and, secondarily, of the awareness of this failing behavior.[6] The problem is then to grasp what can be meant by such a transition. Is it an automatic substitution of the failing for the initial behavior due to the impossibility of maintaining the latter? The so-called failing behavior would then be no more than a random discharge of nervous energy "following the law of least effort." This would return us to a thesis very like James's. Yet Janet seems tempted to move beyond this when he pictures consciousness as no longer restricted to secondary "awareness" but as including intervention and effective operation. Thus consciousness can complete the emotion, making it a true behavior by conferring on the emotional process the meaning of failure in relation to a superior alternative—which continues to be viewed as possible but too difficult. My sudden anger at a friend who persists in failing to understand my arguments is a psychic phenomenon, a true behavior, only inasmuch as it is not mechanically necessitated by the *impossibility* of finding new arguments, being in fact motivated by a difficulty that I elect to evade.

Although Janet may be said to hesitate between two interpretations, psychology cannot be content with conscious behaviors which remain, in Janet's terms, mere "states of consciousness." The very notion of "behaviors" should have value for psychology only as *behaviors of consciousness*.

By bringing out such points, phenomenology can provide the means for understanding the "phenomenon" of emotion. Let us consider examples from which we can draw various conclusions concerning the phenomenological theory of self-knowledge.

Some Examples

A man who is unexpectedly prey to a ferocious beast faints. Upon entering Pierre Janet's office, a patient who comes to make a painful confession is struck

6. [See Pierre Janet, *Les Névroses* (Paris: Ernest Flammarion, 1910), pp. 358–364; *L'Automatisme psychologique* (Paris: Félix Alcan, 1889), p. 465.]

by the professor's prestige and suffers a fit of hysteria. I receive word of the arrival of someone dear to me and I begin to sing, dance, and show a most lively exultation.

It is noteworthy that a single characteristic can be extracted from these three examples: in each, a sort of evasion of the real situation seems to be operating. As we have seen regarding anger—and as Janet appears to have suspected—evasion is not a purely physiological disorder; it is a behavior and it acquires meaning as such only within a conscious intention which, in the above case of dread, is negative. The subject sees clearly that his present situation demands an effort from him. If he accepts that situation, he is obligated to act. But he does not feel equal to this obligation. Its difficulty, appearing unexpectedly and leaving no time for deliberation, makes him dread a lurking impossibility. Moved by defeatism, the subject faints, negating the situation as it presents itself, thereby evading the obligation.

Clearly the man in danger of death and the intimidated patient both attempt, by sharply altering their own attitudes, to ignore the present situation the moment it appears irresolvable. But does this interpretation apply to joy? That it does apply becomes evident if one notes that within the objective conditions of our existence every anticipated satisfaction courts several dangers. At a general level, these dangers are: dissolution, debasement through repetition, and mediocritization as a consequence of the thousandfold exigencies of our time-bound existence. It is normal, therefore, to seek to deny those objective conditions which may be hostile, so as to collect in a sort of instantaneous absolute all the satisfaction we feel entitled to exact. The real situation calls for a positive task of concentration and struggle; we oppose that situation with an imaginary one, thus demanding a right that need not be earned.

It may also be objected that emotion is *expressed* in concrete performances that are, as such, beyond the domain of fiction. But it is precisely in such performances that emotion itself resides, since a subject who was content with a merely mental negation of the situation would be unable to believe in that negation. Emotion is experienced as self-dispossession, as escape from oneself, and it must be so if it is to constitute an evasion. Yet there are critical moments when reverie is no longer possible. Since the subject feels it is impossible to transform the world, he transforms his own manner of being present to the world. In between the possible act of "attention to life" discussed by Bergson[7] and the passive relaxation of dreaming, there is room for an attitude opposed to this positive act but equally intent. A dream is neutral; the attitude we are pointing to is resolutely negative and the body is assigned the task of playing out, of "miming," the self-transformation involved. The body's action ensures our belief either by giving us a new situation or, in the extreme case, by suppressing all situations (fainting).

7. [Henri Bergson, *Matière et mémoire* (Paris: Félix Alcan, 1908), pp. 188–190; *Matter and Memory*, translated by Nancy Margaret Paul and W. Scott Palmer (London: Allen and Unwin, 1919), pp. 225–227.]

As Merleau-Ponty notes, "the body, being our perpetually available means of 'taking up attitudes' and thus of constructing pseudopresents for ourselves, constitutes our means of communication with time as well as with space," and consequently it also constitutes our means of abolishing objective time or space.[8] The subject is indissolubly both consciousness and body, a consciousness which acts, and thus he concentrates all his energy—which had seemed to him insufficient for living through the real situation—on creating a fictive situation or a total absence of situation. His procedure closely resembles the primitive sorcerer's casting of a voodoo spell. It is a magical operation not upon the object itself, which he hopes to affect at a distance, but on a substitute for it. In the case of emotion, the substitute for the world's objective conditions is the subject's own body, which he uses in order to reach and magically affect those conditions. The result is the "death" of the victim whose wax effigy has just been pierced by the sorcerer's needle.

The operation in question is most obvious in subtle emotions, such as aesthetic emotions. Let us simply note that while listening to a piece of music we will often gather ourselves in a total attitude—concentrating our consciousness, tensing our body—in order to "inflate" a single instant with all of the satisfaction which we await, a moment whose perfection lies at the mercy of our neighbors or of the duration of the musical piece itself. The point is to thrill more intensely for fear the thrilling may be too brief. One sequesters himself in a musical universe outside of time and protects this unreal world from real-world incursions through an attitude of one's whole being. We feel shivers on our spine, tears may come to our eyes, our hands may tremble and contract as though to close off all possible leakage; we avoid some irreparable disaster by immobilizing whatever might drain away. Of course we are ourselves in flight toward this refuge whose fragility disturbs us and which lasts precisely as long as we can affect ourselves and thus be affected.

The description of sadness would bring equivalent results. Imagine that one has just learned of one's own bankruptcy; the world remains the same, but one no longer has at his command the same means of action upon it.

. . . lacking the ability and will to carry out the acts we had planned, we behave as though the universe no longer demands anything of us. To bring this off we can act only upon ourselves by "dimming the lights," an attitude whose noematic correlate is what we call *gloom*: the universe is gloomy, that is, undifferentiated in structure. At the same time, however, we naturally assume a withdrawn position, we huddle ourselves. The noematic correlate of this attitude is the *refuge*.[9]

8. *Phénoménologie de la perception*, p. 211; *Phenomenology of Perception*, p. 181.
9. Jean-Paul Sartre, *Esquisse d'une théorie des émotions* (Paris: Hermann, 1939), pp. 36–37; *The Emotions: Outline of a Theory*, translated by Bernard Frechtman (New York: Philosophical Library, 1948), p. 65. The technical expression "noematic correlate" will be clarified in the following pages. [*The Emotions* was the only published part of a systematic work on phenomenological psychology called "La Psyché" which Sartre worked on between 1934 and 1938, abandoning it unpublished

DEGRADATION OF EMOTIONAL CONSCIOUSNESS

One last objection seems to come forth. If emotion is an attitude of the subject and therefore an act of consciousness, how shall we understand the subject's possibility of not being conscious of this act and thus of deluding himself?

Our ordinary language—which is often very revealing—oscillates between the following pair of expressions: "to be moved" ["*être ému*"], 'to be touched,' and "to be moved" ["*s'émouvoir*"], 'to get oneself worked up or excited.' Indeed, we often discover ourselves in the process of inflating the force of our own emotions. Our taste for the sensational is found not only in our entertainments, newspapers, and carnivals; it is also present in the events of our personal lives, before which, however serious and brief they may be, we gladly assume the role of spectators. We are thrilled by our own reactions to what befalls us, keeping score of inner developments as though they were experienced by another person. It thus becomes difficult to distinguish "magic comedy," in which we are taken in by our game, and pure comedy, in which we deliberately overplay for the pleasure of observing ourselves play.

Of course, in order to overplay there must first have been a game. Our awareness that we are overplaying does not entail that we initially wished to play, but only perhaps that we got ourselves excited *from having been excited*. We find the same problem here that we find in the intellectual domain where consciousness, returning upon itself in the process of thinking, forms "the idea of the idea." And it seems the solutions must be identical. First, we must grant that the process has a starting point. Now the problem is that, if this starting point is situated outside of consciousness, it is impossible to understand how it can ever subsequently insert the first idea into consciousness; but, equally, if this starting point is conceived as being a fully constituted idea, then we must call it innate and declare illusory the actual process which progressively constitutes an idea in concrete cases. Clear, reflective consciousness is therefore no more explicable in terms of what is not conscious at all than it is in its own terms. However, we do observe that such consciousness makes its appearance bit by bit and determines itself. It disengages from the plane at which it is still only consciousness of the world, as yet indistinguishable from its own behavior, a plane at which its worldly situation is given only in the form of external exigencies. Life on this plane is of course already that of consciousness, but it is lived unreflectively. And even if we pass to the stage in which we go back to where we left off in one of our numerous daily doings—such as writing—our worldly situation requires a directed behavior that is possible only

---

after writing 400 pages. See Simone de Beauvoir, *La Force de l'âge* (Paris: Gallimard, 1960), p. 326; *The Prime of Life,* translated by Peter Green (Cleveland: World, 1962), pp. 253–254.]

for a consciousness, but it does not require that we recover or reflect upon such behavior.

Thus, in the sense of "behavior" or "act" that we have in mind, there are *unreflective acts*: " . . . an unreflective act is not unconscious, it is aware of itself non-thetically";[10] that is, it is aware of itself without taking itself as a theme. When the world seems "difficult" to me, it is not because it obliged me to judge it so; rather, its having this character is itself a function of the activity that I am endeavoring to carry on in it. Consequently, I need not reflect or return to myself in order to attempt some change whereby the world, qua difficult world, ceases to trouble my enterprise. This also explains why I always discover myself *already involved* in the manifestations of this attempt: what has become involved is, precisely, *myself*.

Consciousness in emotion, therefore, should not be considered passive; it should instead be called passionate in the sense that we empassion *ourselves* for someone or something. "Empassion" brings out the ambiguity of this capacity: consciousness intervenes actively, yet with the purpose of inhibiting itself and, ultimately, of becoming passive in relation to its first intention. This works to the extent that the first intention is not a simple act of a pure consciousness; it must involve an attitude of one's whole being in order to achieve consistency and fullness of meaning.

There is a giddiness to emotion, and the overplaying discussed earlier is not necessarily a hypocrisy since initially, as a natural attitude, emotion is never inevitable. Merleau-Ponty's separation of "psychological hypocrisy" from what he calls "metaphysical hypocrisy" seems apt here:

The former deceives other persons by hiding from them thoughts explicitly known to the subject. It is fortuitous and easily avoided. The latter, however, is a self-deception by means of generality; it may thereby lead ultimately to a state or a situation which is not inevitable, but which also has not been posited and willed as such. It is even found in the "sincere" or "genuine" person whenever he pretends to be whatever he is without qualification. It constitutes a part of the human condition. When the hysterical fit reaches its climax—even if the subject may have pursued that climax in order to escape an embarrassing situation, plunging into it as into a shelter—he hears *almost* nothing, he sees *almost* nothing, he has *almost* become this spastic, breathless being who flounders on a bed. . . . With each passing moment, freedom becomes degraded and less probable.[11]

For a normal person, life itself, which includes attention to life, makes recovery possible: after a night's sleep the world's exigencies can resume their former urgency. But we can also understand those continued emotions ex-

10. [*Esquisse*, p. 32; *Emotions*, p. 57.]
11. *Phénoménologie de la perception*, p. 190; *Phenomenology of Perception*, pp. 162–163.

hibited by certain "manias." The subject's suppression of the objective world pleases him to the extent it succeeds. However, the *degradation* of consciousness that permitted this suppression continues—after this "success" has been achieved—to restrict the chances of a recovery of consciousness that might allow a transformation of the world in the other direction. Once reached, the tempting shelter becomes a prison. One incarcerates himself to save himself. Gribouille acted this way in throwing himself in the water to avoid getting damp, and Camus puts forth a Gribouille who abruptly renders the entire world absurd so as to avoid forever the risk of encountering, in some concrete absurdity, the demand to try to give meaning to things. Camus's Gribouille thereby condemns himself to an absurdism for fear of the absurd. Such is the character we saw in a fit of anger in *The Stranger* in the example we used briefly at the start of this chapter.[12]

Emotional consciousness is degraded because in it the subject surrenders to a defeatist purpose and transforms only his own attitude, while he releases his grip on the actual situation. The behavior involved is artificial but it is not fictitious, since it remains "sincere" and has clear effects. Emotional consciousness is inefficacious because these effects are obtained at the cost of an evasion that is often dangerous and that always indicates a maladaption.

METHODOLOGICAL IMPLICATIONS

The preceding remarks display adequately the ambiguity in unreflective acts. Yet this ambiguity is present as a potentiality only; if the unreflective act appears to us at all, it does so in relation to a reflection, and this obliges us to place it somewhere between that reflective consciousness and pure unconsciousness. This ambiguity becomes explicit only at that level where the subject asks himself—from within a practical perspective in which his own openness to himself is at issue—whether he is condemned to undergo in a reflective manner the emotion he "intends" at the unreflective level. Is self-consciousness also at the mercy of the initiatives of this consciousness of the world? And are there substantive reasons for attributing one's overt acts to unreflective emotion, if indeed self-consciousness—which alone has the means of thoughtfully struggling, rectifying and orienting—remains impotent in the face of the degradation these initiatives bring about?

Thus put, the problem is a moral one. It is a human dilemma par excellence, and of course it is the only one in which ambiguity is actualized, that is, known and lived as such.

12. In the course of this work we have been led to formulate various criticisms regarding certain of Camus's theses. Naturally, these criticisms apply only to the "absurdist" part of his work and are in no way concerned with the new orientation which seems to emanate from a novel like *La Peste* (Paris: Gallimard, 1947); *The Plague*, translated by Stuart Gilbert (New York: Knopf, 1964).

This brings us to the methodological implications of the inquiry we have just pursued with Sartre. These are expressed strikingly by Sartre himself.

First of all, emotion should not be considered an accident. It manifests both its own significance and a consciousness that has assumed a certain attitude, in fact, one of the major attitudes essential to consciousness as such.

But we have seen that this attitude is a spontaneous finality aimed at realizing a magic side of the world. It therefore assumes for its correlative term the appearance of a magical world. This point must be stressed.

Corresponding to each emotion there is a world: a world of the horrible, a world of the gloomy, of the "shifty," of the disturbing, of the intimidating, etc. In general "the social world is at first magical" and "man is always a sorcerer to man."[13] According to Alain's dictum, the magical "is mind loitering among things." So even if it is later rationalized, such a human world can break up any framework imposed on it, abruptly reasserting its original magical aspect. We will then live the magical as such. Even in that case, though, emotion will have nothing accidental about it. It will still be characterized as the return of consciousness to the magical attitude, which is "one of the means by which it *understands* . . . it's 'being-in-the-world.' "[14] The correlate of the rationalizing attitude is the world of determinism, which is modifiable only through the intermediary of specified "implements." By contrast, the correlate of the magical attitude is the magic world, which is "modifiable without intermediary and by large regions." Emotional consciousness understands its situation in terms of its own magical behavior.

All behavior indicates two perspectives: an act of consciousness and a corresponding world in which that act unfolds and to which it gives meaning. The magical appears only to the extent it is lived as such, that is, only where there is magical activity of consciousness. Thus we can state that *to every essential structure of consciousness there corresponds an existential structure of the world*.

This being the case, if we wish to characterize emotion in a global manner, we must call it an existential phenomenon under the "category" of magic, a "simultaneous patterning of body and world"[15] that points to "the totality of relations of human reality to the world"; more precisely, it is a "total modification of one's 'being-in-the-world' according to laws quite peculiar to magic."[16]

If, within this framework, we stress the *living* of meanings, we have the existentialist strain in phenomenology. According to this school of thought, represented by Heidegger, the existential structure of the world is questioned

---

13. [*Esquisse,* p. 46; *Emotions,* p. 84.]
14. [*Esquisse,* p. 49; *Emotions,* p. 91.]
15. Merleau-Ponty, *Phénoménologie de la perception,* p. 220; *Phenomenology of Perception,* p. 189.
16. [*Esquisse,* pp. 51–52; *Emotions,* p. 93.]

in each case inasmuch as that structure is a meaning-bearing situation embodying an understanding or assumption, by "human reality," of its own "being-toward-the-world." This amounts to an *analysis* of human reality, but only within the synthetic totality that is man, whose essence, as we initially said, is to exist in the act of self-understanding. If, on the other hand, we place the stress on the *constitution* of meanings, we have the essentialist strain, represented by Husserl. According to this school of thought, one endeavors in each case "to describe and to fix within concepts" the essential structure of consciousness. To understand any psychic phenomenon—assuming man faces the world—requires that one raise himself from his situation of man-in-the-world to the origins in consciousness of man, the world, and their relation, that is, to a consciousness that is transcendental and constitutive. We get at this consciousness by means of the "phenomenological reduction" or "the placing of the world between parentheses." This operation will be studied in the next chapter. What follows are some of the practical consequences that we can now begin to lay out, having applied a phenomenological method to psychology.

In analyzing anger, Sartre distinguishes two forms of reflection. He calls one of them "accessory reflection"—"which, to be sure, grasps consciousness as consciousness, but ony insofar as that consciousness is motivated by the object."[17] This object is thereafter seen as *possessing* the aspect which has in fact been conferred on it by the magical attitude of consciousness. To "accessory reflection" Sartre opposes that form of "purifying reflection" which is characteristic of the phenomenological reduction. It grasps the emotion insofar as it *constitutes* the aspect conferred upon the object. Instead of saying, "I am angry because he is detestable," we say, "I find him detestable because I am angry." Now it may well seem that this purifying reflection—to which we will later return at length—never passes beyond the level of a sort of mental hygiene. As for its practical significance, this is formulated in conditional terms only, suggesting that the capabilities described have yet to be put to use for a categorical goal. Thus, whether we analyze existential modes of self-comprehension or describe "the essences which preside over the unfolding of the transcendental field," we remain in either case at the level of being, in the latter case the being of pure consciousness, in the former the being of its behavior in the world. Any conciliation of these two viewpoints would therefore naturally tend to be in terms of an "ontology," a study of being, whereas morality is situated at the level of what ought-to-be. And that would be to speak in the indicative mood when what is called for is expression in the imperative.

In the subsequent chapters, by studying Sartre's use of these two perspectives—sometimes separately, sometimes in an effort at conciliation—we shall prepare the groundwork to better pose our principal question: can the moral

17. [*Esquisse*, p. 49; *Emotions*, p. 91.]

imperative come out of any simple theoretical conciliation, or must it be brought in with an added practical attitude?

This evolution in Sartre the phenomenologist, as well as his attitude toward conciliating the two tendencies, will be better understood if, before leaving the emotions, we note some valuable remarks Sartre adds regarding the possibility of framing a total study of man, that is, an *anthropology*.

In his conclusion Sartre insists on the fact that his outline was intended only to "serve as an experiment for the establishment of a phenomenological psychology."[18] It sought to determine in a particular case whether "human reality" —which, given its principles, can appear to classical psychology only "as a collection of varied givens"—is in fact something other than such a collection and, consequently, "whether it is essentially conducive to phenomenological inquiry." The answer is affirmative, since, as we have indicated, emotion is not even completely perceived unless it is viewed as a signifying or meaning-bearing phenomenon, one which indicates the totality of human reality as it empassions itself through the particular emotion in question.

Thus assured of their rights, all inquiries in phenomenological psychology can henceforth "at their inception begin by establishing through *eidetic* reflection"—employing concepts—the *essences* of the phenomena that are interrogated. As we shall see in the following chapter, the psychology of the imagination unfolds in this manner. Instead of beginning with the phenomenon and reascending, through the various perspectives needed for its comprehension, to the essence which validates these perspectives, we shall be able to take the reverse route, immediately laying the foundation of the phenomenon by elucidating its essence.

It nevertheless remains implicit for Sartre that no psychology, not even a phenomenological one, can place "either the man in question, or the world between parentheses."[19] It must take man "in situation." This means that the eidetic reflection mentioned above must be based on a general principle of inquiry that has clear applicability, rather than on a notion of human reality that has been "outlined and fixed by an a priori intuition." Of course this eidetic reflection will start with some idea of this human reality, but it will be an idea in the Kantian sense: a regulative concept or methodological ideal. "The various disciplines of phenomenological psychology are *regressive*, even though the terminus of their regression is *for them* a pure ideal; the disciplines of pure phenomenology are, by contrast, progressive."[20] Phenomenological psychology is regressive in that it is tied down to the phenomenon on which it can reflect through an essentialist procedure but which it can never reach immediately even when it starts with the essence of man. This bondage to the phenomenon can be clearly grasped by noting that although emotion, for

18. [*Esquisse*, p. 51; *Emotions*, p. 92.]
19. [*Esquisse*, p. 12; *Emotions*, p. 18.]
20. [*Esquisse*, p. 52; *Emotions*, p. 94.]

example, is "a realization of the essence of human reality insofar as this reality is *affectivity*," phenomenology is nevertheless unable to "show that human reality must manifest itself in *just such* emotions. That there are such-and-such emotions, and only those, demonstrates the *facticity* (the character of fact) of human existence."[21]

It therefore seems necessary to maintain an existential analysis parallel to an essentialist method. This also entails attempting an ontological psychology in which the lessons of "psychological regression" and those of purely phenomenological "progression" tend to join and enrich each other.

In *The Psychology of Imagination*, "eidetic reflection" is assigned the former task, which it accomplishes with some help from the possibility of such an ontological psychology, full realization of which was later attempted in *Being and Nothingness*.

21. [*Esquisse*, pp. 52–53; *Emotions*, p. 94.]

Chapter 3

The Phenomenology of Imagination

EMOTIVE INCANTATION, IMAGING INCANTATION

In examining emotion we saw one way in which consciousness can become clogged or enmired [*empâtement*]. The initiative that emotional consciousness takes appears as a degradation under these circumstances—a degradation that engulfs consciousness in the very transformations it effects in its own manner of being present to the world. This initiative restricts further initiatives, including those of emotion itself. We are bound by a spell of our own casting, "possessed" by our own rite of possession over the world. We are ourselves subject to magic the more we take magic as the only solution.

We also saw that in the end there is really no difference between a child who puts on fear only to find himself powerless to curb his trembling, and the adult who accepts his fear—investing it with all the vitality he refuses to employ in coping with the situation. Like the power of Orpheus and Amphion, the body's power of incantation transports the stupefied soul to a magical world. Since this world has no rational moorings, it comes unstuck. Lacking perspective and determinate spatiotemporal coordinates, it starts irreversibly to reorganize itself, following the foolish invocation of the sorcerer's apprentice:

> *Astray within my soul where I am master of all around me.*
> *I tremble like a child*
> *Before all I can do.*[1]

In examining mental imagery, we encounter the same kinds of failure, degradation, and stuffing up of consciousness. Sartre indicates quite clearly the similarities between emotion and mental imagery: "The act of imagination . . . is a magical act. It is an incantation aimed at causing the appearance of the object of one's thoughts and desires in such a way that one can take possession of it. There is always something imperious and childish about this, a refusal to consider distance and difficulties. Thus the very young child acts upon the

---

1. Paul Valéry, "Mélodrame d'Amphion," in *Poésies* (Paris: Gallimard, 1942), p. 231.

world from his bed, by orders and entreaties. And the desired objects obey these orders of consciousness: they appear."[2]

To illustrate, we can cite the following brief passage from "The Childhood of a Leader," in *The Wall.* It concerns little Lucien, who tries to persuade God that he loves his mother. However, since God sees everything, Lucien must begin by persuading himself.

> . . . sometimes it was possible to absorb yourself completely in what you said. You said quickly, "Oh, how I love my mommy," pronouncing clearly, and you saw mommy's face and felt consumed with affection; you thought, vaguely, vaguely, that God was watching you and then you didn't even think about it anymore, and you were all creamy with tenderness, and the words came dancing in your ears: mommy, *mommy*, MOMMY.[3]

Here again we find incantation by the utterance of words. This procedure enables one to cause an image to appear, but it also places one in the emotional ambience associated with the image. The incantation may continue, sustained by the rhythm of the basic word, even when its initial goal has faded as a theme of thought.

In this way the word functions as an underlying motif. Its utterance, having mimed the situation desired, is prolonged without purpose. Notice, in this connection, that words can play an immense role in emotion. Take fear, for example. There are two ways in which I can respond to sudden danger. First, I can conceptualize it, grasp it in ideas which I produce in a movement of reflection. Or second, I can foolishly pronounce—privately, if I wish—the words corresponding to these ideas, which then present themselves merely as words, devoid of all spiritual dynamism. If I pursue the latter course, I renounce my power of conceptualizing the situation, of gaining perspective on it by identifying its salient characteristics. Instead, I accede to an unreasoned bodily posture and make myself passive. I yield to my body, whose inertia absorbs all initiatives within me and, with them, any movement that might be directed toward knowledge.

Dr. Coué's famous method of autosuggestion has this same basis.[4] But this method is clearly ineffectual. The conviction it produces cannot in turn bring anything about. In being achieved by surprise, such a conviction is unadaptive to circumstances and torpidly stereotyped.

2. Jean-Paul Sartre, *L'Imaginaire: psychologie phénoménologique de l'imagination* (Paris: Gallimard, 1940; reprinted, 1966), p. 239; *The Psychology of Imagination,* translator anonymous (New York: Philosophical Library, 1948), p. 177. [The literal translation of Sartre's full title would be "The Imaginary: Phenomenological Psychology of the Imagination."]

3. Jean-Paul Sartre, "L'Enfance d'un chef," in *Le Mur* (Paris: Gallimard, 1939), p. 146; "The Childhood of a Leader," in *Intimacy and Other Stories,* translated by Lloyd Alexander (New York: Berkley Medallion, 1956), p. 91.

4. [Emile Coué, *La Santé physique et morale par l'autosuggestion consciente* (Brussels: Bertels, 1933); *Self-mastery Through Conscious Autosuggestion* (New York: American Library Service, 1922).]

Another example of this ineffectiveness, alluded to by Sartre in a recent article, is equally pertinent albeit more complex. In *The Charterhouse of Parma*, Count Mosca, who is in love with Sanseverina, sees her go off in a coach with the young Fabrizio and then remarks: "If the word 'love' arises between them, I am lost."[5] One can imagine two interpretations for this. It may imply that "love is not, in the first instance, a consciousness of love, it is consciousness of the charms of the beloved."[6] In that case the spoken word would provoke in one the *thought* that one is in love, having been charmed by the other all along. Alternatively, however, Mosca's remark may indicate how a word can sometimes free one from a hitherto unnoticed obsession. Naming is often a defense against the threatening power of whatever is named, at least denying that something the privilege of oppressing the unaware.

On closer view, however, we see that a mere word cannot accomplish either of these tasks unless the subject who pronounces it goes beyond the word to the idea it signifies. Strictly speaking, it is the idea which liberates, and all names give expression to ideas. Thus the uttered word may be either reintegrated in a stream of thinking or fixed within its own utterance, evoking all the affective associations that can flow from such a bodily motion left to itself. Our encounter with words is therefore an ambiguous occasion and can be met with either of two responses: (a) an attitude of reflectiveness or (b) some behavior that is unreflective and that reinforces its own unreflectiveness from the start.

So far as concerns love, we believe that the phenomenon of crystallization is more characteristic of this second unreflective response than of the first, although we have seen that reflectiveness can emerge from it.[7] A lover not only contemplates his love, he equally "puts it on," inducing in himself loving *states* which, though unspontaneous, are still sincere.

INTERVENTION BY REFLECTIVE CONSCIOUSNESS

We now have the essentials for a study of images. And we are in a position to use the phenomenological method of "eidetic reflection."[8]

5. J.-P. Sartre, "Qu'est-ce que la littérature?" *Les Temps modernes*, no. 17 (February 1947), p. 789. [Remaining portions appeared in *Les Temps modernes*, nos. 18–22 (March–July 1947). A final version with added notes and passages—none of which is quoted by Jeanson in this volume—was published in a volume of Sartre's collected essays: *Situations, II* (Paris: Gallimard, 1948). The above-quoted passage is on p. 74 of *Situations, II*.] *What is Literature?* translated by Bernard Frechtman (London: Methuen, 1950), p. 14.

6. *L'Imaginaire*, p. 138; *Psychology of Imagination*, p. 99.

7. [The allusion is to the theory of love as "crystallization," expounded by Marie Henri Beyle [Stendhal] in *De l'amour* (Paris: Éditions Garnier Frères, 1959), pp. 8, 345; *On Love*, translated by Philip Sidney Woolf and Cecil N. Sidney Woolf (New York: Brentano, 1916), pp. 5, 368.]

8. [See Husserl's *Ideen I*, §§ 76–78 (pp. 141–159); *Ideas*, §§ 76–78 (pp. 194–213) and Sartre's *L'Imaginaire*, pp. 13–15; *Psychology of Imagination*, pp. 3–4.]

This method consists in reflecting on an image qua image, so as to explicate, describe, and fix its *essence*. If we attempted to deal with imaging without such a method, our study could not get off the ground; reflective consciousness must be brought into play. But recourse to such reflection is itself inadmissible if it does not allow "imaging" to have its fullest sense.

It is helpful to recall here Auguste Comte's rejection of introspective psychology. He omitted it from his list of sciences because, he said, nobody can at once be walking down the street and watching himself from a window. Thus one's anger is no longer what it was, once one begins to examine it. The angry man ceases being an angry man and becomes a psychologist instead, so to speak.[9] Comte's observation is instructive: considered as a prohibition against introspective psychology, it implies that anger, for example, is a state and must therefore dissolve upon the occurrence of an act of reflection—as when the manipulation of a kaleidoscope transforms one pattern of colors into another.

Anger, in that case, would be only a fact about consciousness; it would wane and vanish upon the slightest approach of reflection. But this will not do at all. According to the perspective that Comte criticizes, consciousness is taken either as a static container of its own states and processes or as a passive screen on which they are projected. Were either image correct, however, it is hard to see how consciousness could also be such as to reflect in any way whatever upon what occurs within it. Thus, although Comte was right to reject a certain species of psychology, it does not follow that *all* psychology is to be rejected. The founder of positivism drew a hasty conclusion.

The necessity for a secondary reflection can in fact be reconciled with the continued authenticity of its object, which is the initial consciousness to be described. This consciousness is not a place where events take place. In imagination, for example, consciousness is not composed of or traversed by images. The image is not a thing, either stable or mobile, but a relation instituted by the imaging activity of consciousness as it aims at a transcendent object. This activity does indeed make use of an "analogue," that is, a correlate of the object. But it would be erroneous to take the latter for the image. The image is not the analogue itself but the constituting of the analogue, or, if you will, it is the meaning which consciousness confers on the "analogue" in constituting it as such.

In the attitude of unreflective imaging, consciousness reaches an object by means of the analogue that consciousness gives itself or that is given to it. Reflective consciousness can reach an image's essence only insofar as the imagined appearance of the object implies a psychic given, "a certain material

9. [See Auguste Comte, *Cours de philosophie positive*, vol. 1 (Paris: C. Delagrave, 1892), pp. 34–38. Quoted in William James, *Principles of Psychology*, vol. 1 (New York: Henry Holt and Co., 1890), p. 188.]

that functions as an *analogue*."[10] Now since this material plays the role of analogue only within the intentional synthesis effected by imaging consciousness, reflection on the image can fully grasp "the qualities of the thing aimed at."

Reflection does not disturb imagination, since it simply focuses on the image's essence and its implications. It can grasp the imaging relation as such without suppressing that relation or its psychic contents, since this grasp does not require dislocation of the imaging attitude. Moreover, any unreflective conscious attitude can become reflective without losing itself. This possibility is always present, inasmuch as a consciousness can never be unconscious of itself, on pain of contradiction.

If one wishes instead to reflectively examine the psychic content in isolation, one thereby suppresses the content's role as *analogue*. The relation to the object, which was established through this role, is also suppressed. In short, a reflective inquiry of this sort suppresses the imaging attitude and with it the very content of the image. Similarly, when viewing a painting either we can adopt the aesthetic attitude and take the painting as an analogue of an object which is thereby grasped in an image or we can adopt the perceiving attitude and observe the painting qua object—concentrating on the analysis of its various elements. These two attitudes are irreconcilable: we can reflect upon the first without losing it, but the second suppresses the first.

We shall have to return to these points. Approaching them is necessarily arduous, since it involves a conception of the image that has not yet been justified. But before giving that justification, let us summarize our discussion so far.

Consciousness that imagines aims at a transcendent object. Reflective consciousness can turn back upon such consciousness so as to grasp both (a) the essence of the act of aiming and (b) the psychic correlate that this act necessarily implies. Finally, the nature and composition of this correlate can be studied only on the *hypotheses* of an experimental psychology. To adopt these hypotheses is to abandon phenomenological description; Sartre views this as a move from the certain to the probable.

In what follows we shall focus our analysis on *The Psychology of Imagination* and *Imagination: A Psychological Critique*.[11] Although we shall try not

10. [*L'Imaginaire*, p. 41; *Psychology of Imagination*, p. 23. Sartre's emphasis. The full sentence reads: "And, since I cannot directly call up the perception of him [my friend Pierre], I make use of a certain material that functions as an analogue, as an equivalent of the perception."]

11. [This second-listed work was the first philosophical essay by Sartre to be published (Paris: Gallimard, 1936). However, it was *written* a year after the composition of *The Transcendence of the Ego*, Sartre's first properly philosophical writing (after completing his academic training). See Sylvie Le Bon's Introduction to *La Transcendance de l'Ego: esquisse d'une description phénoménologique* (Paris: J. Vrin, 1978), p. 7. *L'Imagination* is the critical work—dealing with prior accounts

to misrepresent Sartre's thought, our purpose is certainly not to follow the development of these two works step by step. Instead, we hope to provide an elucidation of Sartrism by examining the essential features (as we understand them) of the several stages of its development.

PERCEPTION AND IMAGE

The image, then, is not an object in consciousness. It is rather a relation to some external object and cannot be understood as the mental transposition of that object.

Conceiving of images as objects in consciousness is strongly rooted in our intellectual habits, and this is often supported by seemingly conclusive arguments. We should therefore examine this conception more closely, with a view to elucidating the essence we seek to describe.

One feels that the central question here is how image and perception are related. In general, classical psychology finds no essential difference between the two. This harmonizes with the classical psychologist's preference for attending to the "landscapes" within consciousness to the neglect of its attitudes. We must immediately observe, however, that by making the image an internal perception, the psychologist is logically required thenceforth to consider perception as an image projected upon the external.

In short, one cannot suppress the intentionality of consciousness to any degree without suppressing to exactly the same degree the object intended by consciousness. Of course this is the result of having first interiorized the object. Such interiorization merely postpones the problem, for it is still necessary to explain how these mental objects can be grasped and handled by the mind that "contains" them. To view the objects of consciousness as immanent therein is to tie consciousness to the contingencies associated with their appearance, and this reduces consciousness to the bare succession of these appearances.

Let us provisionally assume precisely such a point of view. We would then have a world of "impressions." We would have to decide which among them are perceptions and which are images. This situates us squarely within "phenomenalism." We have no criteria for distinguishing between external world and imaginary world except those founded upon the external characteristics of these impressions, for example, their comparative intensity or distinctness.[12] (This is a good place to note the strange confusion of those "philosophers" who make use of a weak system of classification when they reproachfully label Sartre's phenomenology as a mere "phenomenalism.")

---

of imagination in philosophy and psychology—after which *L'Imaginaire (The Psychology of Imagination)* came as the positive and systematic sequel. *L'Imagination* has been translated into English by Forrest Williams with the title *Imagination: A Psychological Critique* (Ann Arbor: University of Michigan Press, 1962).]

12. [The allusion is to David Hume's theory of perception: *A Treatise of Human Nature,* ed. L. A. Selby-Bigge (Oxford: Clarendon Press, 1960).]

In any case, according to the view in question, an object is only an exteriorized image and an image is only an interiorized object. Object and image possess the same objective characteristics, the same determinate qualities. This view may be reinforced by the fact that certain images do indeed strike us as *traversing* consciousness, as appearing to it suddenly, and as being no less alien to it than is a meteor to the space through which it plunges.

No doubt there are many images that do not correspond to any "premeditation" of consciousness, images that consciousness has not "decided" to make appear. Coming from who knows where, they do not announce their bearing on our present preoccupations.

Yet we should not forget the points we made about emotions. We saw how magic could be present, evident in our very situation in the world, manifesting itself through a break in our "attention to life" due to some distraction of our rational attitude. But we also saw that, even then, the magical could be grasped as such only if we first consented to adopt the magical attitude. The world of implements [*ustensiles*] may very well be temporarily dislocated, but it does not recrystallize itself in the form of a magical world unless our consciousness gets itself worked up through the process of dislocation and intends the world emotionally. Similarly, in imaging, it may well happen that all the material for an image arises from a failure of consciousness in some prior stance, but this material becomes an image only when grasped again within a new attitude that asserts itself as an imaging attitude. Our thinking has the ability to forget itself, to lose itself and give up, no longer sustaining its products in the tension that constitutes their psychic being, and these products can then offer themselves for the new syntheses. But they will disappear altogether if they are not immediately taken up in a new act of synthesis and reengaged in a new movement of thought. This new movement may sustain them for a while by giving them a meaning, and apart from this meaning they would simply not be conscious at all. In terms we have used before, psychic contents can undergo discontinuity only insofar as they are psychic. And if a content reappears, imbued, for example, with the power of imaging, it is because a conscious intention confers upon it for a time the role of analogue of some object that consciousness aims at through it. In short, consciousness cannot "encounter" anything without itself taking part; even if it had not foreseen the encounter, it inevitably accedes—in accepting the encounter—to some form of understanding of itself within the altered situation. Consciousness orients itself in order to grasp its object, and when what it grasps is an "image," it is at the price of an act of imagination on its own part.

Accordingly, one may expect that the orientation of an act of imagination will be different from that of an act of perception. An image is not a stray impression left to enter into a contingent "association" for which, being capricious, no law is discoverable. Nor, equally, is it caught in the determinism of a world where everything is already completed, a world that is conceivable only and that is therefore inaccessible to imagination. In fact, even such a world must constitute itself progressively, and on the basis of perception alone. And this touches the basic point on which the perceiving and imagining functions are to be distinguished.

The image I have of this chair is really no less exterior, no less "transcendent" to my consciousness than the chair itself that is perceived in its place. My image is in space by the same right that my perception is, though of course the spatiality involved is different. Image and perception have the same object and I aim at this object in both. In the case of my *perception* of the chair, however, the object that I intend is inexhaustible and overflows my perception. I sense clearly, the more I apply myself to it, that I can never finish learning from it. For the object of perception is something that I must learn about, which is to say that I must confront the richness of its determinations. I must do so with the knowledge that I can grasp the object only successively and through particular aspects, thus always to the exclusion of an indefinite number of alternative viewpoints. In considering my *image* of the chair, I find the contrary state of affairs. The object as imaged gives itself to me once and for all in the synthetic act in which I direct myself toward it. At once, the image gives me all it has. There is nothing more to learn of it that I do not already know at the very moment when it first appears to me. My relation to this object is confined to its initial manifestation. My image is "poor" in determinations, having only those I confer on it in forming it. Since this sort of object is constituted neither by the interdependence of its parts nor by its solidarity with the other objects of the world, I do not *observe* it; I can only consider it, a considering that in no way deepens my knowledge of it. Sartre calls this a "quasi observation."[13]

In a perception I am given over to the object. It draws me into the momentum of a total investigation, and I experience the density it derives from the plenitude of its presence to the world. The object of an image, however, is given to me at the level of my own intention, and while adaptation does occur, it involves no effort, inasmuch as it takes place within a stable equilibrium. The appearance of the perceived object holds surprises for us, remaining open to an infinity of different appearances; the appearance of the imagined object is closed in upon itself, limited to whatever determinations it possessed at its origin and without any possibility of evolving.

An image is therefore not the presence "in" consciousness of a "mental object" or "simulacrum" of an external object. The image presents us with an absent object, but it does so in a manner quite unlike the way an object would appear if it were really present. In an image we may well aim at a spatial object, but it appears to us in an original form, namely, in the form of imaging. Determinations do not "unfold" themselves in it, nor are they juxta-

13. [*L'Imaginaire*, p. 26; *Psychology of Imagination*, p. 13.]

posed, as in an object in the world. Instead, its determinations mutually imply and interpenetrate each other in a global impression that is shut off on itself.

BERGSON'S VIEW OF IMAGES

Perhaps we can clarify these remarks by comparing the phenomenological view of images with Bergson's. We shall have in mind the criticisms of Bergson given by Sartre, particularly in *Imagination: A Psychological Critique*.

Bergson's view of images could be the subject of an elaborate investigation. This would itself present problems since, Bergson's statements to the contrary notwithstanding, his psychology and his metaphysics regularly point in different directions.

A rereading of *Matter and Memory* will disclose that the world consists of "images" and that for an object to *be* means that it is a possible image, still virtual only. Such an image can be actualized in a representation solely through the impending action of my body, which isolates it from the entourage of other images that surround it in its capacity as a thing, thus causing it to stand out from them in its capacity as a picture. And Bergson explicitly declares: "Among images there is merely a difference of degree, but not of kind, between *being* and *being consciously perceived*."[14] So it is that perception gets a metaphysical basis: it is said to rest on the encounter between (a) an unconscious consciousness immanent in the objects of the world and (b) discriminations by the action of the subject within that world.

A curious view. It certainly represents a reversal of the classical positions, which took as their model the action of an object upon a subject endowed with consciousness. For Bergson, on the contrary, the perceiving subject is a body whose physical activity—within a world consisting of images—creates the differences of level by which the conscious character of certain images shows forth.

Accordingly, such images are at bottom schemas of bodily activity [*schémas d'activité corporelle*] and, as such, they are devoid of meaning. Bergson must therefore make a fast departure from this level of "pure perception" if he is to arrive somehow at concrete perception. This is accomplished in two ways. First, the inertia of our nervous system condenses or contracts into "relatively simple intuitions" a multiplicity of outlines sketched upon the world. Second, each perception thus subjectivised is also a memory, for such is the way it fixes itself within the subject's duration [*durée*], though it does this, not as a bodily schema oriented toward action, but instead as a congealed representation that has been rendered inactive and indestructible. By later inserting them-

14. [*Matière et mémoire*, p. 22; *Matter and Memory*, p. 30. The emphasis is Bergson's.]

selves into our perceptions, these memories will give the latter their form and meaning. "Perceiving ends up being just an occasion for remembering."[15]

We should observe here that a perception—being a pure object and thus quite meaningless—is hardly able to acquire a meaning, whether by the false "subjectivisation" it undergoes in an impersonal, physiological "memory" or by the intervention of earlier perceptions that have been preserved. The reappearance of these latter, which is puzzling enough in view of their alleged inactivity, is in any case unable to add any meaning to their initial appearance.

Still it is with these two elements (pure perception and pure memory, both of which are metaphysical) that Bergson believes he can account for concrete perceiving and effective imagining. We insist, however, that these initial conceptions cannot have failed to influence Bergson's psychological descriptions and that, insofar as these descriptions are at all satisfactory, the conceptions in question must to some extent have been abandoned in favor of that more direct view of psychic phenomena.

The upshot is that, however flexible the more direct view may be, Bergson is still unable to get beyond the perspective of an inner unfolding. Everything is put on the same level since consciousness is seen as coinciding with its objects, which in turn are seen as its "immediate givens."[16] Even if these "images" have been very deeply subjectivated and interiorized in relation to their material origin and even if they become very explicit, distinct, and lively in contrast to the recollections of inactive spiritual memory, we would still not know how to distinguish images originating in perception from those originating in imagination. What, then, becomes of this "hemorrhaging" from which all perception suffers? And how shall we distinguish perception itself from the image, if the latter is closed in on itself like a seamless tunic?

Such questions require a wholesale critique of the notion of "immediacy." We shall limit ourselves to noting what follows from positing an object that is one with the subject. Such an object is already "conscious" in the double sense that its essential properties include the capacities (a) to make itself present to a consciousness and (b) to inscribe itself on the temporal career of that consciousness so as to be later re-presented in it. This results in making the subject passive and secondary as regards everything that actually unfolds within him. Consciousness is "stuffed up" from the very start and by definition. It is the prisoner of its objects, which weigh on it and in which it loses itself. Generally speaking, this is also the position of the "intuitionists," who, thinking to avoid the distortion of reality which they believe results from turning their look upon it, try to assure themselves of the most authentic knowledge of reality by drowning themselves in it.[17]

15. [*Matière et mémoire*, p. 59; *Matter and Memory*, p. 71.]
16. [The allusion is to Henri Bergson's theory that images constitute the immediate givens of consciousness, as he developed it in *Essai sur les données immédiates de la conscience* (Paris: Félix Alcan, 1889).]
17. ["Intuitionists" refers to Bergson and his exponents; see, for example, J. Segond, *L'Intuition bergsonienne* (Paris: Félix Alcan, 1930).]

At all events it is clear that Bergson frequently vacillates between two perspectives: although he wishes to bring the notion of conscious attitude into a properly psychological context, his basic principles regularly pull him back to the "consciousness of a certain movement of representations."[18] No text is more striking evidence of this vacillation than his study of "intellectual effort."[19] Sometimes the dynamic schema is a representation in motion plus the consciousness of this motion; sometimes it is conceived as a power of organizing which has an implicit knowledge of what it wants to attain but which remains at a distance from images as it directs their movements. In either case we are put in mind of a synthesis without a synthetic act, and this is incomprehensible. Either we are compelled to reject the notion of intellectual effort, together with any attempt to draw psychological distinctions, or we must ask how "knowledge," which is conscious, can be exterior to "images" (the "givens" of consciousness) and how it can guide them while remaining exterior to them.

With this difficulty we come to a key element of the problem before us. To deal with it we must return to the perspective of phenomenology and take up its disagreements with Bergsonism. This should contribute to clarification.

KNOWLEDGE AND THE IMAGE

The object is not in the first instance an object of consciousness. It is only the correlate of a consciousness that remains transcendent to it. It can no more penetrate consciousness than be penetrated by consciousness, being merely the target for consciousness, the terminus of its aimings, the motif of its perpetual intentionality. Perception is one of these aimings, imagination another. Consciousness remains distant from the object but not from its own perceptions or images, since these are no more than its relations to the object. One understands, therefore, why the foundation for the distinction that we drew between perceiving and imaging ought not to be sought in the characteristics that properly belong to the *objects* of perception and imagination, *for these are the same objects*. They serve in either case as target and theme, though the thematization that consciousness makes of them does not carry the same meaning in the two cases. The differences are consequently between various attitudes and the types of relation of consciousness to the world these attitudes contain. This relation is the existential phenomenon, which may be, for example, either perception or image.

It is important to remember that there is no image if there is no imaging

18. [Henri Bergson, "L'Effort intellectuel," *L'Energie spirituelle, essai et conférences* (Paris: Félix Alcan, 1919), p. 163–164; "Intellectual Effort," *Mind-Energy: Lectures and Essays*, translated by H. Wildon Carr (London: Macmillan and Co., 1920), p. 186–187.]

19. "L'Effort intellectuel," *L'Energie spirituelle*, p. 199; "Intellectual Effort," *Mind-Energy*, p. 227.

intention. We should therefore avoid representing the relation between the implicit knowledge that orients images and the images themselves as if it were an external relation. This knowledge subtends the images, which would cave in without it. It orients them, not by guiding them like pieces on a chessboard, but by giving them meaning and, consequently, an internal consistency that allows them to appear and to maintain themselves. This knowledge forms part of the imaging intention itself. It is this knowledge that we must now characterize.

An image, however poor it may be qua image, does possess a number of determinations. These determinations, far from pointing to an infinity of other determinations, immediately give themselves as limited. When, in Peter's absence, I again see Peter's face, I know it is his, for it is precisely to Peter that I address my look. My image exists, not as a mediocre picture of Peter, but as a consciousness of Peter-in-image.

This consciousness is not a mere knowing-about Peter: it gives an absent but intuited Peter, a Peter who is present to my look. As we have seen, this look does not differ essentially from that of perception, except that it is incapable of a genuine *observation*. As thus subtended by knowledge, how does this look differ from the attitude of conception?

These two questions—the nature of this knowledge and the relation of this look to conception—are in fact connected and they mutually clarify each other. If I perceive a cube, it is a cube only hypothetically, since it is always possible that a deeper observation will lead me to change my mind about it. However, if I imagine a cube, I am assured of my object. I know—with evidence and with no risk of surprise—that what I am concerned with is indeed a cube. In the former case we find a knowledge that is still in the process of forming, in the latter, an immediate knowledge. But neither imagination nor perception *is* knowledge. *Conception* is knowledge. We should therefore briefly describe conception if we wish to understand how consciousness can start with conception and then adopt a new attitude which presupposes conception while differing from it in intentional mode, that is, in having either an imaging structure or a perceiving structure.

With this we come across the same problem of reduplication and progression that we had to consider with regard to emotion. Prior to the emotion-augmentation, there is a pure emotion, an emotion-act of consciousness that is unreflectively lived. Prior to the idea of the idea, there is an initial ideation in which consciousness posits its object in a cognitive intention but does not yet take this same positional act as its theme. Similarly, there is a pre-reflective knowledge wherein we think a cube by means of a "concrete concept" which apprehends the cube at its center in a single stroke, attributing to it the minimum of characters through which it can be unambiguously defined. Of course such a knowledge can become more complete, but initially it gives itself in the above manner, without preparation or correction, in a single act of consciousness.

This knowledge is what regulates those determinations of which my image of the cube will be the intuitive synthesis. And the more this preliminary knowledge is developed, the more complex will be my image. However complex my image is, though, it will be closed in on itself from the start.

In perception this knowledge expands. If such knowledge consents to change into the perceptual attitude, thereby conferring an orientation upon itself, it can return to itself and enrich its object with new determinations observed in the perceptual orientation.

In thus contrasting perception and imagination, we find the same degradation in imaging consciousness that we stressed at the start of the chapter, where we compared imaging with emotional consciousness. We now understand the meaning of this degradation. Knowledge, in imaging, is turned not toward perceptual knowledge, with a view to gathering information about the present object, nor toward reflective knowledge, with a view to gaining the assurance that comes from determining itself intellectually; instead, it becomes involved in the formation of an image. Knowledge jettisons its acquired learning in order to cause the absent object to appear, but in doing so it condemns itself to acquire nothing in return.

Impotent satisfaction and sterile defeatism thus seem to be the negative features in consciousness's function of imaging. It is indeed a function of renunciation. Yet any renunciation, if it makes the negative appear, is for that reason a positive act. We must therefore go on to ask what makes the image a negation. But we must also ask how this negation is able positively to serve consciousness, which, for its part, may surrender to it temporarily, without going so far as to become lost in it entirely.

Negative Aspects of the Image

An *image*, as opposed to a perception, is formed when consciousness directs itself toward an object that it considers *absent*. The image is a presentation of the object as absent. This relation, which is lived by consciousness, makes the image a phenomenon of consciousness, forbidding us to see it as an object "in consciousness."

This point completes, and therefore clarifies, the results just obtained. To become assured of it, we must closely examine non-reflective, "non-thetic" consciousness. Non-thetic consciousness must accompany every positional act of unreflective consciousness, insofar as the latter originates in a consciousness at all. Such consciousness posits an object, but it can be ignorant neither of this positing nor of the manner in which it is accomplished, even though it has not yet explicitly reflected. This is why even the most unreflective consciousness can never be unconscious of itself. Now, having brought this consciousness into view, what do we find?

In the image of Peter, he is given as absent to intuition. As Sartre puts it, Peter is not "non-intuitive" but rather "intuitive-absent." The image is "consciousness imaging Peter," and it points toward a sensuous intuition which is presented as incapable of taking place. It is Peter himself who has a certain quality of untouchability, of *not being* at *such* a distance, in *such* a position. My consciousness of Peter is therefore also consciousness of the present non-being of Peter. "However lively or touching or strong the image may be, it gives its object as not being."[20] I can imagine Peter as dead, or as not there, or as far away from me. I can also imagine him without committing myself either to his nonexistence, or his absence, or his existence elsewhere.

No doubt this last noncommittal modality is the most properly "imaginary" one. My consciousness can apprehend this modality only through its own creative spontaneity, in acts which posit, not a particular negation, but rather the very negation of the world as such. This modality crops up in the form of a gratuitous act of imagination when I imagine in order to imagine; I then imagine solely in order to negate the real. Two apparently incompatible consequences emerge from this observation and we must try to illuminate them.

Consider the following example. If I seek to imaginatively call up my absent mother's face because I miss her, I cannot cause her face to appear to me except at the cost of taking the image of her as unreal. The desire for her presence is therefore frustrated in the very attempt to satisfy it. Moreover, my project requires that I continually redouble my efforts to maintain my image, which in turn continually renews my disappointment. But if, to take a contrary case, I sit daydreaming and I come up with imaginary faces "for the fun of it," having no purpose beyond my desire to escape from the present, I can then posit these faces without consideration of time and place. Since in this second case I do not ask my images to remedy specific deficiencies in the objective world but only to oppose this world so as to help me forget it, they will not disappoint me, save perhaps in their general liability to dissolve rapidly despite my will. I will in any case feel more detached in my relations with each image, since I will be busy imagining faces and not preoccupied with imagining one face in particular. I will be more "aware" of being engaged in a gamelike endeavor, for I will have no precise reason to take my pursuit seriously, much less tragically. This is properly designated as reverie and it is "disinterested" in two senses: (a) it lacks a particular goal and (b) it is concerned with avoiding the risk that the objective world may present such a goal. Thus reverie is not interested in any particular thing but instead pushes back a world regarding which it has specifically chosen to be dis-interested.

It is well known that reverie sometimes occurs in a clearly pathological form.

20. [*L'Imaginaire*, p. 33; *Psychology of Imagination*, p. 18.]

Schizophrenia is the extreme type. In this case the patient has absolutely no desire for his image to become a reality. If he were presented with it, he would push it away, incapable of adapting to it. He asks that his images compensate for his inability—which he admits freely—to handle the corresponding real situations. The deficiency here arises, then, not from some particular aspect of the world in which he is situated, but from his own sense of inadequacy for that world. The act of de-realizing does not have for him the meaning it has for me when I want to call up an image of my mother's face. I exert real effort in straining toward the unreality whose appearance I bring about. He, on the other hand, takes pleasure in this unreality and the cost of this is that he de-realizes himself. Living in the unreal, he is satisfied. He is taken in by his own game, captivated by the imaginary.

He is to some extent consciously a captive. Consider the remarks of Marie B., as recorded by Borel and Robin (and noted by Sartre):

> I recall the breakdown I once had. I said that I was the Queen of Spain. At bottom, I was quite aware that this was false. I was like a child who plays with a doll and who knows that her doll is not alive but who wishes to be taken in anyway. . . . Everything seemed enchanted to me. . . . I was like an actress who played a role and wished to be placed inside the skin of her character. I was taken in . . . but not altogether. I lived in an imaginary world.[21]

Let me add a case recounted to me not long ago by Gilbert Maire. It has to do with a person who fancied himself master of an immense fortune. When he spoke of it he would ritually multiply his holdings by stages, first calculating in thousands of francs, then in millions, then in billions. One day he was asked to give twenty francs, which in fact he had in his pocket, to a collection for one of his comrades. He straightaway offered his imaginary fortune, saying, "Not at all, not at all, I'll give everything I have," whereupon he devoted himself anew to his imaginary multiplications. Upon insistence, however, he became stubborn. Finally, faced with a renewed request, he declared, "Ah, but twenty francs, after all that does represent something.... "

Yet the awareness which these persons retain of the fictive character of their behavior does not by itself make them curable. That is because, even when such an awareness is present, they may be quite sincere in professing their need to reject all demands for realistic behavior. And this explains why an unreflective action in the world presents fewer dangers than a more reflective action that is lived (and more or less willed) as an evasion of the world. The former is, in effect, always forewarned against itself by the various exigencies contained in its selected tasks. The latter, an evasion that totally rejects such tasks, can find direction only within itself by falling into step with its own productions. In short, just as there is a passionate fixation of the emotions, there is

21. [*L'Imaginaire*, p. 286; *Psychology of Imagination*, p. 213.]

also a passion of the imagination. The imaginary, which normally crops up only in momentary evasions of behavior, can also become segregated and fixed in a pattern of evasion.

REACTIVE EFFECTS OF THE GAME UPON THE GAME-PLAYER

In addition, the feelings one experiences when one is before one's images are essentially unlike those one can experience before the objects themselves. The former are active, not passive. They are performed feelings. The subject tries to undergo them and to make as if he suffers them, but his love for this woman, his hatred for that enemy, his disgust at some behavior—all are restricted to their impoverished and standardized modes, reduced to being no more than love, hate, and disgust in a formal sense. They are easier to live through when simplified in this way; and this is why—without going as far as the schizophrenic—the normal person may have difficulty recovering contact with reality, even when the simplified object is the person he loves.

At the affective level, then, we find the same degradation of imaging consciousness that we found at the level of knowledge. Such "quasi feeling" is the counterpart of the "quasi observation" by which Sartre distinguished the image from the perception.

The question of "forced," or reinforced, or otherwise falsified feelings no doubt figures centrally in a person's reflections on his own life. To some extent we all resemble those "pithiatic"[22] persons who persist in attempting to persuade themselves of something that they do not really feel and who conduct themselves accordingly. Children first learn feelings from the reactions of others and later from their own experiences. Just as the man alone tries to love his absent mate as if she were still there, so the child tries to feel what he knows one is supposed to feel.

The example of little Lucien in "The Childhood of a Leader" is again pertinent here. It allows us to illustrate some of the preceding analyses of the image's constituent elements.

> . . . sometimes it was possible to absorb yourself completely in what you said. You said quickly, "Oh, how I love my mommy," pronouncing clearly, and you saw mommy's face and felt consumed with affection; you thought, vaguely, vaguely, that God was watching you and then you didn't even think about it anymore, and you were all creamy with tenderness, and the words came dancing in your ears: mommy, *mommy*, MOMMY.[23]

Again we find in this description the intervention of an awareness that "intends" not only a definite objective, the mother's face, but also the corporal

22. [Pithiatic: having to do with those hysterical symptoms that may be treated by persuasion and suggestion. See for example, Merleau-Ponty, *Phénoménologie de la perception*, p. 188; *Phenomenology of Perception*, p. 161.]
23. [J.-P. Sartre, "L'Enfance d'un chef," in *Le Mur*, p. 146; "The Childhood of a Leader," in *The Wall*, pp. 91–92.]

movements (the pronouncing of words) needed to fix that awareness. In this case, however, no feeling presents itself for synthetic unification, in the same intentional act, with this awareness and these movements. It is as if producing the image is only an intermediary goal for Lucien, the true objective being to cause the appearance of a sentiment toward his mother which he does not really feel. To all appearances he achieves his goal. And yet consider the subsequent lines: "That lasted only an instant, of course, as when Lucien tried to make a chair keep its balance on two feet. . . . Lucien gave up this game because it required too great an effort. . . ."

Lucien never really accomplishes more than a change of games. His life passes in "playing," suspended between the need for seriousness and an inability to accept his own feelings as genuine. He must, therefore, constantly mime his feelings and exteriorize them so as to give them the consistency which he *knows* they ought to have. His effort to persuade God of his love for his mother is a way of pursuing seriousness. He strives to acquire a character through the mediation of a being who is sure of himself and inaccessible to doubt since, left to his own devices, he could never succeed in persuading himself he possesses that character. One day the curé asks him if he really loves his mother. Lucien would willingly answer in the affirmative were he quite certain that his mother was the pretty mommy of his fantasies, whom he was eager to adore, and not someone playing at being her. But the doubt lies within him. When the curé asks him whom he prefers, his mother or God Almighty, Lucien, seized by his doubt, flees.

> He ran to the garden and slipped out by the rear door; he had brought his little malacca cane. . . . Lucien whipped the nettles with his cane, crying, "I love my mommy, I love my mommy." He saw the broken nettles, hanging pitiably, oozing white, their necks whitish and nappy, having been frayed as they broke, and he heard a solitary little voice that cried, "I love my mommy, I love my mommy"; there was a big blue fly that buzzed, it was a do-do fly and Lucien was afraid of it, and an odor of the forbidden—powerful, putrid and tranquil—filled his nostrils. He repeated, "I love my mommy," but his voice seemed strange to him; he felt an unbearable fear, and he fled in one stretch to the living room. From that day forward Lucien understood that he did not love his mommy. He did not feel guilty, but he redoubled his niceties because, he thought, one ought to appear throughout one's life to love one's parents, for otherwise one was a bad little boy.[24]

The passion for playing is clearly visible here. It results from the spirit of seriousness which shows up precociously in this child who already wants to model himself after his father, that is, to become a leader. We reuse this example only because it illustrates so well the ambiguity of all "de-realizing" behavior and, more generally, of all artifice.

24. [L'Enfance d'un chef," in *Le Mur*, pp. 141–142; "The Childhood of a Leader," in *The Wall*, pp. 88–89.]

Like the schizophrenic, Lucien performs fictive acts, but, unlike the schizophrenic, he does so in order to "realize" himself, to better insert himself into the real world, upon which he wishes to act and to which he feels maladapted. It would be too simple to say he plays merely to play. Rather, he "plays the game," he accepts the conventions generally accepted around him, he tries to make himself consistent by pursuing the path indicated by his father. In this respect he is not a captive of the imaginary life. He uses the imaginary to reach reality and to become real himself.

For all that, such a procedure has a tethering effect. It induces its user to come back to it. The game that is played here has a built-in angle, and from that angle the player who thinks only of playing can lose sight of his goal.

With regard to images in particular, there arises the problem of determining the value of resorting to them when one is faced with a difficulty. Such recourse seems destined to remain fruitless. As we have seen, an object given in the form of an image is closed in upon itself, never containing more than what consciousness places in it. It can therefore teach consciousness nothing. It can represent to us only our own affirmations, leaving our questions forever unanswered.

What must be acknowledged, though, is that recourse to images is itself an act of thought. Such an act assumes the imaging form "when it wishes to be intuitive, when it wishes to found its affirmations on the *viewing* of an object. In this case, thought summons the appearance of the object in order to *see* it, or better, in order to *possess* it. But this attempt, into which all thought risks being drawn and stuck [*s'enliser*], is always a failure: the objects are infected with the character of unreality."[25]

Hence it is incorrect to say flatly that imagination harms thought. Instead, when thought encounters a difficulty, it may become degraded by settling on that form of itself which induces a sort of fascination. For example, thought can more easily envision a thing of beauty than define the Beautiful.

It is therefore important for thought to avoid fixing irremediably upon its own marvels, to remain instead alert and capable of detaching itself from them. It should not risk losing itself in the nothingness it invokes in its effort to "possess" the object. Since an image is ambiguous, it always implies the possibility of a conflict between what it is and what it represents. Thought can profit from its imaging power if, in forming images, it never forgets their objects, which the images never present with absolute validity.

When I preserve this discontent with images in the very heart of images . . . thought does not suffer from the ambiguity, since I allow no time for the image to develop according to its own laws. I abandon it [*je la quitte*] as soon as it is formed; I never rest content with it. Always ready to become bogged down [*s'enliser*] in the image's materiality, thought may escape it by slipping into

25. [*L'Imaginaire*, p. 235; *Psychology of Imagination*, p. 174.]

another image, and from this one into another, and so on. But in most cases this mistrust of the image, which is like a trace of reflection, does not appear. The laws of development proper to the image are then frequently confused with the laws of the essence that is under consideration[26]

—whereas the image should simply attempt to render that essence intuitive.

The Positive Value of the Imaging Function

We have dwelt on these issues because they contain all the perspectives we shall later encounter and we wished to facilitate their comprehension. It remains to point out the positive counterparts of the dangers we have noted, thereby situating imaging among the essential structures of consciousness.

The preceding analyses hardly prepare us for certain assertions Sartre makes in the conclusion of *The Psychology of Imagination*. The most striking and apparently paradoxical one bears on the same basic problem that guides our inquiry: " . . . the imagination is not an empirical and superadded power of consciousness; it is consciousness as a whole inasmuch as it realizes its freedom. . . ."[27]

This statement seems far from the degradation we have been noting. The paragraphs that follow it might also disconcert us since they speak of a permanent possibility of *transcending* the consciousness which intends reality "toward a particular imaging consciousness which is like the reverse side of the situation and in relation to which the situation is defined." These paragraphs are in fact aimed at showing that "the imaginary represents at each instant the implicit meaning of the real."

A comparison is needed. In Pradines's philosophy one finds an extensive study of emotion, which, as we have seen, merits the same phenomenological treatment as imagination. Emotion appears as a *degradation*, but in the form of an accident that supervenes in the normal functioning of consciousness. Emotion is an irregularity in fundamental feelings, which normally serve to regulate behavior. Consciousness is the victim and the register of this irregularity, which causes behavior to regress from perpetual adaptation in new situations to a stupid automaticity. In short, the degradation of consciousness is not its own work. It is a natural event, as are the adaptations effected by life imbued with the psychic when it confronts obstacles blocking its advance. Emotion is the cord that breaks as a result of having been stretched too far. Thus "emotional associations reach not only into the past: they are also precursors. They sink beneath thought only when thought outruns its resources."[28]

26. *L'Imaginaire*, p. 229; *Psychology of Imagination*, pp. 169–170.

27. *L'Imaginaire*, p. 358; *Psychology of Imagination*, p. 270. [The words "its freedom" (*sa liberté*) are erroneously omitted from this French edition. Cf. *L'Imaginaire* (Paris: Gallimard, 1940, printing of 1964), p. 236.]

28. Maurice Pradines, *Traité de psychologie générale*, vol. 1 (Paris: Presses Universitaires de France, 1943), p. 730.

For Pradines, emotion is clearly not an act of consciousness or an aberrant form that thought may provisionally assume: it is instead a rupture of thought; a rapid, passive consciousness of dislocation—which amounts to a return to the unconscious.

Here, then, is a psychic phenomenon whose whole meaning is to be anti-psychic. Certainly when nature turns against itself it always does so naturally. But how can we speak of degradation or flight, etc., if all this refers to a simple change of direction? One must use a play on words to restore as phenomena of consciousness events one had initially considered to be purely empirical. This reintroduces into these events an ambiguity one had deprived them of earlier, thereby tacitly conferring on them the task of standing for a consciousness whose vocation is not written in nature and does not manifest natural laws. This vocation is already implied in the double-edged character of one's power of consciousness, which is a perpetual escape that *can* bog down in its own flights, a freedom susceptible of nullifying *itself*.

It is this latter form of consciousness that Sartre presents to us in his *Outline of a Theory of the Emotions*. For Pradines the distance between emotion and imagination is that between an accident and a function. In light of the preceding remarks, however, we can see that for him this function must be quite natural, performing its role so long as nothing disturbs it from outside. Sartre, for his part, uses the very same point to accentuate the role of consciousness as a whole. Even the aberrant forms of imagination derive essentially from the capacity of consciousness to make itself "imaging consciousness."

Imagination is not a function residing in consciousness. It is a direction thought may take, but it is prefigured only when thought endeavors to take it, which is to say that imagination issues from a genuine initiative. The problem is therefore to learn (a) whether imagination is an accident or a function and (b) if it is a function, whether it is an accidental function—however important it may be as such—or an essential function. To decide these matters we must ask whether we can conceive of a consciousness that does not and could not imagine. "Can one conceive a consciousness that would never imagine, that would always be entirely absorbed in its intuitions of the real? If so, then the very possibility of imagining, which appears as one quality among others of *our* consciousnesses, would be a merely contingent enrichment. Or rather, from the moment one posits a consciousness at all, must one posit it as always capable of imagining?"[29]

Sartre is preparing for a valuable remark aimed at delineating his opposition to other modern psychologies, Bergson's in particular. It deals with the radical distinction between remembering and anticipating, on the one hand, and imagining, on the other.

We can relive the past or, in our acts, anticipate the future. In neither case,

29. *L'Imaginaire*, p. 344; *Psychology of Imagination*, p. 260.

Sartre holds, do we depart from reality: "All real existence gives itself with structures of present, past, and future; thus, inasmuch as the past and the future are essential structures of the real, they are themselves also real, that is, correlates of a thesis of reality."[30] For example, I can realize Peter in the past by directing my consciousness to yesterday's events in order to find among them the handshake he gave me. Peter is not "*given-as-absent* but is rather *given-now-as-in-the-past*." His handshake of yesterday has not become unreal, "it continues to be real, but past"; it is "placed in retirement" as it were. Similarly, I can foresee the tennis ball's trajectory, but "here the future is only the *real* development of a form initiated by my adversary's gesture. His real gesture communicates its reality to this entire form. If you prefer, the real form, with its real-past and real-future zones, is realized [*se réalise*] wholly through his gesture."[31]

On the other hand, I may isolate this same past or future and cease to live them as real and as foundations of the present, positing them instead in their own right and severing them from all reality by making them appear to me as nothingness. Peter's face as it could have been a moment ago, or as it may appear when I shall go to meet him at the railroad station, is obtainable for me only if I posit it on the margin of reality as a whole, which I must keep at a distance, freeing myself of it by negating it.

In brief, to recall this or that memory is to reopen time, to go looking for the memory at its place in the past, just as in perception one goes looking for an object at its place in space. If the object fails to appear in the real time and space accessible to me, then this time and space must be negated and one must "posit a thesis of unreality."[32] The object then appears with absolute dimensions that are not derived from possible comparisons with other objects: my image of Peter gives him to me as tall or short, independent of all relation with his surroundings. Similarly, the imagined object appears as dateless: this face is the synthesis of what Peter may have been at various times in his life; it expresses a sort of absolute age—as when one says that a certain person should always be forty, that it is "the best period of his life."

For consciousness to imagine, then, it must be able to de-realize. However, "to negate an object one designates as real is to negate the real insofar as one posits that object; the two negations are complementary and the latter is the condition for the former."[33] It follows that, "for a consciousness to be able to imagine, it must escape the world by its very nature, it must be able to draw from itself a position of retreat [*une position de recul*] in relation to the world. In a word, it must be free."[34] "Were it possible to conceive a consciousness that

30. *L'Imaginaire*, p. 350; *Psychology of Imagination*, p. 264.
31. *L'Imaginaire*, pp. 349–350; *Psychology of Imagination*, p. 264.
32. *L'Imaginaire*, p. 351; *Psychology of Imagination*, p. 265.
33. *L'Imaginaire*, p. 352; *Psychology of Imagination*, p. 266.
34. *L'Imaginaire*, pp. 353–54; *Psychology of Imagination*, p. 267. ["*Recul*," which lacks a univocal English translation, means both *the movement* of retreat, especially

did not imagine, it would have to be thought of as totally caught up in what is existent, with no possibility of grasping anything besides what is existent."[35] Here we recognize those psychological views which hold that mental realities exist inside consciousness. Even when those realities transcend the external world, such a view condemns consciousness to a psychological determinism that is the simple homologue of scientific determinism.

Not only would such a consciousness be caught up in the physically existent, but it would also be captive within the world of human feelings. A limiting case of this sort is implicit in the phenomenon of "participation" which certain authors have considered characteristic of the "primitive mentality" but which our civilized societies also manifest in the form of collective hysterics. In the latter case, each individual renounces himself in order to enjoy a commonly experienced feeling. French sociologists have recently brought to light the spontaneous preference exhibited by a German sociologist, Tönnies —as by the majority of his compatriots—for a consanguine community (*Gemeinschaft*)as opposed to a contractual community (*Gesellschaft*).[36]

We find in this preference a nostalgic yearning for some lost paradise where one could feel an animalistic "fraternal" warmth.[37] Yet, if one examines primitive societies themselves, one finds that magic actually disconnects itself from this base of participation with its lived vision of the world and sets up new horizons connected instead with the subject's intervention. Magic thereby demonstrates a capacity for escape. Although the sorcerer would be inconceivable outside the dimension of participation, he is also the one who disengages himself from this natural perspective, liberated from it by the particular use he chooses to make of it.

A passage in Henry Miller's *Tropic of Capricorn* provides a good example of this liberation from a primary human world and from the burden it weighs upon all engaged in it. Miller is writing of his grandfather, whom he always visualizes as follows:

> . . . he would stand with one hand over the other and look out of the window dreamily. I remember the expression on his face, as he stood there dreaming. . . .
> I used to wonder what he was dreaming of, what it was that drew him out of himself. I hadn't learned yet how to dream wide-awake. I was always lucid, in

---

retreat in order to gain perspective on something, and *the space* into which one moves in order to gain such perspective. Thus Sartre is pointing here to the capacity of consciousness to "back away" in order to place its object in perspective (that is, in the context of past and future), yet without movement or alteration, drawing such a perspective "from itself."]

35. *L'Imaginaire*, p. 359; *Psychology of Imagination*, pp. 271–272.

36. Ferdinand Tönnies, *Gemeinschaft und Gesellschaft* (Leipzig: H. Buske, 1935); *Community and Association*, translated by Charles P. Loomis (London: Routledge and Kegan Paul, 1955).

37. See, for example, Georges Gurwitch (Georgii Davidovich Gurvich), *Essais de sociologie* (Paris: Librairie du Recueil Sirey, 1938) and Jules Monnerot, *Les Faits sociaux ne sont pas des choses*, Les Essais, no. 19 (Paris: Gallimard, 1946).

the moment, and all of a piece. His daydreaming fascinated me. I knew that he had no connection with what he was doing, not the least thought for any of us, that he was alone and being alone he was free. I was never alone, least of all when I was by myself. Always, it seems to me, I was accompanied: I was like a little crumb of a big cheese, which was the world, I suppose, though I never stopped to think about it. But I know I never existed separately, never thought myself the big cheese, as it were. So that even when I had reason to be miserable, to complain, to weep, I had the illusion of participating in a common, a universal misery.[38]

Imagination appears here as consciousness's opposing itself to the world by negating the world's "being-there" and by positing a "nothingness" toward which this negation is aimed.

We must also observe, however, that I can oppose an imaginary object to the world in this manner to the precise extent that I am firmly situated within the world. The imaginary is not just anything at all. I can give myself a particular image only according to a "concrete and precise motivation" within a situation, a motivation which excludes the object in question from all accessible reality.[39] Only insofar as Peter cannot be actually present for me, am I able to imagine him as absent. In short, "an image is not *the world negated*, purely and simply, but rather, always, *the world negated from a certain viewpoint. . . .*"[40] The world forced back in this way remains there as a horizon against which the unreal form of the image stands out in relief.

We are at the heart of the imaging function: when imagining, consciousness seems to be momentarily transported from the world; and yet the essential condition for the possibility of this imagining is that consciousness be situated within the world. Thus the object in an image is always a disappointment: it is incapable of appearing to us without indicating its absence. We must also note, however, that this same ambiguity defines consciousness itself, which is also free only insofar as it is in a situation. Just as all consciousness is consciousness of something, so all freedom is freedom within some situation, that is, a negation of a state of affairs, an escape from an objective existence, and a transcendence of this existence in the direction of its meaning. Consciousness is not a prisoner in the real, it is a relation to the real; this is its situation *and* its freedom.

We can now understand those concluding remarks of Sartre's that may have appeared surprising. Imagination, it turns out, is neither an accident supervening in consciousness, nor "an empirical and superadded power of consciousness."[41] It is rather an "essential condition and primary structure" of consciousness inasmuch as it is the same thing for consciousness to imagine

38. [Henry Miller, *Tropic of Capricorn* (New York: Grove Press, 1961), p. 14.]
39. [*L'Imaginaire*, p. 356; *Psychology of Imagination*, p. 269.]
40. *L'Imaginaire*, pp. 354-355; *Psychology of Imagination*, p. 268.
41. [*L'Imaginaire*, p. 358; *Psychology of Imagination*, p. 270.]

something and for it to "nihilate" ["*néantiser*"] the world.[42] On a theoretical plane one could consider this "nihilation" as a mere manifestation of that freedom by which all consciousness distinguishes itself from things and thereby defines itself as consciousness. But on the psychological and empirical plane, although the act of imagining is conditioned by this capacity for freedom, it is just this act which allows that capacity to show forth in the first place. An absolute negation of the world is impossible, since only an absolute nothingness could effect it and to thus oppose the world with an absolute nothingness would be to not oppose it at all. For my part, then, I can negate the world only in relation to some thing or other, a procedure which nevertheless involves negating *all things*. This "other thing" which I oppose to all things must therefore also be a nothing in relation to them and must be given intuitively to me, remaining in some way graspable for me. This nothingness is the imaginary. Imagination is the surpassing of everything existent; it allows me to apprehend the latter as real by disengaging myself from it, also, thereby, allowing me to grasp the particular meaning of the situation in which reality appears to me. "There could be no realizing consciousness without imaging consciousness, and vice versa."[43]

Thus from a transcendental viewpoint—and we shall have to return in the next chapter to the problem posed by such a viewpoint—it is consciousness's power of negation that makes imagination possible. But from an empirical perspective, it is through imagination that this power is manifest. One can escape everything only if the escape is in the direction of some other thing; imagination affords us this perpetual escape; it characterizes the subject's freedom in contrast with the object's inertia.

THE TWO MODES OF EXISTENCE

No description of this contrast is more striking than *Nausea*, Sartre's account of the sickness that grips Antoine Roquentin in his encounter with things. The hero of this novel unconsciously relieves himself of his own existence through the life he gives to the Marquis de Rollebon, on whom he is writing a historical work. But bizarre impressions have already troubled Roquentin on several occasions. Obsessed with them, he breaks off work. Up to that point, he notes in his journal,

42. [*L'Imaginaire*, p. 354; *Psychology of Imagination*, p. 267. "*Néantiser*," Sartre's neologism, literally, 'to nothing-ize,' has been translated as "nihilate"—following Hazel Barnes's cognate English neologism; cf. *EN*, p. 58; *BN*, p. 56. This is Sartre's term for the capacity of consciousness to introduce nothingness between itself and the world, a capacity that Sartre thinks is implicit in our ability to perceive absences, holes, and other particular lacks of being.]

43. *L'Imaginaire*, p. 361; *Psychology of Imagination*, p. 273. ["Realizing" here means 'with a thesis of reality' as opposed to 'with a thesis of unreality' and does not refer either to an actualizing power of consciousness or to the historical development of consciousness.]

I lived in the court of the Czars, in old palaces so cold that stalactites of ice formed over the doors in winter. Today I awaken before a pad of white paper. The torches, the icy festivals, the uniforms, the beautiful shoulders that shivered: all have disappeared. Instead, there is *something* here in this tepid room, something I do not want to see. Monsieur de Rollebon was my partner: he needed me in order to exist, and I needed him so as not to feel my own existence. My role was to furnish the raw material, this material of which I had enough and some to spare, which I didn't know what to do with: that is, existence, *my* existence. His role was to represent. He stood before me having laid hold of my life in order to *represent* to me his own. I no longer noticed that I existed; I existed no longer in myself, but in him. It was for him that I ate, for him that I breathed, each of my movements had its meaning outside, there, right before me, in him. I no longer saw my hand as it drew the letters on the paper, not even the sentence I had just written—but behind and beyond the paper I saw the Marquis who had claimed this gesture and whose existence was prolonged and consolidated by it. I was a mere means of making him live and he was my raison d'être, he relieved me of myself.[44]

Roquentin had been seeking to move beyond his own existence—in which he constantly dreaded feeling imprisoned, which he dreaded feeling at all—towards the imaginary. It could make him forget his existence as such, while conferring upon it a meaning, a value, a sort of justification. In the following passage, however, we see he can no longer sustain the imaginary and make it win out over the real:

I made one final effort, I repeated those words of Madame de Genlis by which I had usually evoked the Marquis: "His wrinkled little face: neat and clean, all riddled with smallpox, where there was a peculiar malice that struck the eye, no matter what effort he made to dissemble it." Again his countenance came to me obediently, his pointed nose, his blue cheeks, his smile. I could shape his features at will, perhaps with even greater ease than before. Only it was no more than an image within me, a fiction. I sighed, letting myself fall against the back of my chair with a sense of intolerable loss.[45]

After that the game was over. Roquentin's existence reassimilates the game and is no longer surpassed by any meaning. "The Thing, which had been waiting, was alerted, it pounced on me and now it courses through me, I am full of it. It is nothing: the Thing is myself. Existence, liberated and detached, again flows back over me. I exist."[46]

This existence—which penetrates him "from everywhere, through the eyes, through the nose, through the mouth"—is his own existence but *in the same mode as that of things.*

44. J.-P. Sartre, *La Nausée* (Paris: Gallimard, 1938), pp. 126–127; *Nausea*, translated by Lloyd Alexander (Norfolk, Conn.: New Directions, 1959), pp. 133–134.
45. *La Nausée*, p. 126; *Nausea*, p. 132.
46. *La Nausée*, p. 127; *Nausea*, p. 134.

Roquentin enters a subway train:

> I rest my hand on a seat but withdraw it hurriedly: it exists. This thing on which I am seated, on which I rest my hand, is called a seat. . . . I murmur, "It's a seat," a little like an exorcism. But the word remains on my lips: it refuses to go rest upon the thing. . . . Things have been relieved of their names. They are there, grotesque, obstinate, gigantic, and it seems imbelicic to call them seats or to say anything at all about them: I am in the midst of the Things, the unnameables. Alone, without words, without defenses, they surround me, beneath me, behind me, above me. They require nothing, they impose nothing: they are there.[47]

At this point it is evident his attempt to escape has again failed. Incantation in words is no more successful than the appearance of Rollebon's face in an image. Consciousness has lost its capacity to go beyond, to surpass; it lets itself get caught among things, mired in existence.

Finally there is the moment of revelation. Roquentin has entered the park: "And suddenly, all at once, the veil was torn away, I understood, I *saw*." Existence no longer lacks merely the particular meaning which gave it its rationale for Roquentin but is now stripped even of its most general meaning, according to which the world is a complex of implements.[48]

> So I was in the park just now. The root of the chestnut tree plunged into the earth just beneath my bench. I could no longer remember that it was a root. Words had vanished, and with them the meanings of things, their uses, the feeble pathways men had traced on their surface. . . . And then I had this revelation.
>
> It took my breath away. Never, until the last few days, had I suspected what "to exist" meant. . . . ordinarily existence conceals itself. It is there, around us, in us, it is *ourselves*, one cannot say two words without speaking of it, and yet, one doesn't touch it. Though I had believed I was thinking of it, I must consider that I was thinking of nothing, head empty, or with just one phrase in it, the phrase, "to be." . . . And then it came, all at once there it was, clear as the day: existence was suddenly laid bare. It had lost the harmless demeanor of an abstract category; it was the very dough of things, this root had been kneaded in existence. Or rather the root, the park's iron fence, the bench, the sparse grass of the lawn, all that had vanished; the diversity among things, their individuality, was only an appearance, a glaze. This glaze had dissolved, leaving monstrous soft masses in disorder—naked, with a terrifying and obscene nakedness.[49]

We see developed here the idea we caught sight of in the preceding passage: the obsessive thought that all justification may be impossible. Roquentin, sens-

47. *La Nausée*, p. 159; *Nausea*, pp. 168–169.
48. *Esquisse*, p. 48; *Emotions*, p. 89.
49. *La Nausée*, pp. 161 and 162; *Nausea*, pp. 170–173.

ing that his own existence is caught in the overwhelming "flexion" and "swooning abundance" of the things around him, experiences a diffuse sensation permeating the world, which had itself become amorphous:

> We were a heap of awkward existing things, an inconvenience to ourselves, not one of us having the least reason for being there, each existing, embarrassed, vaguely alarmed, feeling in the way [de trop] in relation to others. In the way: this was the only relationship I could ascertain between these trees, these fences, these cobblestones. I sought in vain to count the chestnut trees, to situate them in relation to the statue of Velleda, to compare their height with the height of the plane trees; each escaped the relationship in which I tried to enclose it, isolated itself, overflowed. These relationships (which I tried to maintain in order to slow the collapse of the human world with its measurements, quantities, and instructions) felt arbitrary to me; they no longer had their teeth into things. The chestnut tree, in the way, there in front of me a bit to the left. The Velleda, in the way....
>
> And me—flabby, languid, obscene, digesting, shaking with dismal thoughts—I was also in the way. I vaguely contemplated doing away with myself to annihilate at least one of these superfluous existences. But my very death would have been in the way. In the way: my dead body, my blood on the cobblestones, among the plants at the end of this smiling park. And the corroded flesh would have been in the way in the ground that received it; and finally my bones, scoured, peeled, neat and clean like teeth, would also be in the way: I was in the way forever.[50]

Just before this, gripped by his malady in a restaurant, Roquentin had already thought regarding the other patrons: "Why are these people there? Why are they eating? It is true that they are not aware that they exist. I want to leave, to go some place where I would feel truly in my place, where I would fit.... But my place isn't anywhere; I am in the way."[51]

Nausea is therefore the awareness of existing not as consciousness but as thing: "How long did this fascination last? I was the chestnut tree's root. Or rather I was, entirely, consciousness of its existence. Though detached from it—since I was conscious of it—I was lost in it and was nothing else besides it. I was an uneasy consciousness which, nevertheless, released all of its suspended weight upon this inert piece of wood."[52] Roquentin's consciousness almost ceases to exist as such, retaining only enough of itself to feel caught and engulfed in the being of things. "All that really exists in me is existence feeling itself exist. . . . Consciousness exists like a tree, like a blade of grass. It dozes,

50. La Nausée, p. 163; Nausea, pp. 172–173. ["Velleda" refers to a statue representing a druidess and prophetess who lived in Germany during the reign of Vespasian. With Civilis she guided an uprising in part of Gaul and died, captive, in Rome.]

51. La Nausée, p. 155; Nausea, p. 164.

52. La Nausée, p. 167; Nausea, p. 177.

it is bored. . . . But it *never* forgets itself; it is always conscious of being a consciousness that forgets."[53] Thus, "there is" consciousness, but a person no longer dwells within it.[54] And if Roquentin remains ever so slightly detached from things, it is from having lost all power to negate them, in his fascination with witnessing their insolent and absurd self-affirmation.

Even more characteristic of this self-affirmation, as he discovers in reflecting on his encounter with the root, is

> contingency: that's what is essential. I mean that, by definition, existence isn't necessity. To exist is simply *to be there*; existences appear, they let themselves *encounter* each other, but you can never *deduce* them. . . . contingency is not a pseudoappearance or an appearance one can dissipate; it is the absolute, and consequently, it is perfect gratuitousness. Everything is gratuitous: this garden, this city, myself. Once you realize that, it turns your heart upside down and everything starts to float . . . : that's what Nausea is, that's what the Bastards— those on the Coteau Vert and others—try to side with their idea of rights. But what a poor lie: nobody possesses rights. The Bastards too are entirely gratuitous. Like other people, they are unable to cease feeling in the way. And inside themselves, secretly, *they are in the way*, that is, amorphous and vague, sad.[55]

These passages foreshadow several themes in *Being and Nothingness*. It suffices to indicate that in the latter work Being will be this gratuitousness, this contingency of things, while Nothingness will be that by which there may be being for a consciousness, that is, the term corresponding to consciousness's power to nihilate. Nausea reveals Being—that in which consciousness constantly risks letting itself be caught. The "Bastards" are those who allow themselves to be thus caught, who cease to exist qua consciousness and who then constantly pretend to *justify* this thing-like existence. This is later called the Spirit of Seriousness. Since their opposition to being endures, the Bastards must veil their own power of negation and freedom; this veiling is later called Bad Faith. And corresponding exactly with Nausea, which is the unveiling of Being, there is Anguish, which is the unveiling of one's freedom. "Most of the time we flee from anguish in bad faith."[56]

These observations will perhaps help measure the route from psychology to ontology that we have just traversed. The next chapter will try to illuminate this route, introducing the above-mentioned themes in their own right.

Meanwhile, further lessons can be drawn out of Roquentin's liberation from Nausea.

53. *La Nausée*, pp. 212–213; *Nausea*, p. 227.
54. [Sartre develops this thesis at length in "La Transcendance de l'Ego: esquisse d'une description phénoménologique," *Recherches philosophiques* 6 (1936–1937): 85–123; *The Transcendence of the Ego: An Existentialist Theory of Consciousness*, translated by Forrest Williams and Robert Kirkpatrick (New York: Noonday Press, 1957).]
55. *La Nausée*, pp. 166–167; *Nausea*, pp. 176–177.
56. [*EN*, p. 642; *BN*, p. 711.]

THE RIGOR OF ART

As we have seen, Roquentin's own existence appears "in the way" to him as it flows back over him because, just like the existence of things, it is contingent, unjustified, and absurd.

The word Absurdity is now born beneath my pen. A moment ago in the garden I didn't find it, but neither did I look for it. I didn't need it: I thought without words *upon* things, *among* things. Absurdity was neither an idea in my head nor a murmur of my voice, but rather that long serpent lying dead at my feet, that serpent of wood. . . . and without clearly formulating anything, I understood that I had found the key to Existence, the key to my Nausea, to my own life. In fact, everything I was able to grasp henceforth referred back to this fundamental absurdity. Absurdity: still just a word. I am debating against words; back there I was touching the thing. And yet I want to pin down the absoluteness of this absurdity. A gesture, an event in the colorful little world of men, is never more than relatively absurd. It is absurd in relation to the accompanying circumstances. The orations of a madman, for example, are absurd in relation to the situation in which he finds himself, but not in relation to his own delirium. All the same, I just now had the experience of the absolute: the absolute or the absurd. As for the root, there was nothing in relation to which it was not absurd. . . . Absurd: in relation to the cobblestones, to the tufts of yellow grass, to the dry mud, to the tree, to the sky, to the green benches. Absurd, irreducible: nothing could explain it, not even a deep and secret delirium in nature. I did not know everything, to be sure, not having seen the seed develop or the tree grow. Yet faced with this big, gnarled paste, neither ignorance nor knowledge had any importance: the world of explanations and reasons is not the world of existence. A circle is not absurd, it is quite well explained by the rotation of a straight line around one of its extremities. But neither does a circle exist. This root existed—to the precise extent that I could not explain it.[57]

One may imagine he hears in this the voice of Camus. Still, both the tone and the concern are different. The above remarks are not made on the plane of *The Myth of Sisyphus* or *The Stranger*. For Camus, the circle itself would be absurd insofar as it is a vain attempt to rationalize an unreasonable world, that is, insofar as it is a product of mind—which is unadaptable to things. This places the absurd within human behavior, whatever its form. Sartre, on the other hand, situates the absurd exclusively in the mode of existence of things, and in the human domain only to the extent that that domain abdicates its role by losing itself in things. For Camus the absurd is relative to every human effort, whereas Roquentin insists on its absolute character: we do not cause it to be, it *is*, and we have seen how this absolute of Being can be opposed by an unconditioned power of negation.

57. *La Nausée*, pp. 163–164; *Nausea*, pp. 173–174.

Imagination is the term that designates this power, and it is through imagination that Roquentin moves toward his cure. The imaginary—though always motivated by one situation or another—offers up the unreal material of its creations, which can then be made as necessary as one wishes. The circle is one case of a check on absurdity and contingency. Doubtless that is because the circle does not exist. But all sorts of round objects may derive their meaning from the circle; being penetrated—albeit to a lesser degree—by the necessity it embodies, they find some justification for their existence.

"The imaginary," Sartre states, "represents at each instant the implicit meaning of the real." Clearly, though, the imaginary may turn out to be as absurd as the real if, like a simple counterpart, it confines itself to imitating the motivations of the real. At least it cannot thereby become a *work of art*. The work of art challenges contingency. It is a rigorous forming of our various negations of the real. It affords a confrontation between the world and the necessity which issues exclusively from our own freedom. "The real is never beautiful. Beauty is a value applicable to the imaginary only, and this entails the negation of the world in its essential structure."[58] It remains to note that this value, once created in the imagination, endows certain aspects of the real with value while divorcing us from its other aspect of brute existence.

Human superstructures established on the natural world are not solid. Roquentin proved they were fragile and aided in their collapse. They can enclose us in a web of appearances where we are victims—consenting victims at that—of a mirage of justification. We doze there lazily, perhaps losing ourselves in it altogether. Under these conditions Nausea is a happy occurrence, provided it can be surmounted. It is really an awakening, a warning comparable to that dislodging of traditional forms brought about by surrealism. I can create authentic values only if I am first aware of the incompatibility of any such values with my constituted horizon. I must therefore work upon that horizon, trouble it, dislodge it, and institute a new rhythm in it on which I can base this creation. Yet it would be unfitting to enslave myself to this rhythm, to this splendid coursing of "destructured" ["*déstructurés*"] existents through me in which I risk becoming assimilated.[59] In other words, unlike so many surrealists, I should not take the means for the end and forget the true goal, which is free creation.

This mistake is the peril that inevitably accompanies this awakening. Whatever is efficacious is never inoffensive. This danger assumes the form, for Roquentin, of "a horrible ecstasy," a "fascination" to which he is suddenly delivered without knowing how. Finally the park smiles at him and again things point beyond themselves to their meanings. "The smile of the trees, of the clump of laurel, it *meant to say* something; therein was the true secret of

58. *L'Imaginaire*, p. 372; *Psychology of Imagination*, p. 281.
59. [The reader is referred in this regard to André Breton, *L'Amour fou* (Paris: Gallimard, 1966), pp. 96, 100.]

existence."[60] However, this surrender to fascination is, in its very gratuitous-ness, also merely fictive: Roquentin will not achieve salvation through such a vague escape.

Having given up his own existence as consciousness and restored the world to itself, Roquentin is for the moment preoccupied with the existence of things. Caught up in the plenum of his perception—a perception that has again be-come undifferentiated—he lets himself become entangled in the outburst of motiveless forms, just as the surrealist abandons himself to the tumult of visions. At this stage, consciousness submits itelf to the magical category of *the suspicious*:

> Suspicious, that was what they were: the sounds, the smells, the tastes. When they ran fleetingly under your nose like flushed hares and you didn't pay much attention to them, you could believe they were quite simple and reassuring, you could believe a real blue, a true red, belonged to the world, that it had a true odor of almond or violet. But once you held them a moment this feeling of comfort and security gave way to a profound uneasiness: colors, tastes, odors, were never true, never straightforwardly themselves and only themselves. . . . That black there, against my foot. . . . It *resembled* a color but it also resem-bled... a bruise, or a secretion, or a grease stain—and it resembled other things, for example, an odor made up of the smells of moist earth and warm, moist wood, the sort of black odor that spreads like varnish over sinewy wood, evoking the flavor of chewed-up, sugary fiber. I didn't merely *see* this black: *sight* is an abstract invention, a cleaned-up, simplified idea, an idea of man. But that black, that amorphous and drab presence, far surpassed sight, smell, and taste. This richness became confusion; in the end, it was nothing because it was too much.[61]

Roquentin clearly has nothing to expect from a provisional return to a more reassuring world, to a perception distracted by action. He must rigorously set man over against this nature which threatens to recrystallize under the form of the "suspicious." He must have something clear and pure if he is to assert himself against this dense invasion of softness. The circle was already placing the absurdity of existence in check. A further step is required: "In another world, circles and musical tunes keep their lines pure and rigid."[62]

Just so, it is a melody that serves as motif, throughout the work, for Roquen-tin's partial recoveries, finally providing the theme of a fundamental recovery.

Hearing it, he feels happy—at first within the same time in which he lives and encounters his Nausea. However, as the record turns,

> there is another happiness: outside, there is this band of steel, the narrow dura-tion of the music traversing our own time through and through, rejecting it and tearing it out of its dry little points; there is another time. . . . Nothing

60. [*La Nausée*, p. 171; *Nausea*, p. 181.]
61. *La Nausée*, pp. 165–166; *Nausea*, pp. 175–176.
62. *La Nausée*, p. 163; *Nausea*, p. 172.

acts upon the steel ribbon, not the door opening, nor the blast of cold air passing over my knees, nor the arrival of the veterinary with his young daughter: the music pierces these vague forms and passes through them. . . . A few more seconds and the Negress will sing. It seems inevitable, so strong is the necessity of this music. Nothing can interrupt it, nothing from this time into which the world has fallen; it will stop on its own, on beat. . . . And yet I am uneasy, for it would take so little to stop the record: a broken spring, cousin Adolph's whim. How odd, how moving, that this hardness should be so fragile. Nothing can interrupt it and everything can break it.

The last chord has faded away. In the brief silence that follows, I strongly sense it is there, that *something has happened*. . . . When the voice rose . . . I felt my body become tense; the Nausea vanished. It was almost painful to suddenly turn hard and glowing like that. At the same time the music's duration swelled, dilating like a column of water. It filled the café with its metallic transparency, shattering our miserable time against the walls. I was *within* the music.[63]

The characteristics of the music contrast it with the vague, the viscous, the exhaustion of the world of things, and for the moment the things themselves cease to be in the way. The notes exist only for the inflexible order which "gives birth to them and destroys them, never allowing them the leisure to recover themselves and exist for themselves."[64] Then: "my glass of beer shrinks, it settles down on the table: it has an air of density, indispensability." Even Adolph's face assumes "the obviousness, the necessity of a conclusion."[65]

Roquentin, fascinated with this softness that overflows all existent things and that also turns within him, later regains possession of himself by the same means:

The voice, heavy and hoarse, suddenly appears, and the world vanishes, the world of existences. A woman of flesh had that voice; she sang before a microphone in her prettiest costume and they recorded her voice. The woman: bah! She existed like me, like Rollebon, I had no desire to know her. But then there's the other thing. One cannot say it exists. The turning record exists, the vibrating air struck by the voice exists, the voice that engraved the record existed. And I, who listen, exist. Everything is full; existence is everywhere dense and heavy and soft. But beyond all this softness, inaccessible, near yet far, young, merciless, and serene, there is this... this rigor.[66]

Still later the opposition grows stronger between the unconstraint of things, with their inertia, and this necessity that impregnates the melody, that *is* the melody right up to its end. "There's nothing to compare with musical tunes for carrying their own death proudly within themselves like an internal neces-

63. *La Nausée*, pp. 36–37; *Nausea*, pp. 33–34.
64. *La Nausée*, p. 36; *Nausea*, p. 33.
65. *La Nausée*, p. 37; *Nausea*, p. 35.
66. *La Nausée*, pp. 132–133; *Nausea*, pp. 139–140.

sity; except that they don't exist. Everything existent is born without reason, and is prolonged by weakness, and dies by collision."[67]

At this stage we find only an absolute opposition between the rigor of art and the absurdity of things. Will we be condemned to the sterility of such an opposition; must Roquentin wait each time for a piece of music to provisionally save him from Nausea?

THE IMAGINARY AND LIFE

It seems the answer is no. For if action left to itself is not always enough to suppress the appearance of "the suspicious" in the world, and if art merely negates the world's existence to the point of manifesting it, there is still a sort of artistic action, an art of life, that might transform the face of things.

A brief entry in the diary prepares us for this perspective in which rigor and existence are to be reconciled: "My train leaves in twenty minutes. The phonograph. Strong sense of adventure."[68] More exactly, Roquentin describes his need for clear events, for true beginnings that "appear like a trumpet call, like the first notes of a jazz tune, suddenly cutting boredom short, fortifying the passing moment."[69] He notes: "Yes, that's what I wanted, and it's what I still want. I experience such happiness when the Negress sings: what summits would be beyond me if *my own life* were itself the content of the melody."[70]

Yet he is quick to admit that the sense of *adventure* always arises from an account of the events, which, as such, inevitably unfolds those events in reverse. Since an account is oriented toward an ending that is already known, it transforms the elements that precede that ending, drawing them all to itself: "I wanted the moments of my life to follow each other like those in a life that was recollected. You might as well try to catch time by the tail."[71]

Anny[72] arrives at a conclusion of the same order in her study of "perfect moments." There were, for her, "privileged situations," "situations which had a rare and precious quality, a style, if you like."[73] One is supposed to make perfect moments out of them. "Yes, I reply, I understood. In each privileged situation there are actions that must be undertaken, attitudes that must be assumed, words that must be spoken—and other attitudes, other words, are strictly forbidden. . . . In sum, the situation is the raw material: it demands to be worked." "That is it, she says, One must first be plunged into something exceptional and feel one was giving it order. If all these conditions had

67. *La Nausée*, p. 169; *Nausea*, pp. 179–180.
68. *La Nausée*, p. 172; *Nausea*, p. 182.
69. *La Nausée*, p. 55; *Nausea*, p. 54.
70. *La Nausée*, p. 60; *Nausea*, p. 55.
71. Ibid.
72. [Roquentin's mistress, an actress.]
73. [*La Nausée*, p. 185; *Nausea*, p. 196.]

been satisfied the moment would be perfect." "In sum, it was a kind of work of art." "You've already told me that, she said with irritation. No; it was instead... a duty. One *must* transform privileged situations into perfect moments. It was a matter of morality. Yes, you may well laugh: morality."[74] Of course Anny later loses all illusions on this point. Situations and feelings lack sufficient weight by themselves. And acts lack sufficient clarity; their consequences are not sufficiently defined or inevitable. "One cannot be a man of action."[75] In short, there are no adventures. Life stretches out like "a paste that spreads and spreads... so homogeneous that you wonder how men got the idea of inventing names for making distinctions."[76]

Yet this failure is apparent only. The above pages constitute a deepening of the preceding reflections and through them a solution appears.

Roquentin reproaches himself for having wanted *to be*—in the manner of the music.

> I wanted that alone; that's the last word of the tale. Amidst the apparent disorder of my life I see clearly that below all my seemingly disconnected efforts lay the same desire: to chase down existence outside myself, empty its instants of their fat, wring them, dry them, purify myself, harden myself, so as finally to produce the clear and precise sound of a note on the saxophone.[77]

And therein lies the failure. For this flight from contingent existence toward necessary being cannot succeed: it cannot make one forget this real world in which one plods along.

> Once there was a poor fellow who was in the wrong world. He existed, like other people, in the world of parks, bars, commercial centers, and he sought to persuade himself that he lived elsewhere, behind the canvas of paintings, with Tintoretto's doges, with Gozzoli's sober Florentines, behind the pages of books with Fabrizio del Dongo and Julien Sorel, behind phonograph recordings with the languorous, dry moans of jazz. Then, having made a complete fool of himself, he understood. He opened his eyes, he saw that it was all a misdeal. He was in a bar, for sure, before a tepid glass of beer. He rested, worn out, on the café seat. He thought: I am a fool.[78]

This indicates that the imaginary should be conceived not as a model of being but as a reason for acting, not as the possibility of evasion but as the theme of an action. One should not seek to be, like a work of art, one must strive to *bring into being* a work of art. It is not action that should be penetrated by the imaginary and finally renounced altogether; it is rather the imaginary that should constitute the object of an action in the world. The meaning of life will thereby appear in the form of a justification granted it.

74. *La Nausée*, p. 187; *Nausea*, p. 199.
75. *La Nausée*, p. 190; *Nausea*, p. 202.
76. *La Nausée*, p. 189; *Nausea*, p. 201.
77. *La Nausée*, p. 218; *Nausea*, p. 234.
78. *La Nausée*, pp. 218–219; *Nausea*, p. 234.

But it happens that one last time, a few minutes before Roquentin leaves town for good, the Negress sings this melody written by some American Jew:

> She sings. There are two who are saved in that: the Jew and the Negress. Saved. Perhaps they thought they were irrevocably lost, drowned in existence. And yet, no one could think of me as I think of them, with this softness. No one, not even Anny. For me they are a bit like the dead, a bit like the heroes in a novel: they have cleansed themselves of the sin of existing. Not completely, of course, but as much as possible for a human being. . . . The Negress sings. Can one therefore justify her existence? Just a little? I feel extraordinarily intimidated. . . . Couldn't I also make this attempt... Of course it would not be a question of a musical tune... but couldn't I, in another form?... It would have to be a book—I don't know how to do anything else. But not a history book. History speaks of what has existed, and one existence cannot justify the existence of another. My mistake was to want to resuscitate the Marquis de Rollebon. Another kind of book. I don't really know which, but one would have to discern, behind the printed words, behind the pages, something that would not exist, that would be above existence. A story, for example, that could never take place, an adventure. It would have to be beautiful, and hard as steel, and it would make people ashamed of their existence.[79]

When Roquentin leaves us, it is with the hope of one day through this book causing others to think of him, perhaps gaining with this thought an acceptance of himself—but, he admits, "in the past, always only in the past."[80]

The present is, at each instant, unjustifiable. We sense here what will later be brought out more clearly: it is only within the unity of a "project"—which demonstrates both the power of negation and the desire of consciousness to engage itself—that consciousness can become subject and constitute the world and life as meanings. It thereby passes between two reefs: the impersonality of absolute negation and the impersonality of contingent, thing-like self-assertion.

Toward a Practical Meaning of Escape

Roquentin's "liberation" is still only a liberation for its own sake. Though it entails a positive act, its result is purely negative. Prey to Nausea, he is concerned only to detach himself from his existence among things, appealing to the rigor of Art in order to escape an intolerable absurdity and to cease feeling "in the way." But, at this stage, no longer to feel "in the way" could only mean to stop sensing one's very existence. Thus in his journal's last lines Roquentin is aware that any success he obtains will truly hold good only for the past and never totally for the present. The present is there; one can never elude it altogether.

Nausea thus situates us on a strictly theoretical plane, but it does so with

79. *La Nausée*, pp. 221–222; *Nausea*, pp. 236–237.
80. *La Nausée*, p. 223; *Nausea*, p. 238.

regard to what is the true practical problem. In his effort to counteract the contingency of existence, Roquentin finds only the gratuitousness of his own negation. The operation that is described psychologically in this regard is the strict homologue of the operation of reduction which the phenomenologist undertakes when he suspends all affirmation concerning the world, placing the world in brackets.

The freedom arrived at is still only the essence of freedom; it is pure, transcendental consciousness inasmuch as it defines itself as freedom. Apart from concrete considerations, this freedom is the unconditional power to say no, to refuse, to suspend adherence. To be more exact, this freedom appears at three planes: on the phenomenological plane, consciousness can be cut off from the world so it may be studied regarding the essential structures of its intentionality toward the world; on the metaphysical plane, freedom can be opposed to all possible situations in order to demonstrate its power of escape from situations; finally, on the psychological plane, the necessary character of an imaginary creation can relieve us of the feeling of existence, which is the indispensable starting point of any grasp of oneself. On all three planes, however, we sense that the primary term has value only as a means. Pure consciousness, unconditioned freedom, and self-determining imagination: these are all so many instruments at man's disposal, affording him knowledge of himself and guaranteeing his possibilities of emancipation.

This is also the meaning of the discovery of thought within the Cartesian *cogito*: "Is not the very condition of the *cogito* primarily doubt, which is both the constitution of the real as world and its negation from that same viewpoint? And doesn't the reflective grasp of doubt as doubt coincide with the apodictic intuition of freedom?"[81]

And this same meaning is further specified in Sartre's introduction to a selection of Descartes's texts:

Doubt strikes at all propositions that affirm something outside of our own thinking. This means that I can place all existences between brackets, that I exercise my freedom fully when I, who am a nothingness and a void, *nihilate* [*néantis*] or make a nothingness of everything that exists. Doubt is rupture of contact with being; through it man has the permanent possibility of disentangling himself from the existent universe. . . . Although this doctrine may be inspired by the ἐποχή [*epoché*] of the Stoics, no one prior to Descartes had stressed the connection between free will and negativity. No one had shown that freedom comes to man, not because he exists as a fullness of existence among other fullnesses in a world without lacunae, but rather because he *is not*, because he is finite, limited.[82]

81. *L'Imaginaire*, pp. 357–358; *Psychology of Imagination*, p. 270.
82. J.-P. Sartre, "Descartes," in *Descartes, 1596–1650*, Les Classiques de la liberté (Paris: Traits, 1946), pp. 35, 37; "Cartesian Freedom," in *Literary and Philosophical Essays*, translated by Annette Michelson (New York: Criterion Books, 1955), pp. 178–179.

However, the immediate consequence of such a conception of freedom is that it "could not be creative in any way, being nothing." What Descartes lacked, Sartre writes, is "a conception of negativity as productive." Now on these terms there are only two solutions for the subject of the *cogito*. He can enclose himself in a perpetual neutralization of the world. Since limiting himself to ceaseless repetition of his doubt is impossible, the psychological counterpart to this neutralization is imaginary thinking as such, which means he would take refuge among creations whose sole value is precisely that they are unreal. Alternatively, he can reunite consciousness—through a sort of metaphysical postulation—with a being from which one has in advance eliminated all error. Descartes chose the second solution, Roquentin the first. In either case, however, all creation of positive values has been eliminated. On the one hand, creation of art works is creation by opposition only and falls wholly within the motive of negating the real; on the other hand, affirmation of reality by a Cartesian consciousness relieved of doubt amounts to adherence to a Truth that is freely posited only by God himself, yet which somehow ties the human mind to its norms.

In the latter case, the power of negation renounces itself once and for all; in the former, it latches onto its own manifestations and renders itself unable to "operate" the real itself. The mistake consists in conceiving freedom either as a pure suppression of the real or as a self-suppression to the profit of a reality that is thereby rendered valuable. The end result for the subject is either a de-realization of himself or his self-abandonment to an impersonal truth. In both cases consciousness loses itself through repudiation of its relation to the world, whether by suppressing the world as correlative term or by suppressing its distance from the world.

The differences between the two solutions may be even less: is not the constituted Truth to which Cartesian consciousness submits itself an imaginary entity, an ideal reconstruction of the world set against the world that is lived, experienced, and felt? In both cases consciousness has clearly lost sight of the true meaning of its autonomy and is declining to constitute itself as subject. "There is consciousness of..." is all one can say of it.

To sum up these points: negation by itself is valueless; as such it is led either to congeal itself or to disown itself. The purely negative power of consciousness lacks firmness on its own. As in imaginary creation, consciousness is in bad faith if it fails to recognize (a) that the sole value of its acts lies in their resistance to brute existence, (b) that as such this value is purely negative, and (c) that it could become positive only by turning again toward existence in order to endow it with value. In short, to be free and to be in a situation are one and the same. The situation of a being is his existence insofar as his freedom has passed *beyond* that situation and made it significant. Correlatively, however, the freedom of a being could not lie in an escape from all situations, but rather in the passing-beyond of his brute existence toward some particular situation.

The same holds on the concrete psychological plane where we started. If consciousness is liberation from enslavement to existences in *perception*—where consciousness is subjected to contingency in all its infinite proliferation and therefore tends to become a merely passive, impersonal registering—then the formation of *images*, which manifests consciousness's active ability to escape, remains a vain freedom so long as this imaging negation is its own end. In imaging for its own sake, consciousness encounters only the slaves of its own creation; they are unresponsive and unsuited for confirming consciousness in the value of its own existence.

In love, such a being searches for a slave, another being that he can shape as he wishes. He wishes for a look from another that is free of all hostility, a partiality favorable to him, an echo of his own affirmations. But, finding it, he is disappointed and soon rejects it, seeing that a servile approbation is no help and that being loved and judged are worthless except by a freedom equal to one's own. Such is Garcin's failure in *No Exit* as Inès brings him to observe that Estelle's favorable judgment issues only from her physical desire for him.[83] Once one sets this image of himself glowing within the look of another—an image aimed at nullifying one's own sense of existing, whose weight is difficult to support—one immediately senses its vanity, weakness, and unreality. Narcissus believed he ought to love only his own image. Startled by fleshly beings, he repaired to the fountain where he admired his own beauty unceasingly. But he thereby closed this beauty in on itself, condemning it to an unreal existence, losing himself in an image-face he could not truly possess without dissipating it.

> *I am so close to you I could drink you,*
> *O visage!... My thirst is a naked slave...*

But also:

> *I find in the eye such a treasure of impotence and pride. . . .*

And again:

> *How much you resemble all my wishes!*
> *But fragility makes you inviolable,*
>
> . . . .
>
> *The disorder of the shadows will soon shudder!*
> *Tree reaches dark members blindly toward tree*
> *And searches hideously for the tree that disappears...*
> *Thus is my soul lost in its own forest,*

83. J.-P. Sartre, *Huis Clos,* in *Théâtre* (Paris: Gallimard, 1947), p. 161 (scene 5); *No Exit,* translated by Stuart Gilbert, in *No Exit and Three Other Plays by Jean-Paul Sartre* (New York: Vintage Books, 1955), p. 41.

Where power expresses its supreme forms...
Soul, soul of night-black eyes, touching gloom itself,
Becoming immense yet encountering nothing . . .
Between death and itself, a singular gaze![84]

Alternatively, if one faces not an image or a slave but an infinite reality, and if one wishes it to hold surprises, to retain an inexhaustible richness, then, with roles thus reversed, is it not inevitable that one will increasingly become the other's slave? By positing the other as free and attempting no longer to *possess* but to constantly *discover* the other, is one not surrendering to a type of ecstasy in which consciousness alienates and annihilates itself?

Being and Nothingness will describe this double failure of love. But according to the present analysis this failure should not be considered final. It results from the approach we were obliged to take to the study of consciousness. The next chapter will set this approach in relief in order to illuminate its results. We can then grasp the meaning and place occupied in Sartre's work by his enormous treatise, *Being and Nothingness*, which for us will constitute a systematization, elucidation, and development of the themes we have already encountered.

Before entering into these reflections on approach and method, let us draw what we can from the manner in which this failure presents itself.

Consciousness is that ambiguous being which, even in unreflectivity, cannot completely lose sight of or ignore itself. The degradations consciousness undergoes are undergone only if it accepts them, therefore only if it is conscious of accepting them, and therefore only if those degradations are the simple counterparts of its own powers of liberation. Consciousness is caught to the extent that it can escape. If it exists at all it can always break with itself, abolishing its previous attitude for a new one.

We can only conclude (a) that the definition of consciousness that we are sketching—which opposes it to everything that is not itself a power of opposition and escape—already points beyond itself to a fuller definition that gives meaning to its ambiguity; and, further, (b) that, when we have adequately explored the being of consciousness, we will have to posit a corresponding "have-to-be" through which that being will be realized. Consciousness exists in an original mode that still awaits specification. But the specifications we shall obtain will lead us to bring out, albeit still on a theoretical plane, the *vocation* which corresponds to this *existence* and by which consciousness is required to pull itself together in order to become conscious.

The example of love mentioned above can help us grasp this transition. At the level of the study of essences, the lover appears torn between the alternative

84. Paul Valéry, "Fragments du Narcisse," in *Poésies* (Paris: Gallimard, 1942), pp. 110, 114 and 116; "Fragments of the Narcissus," in *Poems*, translated by David Paul, vol. 1 in *The Collected Works of Paul Valéry*, edited by Jackson Mathews (Princeton: Princeton University Press, 1971), pp. 149, 151, 157, and 161.

possibilities presented by positing a thesis either of reality or of unreality. He *can* transpose his love into the realm of the imaginary, tying down the beloved by producing an image for himself and thereby obtaining a perpetually disappointing pseudosatisfaction. He *can* also, in an attitude of indefinite expectation, respect the freedom of this other and dissolve himself in the ecstasy of his contemplation. What *must* love be, then, if not an immense effort to synchronize these two attitudes? And wouldn't this synchronization aim to maintain both the integrity of the loving consciousness and the worth it acquires in reaching toward another consciousness?

The transition is illustrated equally in the case of knowledge, which, since Plato, has so often been compared with love. Here, it is thought that is torn. On the one hand, thought takes care to alienate the object and to assume the advantage over it. It is capable of retracting the object's opacity, which implies the threat of perpetual flight. This attitude corresponds to the immediate awareness of conceptualization. To conceptualize, to name, we have seen, are means of exorcizing things, withdrawing their strangeness, and possessing them. Meanwhile, however, one loses them as things, because one has renounced the attempt to know what is real. On the other hand, thought has a quite different attitude at its disposal: that of perception in all its docility. Here, thought consents to be informed by the things themselves; it is able, therefore, to situate itself at their level. But, in the empiricism to which it thus surrenders, it is thought itself that becomes estranged from itself by merging with the real. In the former case, what it lays hold of is no longer the real. In the latter, thought itself is no longer there to lay hold of anything. The nominalists are correct, but the intellectualists are not wrong. And one can see that science is precisely this attempt by thought to reach the world, without thereby losing itself.

Chapter 4

From Psychology to Ontology

To PASS BEYOND the real (without annihilating it) in the direction of its meaning and to pass beyond consciousness's own act of pure negation in the direction of the value and practical coherence of that act are one and the same. We have just seen this in the cases of love and knowledge.

"All consciousness is consciousness of something"; all consciousness is intentionality.[1] The world is the correlate of consciousness. Consciousness "loves" the world, always reaching toward it and aiming at it. "To aim" derives from the Latin *aestimare* meaning both 'to appraise' and 'to imbue with value.'

Reaching toward the world comes easily to consciousness. Indeed, consciousness finds such ready satisfaction in this normal activity—to the point of becoming ensnared in the world—that it forgets the world comes into being for it only through this relation, which it activates. In practice, then, consciousness omits itself in favor of an objectified world. It sees its own valuations as simple acknowledgements, its own presence as a mirror; it takes objects as being determinate in themselves, possessing as qualities a variety of meanings which, in fact, consciousness alone is capable of giving them. This omission-of-self characterizes the empiricism in "*tabula rasa* consciousness" with its self-imposed role of receiving the world. It is also present in the intellectualism of "transcendental" consciousness, in which the world's Truth is already fully constituted. It is particularly characteristic of the classical psychologists' positions on emotion or imagination. They fail to distinguish adaptive from magical behavior in these two areas because they recognize only (a) objective behavior caused by circumstances (the result of having failed to distinguish between perceptions and images) and (b) "image-things" which are given as such to consciousness.

If consciousness wishes to regain its self-control, to reassume its native power

1. [This is a central tenet of phenomenology in general and Husserl's and Sartre's phenomenologies in particular. According to Husserl, "we understand under Intentionality the unique peculiarity of experience 'to be the consciousness of something.'" *Ideen I*, p. 167; *Ideas*, pp. 242–243. But also note Husserl's caveat regarding "sensory data," *Ideen I*, p. 76; *Ideas*, p. 120. Sartre interprets intentionality dialectically as the capacity for self-transcendence within consciousness itself, a capacity that includes the ability to alter something through the mere fact of being conscious of it. *L'Imaginaire*, pp. 27–28; *Psychology of Imagination*, p. 14.]

of valuation, it must change directions so as to capture its own movement at the source. This source must then be considered in its own right, independently of the incline that makes it a source of movement. Or, rather, this incline will appear as such only to the extent that consciousness attempts to reascend it. From this perspective, however, the incline will present itself as drained of effectual meaning, of practical value, since it will have ceased to be an incline toward that existence that is our own, toward this situation, having become, as it were, no more than an absolute incline. As Sartre specifies in *Being and Nothingness,*

> if the *cogito* necessarily leads outside itself, if consciousness is a slippery incline on which one cannot settle without thereby finding himself dumped out onto being-in-itself, it is because by itself consciousness has no sufficiency of being as absolute subjectivity; from the start it refers to the thing.[2]

We shall be able to discern the theoretical implications of this incline and the manner in which it constitutes consciousness, and hence to describe the major essential attitudes defining consciousness as such. Clearly, though, this analytical *disengagement* will lose all meaning if it is not performed with the aim of illuminating the prior *engagement* implicit in our very existence, without which any such disengagement would be inconceivable.

The Two Tendencies of Phenomenology

It must therefore be determined whether we must first disengage consciousness in a separate theory, in order to illuminate its engagement in the world, or whether we can directly study consciousness situated in the world. In the latter case, "existential phenomena" would be examined without prior elucidation and in their own right, together with the essential structures of consciousness that show forth in these phenomena.

This amounts to asking to what extent a phenomenology must be essentialist. It is to ask to what extent Husserl, phenomenology's originator, was correct, as compared with Heidegger, who seeks to lay hold of concrete existence and to carry out an authentic existentialism without any intermediary.

In the context of phenomenology we willingly contrast Sartre with Heidegger: the latter seems to have influenced Merleau-Ponty's perspective much more directly than he did Sartre's. But insofar as Sartre wishes to carry out an existentialism—considered now solely as a goal and apart from the means leading up to it—his tendencies are obviously Heideggerian, in the sense that Sartre also attempts to pass beyond Husserl's essentialism.

Consequently, we shall find elements in Sartre's conception of phenomenology that distinguish it from both Husserl's and Heidegger's conceptions. Before approaching Sartre's disturbing *Essay in Phenomenological Ontology,* we

2. *EN*, p. 712; *BN*, p. 786.

should take one last look at the characteristics of these two tendencies, as conceived by the French phenomenologists. For this we shall call upon Sartre, naturally, but also upon Merleau-Ponty, whose analyses, whether or not they are opposed to Sartre's, are always remarkably illuminating.

It is Merleau-Ponty who, beginning with the preface to his *Phenomenology of Perception*, contends that any so-called opposition between Husserl and Heidegger should be admitted only as a first approximation, since the tendencies involved had appeared previously as a contradiction within Husserl's own philosophy. Whatever there may be in this point, to which we shall return, there clearly exists a duality of tendencies within phenomenology as it presented itself to French minds. Merleau-Ponty brings this out in the following manner:

> Phenomenology is the study of essences and, according to it, all problems come down to the definition of essences: the essence of perception, the essence of consciousness, for example. But phenomenology is also a philosophy that re-places essences in existence, and it believes one cannot expect to arrive at an understanding of man and the world from *any starting point other than that of their facticity*.[3]

Phenomenology is then a transcendental philosophy which suspends the affirmations of the natural attitude in order to understand them. But it is also a philosophy for which the world is always "already there," before reflection, as an inalienable presence. On the one hand, its whole effort is toward recovering naïve contact with the world in order to give that contact philosophical status. As such, it is a philosophy that aspires to be an "exact science." But it is also an account of the space and time of the "lived" world.[4]

Certainly, for Merleau-Ponty, this duality of tendencies should not be maintained for its own sake. This is attempted by those historians of philosophy more concerned with counting citations and debating over the letter of texts than with grasping their fundamental inspiration. German phenomenology must itself be *understood* by phenomenological procedures; we must recapture it by recognizing in it just what we were expecting, which is not just another philosophy but the value inherent in the philosophical attitude itself. "It is within ourselves that we shall find the unity of phenomenology and its true meaning."[5]

Even with such a unification as our goal, however, methods may vary. The results obtained by searching for what is common to the two tendencies will differ from the results obtained by supplementing one tendency with the other, correcting each one individually so as to push it as far as possible.

3. Their "facticity" is their existence as fact, contingent and unjustifiable (our emphasis). [The quotation is from *Phénoménologie de la perception*, p. i; *Phenomenology of Perception*, p. vii.]
4. Ibid.
5. [*Phénoménologie de la perception*, p. ii; *Phenomenology of Perception,* p. viii.]

Merleau-Ponty has clearly chosen the first method. For this reason we must qualify Alphonse de Waelhens's remark that there is no direct line of descent leading from Husserl to Heidegger and then from Heidegger to the "phenomenology of perception."[6] Merleau-Ponty seems at least to have more authorization than Sartre to lay claim to *filiation*, having retained the elements of kinship between the two tendencies. *Confrontation* seems a more apt characterization of Sartre's work, since he chose the second method and accentuated differences and oppositions.

It is therefore to be expected that Sartre should emphasize his disagreements with Husserl, as with Heidegger, and that Merleau-Ponty should wish to consider only those harmonizing factors which allow the constitution of an all-embracing phenomenological method for French philosophers.

These points will permit us to better understand how, following the same phenomenological pathway, Sartre nevertheless elaborates an ontology whose basic concept remains absent from Merleau-Ponty's work.

Let us say, approximately, and solely to identify ideas, that Husserl elaborates an ontology of pure consciousness, while Heidegger attempts an analysis of the concrete situation. Starting from this, either one could follow Merleau-Ponty in de-emphasizing the ontological aspects of the Husserlian tendency so as to facilitate its increasing coincidence with the Heideggerian approach, or one could follow Sartre in taking the two as complementary in their very opposition and develop an ontology of consciousness in situation.

The analyses offered by Sartre which we have discussed to this point are oriented toward such a perspective. At the start of *The Emotions: Outline of a Theory*, Sartre gives his own noteworthy characterization of the respective contributions of Husserl and Heidegger.

As we have seen, Sartre rejects "psychologism"—which wants to treat phenomena of consciousness as accidents—contrasting such an approach with phenomenology:

> Its founder, Husserl, had at first been struck by this truth: there is an incommensurability between essences and facts, and he who initiates his inquiry with facts will never succeed in rediscovering essences. . . . Nevertheless, without renouncing the idea of experience (the principle of phenomenology is to go "to the things themselves," and the basis of its method is eidetic intuition), one must at least make that idea supple and find a place in it for the experience of essences and values. One must recognize that essences alone permit us even to classify and inspect facts.
>
> If we did not have implicit recourse to the essence of emotion, it would be impossible to distinguish, within the mass of psychic facts, that particular group made up of the facts of emotionality. Inasmuch, then, as one has also had tacit recourse to the essence of emotion, phenomenology prescribes that one now

6. [Alphonse de Waelhens, "Heidegger et Sartre," in *Deucalion I* (Paris: Editions de la Revue Fontaine, 1946), p. 22.]

explicitly refer to it, fixing in concepts the contents of this essence. . . . There will therefore be, for example, a phenomenology of emotion which, having "placed the world in parentheses," shall study emotion as a pure transcendental phenomenon, not by addressing itself to particular emotions, but by seeking to grasp and elucidate the transcendental essence of emotion as an organized type of consciousness.[7]

Such a study is not Sartre's purpose in his outline. He wishes rather to draw from phenomenology a method and lessons for "pure psychology." He retains the observation that the being of the phenomena of consciousness is primary in relation to their phenomenality in this or that form: "Phenomenology is the study of phenomena—not facts."[8]

We remain in agreement that psychology places neither man in question nor the world in brackets. It takes a man in the world as he presents himself through a multitude of situations: at the café, with his family, at war. Generally speaking, it is concerned with *man in situation*. As such, psychology is, as we have seen, subordinated to phenomenology, since a truly positive study of man in situation should have first clarified the notions of: man, the world, being-in-the-world, and situation. But, after all, phenomenology has scarcely been born, and all these notions are quite far from their definitive elucidation.[9]

In the remainder of the *Outline* Sartre limits himself to an "experiment in phenomenological psychology." But it seems odd that opening remarks like those above do not reverberate through the remainder of the work, the more so since inquiry in *The Psychology of Imagination* still moves on the level of psychology, even though it reveals some decidedly ontological preoccupations.

At this point we can obtain some insight into this philosophy's basic trajectory. The transition between the *Outline* and *Being and Nothingness* is continuous, inasmuch as the *Outline* had already laid the groundwork for an ontology of the psychic, while requiring that this ontology be concerned always with man in situation. The same point emerges from the parallelism Sartre finds between Husserl's and Heidegger's basic principles. Sartre seems to want to show that each should be evaluated in terms of the other. The essential structures of consciousness as described by Husserl are set up by Sartre in direct parallel with the Heideggerian theme that human reality has an existential understanding of itself merely in existing.

And he specifies:

. . . *to exist*, for human reality, means, according to Heidegger, to take upon itself its own being in an existential mode of comprehension. *To exist*, for consciousness, according to Husserl, means *to appear*. Since in either case appearance is an absolute [inasmuch as its existence doesn't indicate something else

7. *Esquisse*, pp. 7 and 8; *Emotions*, pp. 9–12.
8. *Esquisse*, p. 9; *Emotions*, p. 14.
9. *Esquisse*, p. 12; *Emotions*, p. 18.

which does not appear], it is appearance that must be described and interrogated. Heidegger believes that within each human attitude considered in this manner—within emotion, for example . . . —we will rediscover the whole of human reality, since emotion *is* human reality that has taken its being upon itself in such a way as to "direct itself emotively" toward the world. Husserl, for his part, considers that a phenomenological description of emotion will bring to light the essential structures of consciousness, since an emotion is, precisely, a consciousness.[10]

To the extent one can separate Sartre's *method* of investigation from its *object*, he is furnished with the former by Husserl and with the latter by Heidegger. This object is "human reality," man in situation. The method will define man as consciousness, center of intentions, and power of initiative, but only insofar as he is all these things within his actual situation.

Thus Sartre reproaches Husserl for taking the method for the goal and for beginning an artificial ontology of the essences of pure consciousness. But he reproaches Heidegger for pretending to immediately reach the object without any distancing and for having begun a sort of natural ontology of unreflective existence.

The point here is that ontology must be *total*; that is, it must never forget that its object is double or, more precisely, *ambiguous*. Genuine ontology must neither mistake itself for an "essential" ontology nor immerse itself from the start in an "existential" analysis. Either way it loses its object and hence the very relationship of essences to existence, of conscious intentions to their motivations. Ontology should therefore have as its sole object that freedom which is manifested either by affirming itself, as when our intentions confer a *sense* upon our motivations, or by renouncing itself, as when motivations tend to become purely and simply *causes* of intentions.

HUSSERL'S INFIDELITY TO HIS OWN PRINCIPLE

Ontology, then, should not be pure phenomenology in the Husserlian sense. This would make an abstraction of *facticity*, which is simply the reverse side of this ambiguous "freedom" and which, as we have seen, we might designate with equal correctness as "situation."

Despite Merleau-Ponty's accentuations of Husserl's hesitations regarding his own method, too many texts reveal that Husserl's confidence in setting forth that method was of a sort that tends to exclude the ambiguous as such.

Let us cite some passages from the preface that Husserl wrote for the English edition of *Ideen I*, dated 1931, eighteen years after the first publication of the work in German:

10. *Esquisse,* p. 10; *Emotions,* pp. 14–15.

Transcendental Subjectivity . . . is an absolutely independent realm of direct experience, although for reasons of an essential kind it has so far remained inaccessible. Transcendental experience in its theoretical and, at first, descriptive bearing, becomes available only through a radical alteration of that same dispensation under which an experience of the natural world runs its course, a readjustment of viewpoint which, as the method of approach to the sphere of transcendental phenomenology, is called "phenomenological reduction". . . . In this book, then, we treat of an *a priori* science ("eidetic", directed upon the universal in its original intuitability). . . .[11]

In the course of this reduction,

psychological subjectivity loses just that which makes it something real in the world that lies before us; it loses the meaning of the soul as belonging to a body that exists in objective, spatio-temporal Nature. . . . Posited as real (*wirklich*), I am now no longer a human Ego *in* the universal, existentially posited world, but exclusively a subject *for* which this world has being, and purely, indeed, *as* that which appears to me, is presented to me, and of which I am conscious in some way or other, so that the real being of the world thereby remains unconsidered, unquestioned. . . . Now if transcendental description passes no judgment whatsoever upon the world, and upon my human Ego as belonging to the world, and if, in this description, the transcendental Ego exists (*ist*) absolutely in and for itself . . . , it is still at the same time evident that, at every conversion of meaning which concerns the phenomenological-psychological content of the soul as a whole, this very content by simply putting on another existential meaning (*Seinssinn*) becomes transcendental-phenomenological, just as conversely the latter, on reverting to the natural psychological standpoint, becomes once again psychological. . . . We have thus a remarkable thoroughgoing parallelism between a (properly elaborated) phenomenological psychology and a transcendental phenomenology. . . . And yet this whole content as psychology, considered from the natural standpoint . . . and related to the world as spread before us, is entirely non-philosophical, whereas "the same" content from the transcendental standpoint . . . is a philosophical science—indeed, on closer view, *the* basic philosophical science, preparing on descriptive lines the transcendental ground which remains henceforth the exclusive ground for all philosophical knowledge.[12]

We have quoted these texts at length because they show a remarkable emphasis on just those elements in Husserl's position which Sartre will refuse to accept. The development of Husserl's thought may sometimes be flexible enough to justify Merleau-Ponty's attempt to establish Husserl's kinship and continuity with existential thinking. But it will be illuminating to demonstrate how certain principles that Husserl put forth as flowing from his principle of

11. *Ideas*, p. 11.
12. [*Ideas*, pp. 14–15.]

intentionality ought by rights to lead at all points to the antipodes of existentialism, more precisely, to an idealism.

For Husserl the issues revolve around the matter of a *total* reduction. Ultimately, he takes this to be possible, although the problem of this possibility is
raised on several occasions.[13] Consciousness, he says, can place itself on the
transcendental plane through a simple change of perspective; a conversion occurs which allows it to make itself transcendental consciousness. At this level
the world is no longer important. Not only does the world cease to be the
theme of our investigations, it plays no further part in them. Its function as
world has been set aside. It no longer exists as a sort of necessary condition
for consciousness, and consciousness can now conceive of itself without taking
account of the fact that the world is always there. Instead, this world, which
used to be there despite consciousness, without soliciting its assent, has now
become the "world for consciousness." Consciousness exists "absolutely in itself
and for itself," and, as a result, its content acquires a different kind of meaning.

What kind of meaning? The suppression of the world is not strictly methodological; at least, it should not remain so. This suppression inevitably reverberates within the ontological perspective. For, unable to effect a total (if
provisional) suppression of the world, consciousness tries to decisively convert
or transpose itself. It produces *in itself* the equivalent of that world within
which it previously had its being. Consciousness no longer needs the world as
such, since it now possesses the world as its own content. The world's being is
no more than "what appears to me, what is presented to me, what I am conscious of in one way or another." Its facticity, the fact that it was imposed upon
me, becomes the facticity of the elements in which the contents of transcendental consciousness unfold. And whatever these elements may be, they remain
only "possibles" for the "capacities" of this consciousness. The fact that these
capacities have already been given indicates that one must go back to experience to learn which of these possibles will be realized. Facticity has thus
become mere theoretical indeterminacy, and the domain in which it is maintained as such is also "immediately transparent to the mind." Husserl's comparison of eidetic science and mathematics is striking in this regard:

> The science of fact in the strict sense, the genuinely rational science of nature,
> has first become possible through the independent elaboration of a "pure" math-
> ematics of nature. The science of pure possibilities must everywhere precede the
> science of real facts, and give it the guidance of its concrete logic. So is it also
> in the case of transcendental philosophy, even though the dignity of the service
> rendered here by a system of the transcendental *a priori* is far more exalted.[14]

13. [Cf. *Ideen I*, § 32 (pp. 56–57), § 33 (pp. 57–60); *Ideas*, § 32 (p. 110), § 33
(p. 113); and also Merleau-Ponty, *Phénoménologie de la perception*, pp. viii–ix;
Phenomenology of Perception, p. xiv.]
14. [*Ideas*, p. 13.]

This says unequivocally that, although they obviously take the form of meanings rather than mental things, possibles are nevertheless contents of transcendental consciousness and as such are perfectly homogeneous with it, immanent in it, and, ultimately, constitutive of it. Henceforth this consciousness is only a pure glance directed upon these possibles which it discovers within itself and which are accessible to it without any distance, within that perfect transparency that the mathematical notion of the circle possesses for the mathematician. However, just as this mathematical concept is transparent because it is the work of mind, so, would it not follow, inasmuch as the world transposed in consciousness also loses its opacity, that it does so in proportion as it too is a work of consciousness?

Sartre takes just this direction in the criticisms to be found in *Being and Nothingness*. Husserl "never passed beyond the pure description of the appearance as such; he enclosed himself within the *cogito*. Despite his denials he should be called a phenomenalist rather than a phenomenologist, and his phenomenalism borders at each point on Kantian idealism."[15]

> All consciousness is consciousness *of* something. This definition of consciousness may be taken in two quite distinct senses: either we understand it to mean that consciousness is constitutive of the being of its object, or else it means that, at the deepest level of its nature, consciousness is a relationship to a transcendent being. But the first interpretation of the formula negates itself: to be conscious *of* something is to be before some concrete, full presence that *is not* that consciousness. . . . the objective will never come from out of the subjective, nor the transcendent from the immanent, nor being from non-being. . . .
>
> Consciousness is consciousness *of* something: this means that transcendence is a constitutive structure of consciousness.[16]

In short, Husserl misunderstood "the essential character of intentionality": consciousness is that being that "implies a being other than itself." This latter is nevertheless not the being of realism, as we shall later show. In reproaching Husserl for sliding toward idealism, Sartre is not committed to repudiating the phenomenological attitude.

Husserl's ontological sliding constitutes a real danger that is already *implied* in the principles of his method. Husserl himself proclaims this method must lead in such a direction: "Within this view of things there grows up, provided the consequences are fearlessly followed up (and this is not everybody's business), *a transcendental-phenomenological Idealism*, in opposition to every form of psychologistic Idealism."[17]

Now what can these consequences mean? Merleau-Ponty characterizes them as follows:

15. [*EN*, p. 115; *BN*, p. 119.]
16. *EN*, pp. 27–28; *BN*, pp. 21–23.
17. [*Ideas*, p. 18.]

For a long time, and even in recent texts, the reduction is presented [by Husserl] as the return to a transcendental consciousness before which the world deploys itself with absolute transparency, animated through and through by a series of apperceptions that the philosopher must reconstitute starting with their result. . . . Thus [my sensation of red] would be the apprehension of a certain *hylè* as signifying a phenomenon of a higher degree, the *Sinn-gebung*, that is, the active operation of meaning-giving by which consciousness is defined, the world would be nothing other than "the meaning: world," and the phenomenological reduction would be idealist in the sense of a transcendental idealism. . . . A logically consistent transcendental idealism rids the world of its opacity and transcendence.[18]

Admittedly, to cause consciousness's intentionality toward the world to appear, one must "stretch" the "intentional threads" that bind it to the world. And certainly, to lay hold of the "facticity" of the world and of existence, as such, one must pass, by means of their ideality, to the plane of essences. But this stretching must not exceed what is properly intentional within intentionality, and this passage to ideality must not eliminate what it is supposed to make manifest, namely, the relation of consciousness to an actual world, without which relation consciousness's own notion of itself would necessarily dissolve. Thus when Merleau-Ponty, having interpreted Husserl through the Heideggerian motifs in his thought, concludes quite naturally that "the eidetic method is the method of a phenomenological positivism that bases the possible upon the real,"[19] we must ask—in light of the cited texts—whether this proposition shows anything more than a simple equivocation in Husserl's own philosophy, bringing out by antiphrasis what Merleau-Ponty was himself compelled to consider aberrant in the Husserlian principles.

REPERCUSSIONS FOR PSYCHOLOGY

If we follow these principles we will encounter the dangers entailed in "placing the world between brackets," and these dangers are best shown by Husserl's conception of psychology. As we have seen, he rejects psychological idealism— the reconstitution of the world inside of psychological consciousness by means of mental impressions—because its method is empirical. He calls it a "naturalism" or "sensationalism," and he considers it as "absurd" as its counterpart, realism.

Thus, Husserl reproaches psychological idealism for making the world a correlate, not of transcendental subjectivity, but of concrete, psychological sub-

18. *Phénoménologie de la perception*, p. vi; *Phenomenology of Perception,* pp. xi–xii. [I have added a sentence and a half at the beginning of Jeanson's extract from Merleau-Ponty in order to provide necessary context and to improve readability.]

19. *Phénoménologie de la perception*, p. xii; *Phenomenology of Perception*, p. xvii.

jectivity, and this procedure amounts to taking the latter as an absolute. "The result of the phenomenological clarification of the meaning of the manner of existence of the real world . . . is that only transcendental subjectivity has ontologically the meaning of Absolute Being, that it only is non-relative, that it is relative only to itself."[20] To be sure, the kind of correlation that "psychologists" find between consciousness and the world is unsatisfactory for a number of reasons. But is this because that correlation is static or because it is relative? Oddly, Husserl replaces this correlation with yet another form of "correlation," namely, the transcendental, which is characterized precisely by the fact that it is a relation without distance, a relation within the Absolute. Husserl thereby successfully upholds the notion of intentionality, but only by emptying it of its inner consistency. Such an intentionality could maintain itself only by furnishing, through accessory acts, the very objects of its intentions; hence, it would embrace only itself and its own products. The notion of a God capable of having desires would seem to be a good illustration of Husserl's conception.

Obviously, intentionality does not draw its meaning from its own movement. But Husserl's conception of consciousness as a dynamic Absolute is no improvement in this regard over the static relativity of the "psychologists." An intention is such only through the irreducible distance separating it from its object. Transform the object into a meaning, retract its opacity, its strangeness, its being-there, and you render it directly accessible to consciousness. But the latter thereby becomes no more than this meaning. What has been forgotten is just that no meaning could ever arise from an Absolute considered by itself.

This becomes evident if one attempts to apply the Husserlian method—as did Husserl himself—to imagination, for example. The issue is as follows: if we effect the phenomenological reduction and can therefore grasp no differences between images and perceptions besides those ingredient in their intentionality, then "how is it that there can still be images and perceptions? How is it, once we allow the barriers of the phenomenological reduction to come down, that we can find a real world and an imaginary world?"[21]

Husserl would ground all philosophy on a transcendental basis. But a simple inability to answer the above question—which entails that phenomenological psychology itself crumble most directly—shows the inadequacy and superficiality of such a foundation.

This is in fact what occurs. Husserl says that, after the reduction, a certain affair subsists in consciousness which, with Sartre, we have called a "psychic given," a "content." But this content is an object for consciousness only through a "sense," called the "*noema.*" And just as, before the reduction, one could distinguish world and consciousness, so also here one distinguishes the noema and the concrete psychic reality or "*noesis.*" The noesis is the content insofar

20. [*Ideas*, p. 21.]
21. *L'Imagination*, p. 155; *Imagination: A Psychological Critique*, p. 140.

as it is animated by some intentional act.[22] Let us say that I perceive a flower-ing tree: my noema is then this meaning "flowering-tree-perceived" which comes to inhabit my noesis. But from whence comes the meaning "perceived" that the tree assumes for me? Certainly not from the noema: this inhabits con-sciousness in precisely the same way as does a "flowering-tree-imagined." The difference could proceed, then, only from the different intentions characteristic of perception and imagination. On the level of noemas, "tree-perceived" equals "tree-imagined." In placing the world between brackets I have replaced the tree by the meaning "tree." This meaning is henceforth incapable of surpassing itself in the direction of some real complement of meaning, which could give the tree either as perceived or as imagined.

In other words, the noema's indeterminacy in this case is due to its un-reality. In *Being and Nothingness* this criticism will be more explicitly directed at Husserl: "But, it will be said, Husserl himself defines consciousness as a transcendence. This is what he actually posits, and it is his essential discovery. But from the moment he makes the noema an unreality correlative to the noesis such that its *esse* is a *percipi* (that is, its being comes down to the fact of being perceived), he is totally unfaithful to his principle."[23] The point here is that for something to be perceived, it must evince an irreducible transcen-dence in relation to consciousness. Thus, to be there and not to be there are the same when one is concerned with an object posited solely as such by con-sciousness (posited, that is, as either real or imaginary, but in either case as transcendent to consciousness). For Husserl, the distinction can depend, from this point on, only on the intention. But how could the intention wish to be either a perceiving or an imaging intention? What value would its choice have, being reduced to the purely arbitrary? It is still necessary to be able "to distin-guish after reduction the centaur I imagine and the flowering tree I perceive."[24] In the two cases there is an impression-matter that must first have an intention directed toward it if a meaning is to appear and fill this intention. But where could such an intention find "the motivations for shaping a matter into a mental image rather than into a perception?"[25] Sartre responds: ". . . if the matters are of the same nature there can be no valid motivation. . . . the dis-tinction between mental image and perception could not come from intention-ality alone. It is necessary that the intentions differ. But that difference alone is not sufficient. The matters must also differ."[26]

In sum, one must take the object into account. As we saw in the preceding chapter, this is what allowed Sartre to distinguish imagination from perception in *The Psychology of Imagination*. In perception, consciousness shows a sort

22. [For Husserl's introduction of these terms, see *Ideen I*, pp. 192, 200; *Ideas*, pp. 249, 258.]
23. *EN*, p. 28; *BN*, p. 23. [The parenthetical explanation is Jeanson's, not Sartre's.]
24. [*L'Imagination*, p. 154; *Imagination: A Psychological Critique*, p. 139.]
25. [*L'Imagination*, p. 156; *Imagination: A Psychological Critique*, p. 141.]
26. *L'Imagination*, pp. 156 and 158; *Imagination: A Psychological Critique*, pp. 141–143.

of subjugation to the objects of the world in which it is situated. Imagination, on the other hand, requires consciousness's momentary denial of these objects, an evasion of the real situation by means of a negating intention directed toward *this* time and *this* space. Over against what is, consciousness can thereby set what is not, resolutely grasping it as such. To this end, consciousness makes use of elements of prior knowledge without aiming at them as such. In particular, it does not aim *at* the "meaning" furnished by such prior acquaintance, but rather *through* these meanings toward the object itself. This is the price that consciousness must pay in order to be able both to affect the object with unreality and to posit it in an intuition as something "given-absent."

We know that the act of imaging takes place only when motivated by a concrete situation. By itself, the object cannot compel my recognition of it in just the form I wish to see it. Thus imagination is meaningful as a function in relation not only to reality but also to my attitude *toward* reality. Husserl's error will henceforth be characterized for us by his conviction that it is still possible to describe the *essential structures* of consciousness even after it has been emptied of all reference to the *fundamental attitudes* of the subject in the world. Husserl, we have noted, grants that transcendental subjectivity "has ontologically the meaning of Absolute Being." He thus attempts an ontology of a being which is defined by its behavior alone. However, he situates this being on a plane where its behavior ceases to be motivated. The result is that he closes himself up within an artificial ontology which has no possibility of ever passing back to that effective aspect of behavior which he resolved to set aside at the start. In other words, Husserl's Absolute Being comes down to an absolute relativity. An ontology must have as its sole object the ambiguity of being, that is, the shock of a presence that is not *oneself*, a presence that confronts a self who can define himself in opposition to it, but only by starting out from that presence and from the shock that constitutes the *being* of that self.

THE ONLY POSSIBLE ONTOLOGY

A too brief analysis of a complex philosophy will inevitably accentuate certain lapses. Husserl's phenomenology nevertheless appears to us as verging on the disowning of its most fruitful principle. It tries to study intentionality outside the reach of those "motivations" through which the world's irreducible existence guarantees that movements of consciousness will have the character of present, active attitudes.

This difficulty is an inversion of the one we discovered in the distance between the phenomenon and the psychologist's apprehension of it.

As Merleau-Ponty notes: "As contemplative subject we are never the unreflective subject we seek to know; but neither can we become wholly consciousness, or make ourselves into transcendental consciousness."[27]

27. *Phénoménologie de la perception,* p. 76; *Phenomenology of Perception,* p. 62.

The transcendental subject is not somehow "entitled" to exist. The structures of consciousness by which the world is given are not *necessarily* explicated somewhere. For their relative autonomy to be recognized they need only be lived as attitudes. But any transition to the limiting case, in which this autonomy becomes absolute, is condemned to remain theoretical and utterly vain. The only basis this autonomy can have is the actual operation by which a concrete consciousness breaks its spatial and temporal ties. And we know such a rupture is psychologically possible only within the instant, in an empty act of negation whose essential gratuitousness is inconsistent with such a rupture. In a little book which takes up, from the specifically sociological viewpoint, Raymond Aron's argument for the Husserlian thesis, Jules Monnerot gives a picturesque description of such an attempt. Observing that one could accede to the theoretical possibility of "suspension" only at the cost of an effort that is total and perpetually reinitiated, he adds:

> This is not a situation in which one can feel at home. Whoever would pride himself on having once and for all succeeded would in fact play the *comical* role of a *cogito* without a *cogitatum*, a *cogito* so important and busy, with so many pressing appointments, that he hasn't a minute to devote to the *cogitatum*. . . . I am not asserting that the attempt to reach the situation of a *cogito* without a *cogitatum* should not be undertaken or that it is not a desirable human experiment, as are all other human experiments involving the transgression of limits. But an examination free of complacency would see that such a situation —which would not be one of rest, being maintained only by an impulse that would inevitably be truncated, given human limitations—could be creative only as the result of a stubborn asceticism maintained on the scale of an entire life. If it existed at all, such an asceticism would connect the life of the phenomenologist with the practices of Yogis who *realize* a doctrine within themselves by active execution. He thereby passes from the level of having into that of being; he is made into a new person.[28]

The same point is made by Merleau-Ponty when he recognizes that Husserl's perspective allies him, like it or not, with the usual outlook of transcendental idealism. Merleau-Ponty's own criticism of Husserl's position is that it would be "necessary to become the transcendental subject in order to have the right to affirm it."[29]

Conversely, though, it would be equally vain to presume to directly apprehend the unreflective as such. The lived understanding of oneself characteristic of human reality may be immediate, but, if it is indeed a form of understanding, it must in turn lay hold of itself as such. This requirement cannot be avoided. The purely unreflective is just as inaccessible to philosophy as the purely transcendental. Inasmuch as consciousness wishes to grasp itself by op-

28. Jules Monnerot, *Les Faits sociaux ne sont pas des choses*, p. 30.
29. *Phénoménologie de la perception*, pp. 73, 75; *Phenomenology of Perception*, p. 61.

posing the world, it must be what it is not; but inasmuch as it attempts to grasp the world without any reflectivity, it discovers the impossibility of being what it is.

This point approximates certain formulas that recur in *Being and Nothingness*. We sense that consciousness will turn out to be this being which exists in the mode of non-being. Such is the basic mark of authentic ambiguity, for whatever simply *is* could not be ambiguous. The ambiguous can only be a relation that is active, a situation actively *surpassed*, a freedom-in-situation. This also confirms that the consciousness of which Sartre speaks is aware that its very presence to itself—that is, its existence as consciousness—is conditioned by the existence of the world. The only possible ontology is therefore one concerned with this presence-to-self, which is simply the other name for authentic presence to the world.

We shall of course have to inquire whether this ontology, the *only* possible ontology, is *possible*. This amounts to asking about its successfulness, its fecundity. We have sought to bring out here that an ontology of pure consciousness is as impossible as an ontology of the object. It clearly remains to determine whether the relation consciousness-world (or freedom-situation), which thus becomes the sole object of a philosophy, lends itself to an ontology. The issue is whether this kind of reconciliation, following such a variety of abstractions, should be effected at the level of the general, of notions, or on the level of the singular, of concrete phenomena. Should we proceed (a) directly to an essentialist ontology, or (b) directly to an existential analysis, or (c) successively, with the former followed by the latter?

A passage from *Being and Nothingness* permits us both to bring together our preceding remarks and to situate this problem of method as it poses itself for Sartre. Criticizing the various uses of the *cogito*, Sartre holds that it always yields precisely what one asks of it:

> Descartes interrogated the *cogito* under its functional aspect: "I doubt, I think" and, desiring to pass without any conducting wire from this functional aspect to the existential dialectic, he fell into the error of substantialism. *Husserl*, instructed by this error, remained apprehensively on the level of functional description. As a result, he never moved beyond the pure description of the appearance as such, enclosing himself within the *cogito*. Despite his disclaimers, he should be called a phenomenalist rather than a phenomenologist; and his phenomenalism borders on Kantian idealism at all points. *Heidegger*, wishing to avoid this phenomenalism, which leads to the megarian and antidialectical isolation of essences, approaches existential analysis directly, without passing through the *cogito*.[30]

But if we take this last route, Sartre observes, human reality finds itself deprived of the dimension of consciousness. If one wishes to endow that reality

30. [*EN*, p. 115; *BN*, p. 119. Jeanson's emphasis.]

with an understanding of itself, one must recognize its consciousness of being that understanding. "In fact one must start from the *cogito*, but one can say of it, parodying a celebrated formula, that it leads to everything on condition that you depart from it." Thus we must secure the conducting wire Sartre mentioned above: "that dialectical instrument that would allow us to find, in the *cogito* itself, the means to escape instantaneity toward the totality of being which constitutes human reality."[31]

In this way, the goal pursued by *Being and Nothingness: An Essay in Phenomenological Ontology* begins to define itself for us. This work is an attempt to give an account of the very essence of the ambiguity that characterizes our being. Ontology can, in effect, be only the ontology of our actual being. And it would be unable to satisfy this requirement without appealing to that discipline which alone permits us to give due respect to ambiguity as such, that is, to a total phenomenology, one which balances the Husserlian tendency by considering the existence of essences and which also balances the Heideggerian tendency by considering the essence of existence.

This amounts to an essentialist phenomenology. But in it the very essence of consciousness would appear as valid only when placed in contact with the essence of its manner of being toward the world. Under this procedure, we would obviously reach only the essence of ambiguity, thus merely establishing its possibility. Yet this is just what Husserl did not do. On the other hand, Heidegger's error was to have tackled, directly and without prior elucidation, the essential conditions underlying understanding.

Our ontology can therefore furnish us only a duality of terms, a duality of essences. It does so, however, on the understanding that it never retract from either term the incomplete character in virtue of which that term refuses to become the sole object of ontology to the exclusion of the other term. As envisaged by a phenomenological essentialism, actual ambiguity or lived ambiguity would not disappear. This ambiguity would, however, change into its essence, which is to be a duality each term of which manifests its own insufficiency. On the one hand, the object, being-in-itself, is sufficient unto itself in its contingent being-itself but nevertheless lacks a justification of its own *presence*. On the other hand, consciousness, being-for-itself, appears to be sufficient unto itself in its theoretical consciousness for-itself but nevertheless lacks an account of its own *existence*.

The same type of lack or insufficiency is not present in the two cases. Though it is true both that "consciousness considered by itself is only an abstraction," and that "the for-itself without the in-itself . . . could no more exist than could a color without form or a sound without pitch or without timbre," it is equally true that "the in-itself itself has no need for the for-itself in order to be." The in-itself needs the for-itself only in order to appear. "The *phenomenon* of the in-itself is indeed abstract without consciousness, but its being is not."[32]

31. *EN*, p. 116; *BN*, p. 120.
32. *EN*, pp. 715–716; *BN*, p. 791.

It will no doubt be necessary to reemphasize this point. It ties in directly with the lessons we derived from phenomenological psychology, and its misapprehension would lead unavoidably to misinterpretation of the very meaning of ontology. Thus, if, within the duality "consciousness-being" which is ontology's object, the two terms were made to correspond rigorously by implying each other in the same way, we would fall back into an absolute *dualism*. Then to surmount this dualism we would have to force an interpretation of it, either toward a realism in which we abandon consciousness for an unthinkable "being" or toward an idealism in which we would abandon being for a mysteriously active consciousness. It is apparent that if we conceived of our duality as being symmetrical it would be ontologically a pure nothingness. The axis "consciousness-being" has a *sense* [*sens*]; it is not a simple straight line, but rather an *oriented vector*. If dealing with the notion of intentionality has taught us something, it is that the movement of consciousness toward being—whereby consciousness exists and being appears—is not reversible.

There is therefore nothing shocking in affirming that Sartre comes down in favor of "the ontological primacy of the in-itself over the for-itself."[33] This in no way signifies—as Roger Troisfontaines would have it[34]—that Sartre has chosen or opted in favor of matter as against spirit. For, at the level of ontology, there could be no valuing option or "moral" preference; there could only be the question of choosing a valid foundation for all subsequent determination of man's effort to infuse his personal existence with value. If a comparison is acceptable here, the physicist can "choose" among various idealist and realist visions of the world, but he must also "choose" (in a quite different sense) among various geometries, selecting the one that will best facilitate development of his knowledge of the world. Moreover, it would take considerable ill will to ignore, through a misplaced interpretation of an ontological conclusion, the fact that all of Sartre's works testify, not only to the shock he experiences in the face of things or of persons who live like things, but also to his need to oppose them with the authentic existence of a consciousness, a pure freedom. And this certainly amounts to a choice against the in-itself and in favor of the for-itself.

We are firmly convinced—having experimented often, not only in works of "criticism" but in conversations with readers of such works—that one must first clear the terrain by bringing certain distorting approaches to light if one is to make an honest effort to understand the work which will now occupy us.

We are familiar with its essential principles. We have seen the continuous development by which Sartre reaches this level where themes are no longer merely applied to concrete examples but are systematized. We can now approach the new themes that such a systematization will inevitably bring out.

33. [*EN*, p. 713; *BN*, p. 787.]
34. Roger Troisfontaines, *Le Choix de J.-P. Sartre* (Paris: Aubier, 1946).

PART TWO

The Ontology of Ambiguity:
The Human Condition

Chapter 1

"Being and Nothingness":
The General Shape of the Work

THE PHILOSOPHER ENCOUNTERS HIS OWN EXISTENCE

The most delicate part of our journey is behind us. We shall now find increasingly sure terrain under foot—at least to the point where we must rediscover life's complexity, and that is an altogether different task. The firmer terrain now before us will serve as a solid steppingstone as we proceed toward that less certain field of action.

Like a stowaway who abandons the ship's false security by throwing himself into the water in the hope of reaching shore and freedom, the honest philosopher renounces the comforts that put others to sleep. He defies the abyss. He jumps and swims, in his own way, toward an unknown land. Perhaps he has asked too much of his capacities and will sink. Or perhaps his boldness will be sustained by enough tenacity for him to finally touch soil. But the ground falls away again, obliging him to resume the struggle and to deal for the second time with the distress in his legs. The body's exhausting rhythm reemerges. The beach gradually ceases to be a linear image at the mercy of the waves. Its sandy surface and rocky masses develop, confirming the meaning he has doggedly imposed upon his efforts. On reaching shore, the wind is calm and the sand invites rest. Giving in to his fatigue he reflects, looking back at the ship and measuring the distance he has covered. Then, perhaps with nightfall, somber thoughts come to him. He is indeed free of reassuring hypocrisy, of the unbreathable atmosphere in which to think is only a way not to see. But he knew he must learn to see again, to look life in the face. He had thoroughly upset the scenery of the old theatre, having become disgusted with the daily task of mounting a play in which everyone tried to forget himself for some anonymous role. He is free; that test is passed; through his hard journey he has gained simple, unadorned positions that are outspoken and brutal. He has been revealed to himself through the consistency of his refusals and through the purity of a purpose free of both the subtleties of casuistry and the refinements of bad faith.

He is free, but alone. Those he has left have already disowned him. He can-

not go back. Those he moves toward neither know him nor await him. Perhaps he will trouble them: a traveler without baggage, an unknown in whom
they will see only revolt and negation. It will not matter to them that negation
was the necessary first step, even if he was then unable to go further. Nor will
they care whether he makes his decisions according to the demand within himself for authenticity. Who among these new strangers, any more than among
his former accomplices, will be concerned with authenticity? Will anyone, anywhere, ever take on that weight of freedom which he has elected to assume?
How shall he answer the questions he expects to see on their lips: "What use
is your freedom to you? For which cause have you come to do battle? Are
you one of us?" He is certainly not a member and he has not come for the
approval of others. Yet it is again among these others that he will ultimately
have to live. Will he consent to sign up, to affirm, thereby reconfirming,
through a definite act, the meaning of his own endeavor? Or will he remain
the perpetual opponent, the dangerous mystic of freedom who will be only
an indefinite refusal?

At this point he must collapse. He now faces the self-revelation he let himself in for. The beach is well suited for a solitary purification. He is between
two kinds of existence: that from which he comes, which was a sort of mind-
less agitation, and that toward which he must go, in which he foresees how an
act becomes authentic. This sort of absolute place lends authority to his reflection. It also reminds him of the very path that brought him there, that is, his
starting point and its meaning.

The experience of having an attitude is what must be understood, and an
extreme attitude is here in question. All the bridges have been cut; one effects
a negation at the risk of enclosing himself in it. One must understand or die,
for to proceed without understanding is to drain all meaning from the initial
movement, killing that in it which was its raison d'être—since in the first place
it was, precisely, a reaction against blindness. But it is equally possible that he
will understand, then die for having done so. After all, there are ultimate experiences of frontier zones from which one does not return. Perhaps the human
dimension is barred from surpassing itself toward its limit, and the penalty for
trying is an overextension that precludes backtracking. It may be that a truly
free look at things will uncover the horizons of failure without even affording
the enriching "wisdom" that permits a return to some enslavement or other,
in order to adjust to it.

Having passed through the boundaries of psychoanalysis, Koestler's hero can
again take pleasure in a "crusade without a cross."[1] It is enough for him to
sense that his tasks overflow others' interpretations of them, that his inner tension cannot be dissolved in the events of his past. More formidable, however, is

1. [The allusion is to Arthur Koestler's novel *Arrival and Departure* (New York:
Macmillan, 1943). Its hero is Peter Slavek, a student who joins a revolutionary
organization and is arrested and jailed.]

the psychoanalysis in which being places itself in question inasmuch as it has apprehended and lived the infernal exigency of freedom. One who practices this psychoanalysis can no longer be content to sustain his initial action by some causal explanation, thereby dismissing all possible reasons he may have for maintaining the value of that action; he must question this value itself, dismissing it also if it fails to issue strictly from his own free decree, which is that element of the absolute that is his own. It places him on the far side of all those irritating "because of's," but also beyond the too conciliatory "despite's." No longer can he tell himself it does not matter what he wants so long as he wants it strongly, irreducibly. Henceforth he must "psychoanalyze," not the relative purity of his will, but the meaning and implications of the fact that he himself *is* a will—an absolute initiative—not a force but a freedom.

It may be said that this freedom could only be the double requirement to remain free—that is, never to *be* anything—and yet to exist by some absolute plenitude that allows it to enjoy itself and fully unfold as a freedom. Never tied to itself yet always sampling, being *and* not being, at once ignoring itself totally and possessing itself, it would manifest itself without ever letting itself go. Thus it would constantly say no and flee so as to evade others and itself, surpassing all and escaping all, seeking self-assurance by affirming itself in this negation. It would thus aim to be this Nothingness, but after the manner of Being itself. Its goal would be to be God, the supreme Being.

Peter Slavek senses in himself a passion unrelated to any external cause. He too swam toward a free shore. But he had left in order to serve. Having slept, he set out in the morning toward men who ultimately disappointed him, though they did not discourage him. He went towards them before trying to understand what it meant to go towards something. For him it was enough that there was something that needed doing. But our solitary person will have to remain longer on the beach. He left not in order to serve but in order to live an authentic existence. He will not be disappointed, for he knows what he has left behind, but he does risk being discouraged. He seeks the absolute goal that others avoid owning up to. Will he not therefore fail absolutely, learning in solitude that man exceeds his rights when he employs his powers to the utmost, that man must give up fulfilling himself and abjure his most fundamental demand, in short, that man is a useless passion?

An Ontology of Failure

Ontology is that beach. It is a no-man's-land between life and life, a reflection on self, a definition of failure without which no valid endeavor could be undertaken.

A revolutionary psychology has uncovered the hypocrisy of conceiving consciousness in a tendentious way which deprives it of all responsibility for what transpires within it. This conception implies either a naturalism or a transcendentalism: it makes consciousness a mere witness, either of a universal mechanism or of the activity of some objective Spirit. But consciousness is precisely what is not the object. It is instead transcendent to every possible object. And even if it experiences the temptation embodied by the object, it can never entirely forget itself since "it is consciousness of being a consciousness that forgets." Its flaw is its inability to consummate the betrayal of itself: it always apprehends itself as the source of its self-denials. Free in its initiatives, it is nevertheless unable to ignore its own corporeal existence. This presence to the world is the means by which the freedom of consciousness acquires a meaning. However, such *existence* always remains both inescapable and "in the way." It can never be justified by reference to an absolute dimension. Through Nausea a being is shown its inability to flee itself—its rootedness or captivity within life—as well as the fact that this life is not, of itself, valid. Scarcely has an initiative within this life produced effects, when it tries to prolong itself in them, thereby entering a degraded form. One cannot always refuse everything, but even to accept is still and again to renounce.

Men have invented the notion of "rights" in order to conceal this essential margin or overhang of their existence. Psychologically, a right means a title to claim innocence if one considers himself determined. It means being responsible —but responsible solely for one's own "merit." Such responsibility rests on the moral comfort that comes with enslavement of one's consciousness to objective values that have been founded outside one's consciousness by impersonal Reason. Fear of self guides men. They repress this fate of freedom for the same reason that they repress the fatal nature of their individual situation, namely, to avoid placing themselves in question. To be sure, they think often of their lives, their successes, their difficulties and obligations. But they never think of their existence, the elusive but total responsibility which they assume merely in existing. They find refuge in the anonymous, reassuring themselves within the Species. They create separate, inanimate, unsituated "souls" and inflate them to God-size. They dread most the slippery solitude of their own subjectivity in the here and now. They dread the unjustifiable role each must play in this earthly crawling—for this is also themselves. They never stop analyzing themselves, but it is only to dissolve themselves into either Matter or Spirit. To become thus sophisticated about oneself, either as casuist or as savant, is like losing sight of oneself by using the microscope in order to ignore what the naked eye cannot avoid. To look with the naked eye is an absolute act that compels one's being to take upon itself an existence that it did not create, within a world that is irreducibly there.

Man is constantly attempting something. He has to thrust himself into the future. His failures must be circumnavigated by new attempts. He cannot act without at each moment giving some meaning to his situation, his action, and the tests and obstacles in his path. In this way he establishes his freedom. But, establishing it, he may refuse to experience it. To avoid distinguishing the two he may throw himself into activity or into the sleep of the perpetual sleep-walker. He thereby evades the only question that might transform this agitation (characteristic of a natural being carried along by momentum) into the action of a subject, the question, namely, of the fundamental meaning of any endeavor. This question issues from the absolute meaning Failure possesses as the foundation of all attempting that deserves the name.

The freedom of consciousness therefore rests on the contingency of its existence in the world. Its transcendence rests on its facticity. Nothing can be meaningful which does not develop on a basis of absurdity. Equally, if the absurd exists, it is because there is meaning. Indeed, a consciousness cannot even appear without standing out on a horizon of absurdity against which everything that it cannot "penetrate" in a practical sense is pushed back.

This is because man is free. His is an existing freedom and he is an absurd being, a useless passion—"useless," that is, incapable of justification by reference to some preestablished plan or preexisting goal, or to a transcendent principle capable of imposing a unique meaning on it. Being useless, man is already destined for an objective failure unless he invents his own value by setting practical goals that affirm such a value. Failure is the ontological climate of man's subjectivity. It shows up in the distance between his present and its eventual realization, in the requirements to realize his existence and to become himself without being enslaved to himself. Any chance of overcoming this failure is clearly based on recognizing it as such and defining it with precision.

The Treatise's Solidity and Raison d'Etre

From the perspective we have taken, *Being and Nothingness* is easily understood. This philosophy will not be difficult to interpret regarding its initial impulse, its essential movement, or its ultimate aim. Sartre knows what he wants to say and expresses himself without equivocation. His undisputed dialectical ability even leads him on occasion to prolong certain arguments beyond what would be required for the reader's comprehension. He creates expressions, forces syntax, and accumulates verbal confluences, all of which weigh down his text. But they permit him to better delineate his thinking, and the resulting precision justifies such procedures.

These procedures may have a disheartening effect, especially for the French reader, who looks for suppleness and elegance above all. But if philosophy were simply literature one could dispense with philosophizing. For our part, we disapprove of any abuse of technical terms, any scholasticism that merely names what it fails to grasp, in order to create the illusion of having "explained" it. The so-called "soporific power" of opium is a case in point. Sartre, however, is not concerned to explain; he confines himself to uncovering meanings already implicit in human reality. His neologisms and complex expressions aim only at formulating these uncoverings more precisely. Koestler attacks the same problem in the preface to his collection of essays, *The Yogi and the Commissar,* when he writes:

> I admire simplicity of style, but not if it leads to oversimplification or that kind of linguistic asceticism of the Ogden school which actually obscures the content. The far-fetched is often nearer to the truth than the short-cut of common sense. My comfort is what Einstein said when somebody reproached him on the grounds that his formula of gravitation was longer and more cumbersome than Newton's formula in its elegant simplicity: "If you are out to describe to truth, leave elegance to the tailor."[2]

Being and Nothingness is also a work that few have read and that others like to consider unreadable. Some readers talk of the author's "verbal juggleries" while admitting it is understandable that Sartre, who considers himself a philosopher, should draft his own treatise of formal philosophy. This perspective allows one to consider Sartre a literary man at heart and existentialism merely a novelist-playwright's publicity gambit. To make this judgment, though, is to resolutely deprive oneself of the last possibility of comprehending even the more attractive literary works, such as *Nausea* and *The Roads to Freedom,* or successful plays that "one must see," like *No Exit* and *Men Without Shadows.*

In closing the last chapter we pointed out the error, committed particularly by Roger Troisfontaines, in accusing Sartre of having "chosen" the in-itself as against the for-itself by privileging the object as against the subject. It would probably be impertinent to counter this with a statement made by one of his colleagues, Luc-J. Lefèvre, who reproaches the same Sartre for systematically ignoring the perspective of being and for resting content with a solitary and groundless subjectivity. We suggest it is vain to judge a man's work from only one of its aspects. As we see every day, similar misapprehensions can easily flow from limiting one's reading to Sartre's novels, where it would clearly seem the author views man as a rather poor idea.

Recently we have even seen a journalist do battle with Sartre in a student weekly by building his argument on the simple postulate that Antoine Roquentin was the existentialist hero and that permanent nausea was therefore required of anyone wishing to live according to Sartre's philosophy. One cannot help thinking that for this battle Erostratus—the character in the story in *The Wall* whose obsession lead him to fire his revolver on the passersby— would better assist the desired discrediting.

In order to achieve an understanding, we must forgo such pleasantries. We know that the first reader to come along is not responsible for the fact that Sartre's various works are sold and read separately and out of sequence. Having neither time nor taste for philosophical problems, he may be tempted by those

2. [Arthur Koestler, *The Yogi and the Commissar* (New York: Macmillan, 1965), p. 11.]

works that seem most accessible to him, without having been warned against the danger of such a choice. But, if all the philosophical aspects of these works escape this reader, one may rightfully ask that he abstain from formulating other than literary judgments, that he not talk of nihilism, pessimism, or immoralism, for he can only have read descriptions of various nullities, failures, and immoralities. As for pornography, which he may also believe he has encountered, those who dwell on this are precisely the ones who, book in hand, rapidly turn those pages on which "nothing happens."

But we must renounce more than the interpretations circulating in fashionable circles and sects. Socialites and sectarians are busy people, the former because of idleness, the latter because of concern to avoid new perspectives that might put them off course. Philosophers are less busy. In their company we shall have to guard against other pitfalls. We can set aside those who refuse to take an author seriously when his successes in other domains appear to be of poor quality. Yet for anyone resistant to prejudice and conformism who may have taken on *Being and Nothingness*, this enormous treatise sometimes seems to digress excessively and to encourage infinite haggling over detail.

We are interested, not in details, but in broad themes and their guiding spirit. It is more important to inquire about their eventual convergence than to trace their divergencies, which may cause the light provided by more ample viewpoints to fade.

We hope the brevity of the following analysis will not inhibit a firm grasp of this guiding spirit—in all its frankness and internal vigor—while retaining its continuity with the themes examined earlier.

We will judge the moral significance of the ensemble later. At that time we should not feel compelled to revalidate within the moral perspective what may have seemed perfectly clear to us in the theoretical perspective. Rational coherence and practical value are easily confused. By the same token, integrity calls for bracketing the view that a philosophy is fantastical and incoherent solely because one has already decided to condemn it on the practical plane. This is the only "rule of the game" we would like to have observed regarding the book we are examining, a work that is not necessarily an attempt at mystification.

THE TEXT'S STRUCTURE AND DIFFICULTY

The overall plan of this book is simple. As we have indicated, it puts forth an ontology of freedom or, if you will, an ontology of being in situation.

An introduction, "The Pursuit of Being," presents the two mutually irreducible forms of being—being that is transcendent to consciousness, and consciousness itself—and raises the question of the meaning of their relationship.

In the first part, "The Problem of Nothingness," the philosopher's consciousness interrogates itself regarding its own ontological interrogation. It discovers a basis for negation, the source of all the nihilations that characterize it.

A second part, "Being-for-Itself," treats that form of Being through which Nothingness comes to the world.

A third part, "Being-for-Others," introduces a problem we have not explicitly encountered up to now: the existence of other selves and the repercussions of this for the for-itself, inasmuch as the latter is then also seen to exist for-others.

The fourth and last part, "Having, Doing and Being," is then able to approach, from the angle of action, the fundamental question of freedom. By that stage the various elements of the ontological situation in which this freedom shows forth, as well as its basic mode of manifestation, have all been examined in turn.

Finally, the conclusion leaves to metaphysics certain hypotheses that attempt to explain this situation genetically, and, above all, it lays out the perspectives of a moral theory.

Naturally we would like to be able to rely on the reader's patience and tenacity to make up at this point for our inability to make the present chapter and the following one more attractive. In relation to the preceding analyses, these chapters may appear to be a sort of marching in place that would not be advanced by being easier to read. But we have not sought to avoid all effort, and thus we have said nothing rather than something superficial. An effort is always indispensable to authentic understanding. As for marching in place, we believe there is no harm in cross-checking perspectives, approaching the same themes from ever-varying angles, reviewing in a group portrait where these themes are situated, and putting them within reach of a richer comprehension by infusing them with an atmosphere and a life they may have lacked to that point. One gains by immersing oneself at some length in these thoughts. The reader will decide if the resulting advantages compensate him for the relative difficulty of the coming pages.

Chapter 2

Consciousness Encounters Being

In the first pages of his introduction, "The Pursuit of Being," Sartre attacks the problem of the being of the phenomenon, which he distinguishes from its appearing. The phenomenon is *phenomenon*, he explains, insofar as it is for us and appears to us. But it simply *is*, purely in itself, insofar as it is irreducibly set over against us, so as to be able to appear to us. Thus, at the start Sartre takes on the question of principle, the very justification of his attempt— *"An Essay in Phenomenological Ontology."*

This expression alone is shocking. We have so far shown that an ontology is desirable only if it takes as its object the same ambiguity of human reality which permitted the emergence of the phenomenological discipline itself. What is now at issue is not the character of this ideal ontology but the possibility of its existence under this phenomenological rubric.

Reactions are quite violent on this point, even among Sartre's most qualified critics. Jean Wahl—who could not fairly be suspected of partiality regarding the opinions of others—speaks of the *failure* of this ontology and ponders whether one must not see in that failure "a corroboration of the philosophy of existence insofar as it is opposed to all ontology." He calls for "a revision of the fundamental concepts on which *Being and Nothingness* appears to be founded . . . so that everything that is valuable in the remainder of the work may be preserved."[1] Like us, Wahl addresses himself to the introduction and the first chapter. He considers them incapable of providing a real foundation for the subsequent analyses, whose true value is for him situated outside of all ontological perspectives.

The same criticism is advanced by Roger Troisfontaines, but from a different viewpoint. Aside from his attempts to discredit Sartre's work, his viewpoint is interesting because it results in one of the fundamental errors possible here: "Does the word 'ontology' retain any meaning? Hasn't phenomenalism reduced the existent to the series of its appearances? Where can one find a being outside of the appearing?"[2] And, further along: "Does one act in con-

---

1. Jean Wahl, "Essai sur le néant d'un problème," in *Deucalion I* (Paris: Editions de la Revue Fontaine, 1946), p. 71.
2. Roger Troisfontaines, *Le Choix de J.-P. Sartre* (Paris: Aubier, 1946), p. 11.

formity . . . with the phenomenological method in designating as nonrelative to consciousness a Being which appears only in its relation to consciousness?"[3]

Thus, according to both major lines of criticism, Sartre arbitrarily decides to build a "systematics" of being, starting with methods and principles which should limit him to the domain of description. He is accused, in the first instance, of failing to confine himself to an existential phenomenology, and, in the second, of unduly prolonging the subjective consideration of those phenomena within a study of their objectivity.

METAPHYSICS AND ONTOLOGY

Concerning the first accusation, we have already seen that authentic phenomenology cannot be exclusively existential. In effect, Wahl criticizes Sartre for having adopted the phenomenological method in the first place. Basically, he regrets that Sartre does not retain a directly existential philosophy, like that of Kierkegaard or Heidegger, and is consequently unable to emphasize elements opposed to Husserlian perspectives. Such objections bring us back to the worries expressed by many "existential Frenchmen," Benjamin Fondane in particular. Just before his deportation to Germany, Fondane raised the question

> whether the existential philosophy of our time continues in some way the mother philosophy of its initiators (Kierkegaard, Dostoyevsky, Nietzsche, Shestov, etc.) or whether it retains only the *existential* name, applying it to a philosophy which, in essence, would submit its teaching to universal reason. . . .[4]

This question in turn implies a formidable problem: that of the possibility of a "philosophy" that is purely existential. According to Benjamin Fondane— who speaks of ontology, though obviously in a very different sense than that

3. Ibid., p. 41.
4. Benjamin Fondane, "Le Lundi existentiel et le dimanche de l'histoire," in *L'Existence: essais par Albert Camus et al.*, edited by Jean Grenier (Paris: Gallimard, 1945), p. 29. [The parenthetical addition is Jeanson's. The editor, in introducing Fondane's essay, writes: "This study was submitted to us by Benjamin Fondane in February 1944, a few days before his arrest by the Gestapo. Benjamin Fondane has not come back and his family, whose anxiety we share, has received no news of him." It was later learned that he had been gassed at Auschwitz on 3 October 1944. Originally from Rumania, of German-Jewish origins, Fondane was a poet, avant-garde film maker, and philosopher. See *Benjamin Fondane: A Presentation of His Life and Works*, by John Kenneth Hyde (Geneva: Librairie Droz, 1971), pp. 10–20. In Paris Fondane came under the influence of the Russian existentialist Léon Shestov and, like Shestov, opposed infusion of Husserlian "rationalism" into the essential insights of existentialism derived from Kierkegaard. Fondane argued in his major philosophical work—*La Conscience malheureuse* (Paris: Denoël and Steele, 1936)—that philosophy had never come to grips with human misfortune; by sacrificing the desire to *be* to the desire to *know*, it could end only by showing the *necessity* for such misfortune, thereby perpetuating it.]

rejected by Jean Wahl[5]—it seems that such a philosophy can only be made up of lived emotions, despair, passions and screams:

> Enigmatic philosophy! without terminology, method or technique! offering us no Rules by which to judge the truth; in which the "I" is not revealed as a reasoning being whose legislation rests on something; which allows itself to pass for empty discourse and poetic metaphor; which even prides itself on this.[6]

We are quite aware of the dangers facing a philosophy of existence that loses sight of the existing, the concrete, favoring instead a universal systematization, a logicizing that tries to overcome all problems. But a whole world lies between simply living amidst masses of problems, and forgetting to live at all because of the kind of thinking that expresses in equations problems that have become fictive. The world between these two opposed attitudes is in fact the domain proper to philosophy. Philosophy's role is precisely to *live* the problems *as problems* and to delineate that fundamental problem raised by its own existence. Sartre, from his first works on, has insisted on the necessity of an eidetic method and an essentialist attitude. These alone can transform the psychologist's simple auto-observation of the "I" into an understanding of the self that has philosophical value. Sartre is therefore concerned to collect the results thus obtained. He does not seek to suddenly resolve the difficulties of being human, but, on the contrary, to cause men to realize that man is only a discontented striving, an obstinacy that is perpetually disappointed in its basic purpose, a useless passion.

So let us repeat: man merely has the *chance* to grasp himself as such, and perhaps, to glimpse on which plane (and at what price) his effort would hold meaning. Thus the "human condition" itself demands formulation in that it is lived merely implicitly. If man is indeed a perpetual future, it is fitting he should attempt to understand the fundamental intention in himself to come "to *oneself!*" in Heidegger's phrase.[7] The passage from the inauthentic to the authentic is just this effort by the individual to grasp his essential condition. Again following Heidegger: "while man exists there will be philosophizing of some sort."[8] But although the natural attitude may well carry its own self-understanding in itself, it perpetually dissipates this understanding by living it. Man must disengage himself from his life to live it as man. Freedom and failure become such only after they are first thematized, made explicit, and this

5. Making use here of the Heideggerian distinction between the ontic and the ontological, we would willingly call Fondane's ontology an "onticism."

6. Fondane, "Le Lundi existentiel," p. 48.

7. Martin Heidegger, *Sein und Zeit*, 8th edition (Tübingen: Neomarius Verlag, 1957), p. 330; *Being and Time*, translated by John Macquarrie and Edward Robinson (New York: Macmillan, 1962), p. 378.

8. Martin Heidegger, *Qu'est-ce que la métaphysique?* French translation in *Bifur*, no. 8 (June, 1931), p. 27; *Existence and Being*, English translation by R. F. C. Hull and A. Crick (Chicago: H. Regnery, 1949), p. 379.

can be done only within an ontology that defines and situates the poles between which they become manifest. The intervention of ontology frightens us only insofar as we understand this term in a traditional and negative manner that would assimilate it to "metaphysics." Sartre has exactly and emphatically delineated the differences he conceives between ontology and metaphysics: the former situates the human condition; the latter tries to explain it, deducing it from other hypotheses.

Two remarks are needed in this connection. First of all, such a distinction is required if ontology is to avoid turning into ontologism. Secondly, phenomenology alone permits such a distinction, since traditional metaphysics is precisely the effort to ground the supreme "realities" without first inquiring about the concrete reality of the human dimension. We would even say that metaphysics is gratuitious theory, theory for its own sake, while ontology, in Sartre's sense, is theory that issues from concrete psychological description and that is oriented toward the practical. Ontology, then, is continuous with description, it *makes explicit*; metaphysics is continuous with science, it seeks to *explain*. So, if one gives up seeing ontology as a science of sciences "beyond physics" (according to the etymology of "metaphysics"), there is no further reason to hesitate to approach it. Through ontology we can determine the human condition to the exact extent that it is posited for itself, fixed in concepts, and defined regarding its essential components. Briefly, when Jean Wahl speaks of "the failure of ontology" it seems to us he has not taken adequate account of the philosophical necessity of an "ontology of failure." He has attacked aspects of this ontology as though it were a metaphysical theory.

PHENOMENALISM AND PHENOMENOLOGY

On the second point, discussion will be made easier for us. We shall return to the perennial confusion of phenomenology with phenomenalism, but only in order to add two supplementary remarks that seem to us central.

With regard to Roger Troisfontaines's criticism, there are two ways to conceive the relation of being to consciousness. Troisfontaines plays heavily on words in reproaching Sartre for making being-in-itself into an absolute, thereby cutting it off "from all relations."[9] After this inference, one cannot be surprised when Troisfontaines treats this in-itself as a kind of "imaginary entity," relying on the already discussed thesis according to which the imagined object, unlike the perceptual object, sustains no relation with the rest of the world. But the analogy between the in-itself and the object of imagination is lame, for Sartre's in-itself in no way gives itself as *an* object that one could pick out from among others and set against all possible objects, and it is therefore situated neither on the perceptual nor on the imaginary plane. Instead, the in-itself conditions all affirmation, all questioning, and all negation concerning the presence of

9. *Le Choix de J.-P. Sartre*, p. 41.

this or that object. As we have already suggested, and as we will see more clearly a little further along, an affirmation can be understood only in reference to a question, which in turn implies the possibility of a negation, a retreat in relation to things. In other words, to affirm is always first to place in question, to introduce a distance in relation to the object. Clearly this questioning, and the retreat it implies, are meaningless if severed from being, with respect to which they constitute actual relations, relations which bring out the irreducibility of that being and the inalienability of its presence under whatever form. Infinitely diverse, these relations generate essentially relative phenomena, thereby merely underlining the absolute—and in a sense fated—character of the *being* of these phenomena. And this is why phenomenological description is not phenomenalism; the discovery of intentionality makes it impossible for us to make objects homogeneous with consciousness.

Thus we cannot follow Troisfontaines in considering being as absolutely relative to consciousness. "Relative to" can mean either 'absolutely dependent' on or 'always compelling the recognition of.' Phenomenalism understands the relation of being to consciousness in the first sense; phenomenology reserves the right to understand it in the second. As Sartre writes:

> . . . the phenomenon is the relative-absolute. The phenomenon remains relative, for "to appear" essentially presupposes someone to whom to appear. But it does not have the double relativity of the Kantian appearance [*Erscheinung*]. It does not point over its shoulder to some true being that would be, for it, absolute. Whatever it is, it is absolutely, for it reveals itself *as it is*.[10]

Sartre is being taken to task for an "absolute" in-itself as if it were the Kantian "noumenon," a metaphysical notion designed to explain phenomenality without itself being able to attain it (since "that which explains everything explains nothing"). Such a notion is unthinkable and undisclosable because all disclosure denies it. It calls for its own abandonment, in order to give way to an idealistic phenomenalism. Sartre specifically rejects the noumenon, and, as we shall see, this is linked to his rejection of a phenomenon that is absolutely dependent upon consciousness.

To bring out the absolute character of being, phenomenology points to its inexpungability and irreducibility. One cannot elude it from a given viewpoint without confirming it as something overflowing in relation to all possible viewpoints. This causes Sartre to say "all the *whys* are in effect posterior to being and presuppose it."[11] It is also the reason Sartre distinguishes ontology from metaphysics. Metaphysics may well inquire and form hypotheses regarding the origin of the for-itself, but it can never inquire regarding the origin of the

10. Jean-Paul Sartre, *L'Etre et le néant: essai d'ontologie phénoménologique* (Paris: Gallimard, 1943), p. 12; *Being and Nothingness: An Essay in Phenomenological Ontology*, translated by Hazel E. Barnes (New York: Washington Square Press, 1966), p. 4.

11. *EN*, p. 713; *BN*, p. 788.

in-itself. There are two options. First, one may question the in-itself *in its being*. But then the question "how does it come to be that being is?" has no meaning, since that question is conditioned by this very being. Consequently, this being has already been taken as absolutely contingent, "without reason, without cause and without necessity." The second alternative is to question the in-itself insofar *as it appears*. The question becomes "why is there a world?" and the answer is supplied by ontology: there is a world through the presence of the for-itself.

There is consequently no tautology or simple application of the principle of identity in asserting the phenomenon *is* phenomenon. Of course this emphasizes the phenomenal character of the phenomenon, but the phrase also accents its "transphenomenal" character, by which the being of the phenomenon is irreducibly set over against consciousness. Our turning to phenomenology requires that we further admit that this being can be *studied* rather than *explained*. Therein lies all the difference between phenomenalism, or the metaphysics of the phenomenon, and phenomenology, or description of the phenomenon that is conscious of ontological implications. No phenomenon is an absolute as such. But phenomenality, the being of phenomena, is an absolutely objective in-itself beyond the manifestations in which it develops.

FIRST DETERMINATION OF THE IN-ITSELF

What can this study of the in-itself teach us? Is this being of the appearance itself an appearance? Perhaps this absolute of phenomenality is revealed in the case of Nausea, for example. Nausea is a means of immediate access to being. Sartre calls it a "phenomenon of being." Of course there can and must be other "phenomena of being," for "being shows itself in some way to everyone, since we speak of it and have a certain understanding of it."[12] Let us recall Roquentin's discovery of the concrete meaning of the word "existence." All at once existence flowed back *on* him. It was no longer the existence of this or that nameable, usable thing, with its relative meaning limited to the definition imposed by our practical behavior. As Lévinas writes:

> It is like vertigo for thought to lean over the emptiness of the verb "to exist,"
> of which it seems nothing can be said and which becomes intelligible only in its
> participle, "existing," that is, only in that which exists. Thought glides imperceptibly from the notion of being qua being—that by which an existent exists—
> to the idea of a cause of existence, an "existing in general," a God.[13]

Here we rediscover the difficulty of resisting the temptation of explanatory metaphysics. This temptation issues from the conviction that being can be

12. *EN*, p. 14; *BN*, p. 7.
13. Emmanuel Lévinas, "Il y a," in *Deucalion I* (Paris: Editions de la Revue Fontaine, 1946), p. 143.

reached only by means of a causal regression toward some productive principle, rather than by virtue of a pure event. For Lévinas, being as such can be grasped in an experience and articulated after a fashion. This privileged experience is that of "night." It reveals being under the form of "there is"; "a consummation of being that is impersonal and anonymous, but also inextinguishable, it murmurs at the bottom of nothingness itself."[14]

Lévinas cites a curious passage from Edgar Poe, the final lines of which remind us of Roquentin's Nausea:

> There is, I find, no hereafter but this. This—this—this—is the only eternity!— and what, O Baalzebub!—*What* an eternity!—to *lie* in this vast—this awful void—a hideous, vague, and unmeaning anomaly—motionless, yet wishing for motion—powerless, yet longing for power—forever, forever, and forever![15]

Emphasis is placed here on the amorphousness of the subject rather than on the amorphousness of things. Roquentin also ended up feeling "in the way" for eternity, just like things. This is because at the level proper to such an experience "the anonymous current of being invades and submerges everything: subject, person, and thing."[16]

> The light touch of the "there is": that's the horror. . . . To be a consciousness is to be snatched out of the *there is* because the existence of a consciousness constitutes a subjectivity, a subject of existence, and hence to some extent, a master of being, a name. . . . Horror is like a movement that strips consciousness of this "subjectivity." It does so, not by soothing it with the unconscious, but by plunging it into an impersonal vigilance, a *participation* in Lévy-Bruhl's sense. The subject is petrified.[17]

One need only recall here the expression that constantly recurs in Roquentin's journal: "there is consciousness of . . . "

We have had recourse to this confrontation of two experiences or "phenomena" of being for two reasons. First, their confrontation brings out the ontological insufficiency of each. Second, it allows us to better understand that ontology is not a "noumenalism" and that the in-itself is not a substantial foundation of the appearing object but only the character of its being (which is closed in on itself, full of itself, and inert). Moreover, these two reasons are internally linked, a point that is suggested in a remarkable manner in the last paragraph of Lévinas's article, where he raises the question

14. "Il y a," p. 145.
15. ['Il y a," p. 148. Poe excised this passage from "Loss of Breath." *Collected Works of Edgar Allen Poe*, edited by Thomas Ollive Mabbott, vol. 2, *Tales and Sketches, 1831–1842* (Cambridge, Mass.: Belknap Press of Harvard University Press, 1978), p. 80. Poe is here describing the experience of a man who believes he has died.]
16. "Il y a," p. 145.
17. "Il y a," p. 149.

whether, nothingness, which is unthinkable either as limit or negation of being, may not instead be an interval or interruption; whether consciousness, with its power of forgetting, of suspension of being . . . has no recourse against the existence it participates in; whether, in the universality of the *there is*, this interval of nothingness, this stopping, this instant, is not the very condition of the *hypostasis* (the appearance of a substantive, a name, a particular) in the bosom of the anonymous and universal rumbling of the *there is*.[18]

The ontological insufficiency of such experiences of the in-itself is pointed to here. Ontology is not the simple description of this phenomenon, in which consciousness runs the risks of losing itself. It is rather the description of it as the phenomenon or revealing of a being that is in all respects *opposed* to this nothingness by which consciousness wards off such loss of itself. Ontology describes the in-itself insofar as it is, in itself, an absolute affirmation of itself, that is, insofar as it embraces everything, with the sole exception of this escape to the self, this refusal, this perpetual power of negation, which is the for-itself. Whether or not the latter originates in the former is not important; that is a metaphysical question. What counts is that the in-itself defines itself as that against which the for-itself opposes its own power of escape. Consequently, ontology must take note of this massive undifferentiatedness [*indifférenciation*] of the phenomenon of being. Thus, ontology proclaims and reveals being, a revelation that would be impossible if it were not conditioned and tied down by an absolute opposition of being to the consciousness that reveals it—a consciousness which for its part is perhaps quasi-impersonal.

In short, we again grasp here the demand for an ontology that would be neither a pure metaphysical abstraction nor a simple life launched within the heart of being. The latter would allow itself to become confused with being even as it discovers this confusion. Instead, this ontology is a revelation effected by starting from a lived revelation. The phenomenon of being corresponds to the lived revelation; the being of the phenomenon constitutes the object of the ontological revelation.

From this perspective it appears that

> if the being of phenomena does not resolve itself into a phenomenon of being, and if we can *say* nothing about being without consulting this phenomenon of being, then the exact relationship that unites the phenomenon of being to the being of the phenomenon must be established before all else.[19]

And one imagines this relationship will be established precisely in a first definition of consciousness, since the phenomenon of being is being as revealed to consciousness, *encountered* by it, while the being of the phenomenon is *apprehended* by it as the objectivity that inevitably overflows and grounds any knowledge that consciousness has of it. We should add here only that the

18. "Il y a," p. 154.
19. *EN*, p. 15; *BN*, pp. 8–9.

objectivity in question is not that of the object qua *object* of some kind or other, but rather of the object qua unavoidable *objective*: always there, soliciting the intentionality of consciousness, but also simultaneously casting a spell over it—to the point where consciousness overlooks its own intentional character.

THE CONSCIOUSNESS OF SELF

The principle of intentionality is that "all consciousness is consciousness of something." Husserl thereby asserts in effect that consciousness has no contents but is instead the "positing" of a transcendent object. Sartre adds that

> the first undertakings of any philosophy should . . . be to expel things from consciousness and to reestablish its true relation with the world, to learn, in short, that consciousness is positional consciousness of the world. All consciousness is positional in that it transcends itself to attain its object, and it exhausts itself in doing so. The *intentionality* of my present consciousness is its directedness toward the outside, toward the table. My judicative and practical activities, my passing affectivity, all transcend themselves, aim at the table, and are absorbed by it. However, for my knowing consciousness to be knowledge *of* its object, the necessary and sufficient condition is that it be consciousness of itself as being this knowledge.[20]

Here we touch on the essential point. It will determine all that follows. We must ascertain with the greatest precision possible what this "consciousness of consciousness" might be. We have encountered it in psychological analyses, especially in the domain of the unreflective.[21] Sartre warns against an error we have already noted: construing this consciousness of consciousness as a sort of knowledge of knowledge, or an idea of an idea. We would then have a positional consciousness of consciousness itself, that is, a consciousness of consciousness in a *reflection*. The reflecting consciousness would be directed toward the reflected consciousness, transcendent in relation to it, exhausting itself in aiming at it, just as the consciousness reflected upon exhausts itself in aiming at its objects. The object of this reflecting consciousness would therefore itself be a consciousness. Such a perspective, like a hall of mirrors, entails an infinite regression since the knowing reflection would in turn have to be known by a new knowing reflection that would take *it* as object.

This emphasizes that "consciousness of self is not binary" but must be "an immediate and noncognitive relation of self to self."[22] Consciousness of self is not knowledge, it is not a reflection on a prior consciousness taken as object. Instead, reflection itself, and also the prior consciousness that it reflects, are each indissolubly both consciousness of self and consciousness of an object. *All*

20. *EN*, p. 18; *BN*, p. 11.
21. [See above, p. 31.]
22. *EN*, p. 19; *BN*, p. 12.

consciousness of an object is already also consciousness of self, without requiring the least "reflection": such is its very character as consciousness.

> All positional consciousness of an object is at the same time non-positional consciousness of itself. If I count the cigarettes in that box, I have the sense of uncovering an objective property of this group of cigarettes: *they are twelve.* This property appears to my consciousness as existing in the world. I may well have no positional consciousness of counting them. I do not "know myself counting." . . . And yet the moment they reveal themselves to me as twelve I have a non-thetic consciousness of my additive activity.[23]

I am conscious that I am counting but this is not a secondary reflection whose intervention is necessary in order to reveal my consciousness in the process of counting. "On the contrary, unreflective consciousness is what makes such reflection possible."[24] This means the *"cogito"* in the Cartesian sense—"I think that I am counting"—is based upon a *pre-reflective cogito*—to wit: "I count consciously, I am conscious of counting"—that is its condition. In the very additive activity of consciousness there is an "operative intention" unifying the various moments of the addition. It can exist only as "revealing-revealed," a Heideggerian expression that Sartre uses to indicate that consciousness cannot reveal an objective quality in the world without being revealed to itself in this very operation of revealing. "The initial consciousness of consciousness . . . is one with the consciousness of which it is conscious. It determines itself at a single stroke as both consciousness of perception and as perception."[25]

Difficult though it is to express, we have just conferred on the term "self-consciousness" its authentic meaning, which no philosophy has heretofore pinned down. For intellectualist philosophies and for reflective philosophy generally, self-consciousness is consciousness of something else besides itself, of an anterior and separate consciousness in the same stream. Such an approach has several consequences. If my consciousness can grasp itself only by becoming distinct from itself, if I cannot be conscious of myself without making myself double, then there must be an irreducible duality between the "I" that I am as reflecting subject and the "me" that I also am as the unreflective subject who acts and lives. This scission would have incalculable practical repercussions. I would have to oppose myself, condemn myself—regardless of any particular motives—since the "I," once it is split from the "me," could only be a pure activity of judgment and government. Where, then, could I draw not only the motives but also the energy needed for action? I am in effect asked to turn away from myself in favor of an impersonal "I." But this "I" is no longer able to refer to its duty except theoretically and vainly, through ideal formulations. Thus my being is divided into two alien parts: a "psychological" consciousness

23. *EN*, p. 19; *BN*, p. 13.
24. *EN*, p. 20; *BN*, p. 13.
25. *EN*, p. 20; *BN*, p. 14.

that is passive, brute, and meaningless and a "transcendental" consciousness that is normative, "moral," logical, and constituted entirely of pure and ideal forms, an imperative without power. This difficulty does not arise for empiricist philosophies, since, as we have seen, they eliminate all activity of consciousness, limiting it to the impressions received, which are baptized with the epithet "conscious."

More specifically, we can note the following paradox. If, with Husserl, one emphasizes consciousness's intentional directedness toward something, its obligation to constantly posit an object, one ends up making consciousness constitutive of its objects and transparent to itself, giving itself a world through the meanings it holds in itself. If, with Heidegger, one emphasizes the lived self-understanding characteristic of human reality, one then allows the latter to lose itself in its own "reality," to become ensnared in its unreflective mode, its freedom dissolved in its situation. In the one case, one takes account of the object only in order to rescue the subject from it; in the other, one takes account of the subject only to confound it with the object. The resulting absolute liberation and the atmosphere of confusion are equally troublesome. We must conclude from these remarks that consciousness is definable only as being both of the above aspects simultaneously: all consciousness is at once consciousness of something and also of itself as being conscious of something. It is not necessary either to close off consciousness from the start within Descartes's reflective *cogito* or to make its behavior blindly unreflective, thereby suppressing its further chances of rising to reflection.

Consciousness, then, can never be unconscious of itself. But we also perceive in this that consciousness is always in some sense ignorant of itself. For either consciousness renounces all reflection and knowledge by remaining at the unreflective level or reflection constrains it to double itself, in which case it apprehends only a prior consciousness of which it has knowledge. As for itself, qua reflecting consciousness, it can only be conscious of itself; it cannot know itself. Thus authentic self-consciousness is always consciousness's "non-positional consciousness of itself." "However," says Sartre,

> we can no longer use this expression in which the "of itself" calls up the idea of knowledge. (Thus we shall henceforth place the "of" between parentheses to indicate that it merely serves a grammatical requirement).
>
> This consciousness (of) itself should be considered not as a new consciousness but as *the only mode of existence that is possible for a consciousness of something.*[26]

This adjustment has consequences for the being of the phenomenon. We have in effect liberated the consciousness of being from pure phenomenality. By bringing out self-consciousness in its authenticity, we have shown that consciousness is not the mere existence or epiphenomen of being and that being is

26. Ibid. [The sentence in parentheses is Sartre's.]

not the mere determination or product of consciousness. We have instead pointed to the transphenomenality of consciousness at the same time that we indicated the transphenomenality of being. By recognizing that the being of an intention must itself be consciousness, we were able to avoid making the intention a thing within consciousness. This in turn has allowed us to preserve the ambiguity or double phenomenal character of the intention: it indicates two transphenomenalities at once—the intended object and the subject who intends that object while remaining irreducibly transcendent to it.

BEING-IN-ITSELF

This completes what Sartre calls "the ontological proof." Consciousness (of) consciousness *is* absolute subjectivity. It is immanent to itself and it amounts to the identity of appearing and existing: consciousness exists to the extent it appears to itself.

However, this consciousness (of) consciousness must

qualify itself in some way, and it cannot qualify itself except as a revealing intuition, otherwise it is nothing. Now a revealing intuition implies something revealed. Absolute subjectivity can constitute itself only over against the revealed; immanence can define itself only in its grasp of something transcendent. . . . in its being, consciousness implies a being that is non-conscious and transphenomenal. . . . To say that consciousness is consciousness *of* something is to say that it must produce itself as the revelation-revealed of a being that is not itself, a being that gives itself as already existing when consciousness reveals it.[27]

Let us look back over the route we have just covered. Although we started by taking sides with the phenomenon, we ended with the conclusion that the phenomenon does not support itself as such. The world is not merely phenomenal, not merely world-for-us; it *is*; it is in-itself; it exists independently of consciousness and is not reducible to it. And consciousness itself is not just phenomenal: it is absolute subjectivity, irreducible to the world's mode of being.

In thus passing beyond the phenomenon toward each of the two types of being that it indicates, we have avoided a double danger. On the one hand, we avoid the phenomenalism of those idealistic philosophers who would make the very being of the object a constituted product of pure consciousness, thereby referring all being back to the being of consciousness. On the other hand, we avoid the epiphenomenalism of realist philosophers who construe the object as acting upon a passive consciousness, thereby referring all being back to the being of the object. Clearly, then, we have posed the problem of the communication between these two types of being which are irreducible to one

27. [*EN*, p. 29; *BN*, pp. 23–24.]

another. It is also clear that the in-itself can be finally defined only within the context of a resolution of this problem.

We can start by indicating the essential characteristics of these two types of being as they show forth in the preceding reflection.

First point: Being that is transcendent to consciousness is neither active nor passive. It is beyond such categories, which themselves derive their meaning from it. Consequently, being is not *explainable* by some creation. Even if it had been passively created its essence would require that it not retain a trace of this event, but rather that it affirm itself as cause of itself from the first moment of its existence. *It consists of itself* and this is all one can say in this connection.

Second point: Being that is transcendent to consciousness is beyond the categories of affirmation and negation. It is an absolute inherence in itself, an affirmation that is full of itself yet is incapable of self-affirmation since to affirm itself it would have to be at some distance from itself. For this reason, the expression "in itself" that sums up these two points of our inquiry, is, strictly speaking, defective. Being in itself does not refer back to itself like consciousness (of) self. It is this "self," "opaque to itself precisely because it is filled with itself."[28] Being is a "self" that is identical to itself and therefore does not exist for itself. Put another way: *being is what it is*. Being is an absolute synthesis with itself that is isolated and incapable of moving outside itself, either to relate itself to itself or to enter into relations with what is not itself. It is what it is: all becoming is denied it for it is beyond becoming—it is the being of becoming. It cannot even posit itself as being *other* than another being for it ignores the other and alteriety generally, being beyond all negation. It lacks the resources to posit itself as opposition to what it is not.

Third point: Of being in-itself we can say neither that it is possible nor that it is necessary. A phenomenal existent may be derived from another existent only qua phenomenal and not qua existent. By the same token, a phenomenal existent is *contingent*: ". . . never either possible nor impossible, it *is*. This is what consciousness expresses—in anthropomorphic terms—in saying [such being] is *in the way*. . . . "[29] Here we rejoin the phenomenon of being we have uncovered as Nausea.

THE RELATION BETWEEN THE TWO TYPES OF BEING

We have dwelt on these matters—which may look like mere technical subtleties—in order to characterize the spirit in which Sartre's ontology appeared to us. This spirit has been misunderstood fully as much as it could have been, and the reasons are easy to see. We have indicated the main one:

28. *EN*, p. 33; *BN*, p. 29.
29. [*EN*, p. 34; *BN*, p. 29.]

Sartre's research into being has been interpreted as a metaphysical procedure that more or less arbitrarily grounds the consequences that flow from it, which consequences are therefore best viewed with suspicion. We now know this interpretation is worthless and this fear unjustified. Sartre's being in-itself is refractory to all theological and metaphysical contexts. It merely points to a pole of a description whose conceptual form is strictly implied by the meaning of that description. We are dealing with *abstractions*, then, only to the extent that all thought necessarily abstracts. This is not dangerous so long as thought does not allow itself to become attached to these abstractions, thereby taking them no longer as instruments, but as ends, no longer as means for concrete elucidation, but as realities in their own right that can govern the concrete.

The positions heretofore established are essential as determinations of the elements of our situation in the world. But they do not involve necessary consequences, as do the principles of certain metaphysical systems. They must instead be set against other positions which will also themselves compel our recognition through new elucidations of the concrete.

It is to the concrete, then, that we must now return. At no point will we try to reconstruct the concrete with abstractions that themselves emerge from it. We are looking for the relation between the two types of being that we have distinguished—consciousness, and being that is transcendent to consciousness—the second of which we have just provisionally defined. It is not for us to establish this relation; we need only bring it into relief. Our aim is therefore an authentic return to the concrete and not an artificial reconstruction based on the abstract.

> From this point of view consciousness is an abstraction, for it conceals in itself an ontological source in the region of the in-itself. Conversely, the phenomenon (by which we understand: the phenomenon insofar as it exists) is also an abstraction since it must "appear" to consciousness. . . . The concrete is man in the world, in that specific union of man to world that Heidegger, for example, calls "being-in-the-world." . . . The relation between the regions of being is a primitive gushing forth that belongs to the very structure of each of these beings.[30]

30. *EN*, pp. 37–38; *BN*, pp. 33–34. [The phrase in parentheses is added by Jeanson.]

Chapter 3

Consciousness Rejects Being

IN LIGHT OF the preceding, we must interrogate man as he exists in the world, describing certain of his behaviors in the hope of finding the deepest meaning of the "man-world" relation. Initially, I address such questioning only to myself. However, Sartre discerns therein an interrogative attitude that can be considered in its own right, "for it matters little whether the questioner be myself or the reader who reads my work and questions along with me." Questioning is already "a human attitude endowed with meaning" and should illuminate the synthetic relation tying man to the world.[1]

The first clue is that all interrogation addresses itself *to* a being. Whether we inquire about its way of being or its being itself, we are asking about that in virtue of which this being participates in the general transcendence of being. Thus the first lesson to draw is that interrogation presupposes, and does not create, man's relation to being-in-itself. Moreover, it seems the dialogical question is only one form of interrogation. If you interrogate a person he will first have to interrogate being in order to respond to you. Being is therefore capable of giving negative answers.

Transcendent being—which is an absolute positivity beyond affirmation and negation—thus presents itself through interrogation as a perpetual response to human efforts. This response may be put as follows. "Being is that, and outside of that, *nothing*."[2] By the fact of interrogation alone there is a revelation of being, which thereby presents itself as the equally transcendent foundation of *non-being*.

Verifying this involves less paradox than it may seem. It is true that the in-itself—which is one pole of a description based on the concrete—can manifest its absolute character only by becoming relative in this very manifestation. This underlines the in-itself's nonmetaphysical character. Its nature excludes any dependence of being upon consciousness that would enable consciousness to seize it, absorb it, and reduce it to itself. Being is therefore absolute in that it imposes itself on consciousness. At the same time, the fact that consciousness can question being means being is not everywhere and is not everything. Con-

1. *EN*, pp. 38–39; *BN*, p. 35.
2. *EN*, p. 40; *BN*, p. 36.

sciousness can interrogate being only because being imposes itself on consciousness; however, being does this, not by obliterating consciousness, but by responding to its interrogation with a yes or no. In short, being is "haunted" by non-being, by nothingness.

Negation cannot be a merely mental category, an occasional imprint on judgments which themselves remain essentially affirmative. There are genuinely negative judgments. But negation can tear us away from "this wall of positivity that encloses us," to the precise extent that there is, literally, nothing besides being, nothing besides positivity. "The necessary condition for the possibility of saying *no* is that non-being be a perpetual presence in us and outside of us, that is, that nothingness haunt being."[3]

WHAT NOTHINGNESS IS NOT

Nothingness [*le Néant*], then, stands out as the first condition for interrogative behavior. For there to be interrogation there must be the possibility of negation. Moreover, "for there to be negation in the world, and for us to thereby have the capacity to raise questions concerning Being, Nothingness must in some way be given."[4]

How, then, shall we conceive this Nothingness? Four basic points must be made:

1. Nothingness cannot be "outside" of Being as its abstract complement. Nothingness cannot come after Being. It needs Being to maintain its own nihilation [*néant*] of Being, though Being does not imply the existence of Nothingness.

2. By the same token, Nothingness is not "outside" of Being as some infinite milieu in which Being is suspended. This is shown by the existence of lived realities like "distance, . . . absence, change, otherness [*altérité*], repulsion, regret, distraction, etc." Such realities are "experienced, combatted, dreaded, etc., by the human being." Sartre calls them "negativities" ["*négatités*"]. "The inner structure of these realities is inhabited by negation [*la négation*] as by a necessary condition of their existence. . . . they are dispersed in being, sustained by being and by conditions of reality." Within the very bosom of the world there is "a swarm of ultramundane beings which possess as much reality and efficaciousness as others but which enclose non-being in themselves." Nothingness can be given, then, only "in the bosom of Being, in its heart, like a worm."[5]

3. Nothingness cannot be conceived apart from Being, which, for its part, is a full positivity that neither entails nor implies Nothingness.

4. Finally, Nothingness cannot be conceived by starting with itself. Since

3. *EN*, pp. 46–47; *BN*, pp. 43–44.
4. *EN*, p. 58; *BN*, p. 56.
5. *EN*, pp. 56–57; *BN*, pp. 55–56.

Nothingness is "non-being, it cannot draw from itself the power necessary for *nihilating* [*néantiser*] itself."[6] From whence, then, does this power come?

The question has little meaning in this form. First of all, each of the preceding remarks leads to this central conclusion: Nothingness *is not*, for otherwise it would be confused with Being. Strictly speaking, there cannot be Nothingness, only "being-that-is-nihilated." Or, if you will, there can be a being that, as nothingness, is carried along, sustained, assured, by Being. And, as we have seen, the kind of Being that plays this role is not Being-in-Itself.

THE ROLE OF NOTHINGNESS

Understanding is needed here and the following analogy, despite its defects, may help. Life exists, there is life. From a certain point of view—that of the nitrogen cycle, for example—the death of a living being transforms life but does not negate it. Death is life's future; it is a phenomenon whose very phenomenality is founded on the being of life. What, then, would suicide be with regard to life? It would be life's negation, though one not implied by life. Neither would it be added from outside, for suicide is brought about in the very heart of life. Suicide is nothing, it changes nothing with regard to life; yet suicide denies life [*la nie*], refuses it. For a being that is capable of killing itself, it is through this *nothing* [*rien*] that life takes on a meaning, and it could not do so if this nothing did not in some way exist. Its way of existing is evinced by a man's act of annihilation [*anéantissement*] against the life that encloses and smothers him. Life does not imply suicide, but suicide borrows from life the kind of existence that is nothing.

Life is contingent, absurd, and unjustifiable in that one can neither find a raison d'être within it nor explain it by anything outside itself. It is beyond all value. Suicide is that possibility that gives a value to the very life from which, qua possibility, it draws its semblance of existence. It alone enables life to leave its massiveness and being-in-itself and to transcend itself toward all other possibilities.

Suicide *is* nothing; it exists as an ever-present contingency, as something that may happen to life at any time. Clearly, then, a being that *is what it is* could have no relationship with such a nullification [*néant*] of being. That which is merely possible could come to such a being only through the intervention of another being, one that is *not what it is*. The man who is going to kill himself interrogates himself about his life. Through him, suicide will occur in his life. But this is because there was already the possibility of suicide, which amounts to the possibility of the negation of life from within itself. Consequently, this man's anguished question indicates a fundamental negation [*négation*] which lies at the source of every question and every anguish but which *is* nothing if it is not *actualized* in this question.

6. *EN*, p. 58; *BN*, p. 56.

To sum up this analogy: just as suicide implies the possibility of calling life into question, so Nothingness implies the possiblity of calling Being into question.

> . . . nothing can happen to being through being itself—except for nothingness. Nothingness is the possibility that is proper to being, and it is being's unique possibility. Yet this original possibility appears only in the absolute act that realizes it.[7]
>
> . . . the in-itself, being by nature what it is, cannot "have" possibilities. Its relation to a possibility can be established only in an exterior manner, that is, only through a being that does in fact stand before these possibilities.[8]

Such a being "*is* its own possibility,"[9] it is its own negation of being. As such, it is *nothing* "besides the original project of its own nothingness."[10] By virtue of the possibility of suicide both life and that "phenomenon of life" which is death take on a meaning. Similarly, by virtue of nothingness both being and that phenomenon of being which is the future, the changing, take on a meaning. It is because suicide is possible that life *appears*, rising out of a ground of non-life, of other-than-life, of death. Similarly, through nothingness, being *appears*, rising out of a ground of non-being, of other-than-being.

We use this last term with a purpose. First of all, it seems to carry through the analogy we have drawn between Nothingness and the "phenomenon of life" called death—"the moment of life that we never have to live." Second, we refer to imagination, a form of nihilation [*néanisation*] with which we are already familiar, because it will allow us to further specify the Being that is not Being-in-itself. The latter is a being whose "property is the nihilation effected by nothingness" and it is that "*by which nothingness comes to things.*"[11]

THE BEING THAT SUPPORTS NOTHINGNESS

The Being capable of supporting Nothingness in the heart of Being-in-itself must itself be the Nothingness proper to Being-in-itself. Sartre's formula for this looks like a barbarism: "The Being by which Nothingness comes into the world is such that in its Being the Nothingness of its Being is in question."[12] Any "translation" of this into ordinary language is probably useless. But the analogy we established above with the pair Life-Suicide is again relevant here for it applies to the role that phenomenology attributes to the imaging function. The man who envisages suicide is one who places himself in question. He carries within himself the power to annihilate both himself and the world.

7. *EN*, p. 121; *BN*, p. 126.
8. *EN*, p. 144; *BN*, p. 152.
9. *EN*, p. 144; *BN*, p. 151.
10. *EN*, p. 121; *BN*, p. 126.
11. *EN*, p. 58; *BN*, p. 57. [Sartre's emphasis.]
12. *EN*, p. 59; *BN*, p. 57.

Similarly, to imagine is to nihilate simultaneously the world and oneself; the act of imagination is a sort of provisional suicide. Thus one places oneself in question only to the extent one is one's own Nothingness. Our analogy thus seems to point to a sort of breaking of limits and it indicates that man is the being we seek. We are looking for "a being that makes Nothingness burst forth in the world inasmuch as, to this end, it affects itself with non-being." And: "Man is the being by which nothingness comes to the world."[13]

Clearly, though, "human reality" cannot "annihilate the mass of being, even provisionally." Human reality can only place being in question, that is, hold it in view as a totality while placing itself *outside*. Hence, Sartre continues,

> human reality can modify only its *relationship* with this being. For human reality to put a particular existent out of circuit is to put itself out of circuit in relation to that existent. In this case it escapes that circuit; it is out of reach; it cannot be acted upon for it has retreated *beyond a nothingness*. Human reality's possibility of thus secreting a nothingness which isolates it has been given a name by Descartes, following the Stoics: it is *freedom*.[14]

We have explored the imaging attitude above. In the present context, this attitude presupposes that human reality, as freedom, has the power to effect within itself a rupture with being. It is a tearing away from itself in order to tear itself away from the world; it is an escape from itself in order to escape from existent things. Human reality-as-freedom can therefore also put its own past out of action "by secreting its own nothingness."

> Every psychic process of nihilation implies . . . a cleavage between the immediate psychic past and the present. This cleavage is nothingness. . . . That which separates the previous from the subsequent is precisely *nothing*. And this nothing is absolutely impenetrable just because it is nothing. . . . The previous consciousness is still *there* (though now with the modification "pastness"— existence in the past); it still maintains a relation of interpretation with present consciousness. But on the basis of this existential relation the past is put out of action, out of circuit, between parentheses—just as the world within himself and without is put out of action in the eyes of one who practices the phenomenological "*epoché*."[15]

There is a present for a consciousness to the extent this nihilating power disengages that consciousness from a causal series each of whose states is a prolongation of prior ones. It has a present to the extent it can introduce this "nothing" between the current state and the earlier one, thereby changing the latter into a past. Similarly, as we saw, there is a *situation* for consciousness to the extent it views existent things in their totality and in their relation to itself, arranging them as a world around itself.

13. *EN*, p. 60; *BN*, p. 59.
14. *EN*, p. 61; *BN*, pp. 59–60.
15. *EN*, pp. 64–65; *BN*, pp. 63–64.

FREEDOM AND ANGUISH

Human reality, inasmuch as it is conscious, is therefore freedom. It *is* its own past (as it is also its own future) through nihilation of it. Consequently, consciousness both is and is not this past and this future. We also saw that the being capable of thus setting Nothingness over against Being-in-itself (which *is* what it is) must be one which in some way both is not what it is and is what it is not. It must be a being that is never identical with itself.

Just as imaging consciousness must be conscious (of) itself as imaging, so consciousness as freedom must be conscious (of) itself as such. *Anguish* is the form this consciousness (of) freedom takes: "it is in anguish that freedom is a question for itself in its being."[16]

We shall understand anguish by first contrasting it with fear. "Fear is fear of beings in the world and anguish is anguish before myself. Vertigo is anguish to the extent that I am in dread, not of falling over the precipice, but of throwing myself over."[17] The soldier's fear becomes anguish only when he asks himself whether he can resist. Anguish is "fear of being afraid." I am afraid to the extent I am caught within the determinism of things; I free myself from my fear by setting my possibilities of action over against it. However, these are mere possibilities that lack inner solidity, and so I find myself suspended in the void, as it were. All behaviors available to me are presented together and no one besides myself can decide which one to effect. It is just as possible that I shall throw myself over the precipice as that I shall set about resolving the problems presented to me by the narrowness of the path. I depend henceforth only on myself and no psychological determinism can intervene to decide for me. Even my horror of the precipice is not determinative in relation to my possible behavior. It certainly calls for a definite behavior, but it is not the *cause* of that behavior and nothing can oblige me to choose it. In sum, I depend on my future insofar as my future is not strictly contained in my present. Of course it is I who will shortly recover my balance, but there is nothing in me now that conditions this possible recovery: "The decisive conduct will come from a self that I am not yet." By the same token, in the behavior of the gambler, for example, we observe "anguish in the face of the past."[18] This results from the total inefficaciousness of prior resolutions to give up gambling.

Freedom is therefore "discovered within us in anguish and is characterized by the existence of this *nothing* which insinuates itself between motive and act."[19]

Consciousness escapes its motives because they are not *in* it but only *for* it.

16. *EN*, p. 66; *BN*, p. 65.
17. Ibid.
18. *EN*, p. 69; *BN*, p. 69.
19. *EN*, p. 71; *BN*, p. 71.

Consciousness posits them as motives, and it is incumbent on consciousness to confer upon them their meaning and importance.

Anguish, as manifestation of freedom facing itself, means that man is always separated from his essence by a nothingness. . . . Essence is what has been. It is everything that one can indicate about a human being by the words "that *is*." And because of this fact, it is the totality of characteristics which *explain* the acts. But each act is always beyond this essence; it is a human act only insofar as it surpasses any explanation one might give of it, precisely because everything one can designate in man by the formula "that is" is caused by that very designation to *have been*. . . .

In anguish, freedom is anguished before itself, inasmuch as it is solicited and bound by *nothing*.[20]

If anguish is rare it is because *in action* consciousness is unreflective. It is always discovering in the world demands and immediate urgencies which hide from us our farthest-reaching goals and essential possibilities: ". . . we are at each moment cast into the world and engaged there."[21] Action reassures us by circumventing the question of value. An act has an immediate directionality that pulls us along and allows us to avoid asking ourselves about its meaning. Now this meaning, this *value*, can be based only on our freedom: man is the being by which values exist. Moreover, his freedom

is anguished over being the unfounded foundation of values. . . . I do not and can not have recourse to any value in opposing the fact that it is I who maintain values in being. Nothing can protect me against myself. Cut off from the world and from my own essence by this nothingness that I *am*, I must realize the meaning of the world and of my essence: I make my decision concerning them— alone, without justification, and without excuse.[22]

Anguish appears, then, to the extent my freedom disengages me from the world in which I was engaged. It contrasts with *the spirit of seriousness*. In the latter attitude one grasps values by starting with the exigencies of the world, while at the same time denying that these exigencies proceed from the sense one's own freedom gives that world. In *Nausea* these are the people on the Coteau Vert; Roquentin calls them the "Bastards."

The analogy with suicide again applies here. It is in proportion as I know I can end the life within me that it becomes my own. Suicide—which we have made to stand for Nothingness—implies man's unconditioned freedom. Through representation of this possibility a person can decide whether he will accept or reject his situation in the world. If he decides on acceptance he forever retracts his innocence. This decision makes him responsible for his very existence, as if by a reoccurrence of it.

20. *EN*, pp. 72–73; *BN*, pp. 72–73.
21. [*EN*, p. 75; *BN*, p. 75.]
22. *EN*, pp. 76–77; *BN*, pp. 76–78.

FROM ANGUISH TO BAD FAITH

Psychological determinism assumes a particular meaning in this light. We have already rejected it as a method. We have seen that it constitutes a behavior of flight vis-à-vis anguish, a reflection that attempts to neutralize the evidence for freedom provided by reflective intuition.

> Psychological determinism, before being a theoretical conception, is first a behavior of excuse or, if you will, the basis of all behaviors of excuse. . . . it provides us with a *nature* that produces our acts . . . ; at the same time, by reducing us to *being always just what we are,* it reintroduces in us the absolute positivity of being-in-itself and thereby reintegrates us into the bosom of being.[23]

However, psychological determinism is only a postulate or hypothesis; by itself it cannot distract us from anguish. A more concrete effort of flight is involved. What is this effort and how is it able to dissimulate our anguish? We can immediately observe: I cannot suppress the anguish that I *am* as a freedom, and any attempt to flee it only shows that I am not ignorant of it. "I must think of it constantly in order to take care not to think of it. . . . I flee it in order to ignore it but I cannot ignore the fact that I flee, and flight from anguish is merely one way of being aware of anguish." It therefore seems that

> I can be my anguish in the mode of "not being it," in other words, that I can make use of a power of nihilation in the very heart of anguish itself. . . . This is what has been named *bad faith.* . . . I can place myself in bad faith in the apprehension of the anguish that I am, and this bad faith, which is intended to "fill in" the nothingness that I *am* with regard to myself, implies the very nothingness that it suppresses.[24]

We have so far encountered nihilation only as an empirical freedom in the form of constantly maintained distances between a being and his past and future. He transcends himself, as it were, by constituting what he had been or would be as in-itselfs in relation to which he effects a nihilation in his present. Human reality seems to have two alternatives in this context: to throw itself into the in-itself or to engage itself in its own non-being. Either way, the foundation of all negation must reside "in a nihilation that would be exercised *in the very bosom of immanence.*" Thus we encounter "the original act by which man is for himself his own nothingness." This original act must be effected by itself, to itself, within the instant, "in absolute immanence, in the pure subjectivity of the instantaneous *cogito.*"[25]

Now bad faith manifests, in a single consciousness, "the unity of being and not-being as being-in-order-not-to-be."[26] We must therefore turn to it to define this fundamental nothingness.

23. *EN,* p. 78; *BN,* pp. 78–79.
24. *EN,* p. 82; *BN,* p. 83.
25. [*EN,* p. 83; *BN,* p. 84.]
26. [*EN,* p. 83; *BN,* pp. 84–85.]

BAD FAITH AND THE LIE

In bad faith, consciousness's negation is directed, neither to what is outside itself nor to non-present states of itself, but to itself in its very presence to itself. This must be grounded in an essential aspect of consciousness's mode of being. The analysis of bad faith—though it rests on and develops previous insights—will therefore be entirely new for us. If philosophy itself is primordially an attempt at authenticity, bad faith is of central importance and misapprehending its meaning would have grave consequences. We must therefore reemphasize that ontology limits itself to determining and describing the elements of the human condition and in no way prescribes the attitude that man should adopt in order to realize himself. It indicates obstacles, but only in order to suggest which horizons are radically blocked off and which might allow a path to be cleared.

Bad faith is first of all not mere lying. Or, if you will, it is a lie to oneself, which differs considerably from the lie *simpliciter*. The latter always implies a real separation between deceiver and deceived. "Bad faith, on the other hand, essentially implies the unity of *one* consciousness."[27] A situation may elicit it, but it does not come to consciousness from without. Consciousness neither undergoes bad faith nor falls victim to it, as with a deception. Instead, consciousness

> affects itself with bad faith. This requires an initial intention and a project of bad faith. . . . I must be aware, in my capacity as deceiver, of the truth concealed from me in my capacity as deceived. . . . and all this occurs not in two different temporal moments . . . but in the unitary structure of a single project.[28]

How can there be a lie without a real separation? And how can I attain bad faith intentionally? In short, how can an absolute subjectivity that is left to itself in immediacy be other than totally cynical or totally sincere?

THE PSYCHOANALYTIC SOLUTION

We know how psychoanalytic theory would answer these questions. It reinstitutes the deceiver-deceived duality within the psychic realm. The deceiver becomes the unconscious, with its primary and combined tendencies. The deceived becomes consciousness, which expresses in phobias, mistakes, and dreams the symbols provoked by the unconscious. Thus, on the one hand, there is the kind of instinct that is "neither *true* nor *false* inasmuch as it does not exist *for itself* at all,"[29] while on the other, there are genuinely psychic phenomena provoked by this instinct, and between the two there is a demarcation line called the *censor*.

27. [*EN*, p. 87; *BN*, p. 89.]
28. *EN*, pp. 87–88; *BN*, p. 89.
29. *EN*, p. 88; *BN*, p. 90.

On this scheme "the subject stands before the psychic phenomena within himself as the deceived does before the behaviors of the deceiver. He confronts them as realities and must interpret them."[30] These phenomena thus possess a certain "truth," namely, that of the subject's own symbolic acts.

As it happens, this truth is objective. The psychoanalyst alone can discover it, which he does by reconnecting the phenomena with the patient's past, with his unconscious complexes, and with the censor's obstruction. The subject cannot avoid being deceived regarding the *sense* of his own behaviors. He attests to them, but their psychic constitution remains as alien to him as the psyche of another. The subject *is* his own conscious behaviors inasmuch as he can so attest, but he *is not* those behaviors inasmuch as he undergoes them and must engage in scientific conjecturing to discover their meaning. Clearly, though, this account does not explain bad faith. Instead it substitutes for bad faith "the idea of a lie without a liar, and it explains how I can *be lied to* in the absence of any lying."[31] To be precise, the moment of bad faith resides in the *censor*. To act discerningly, to resist the psychoanalyst's discovery of the repressed tendencies, the censor "must know what he represses."[32] Now the role given the censor by psychoanalytic theory requires him to be conscious (of) himself, a type of consciousness with which we are already familiar. It is a "consciousness (of) being conscious of the tendency to repress, but precisely *in order not to be conscious of it*. What can this mean if not that the censor is in bad faith?"[33] But this merely names what one sought to elude; the problem itself remains intact. Bad faith implies a lucidity pervading all consciousness, and what is called "the unconscious" either plays the role of motivations or no role at all. The subject's behavior, being conscious, is not caused by these motivations, and it is a Viennese psychiatrist who writes: "Each time I was able to push my investigations far enough I confirmed that the crux of the psychosis was conscious."[34]

FACTICITY AND TRANSCENDENCE

This brings us back to our initial question: "What must be the being of man such that he is capable of bad faith?"[35] Sartre's analyses of concrete examples of bad faith—which merit lengthy quotation for their profundity and clarity—lead to the same answers. All behaviors of bad faith involve a play on

30. *EN*, pp. 88–89; *BN*, p. 90.
31. [*EN*, p. 90; *BN*, p. 92.]
32. [*EN*, p. 91; *BN*, p. 93.]
33. *EN*, p. 92; *BN*, p. 94.
34. Quoted in *L'Etre et le néant*, *EN*, p. 93; *BN*, p. 95. [Sartre is probably quoting a foreword to the French translation. See *Frigidity in Woman* by Wilhelm Stekel, translated by J. Van Teslaar (New York: Grove Press, 1926).]
35. *EN*, p. 94; *BN*, p. 96.

the two properties of human being: "to be a *facticity* and to be a *transcendence*";[36] one exists both in the mode of "being what one is" and in the mode of "not being what one is." Or alternately: in bad faith one exists in the mode of the in-itself and also in the mode of escape and flight from the in-itself. The "playing" consists in avoiding self-reproach either (a) by considering oneself a transcendence, though in the mode of a facticity, or (b) by considering oneself a facticity, though in the mode of a transcendence.

To dissipate his sense of guilt, the homosexual denies that homosexuality characterizes his *being*. He claims the latter overflows this definition of himself, surpasses it, and infinitely transcends it.[37] What he wishes is to be this transcendence alone. He conceives it as a facticity, as though it could surpass his homosexuality toward anything else whatever in an absolute and final manner. He seeks to place himself out of reach, to constitute himself a "non-homosexual" in the manner of the in-itself. All this is aimed at transcending the facticity of "being homosexual"; but in order to lay hold of this transcendence he reinserts it in the cognate facticity of "not-being homosexual." He is in bad faith.

Conversely, the young woman who is being courted wants to be in a position to reject her own and her partner's behavior at the level of facticity.[38] This is because she seeks both to savor her own excitement and to reduce the man's words and gestures to objective qualities, thereby disarming them of their meaning as "first approaches." But she also wants to consider her excitement at the level of transcendence, as something beyond mere physical desire. While remaining within facticity she pretends to have neutralized the situation's real meaning. She allows her hand to be taken in his "without noticing it." Yet it is precisely in order to reclaim this facticity that she transcends it toward a meaning that permits her to extract the maximum pleasure from it. She is in bad faith.

> . . . thanks precisely to transcendence I am not implicated by anything that I am. . . . I am on a plane where no reproach can reach me since what I really *am* is my transcendence. I flee from myself, I escape myself, leaving my tattered garment in the hands of the faultfinder. However, the ambiguity necessary for bad faith derives from affirming I *am* my transcendence in the mode of being of a thing.[39]

Conversely, thanks to facticity, I am not subject to any duties that might encumber me; I make myself excusable, pitiable. Sartre conveys this in a formula from Sarment: "I am too great for myself."[40] The ambiguity that constitutes

36. *EN*, p. 95; *BN*, p. 98.
37. [*EN*, pp. 103–104; *BN*, pp. 107–108.]
38. [*EN*, p. 95; *BN*, pp. 97–98.]
39. *EN*, p. 96; *BN*, p. 99.
40. [*EN*, p. 96; *BN*, pp. 98, 99.]

the bad faith here derives from my affirmation of my facticity insofar as I may be judged, pardoned, or pitied, that is, as someone who already transcends his facticity.

These matters go to the heart of subjectivity, which Sartre characterizes ontologically as inherently susceptible to bad faith, hence, as *necessarily ambiguous*. This ambiguity is a condition, not an ideal, and bad faith plays upon it, instead of starting out from it in an effort to surmount it in a coordinated synthesis.

> These two aspects of human reality (facticity and transcendence) are and must be capable of valid coordination. However, bad faith seeks neither to coordinate them nor to surmount them in a synthesis. It merely affirms their identity while conserving their differences.[41]

Thus to call Sartre a "theoretician of bad faith"[42]—itself an ambiguous description—shows little desire for understanding, either of the spirit of Sartre's work as a whole or of the explicit statements found within it. We shall return to this point.

BAD FAITH AND SINCERITY

The reader may easily be frightened into skipping the next part of Sartre's chapter. Not content to give the "theory" of bad faith, Sartre expressly states that "for bad faith to be possible, sincerity itself must be in bad faith."[43] This may upset the most authentic champions of objective "virtues." Yet the briefest reflection shows: (a) a virtue in-itself has neither meaning nor value and (b) sincerity would not be "virtuous" were it not precisely an ideal all attempts at which are foredoomed to failure.

Sincerity presents itself as a requirement and not as a state. It is an ideal to strive for and consists in a person's being *for himself* what he *is*. However, this is to desire to constitute oneself in the mode of being of things, while simultaneously revealing that this mode is not that of human reality. Moreover, "if a man is what he is, bad faith is impossible and frankness ceases to be his ideal and becomes his very being."[44] Indeed, frankness itself ceases to exist, for one cannot attain being as what he is *and* as consciousness of what he is.

It is impossible for man to be what he is in the mode of being-in-itself, as we learned from the descriptions of imagination and emotion. In imagination, man

---

41. *EN*, p. 95; *BN*, p. 98.

42. R. Troisfontaines, *Le Choix de J.-P. Sartre*, p. 44. [Sartre has since described *Being and Nothingness* as "an eidetic of bad faith." "Merleau-Ponty vivant," in *Situations, IV* (Paris: Gallimard, 1964), p. 196n; "Merleau-Ponty," in *Situations*, translated by Benita Eisler (New York: George Braziller, 1965), p. 234n.]

43. *EN*, p. 108; *BN*, p. 112.

44. [*EN*, p. 98; *BN*, p. 101.]

makes himself this or that, he *plays at being* this or that, as little Lucien played at loving his mother. Similarly, the sad man makes himself sad; sadness is not what he *is*:

> . . . being-sad is not a ready-made being that I give myself as I might give this book to a friend. I am not in a position to affect myself with being. If I make myself sad the full duration of my sadness must be sustained by me. I cannot ride along on the newly acquired initial impulse, as though my sadness could flow along without my perpetual creation and maintenance of it, like an inert body continuing in motion after the initial impact. There is no inertia in consciousness.[45]

We saw that this illusion of inertia and of acquired motion is really an active stepping up by consciousness of its own emotionality.[46]

These theoretical remarks are confirmed practically by the man who wishes to be sincere and presents himself as *being* the person who did such and such, but then "becomes indignant at the reproach of another and tries to disarm it by asserting he is no longer what he was."[47] Similarly, the apostle of sincerity usually requires the guilty party "to constitute himself a thing precisely in order [for the apostle of sincerity] no longer to treat him as such."[48] He demands that the guilty one "be what he is in order no longer to be it,"[49] that he sink into his facticity to save his transcendence. In sum, "one asks a consciousness, under its character as conscious, to radically destroy itself as such, while instilling in it the hope of renaissance after this destruction." We must conclude that "the champion of sincerity, . . . to the extent he asks a freedom to freely constitute itself as a thing, is himself in bad faith." The sincere man follows an analogous procedure in relation to himself: he evades his evilness by making himself an evil *thing* which he can contemplate as something quite outside his own freedom. In the end "the essential structure of sincerity does not differ from that of bad faith since the sincere man constitutes himself as what he is *in order not to be it*."[50]

In one of Sartre's brief remarks a difficulty seems to arise whose elucidation may clarify our problem:

> There is certainly a sincerity regarding the past, but it does not concern us here: I am sincere if I acknowledge *having had* such and such a pleasure or intention. We shall see that this sincerity is possible because, in falling into the past, man's being is constituted as a being-in-itself. Our concern, however, is with sincerity that seeks to realize itself in the immanence of the present.[51]

45. *EN*, p. 101; *BN*, p. 104.
46. [See above, pp. 31–32.]
47. *EN*, p. 103; *BN*, p. 106.
48. *EN*, pp. 104–105; *BN*, p. 109.
49. *EN*, p. 104; *BN*, p. 108.
50. *EN*, p. 105; *BN*, p. 109.
51. *EN*, p. 106; *BN*, p. 110.

Sincerity seems possible here only as that precision a person willingly exhibits with regard to a past he considers detached from himself. This is altered, though, if I own up, not only to *having had* this pleasure or that intention, but also to being still capable of having it, if, that is, I also attribute that past facticity to my present transcendence. The question is then posed anew for me, by me, in the "present immanence" of my subjectivity, and it is certainly a question of sincerity. Thus, sincerity and bad faith are reconfirmed as problems to the extent a being places itself fundamentally in question. And this is possible only if that question is open-ended—if, having made its appearance in the past, the questioning persists within a present that explicitly continues it.

Bad faith is therefore possible to the extent that sincerity is absent and that one is conscious, not only of this absence, but of the fact that sincerity itself "by nature fails of its goals."[52] If, in my cowardice, my cowardice were not itself "in question," if my being-cowardly were not itself *a* question, my sincerity would then be no problem for it would be natural (which is to say it would no longer be sincerity). But neither, in that case, could I be tempted to see myself in bad faith as *not being cowardly*. It is therefore in some sense necessary both that I *am* and *am not* totally cowardly. If the latter condition did not obtain, I could not even attempt bad faith; if the former did not obtain, I would simply be in good faith in declaring that I am not cowardly.

THE FAITH OF BAD FAITH

One point must be further clarified. The difference that we noted above between bad faith and the lie is the true problem of bad faith and issues from the *faith* implicit in it. Bad faith is neither a cynical lie nor a conviction based on evidence (for that would be good faith). The intention, the very project of bad faith, contains from the start a decision as to what shall constitute truth. The subject surrounds himself with a world of bad faith in which a unique form of evidence appears, namely, "*nonpersuasive evidence.*"

> In this way bad faith . . . decides the exact character of its requirements. It asserts itself wholly in the resolve *not to ask too much*, to consider itself satisfied when still ill persuaded, to force by decisions its adherence to uncertain truths. This initial project of bad faith is a decision in bad faith on the nature of faith. Let us understand clearly that this is not a reflective or voluntary decision but a spontaneous determination of our being. One *puts oneself* in bad faith the way one puts oneself to sleep and one is in bad faith the way one dreams. Once this mode of being [*ce mode d'être*] has been realized, it is as difficult to get out of it as it is to wake oneself. . . .[53]

We recognize in this the voodoo practiced by some of the fundamental attitudes of consciousness. Voodoo yields a magical world made to conscious-

52. [*EN*, p. 107; *BN*, p. 111.]
53. *EN*, p. 109; *BN*, p. 113.

ness's order, but it also limits the future occasions when consciousness might regain its self-possession.

Such willfully unpersuaded faith is no anomaly. For example, every belief, being consciousness (of) *believing*, rests in a way on not-believing. The very fact of consciousness in this case destroys itself *as* a fact:

> No belief is ever belief enough: one never wholly believes what he believes. The primitive project of bad faith is therefore simply the exploitation of this self-destruction of the fact of consciousness. If every belief in good faith is an impossible belief, then there is a place for every impossible belief. My inability to *believe* I am courageous will not discourage me since all beliefs involve not quite believing.[54]

This would seem to assimilate good faith to bad faith. But Sartre adds a cautionary footnote that confirms our comments on his distinction between description of the human condition (psychology, ontology) and man's recovery of himself on the basis of that condition (ethics, morality):

> If it is a matter of indifference whether one is in good or in bad faith—since bad faith reassumes good faith and goes back to the very origin of the project of good faith—that does not mean one cannot radically escape bad faith. However, this presupposes a recovery of the corrupted being by itself which we call authenticity, description of which has no place here.[55]

From Sincerity to Cynicism

Bad faith inevitably results from certain conceptions of sincerity, for example, when it is seen as a perfect coincidence of self with self. So conceived, two attitudes toward sincerity are possible.

On the one hand, one may believe he can achieve this coincidence. The closer one comes, though, the more one tends to exist in the manner of things, which always are what they are. Thus the cynic believes he exhibits his lucidity by saying: "I am cowardly." But his lucidity is that of a camera or of a consciousness in the process of depersonalization, that is, a consciousness that no longer functions, having been reduced to a kind of light vapor or trembling on the surface of being. This would be an "epiphenomenal" consciousness like that of Roquentin in *Nausea* and one can say of it only: "There is consciousness of cowardice." The "realism" popular in the last century and still enjoying amazing success is remarkably well named: it is the systematic transformation of the human into the thing-like. It is a reification, a "thingification" of consciousness. This realism applies to consciousness a scientific attitude that is valid only for nature and so one may equally call it "naturalism." As we have seen, a complete psychology rested on this base of scientism, which also ex-

54. *EN,* p. 110; *BN,* p. 115.
55. *EN,* pp. 111n; *BN,* p. 116n.

cluded all moral perspectives. What is important for us here is that man is not nature, though he may tend indefinitely to naturalize himself. The results of such a tendency are always relative and can only attest to an intervening attitude which manifests the very freedom and distance from oneself that it attempts to deny.

The second possible attitude toward this conception of sincerity is to take such a coincidence as unachievable, thereby promoting it to the rank of an ideal. As against the "cynic," we then have the person who is "modest" or "resigned." Though he knows sincerity is unreachable, he nevertheless takes it as desirable. He says: I never know what I am, I can never capture myself in an idea, I can never have self-confidence. Conscious of his impotency, he loses himself in infinite analysis of the causes and motives behind his acts and of the deep reasons for his feelings, all of which leads to the conclusion that he is never what he is and that he is unknowable to himself. After this every lie to himself becomes possible since, however one construes it, there is always a lie present anyway.

The idealism of sincerity results in an apologetic for bad faith. "Oh, if I could only be sincere.... but I cannot. I live in perpetual unconsciousness of myself, I cannot attain my own truth. My own truth does not exist . . ." We are clearly on the road to casuistry. Wishing the truth about himself to be a thing, he must admit this thing does not exist. And this very inconsistency provides him the refuge from which he rejects all value judgments about him by others or by himself. Finally, if he is religious, he may even pretend to bare himself to God's look, since the examination of his own conscience may have become so refined as to seem impossible. If such a man goes to confession, he renounces any self-examination in advance. The important part of his confession—once he has gone through impersonal sins like greed, cupidity, sexual desire—consists in a blanket accusation of all the sins one never thinks of. He accuses himself of breaking contact, of acts done behind the smoky limits of recognition, of "sins of omission." This last humility is a secret self-defense— what the military call a strategic withdrawal. He carries it out with the self-satisfaction of one who admits the possibility of his guilt, but the concession does not make him feel deeply impaired. "We, the meek.... "

Perhaps nothing better illustrates these two attitudes toward sincerity than the Pascalian formula: "Whoever would play the angel plays the fool."[56] This formula permits two symmetrical applications: (a) he who pretends to have achieved sincerity actually transforms himself into a force of nature that is thereafter incapable of any lucidity; and (b) he who takes sincerity as an inaccessible ideal renounces it in practice with that much greater ease. In the

56. [The full sentence from which Jeanson quotes is: "Man is neither angel nor beast, and it is his bad luck that whoever would play the angel plays the fool." Fragment 358 of Les Pensées, edited by Léon Brunschvicg (Paris: Librairie Garnier Frères, 1930), p. 165; Pascal's Pensées, translated by W. F. Trotter (New York: E. P. Dutton, 1958), p. 99.]

former there is a positive attitude of naturalization, in the latter a negative attitude of renunciation. In both cases consciousness abdicates, rendering itself incapable of acting upon itself: either it considers itself unable to know itself—which *makes* it unable to do so—or it simply *stops trying*, in light of an unattainable ideal.

We must conclude—as Sartre invites us to do—that even though "bad faith" in the ontological sense of "non-coincidence of self with self" is a disease of consciousness, if not its very mode of existence, this description does not ascribe any positive moral meaning. Like all concepts defining the human realm, it is ambiguous: man exists in bad faith but, starting from that, he may either realize himself in bad faith or he may make himself authentic.

From the In-Itself to the For-Itself

In conclusion: "If bad faith is possible, it is in the form of an immediate and permanent threat to every human project, and it is because consciousness, in its being, at once is what it is not and is not what it is."[57]

Now we can see where this places us. We sought to elucidate the "man-world" relation. We interrogated our own interrogative attitude in that regard. This brought us back to negation, which in turn referred us to human reality as freedom. Freedom was revealed to us in anguish, which allowed us to see that consciousness, at the level of temporality, flees all motivation. Finally, these various behaviors of bad faith appeared to imply that consciousness is itself a flight from itself within the instantaneous immanence of its presence to itself.

The last point is the essential one. With it we attain a viewpoint from which we can look back over the complete development of ontology. This progressive storing of attainments, this transition to the essential, must be clearly grasped.

One's most general behaviors are penetrated by interrogation. Human reality is that being for which, in its being, its being is itself in question, and it places itself in question regarding the least of its behaviors. But we have seen that this interrogation, which gnaws away within us, even undermining our most formal affirmations, implies the correlative possibility of non-being in the very heart of being and a power of negation belonging properly to consciousness. At this stage, however, we might still think that consciousness rejects transcendent being so as to assert itself in its immanence; that consciousness denies itself insofar as it is *no longer* or *not yet* this or that, so as to assert its total *presence* to itself. The consequence of such a perspective, which would found negation on the fullness within the instantaneous being of consciousness, is that the Cartesian *cogito* would be admitted as an ontological foundation for human reality, with all its substantialist implications. I doubt the world exists, I suspend the world's existence, and I simultaneously doubt that I previously

57. *EN*, p. 111; *BN*, p. 116.

existed and that I will exist subsequently. I deny everything that is not my doubt itself, my refusal in its instantaneous manifestation. But I thereby apprehend myself as *being* this doubt or refusal; I *am* my thought at the moment it thinks. I coincide with it, and within the instant it is a fullness of being.

We know the difficulty Descartes encountered with this conception: he enclosed himself in the instant from the start because he considered the instant a full thought, a thought-substance, a thinking being. He could then break out of it only by appeal to a metaphysical subterfuge: God guarantees the connection of instants with each other, he sustains consciousness by assuring it from without of a permanence it could never find in its own essence. But this intervention—even assuming it saves the temporal existence of consciousness—imposes on it a compact and massive form of existence by granting it the kind of infinite density that belongs only to the being of things. Thought emanating from the *cogito* would always be filled with its own substance. It would confuse itself with the evidence it wishes to gather, fastening on its own intuitions. One scarcely sees how deduction—the passage from one intuition to another—would be possible. Such a passage implies (for true deduction) that thought ceases to coincide with itself. Deduction is neither the initial intuition nor its simple denial but rather its denial in the direction of something other than itself, a denial that retains it in surpassing it, a signifying movement in which thought must remain at a distance from itself, its objects, and its goal.

In this we can perhaps understand why Spinoza, a Cartesian, was led to conceive consciousness and things—under the headings of thought and extension, respectively—as two strictly corresponding modes of expression of the divine substance. In thus pushing the thesis to its logical conclusion, one sees the collapse of that illusory freedom Descartes had accorded consciousness. We can think solely according to what is true as our thoughts are predetermined to rigorously express the reality of the supreme Being. Truth and reality are here confounded. Error is a non-being, a thought that is not even false but rather illusory, an imaginative mirage due to an illegitimate compromise between thought and extension.

Perhaps Spinoza illuminates the Cartesian tendency only at the cost of caricaturing it. Descartes believes in a power of doubt or suspension of judgment, a freedom in refusal that is quite absent in Spinoza. Yet—and this is the most instructive point in our reference to the Cartesian *cogito*—this very freedom in refusal congeals consciousness in its negation: consciousness *becomes* refusal and only that. Indeed, one has trouble seeing how consciousness might ever renounce its refusal, disown its negation, so as to regain belief and affirmation. Consciousness is closed in on itself by its own consistency and self-sufficiency. No longer can it surpass itself toward what it has been or shall be, or toward the world—which has ceased to be its inevitable object. The Cartesian *cogito* is nontemporal and lacks a situation in the world.

The reason for this is clear: the *cogito* in question has lost its direct, natural complement, and yet it is taken to be the initial *cogito*, the universal foundation of all particular thought.

Instead of starting with "I think such and such," one starts with "I think that I think." One is straightaway at the level of reflection, as if consciousness could be revealed to itself without also being the revelation of what is other than itself. This last role is forever lost, for if this revelation's object is suppressed at the start it cannot be regained at the finish. Moreover, this presumed thought about thought is merely thought *simpliciter,* thought in-itself, thinking nature.

However, we have seen (a) that all particular thought, insofar as it is conscious thinking, contains its own foundation and (b) that this foundation is just what grounds the possibility of a reflection, and not the reverse. The reflective *cogito* asserts "I think that I think such and such," but it rests upon a pre-reflective *cogito* which is "consciousness (of) itself inasmuch as it is consciousness *of* something." There is no thinking that does not posit an object. But all thinking carries in itself this intimate separation whereby it apprehends itself as positing an object. All consciousness (of) belief is belief *of* such and such. But, inversely, all belief is consciousness (of) belief.

Thus belief can never be full belief, since, by being apprehended as belief, "it is already no longer belief, it is troubled belief."[58] At the same time, consciousness (of) belief can never be simply that, for it thereby becomes the reflective consciousness *of* the attitude of belief. As we noted regarding emotion, this would make such phenomena incomprehensible, since emotion occurs only to the extent consciousness moves itself—but without saying so, without "thetic" consciousness of doing so. Emotion is conceivable only in the realm of the unreflected, which is where consciousness (of) itself is to be found.

We may conclude that the reflective, Cartesian *cogito* withdraws consciousness from time and world, effecting a brutal and final separation. Consciousness is thereby portrayed as an instantaneous substance that faces a material substance which also exists solely in the instant. Now let us abandon the grasp of consciousness implicit in this *cogito* and return to the *cogito* preceding reflection, to the pre-reflective presence of consciousness to itself. To be sure, we also find a separation here, a fissure, a sort of "distance-nothingness" that is irreducible. But it has meaning only on the basis of intentionality, that is, of temporality and presence to a world. In this way we uncover the transcendence (either toward oneself—as other than what one is—or toward things) that lies in the heart of immanence. We shall henceforth be able to understand every attitude of consciousness by starting with this negation, this nothingness that constitutes consciousness as such. This is because we are no longer enclosed in the instantaneity of such a negation. We can instead rediscover this negation as the very meaning of every positive behavior.

58. *EN*, p. 117; *BN*, p. 121.

The work's design will henceforth be more visible: a movement of essential-ization [*un mouvement d'essentialisation*] in order to understand existence, an effort that starts from the concrete and aims at disclosing that which consti-tutes the meaning of the concrete. Because of the initial descriptions this effort afforded, we have secured from consciousness its essence; it remains to show that this essence is such that we are in no danger of remaining its captive. And after that we shall bring out the various aspects of the existence of this consciousness in situation.

The reader can rest assured that the essentials have now been covered. From here on we shall take much larger strides, analyzing only those positions that are important for us, namely, those that concern our perspective in this work.

Chapter 4

================

Solitary Consciousness

We must recognize what we have just described: a being that is, to itself, its own nothingness. This being nihilates itself because it is the perpetual project of not being itself in order that it may be present to itself. "The law of being of the *for-itself*, as the ontological foundation of consciousness, is to be itself in the form of presence to itself."[1]

We have also seen that while consciousness causes its own manner of being through its nihilating power, *nothing* is the cause of consciousness itself.[2] The presence of consciousness cannot be explained either by what is other than itself or by itself. The for-itself "exists because there is something in it of which it is not itself the foundation, namely, its presence to the world." This explains why "in our apprehension of ourselves, we appear with the characteristics of an unjustifiable fact."[3]

Phenomenologists call this contingent condition of the for-itself its *facticity*, its presence as a fact. On the one hand, the for-itself is the negation of this condition, which is simply its own being-there: in relation to that condition the for-itself is a freedom and a nothingness, never ceasing to nihilate and surpass it. Yet, on the other hand, the for-itself is connected with the in-itself through this same condition: "The for-itself is sustained by a perpetual contingency for which it assumes responsibility and which it assimilates into itself without ever being able to suppress it."[4] It retains this contingency as a "memory of being,"[5] and as a result, it experiences "nausea." In this context nausea corresponds to anguish: "Just as my nihilating freedom apprehends itself in anguish, so the for-itself is conscious of its facticity: it has the feeling of its total gratuitousness, it grasps itself as being there *for nothing*, as being *in the way*."[6]

Whereas transcendence is the evasion and surpassing of oneself, facticity is existence in the mode of things or consolidation within being. Bad faith rests

1. *EN*, p. 119; *BN*, p. 124.
2. Cf. *EN*, p. 22n; *BN*, p. 16n.
3. *EN*, p. 122; *BN*, pp. 127–128.
4. *EN*, p. 125; *BN*, p. 131.
5. [*EN*, p. 127; *BN*, p. 133.]
6. *EN*, p. 126; *BN*, p. 132.

on this opposition. Sincerity's ideal is for consciousness to be what it is, yet to be so in the mode of transcendence; it wishes to say "I am this or that" without thereby placing that very affirmation in question. From now on we shall have to consider such affirmations futile: I affirm something of myself only because it is not obvious; however, in doing so I make myself a presence that is ambiguous, even in my own eyes. When one questions oneself on what one most fundamentally is, concern is usually focused not on hair color but on what one is in the mode of transcendence, hence, on what one can never fully be. This concern arises in answer to oneself, a self that must itself be surpassed in order to be thus answered. Consequently, the only being that can answer itself is one that is not what it is, that can place itself in question yet hold itself together in taking on the weight of the answer it receives from itself. Anguish is the obsession to perpetually answer. It is experienced because one has not yet answered, one is not yet defined, one remains utterly free and unforeseeable.

The for-itself, anguished over being *for* itself and therefore merely yet-to-be, wishes also to be *in* itself, to already be this or that, yet without ceasing to be itself. It suffers from its lack of thickness and of being, but it does not wish to be utterly abolished within being. It dreams of being in-and-for-itself, thereby retaining the benefits of presence to self that are assured by its nihilating power, without the inconveniences of distance from self. It dreams, in short, of *being-itself* [*être-soi*].

> Thus the perpetually absent being that haunts the for-itself is precisely itself congealed into an in-itself. It is the impossible synthesis of the for-itself and the in-itself: it wishes to found itself as a being rather than as a nothingness, retaining the necessary translucidity of consciousness along with the self-coincidence of being-in-itself. It wishes to conserve that return to self which conditions every necessity and grounding. But this return to self would be effected without distance; it would be an identity with self and in no way a presence to self. . . . In this way, human reality arises in the presence of its own totality or self as lack of that totality.[7]

This basic wish to attain selfhood is the same need to *be* that haunted Roquentin. This was a need to found his own existence, to make it necessary and "solid." He seeks to live "adventures," which Anny calls "perfect moments." These are morsels of life closed in on themselves, full and dense, like feelings that never get outside of themselves.

> This need also underlies the drama of Baudelaire's life, according to Sartre: Baudelaire's famous lucidity is simply an effort at *recovery*. He must recover himself and—since to see is to appropriate—he must see himself. . . . He sought his own *nature*. . . . Instead his glance met the human condition. This condition of freedom, gratuitousness, and abandonment which made him afraid is

7. *EN*, p. 133; *BN*, p. 140.

the lot of every man and not his in particular. Can one ever touch or see *himself?* Perhaps the fixed and singular essence he sought is visible to others only. Perhaps one must be *outside* to grasp its characteristics. Perhaps one *is* not for himself in the manner of a thing. Perhaps one *is* not at all. If one were always in question, always in suspense, perhaps one would be perpetually obliged to *make* himself. . . . To recover oneself within one's inner life means considering consciousness a thing so as to embrace it. . . . Moved by pride and rancor, Baudelaire sought throughout his life to *make himself a thing* in the eyes of others and in his own eyes. He wished to stand aloof from the great social fete like a statue: definitive, opaque, unassimilable. In a word, he wanted to *be*, by which we understand the stubborn and strictly defined mode of being of an object. But Baudelaire would never for a moment have tolerated in this being, which he wanted to force on the attention of others and enjoy himself, the passivity and unconsciousness of an implement. He certainly wanted to be an object, but not simply a chance fact. This object was to truly be his own; it would *save* him, provided it could be established that it was self-created and self-sustaining. But this refers us back to the mode of presence belonging to consciousness and freedom which we shall call *existence*. . . .[8]

The notion of failure reappears here. "In its being, the for-itself is failure since it is the foundation *only* of itself as nothingness."[9] Consciousness is always unhappy, being constantly haunted by its own totality, "which it is without being able to be it."[10] Indeed, consciousness is consciousness only through its own lack regarding that totality.

This totality is *value*: "there can be no consciousness that is not haunted by its value," and, moreover, "human reality in the wide sense encompasses the for-itself and value." As such, value is both "present and out of reach, lived simply as the concrete meaning of that lack which constitutes my present being."[11]

What a given for-itself lacks in order to *be itself* is that which it is not but must be in order to complete itself. Desire, for example, would like to be perpetually satisfied, which entails never ceasing to exist qua desire. Desire lacks satisfaction. However, satisfaction is desired, not so that it can take the place of desire, but so that it can complete the desire in a perfected totality. A thirsty person is haunted by a person who drinks and whom the former would become without ceasing to be thirsty, for that entails ceasing to take pleasure in drinking.

This absent, drinking, for-itself, which is lacked by the present, thirsty, for-itself, is the latter's *possibility*. Human reality is for itself its own possibility

8. [Jean-Paul Sartre, Introduction to *Ecrits intimes de Baudelaire* (Paris: Gallimard, 1947), pp. 28–29, 46–47, 77 and 90; *Baudelaire*, translated by Martin Turnell (Norfolk: New Directions, 1950), pp. 25, 41–42, 68 and 79.]
9. *EN*, p. 132; *BN*, p. 139.
10. [*EN*, p. 134; *BN*, p. 140.]
11. *EN*, p. 138; *BN*, pp. 145–146.

and defines itself accordingly. It defines itself by that part of itself that it is not or, in other words,

> as escape from itself toward.... Doubt can be understood only on the basis of the constantly open possibility that future evidence may "remove" it. . . . No fact of consciousness is ever *this* consciousness, properly speaking . . . —a consciousness, once one wishes to define it as doubt, perception, thirst, etc., always refers us to the nothingness of what is not yet.[12]

In so doing, it already is that nothingness as its own possibility.

We are now in a position to understand (a) that "the nothingness which separates human reality from itself is at the origin of time"[13] and (b) that tied to this nihilation of human reality is the nihilation of the totality of being—which enables there to be a "world." The possible for-itself that the present for-itself needs in order to become self-identical can be situated only in relation to a world.

The world is "what human reality surpasses toward itself or, to borrow Heidegger's definition: 'that starting with which human reality proclaims what it is.' "[14] It is "the infinite distance separating us from ourselves"[15] and "the being beyond which the for-itself projects the coincidence with itself . . . [,] the distance of infinite being beyond which man must rejoin his possibilities."[16]

THE MEANING OF THE PAST

In this way being for itself

> is transcended under our eyes toward value and possibilities; we have been unable to contain it in the substantialist limits of instantaneity of the Cartesian *cogito*. . . . if the *cogito* rejects instantaneity and transcends itself toward its possibilities, it can only be through a temporal surpassing. It is "within time" that the for-itself is its own possibilities in the mode of "not being" them; it is within time that my possibilities appear on the horizon of the world which they make mine.[17]

Let us therefore attempt briefly to fix and describe the principal aspects of Temporality.

First of all, *the past* is always this or that past, which means it is always the past of this or that present. Far from explaining the present, the past acquires

12. *EN*, pp. 144–145; *BN*, pp. 152–153.
13. *EN*, p. 146; *BN*, p. 154.
14. *EN*, p. 148; *BN*, p. 157.
15. J.-P. Sartre, "Qu'est-ce que la littérature?" *Les Temps modernes*, no. 17 (February 1947), p. 801; *Situations, II* (Paris: Gallimard, 1948), p. 108; *What is Literature?*, translated by Bernard Frechtman (London: Methuen, 1950), p. 42.
16. *EN*, p. 146; *BN*, p. 155.
17. *EN*, p. 149; *BN*, p. 158.

its meaning only in relation to the present. Consequently, the past can appear as such only for a being who in some way *is* his own past: ". . . the only beings who have a past are those for whom—in their being—their past being is in question; these are beings who *have to be* their past."[18]

A similar point is made by Raymond Aron in his remarkable *Introduction to the Philosophy of History*:

> . . . history is inseparable from man's very essence. . . . man has a history because he becomes through time, because he constructs works that survive him, because he collects the monuments of the past. . . . humanity has a history because it is seeking a vocation. . . . Man alone has a history because his history forms part of his nature or, better, is his nature. . . . we have distinguished human history, which is defined by the conservation and conscious revival of the past, from all natural history. . . . The human species alone is engaged in an adventure whose end is not death but self-realization.[19]

But how can the past that is mine when I say "I used to be tired" also be mine in the present? How does it happen that I can say of my past both that it *used to be* and that it *is* my past? This conjunction is possible because in a sense I *am* my past. I do not disconnect [*désolidarise*] myself from it. If I do so voluntarily on some particular point I only confirm the responsibility I spontaneously assume for the whole of it. "At the limit [of my life], at that infinitesimal instant of my death, I am henceforth only my past. It alone will define me."[20]

Sartre cites Malraux's formula: "What is terrible about death is that it transforms life into Destiny."[21]

This is one of the essential themes in Sartre's play *No Exit*. We see Garcin at odds with his cowardice, but this cowardice is *totally in the past*: being dead, he can neither return to it nor assume it. He is now only what he has been. The chips are down and the final card has been played.

> Death reunites us with ourselves. Through it, eternity has changed us into ourselves. At the moment of death we *are*, that is, we are defenseless before the judgments of others. They can now decide *in truth* what we are. We no longer have any chance of escaping the summation that an all-knowing intelligence might draw up.[22]

Yet we hear Garcin saying of his former comrades:

18. *EN*, p. 157; *BN*, p. 167.

19. Raymond Aron, *Introduction à la philosophie de l'histoire* (Paris: Gallimard, 1938), pp. 37–44; *Introduction to the Philosophy of History: An Essay on the Limits of Historical Objectivity*, translated by George J. Irwin (Boston: Beacon Press, 1961), pp. 36–43.

20. *EN*, p. 158; *BN*, 169.

21. [Quoted in *EN*, pp. 156, 158; *BN*, pp. 165–166, 169.]

22. *EN*, p. 159; *BN*, p. 169.

I left my life in their hands. . . . In those days I used to be a man of action . . . If I could only rejoin them for a day... I'd fling their lie back at them! But now I'm out of the running; they'll pass judgment without me, which is their right since I'm dead.[23]

And later: "I died too soon. I wasn't allowed time to carry out *my* acts." To which Inès answers: "One always dies too soon—or too late. And yet life is over with, finished; the deed is done and you must add it all up. You are only your life."[24]

The past appears here as that in us of the *in-itself*: ". . . the past is the ever-growing totality [*totalité*] of the in-itself that we are. Yet, so long as we are not dead, we are not this in-itself in the mode of identity. Instead, we *have to be it.*"[25]

We do not coincide with our past, and this is precisely why we must assume it.

Put another way: I *am* not my past to the extent that I *was* it. The for-itself "can assume its being only through a recovery of it, which places [the for-itself] *at a distance* from it."[26] To seize upon this or that particular past is always to seize upon the past as something one has already ceased to be. "The past is the in-itself that I am insofar as *it has been surpassed.*"[27]

In all this, the past is the facticity peculiar to the for-itself. Consciousness obviously cannot reenter its past since the latter is in-itself while the former is for-itself. Instead: ". . . the past is what I am without being able to live it. The past is substance."[28]

This last observation sheds light on the difficulty we found in the Cartesian version of the *cogito*. We have criticized it as a substantializing of consciousness by enclosing the latter in the instant. We can now be more exact: the Cartesian *cogito* can only enclose consciousness in a *past* instant, which as such transforms it into a thing, and so, strictly speaking, one should say: "I think, therefore I was." As a result, though, the "I think" is rendered incapable of acting upon the "I was." Since consciousness had not been apprehended at the unreflective level of consciousness (of) self, it had to be radically severed from oneself and posited as a psychism, thereby compelling one to regard it reflectively as inefficacious.

Psychologists make the same mistake. "Because they looked at the psychic

---

23. J.-P. Sartre, *Huis Clos*, in *Théâtre* (Paris: Gallimard, 1947), p. 160 (scene 5); *No Exit*, translated by Stuart Gilbert, in *No Exit and Three Other Plays by Jean-Paul Sartre* (New York: Vintage Books, 1955), p. 40.
24. *Huis Clos*, in *Théâtre*, p. 165 (scene 5); *No Exit*, pp. 44–45.
25. *EN*, p. 159; *BN*, 169.
26. *EN*, p. 162; *BN*, p. 172.
27. *EN*, p. 162; *BN*, p. 173.
28. *EN*, p. 163; *BN*, p. 173.

mechanism *in the past*, psychologists supposed consciousness to be a quality that might or might not affect the past but without modifying the latter in its being in either case."[29]

We must remark, finally, that the past is the exact inverse of value. A being who moves toward value seeks the solidity of the in-itself in the mode of the for-itself: he wishes *to be* without ceasing to be *conscious*. However, in "passing" into the past, the for-itself is "reassumed and inundated by the in-itself."[30] Being *simpliciter* takes possession of conscious being. But since the past and value are each syntheses of the in-itself and the for-itself, a consciousness wishing to flee value as such, that is, to abolish the anguish implicit in value's perpetual lack of being, will turn to the past in order to *realize* value in it. We are reminded of Roquentin's observation that the various attempts to ground his being are capable of justifying his past only.[31]

This is why Baudelaire's project of self-recovery entails a flight into the Past.

> To see himself not as he had made himself but . . . as he was, he would have to grasp his own Nature. And this Nature belongs to the past. What I am is what I was, since my present freedom always places in question the nature that I have acquired. Yet Baudelaire had not chosen to renounce this lucid consciousness that constitutes his dignity and uniqueness. His dearest wish is *to be*, like a stone or a statue, in the tranquil repose of immutability; but he wished this impenetrability, this calm and permanence, this total adhesion of a self to itself, to be conferred precisely upon his free consciousness as such. The Past is what offered him the image of this impossible synthesis of being and existence. My past is me. But this me is definitive.[32]

> . . . he asked from the idea of suicide this small service, this chicanery, which would allow him to consider his life irremediable and complete, like an eternal destiny or, perhaps, a closed-off past. Above all, he saw in the act of ending his days the ultimate recovery of his being: he will be in the driver's seat. By ending his life he will transform it into an *essence* that will be both always given and always created by himself. In this way he would deliver himself from the unbearable feeling of being *in the way* in the world. However, to enjoy the results of his suicide, he obviously must survive it. This is why Baudelaire chose to constitute himself as a *survivor*. And if he did not kill himself in a single blow, at least he makes as though each of his acts is the symbolic equivalent of a suicide he could not commit.[33]

29. *EN*, p. 163; *BN*, p. 174.
30. [*EN*, p. 164; *BN*, p. 175.]
31. [See, for example, J.–P. Sartre, *La Nausée* (Paris: Gallimard, 1938), pp. 49, 50; *Nausea,* translated by Lloyd Alexander (Norfolk, Conn.: New Directions, 1959), pp. 48, 49.]
32. Introduction to *Ecrits intimes de Baudelaire*, p. 148; *Baudelaire*, p. 170.
33. Introduction to *Ecrits intimes de Baudelaire*, p. 166; *Baudelaire*, p. 189.

THE MEANING OF THE PRESENT

The Past is in-itself. The Present is for-itself.

"We claim first of all that it is impossible to grasp the Present in the form of an instant, since the instant would be the moment when the present *is*."[34] As we have seen, however, this is a character of the past and not of the present.

The Present is the presence of the for-itself to something. This "something" can only be the in-itself. The Present comes to being through the for-itself, which "presents" the totality of beings as simultaneously existing. But if two worldly beings need a for-itself as witness in order to co-exist and to be present to each other, then the for-itself must be able to be its own witness of co-existence, witness of its own presence to being. How can this be done? Actually we acquired much earlier the elements for an answer: the for-itself's presence to being is its intentional directedness outside itself, toward being. As we learned from the study of the imagination, however, intentionality must be conceived as an internal bond: consciousness can not reach toward a being without also denying it is itself that being. We have since seen that negation is also the essential attitude of consciousness toward itself. And we can now see that this same relation indissoluably links consciousness to the world. Consciousness and world are not two juxtaposed realities: the world appears *only as* nihilated by a consciousness that refuses to be it. Consequently, the for-itself is "witness of itself to itself as *not being*" being in-itself. It is

> witness of itself in the presence of being as not-being this being. . . . the For-itself constitutes itself outside, starting with the thing as negation of it. . . . And the present is precisely this negation of being, this escape from being inasmuch as being is *there* as that from which one escapes. The For-itself is present to being in the form of flight; the Present is a perpetual flight before being. . . . the present is not; instead it presentifies itself [*se présentifie*] in the form of flight.[35]

The present is, then, the presentification of the for-itself. Yet, since the present is the non-being of the for-itself, "it has its being outside itself, in front and behind. Behind, it *was* its past and in front it *shall be* its future. . . . At present it is not what it is (past) and it is what it is not (future)."[36]

THE MEANING OF THE FUTURE

The mark of the present is therefore a flight, an "escape from being toward...."[37]

Toward what? Obviously toward whatever the for-itself lacks in order to

34. *EN*, p. 168; *BN*, p. 179.
35. EN, p. 167–168; *BN*, p. 178–179.
36. *EN*, p. 168; *BN*, p. 179.
37. *EN*, p. 170; *BN*, p. 182.

be itself. The for-itself flees toward that possible with which it must coincide if it is to be. The Future is just this lack. The future tears the present away from the in-itself of the instant.

> There is not a moment of my consciousness that is not . . . defined through an internal relationship to a future. Whether I write, or smoke, or drink, or rest, the meaning of my consciousnesses is always at a distance, down there, outside.[38]

Heidegger expresses this by saying that man is "a being of distances."[39] To this Sartre adds—referring to the meaning the existing individual draws from what is not yet, a meaning he thinks Baudelaire clearly perceived—that man is a being "who is defined much more by the goal and terminus of his projects than by what one can know of him when limited to the passing moment."[40]

Those aspects of the possible described above allow us to understand that

> . . . this Future that I have to be is simply my *possibility* of presence to being that is beyond being. . . . I am my Future in the constant perspective of the possibility of not being it. The anguish we have described above, which results from my not being sufficiently that Future which I have to be and which gives its direction [*sens*] to my present, this anguish is because I am a being whose meaning [*sens*] is always problematic.[41]

Because of my being free, the Future is never *realized.* I can never rejoin it qua Future, for otherwise it would pre-determine my for-itself that is to come: the Future is not; it possibilizes itself.

PSYCHIC TEMPORALITY

We must pursue Sartre's description of the weighing down and objectifica-tion suffered by this original temporality when it comes under the glance of "impure" reflective consciousness. There is an "initial, spontaneous (but not *original*) reflective movement"[42] that is as yet unaware of the necessity accord-ing to which the for-itself must *be* for-itself. Consequently, it apprehends the unreflective as an in-itself. Henceforth this consciousness *of* enduring consti-tutes "the psychic": the psyche in the form of a succession of psychic facts. The three dimensions of original temporality are *captured* within it.

> Psychic time is only the linked collection of temporal objects. But its essential difference from original temporality is that it *is*, while the latter temporalizes itself. As such, psychic time must be constituted out of the past only, and the future can only be a past that will come after the present past.[43]

38. *EN*, p. 170; *BN*, p. 181.
39. [*EN*, p. 54; *BN*, p. 52. See *Sein und Zeit*, pp. 105–110; *Being and Time*, pp. 138–144.]
40. Introduction to *Ecrits intimes de Baudelaire*, p. 26; *Baudelaire*, p. 38.
41. *EN*, pp. 173–174; *BN*, pp. 185–186. ["*Sens*" can mean both 'sense', or 'meaning', and 'direction'.]
42. [*EN*, p. 207; *BN*, p. 224.]
43. *EN*, p. 218; *BN*, p. 236.

This helps us to understand the psychologists' error in addressing them-selves to an objectivated, exteriorized psyche quite opposite to the Cartesian *cogito*. Believing they grasp consciousness in an instantaneous intuition, they in fact grasp it reflectively, hence, necessarily, as past.

Sartre's final observation on the "objectivation of original temporality in the in-itself" is noteworthy:

> It constitutes the initial sketch of an "outside"; the for-itself sees itself almost as conferring an outside on its own eyes. But this outside is purely virtual. We shall later see being-for-another *realize* the sketch of this "outside."[44]

KNOWLEDGE

Sartre starts the chapter on transcendence by looking back over the terrain covered and the problem at issue, which is that of the original relation of human reality to the being of phenomena (or being-in-itself).

The solution did not lie in positing an external relationship to unite two initially separate substances since: "The concrete appears as the synthetic totality of which both consciousness and the phenomenon alike are only articu-lations."[45] We should be on our guard even here: "consciousness" and "phe-nomenon" are abstractions in relation to this synthetic totality because they depend on and reflect one another. At the same time, however, "the being of phenomena, as an in-itself that is what it is, cannot be considered an abstrac-tion. It needs only itself in order to be and refers only to itself."[46]

This underlines the ineluctable being-there of that absolute term, the in-itself, in relation to which the intentionality of consciousness is defined. It also re-minds us that the for-itself must itself be a presence to the in-itself.

> One must search solely in the for-itself for the key to that relation to being that is called, for example, knowledge. The for-itself is responsible in its being for its relation to the in-itself, or, if you prefer, it produces itself originarily on the foundation of a relation to the in-itself.[47]

The for-itself does not create the in-itself. But the in-itself cannot cause its own presence to the for-itself, since, by nature, being in-itself is *without rela-tions*. The for-itself must therefore constitute itself as a relation to the in-itself.

And this is the problem posed by knowledge. In our study of this problem we shall obviously have to emphasize thetic consciousness *of* the object. Such consciousness has concerned us up to now only as the indispensable condition for all non-thetic consciousness (of) self.

The first result of the investigation of this problem is that

44. *EN*, p. 218; *BN*, p. 237.
45. *EN*, p. 219; *BN*, p. 238.
46. *EN*, p. 219; *BN*, p. 239.
47. *EN*, p. 220; *BN*, p. 239.

to know is to *realize,* in the two senses of that term. To know is to cause there to be being while having to be the reflected negation of this being: the *real* is *realization.* We shall define transcendence as that internal, realizing negation which uncovers the in-itself while also determining the for-itself in its being.[48]

That is to say, the for-itself knows itself through being only by uncovering the positive characters of being. For example, if the in-itself were suppressed, the for-itself would grasp itself neither as extended nor as unextended; it would be "a-spatial" in a manner quite beyond these two categories. However, the presence of the for-itself to being reveals the for-itself to itself as unextended while revealing being as extended. The consequences of this double revelation are complicated by the fact that *concrete* consciousness is both a nihilating for-itself and a psychism, that is, an in-itself. As a result, such consciousness can never grasp itself absolutely under the categories either of the unextended or of the extended. Yet it would have to be able to do so if consciousness and world had been posited a priori as the purely unextended and the purely extended, respectively. In point of fact, though, consciousness must perpetually *realize* its unextended character; it must always counteract passivity, materiality, and inertia through the forms in which it causes the in-itself to appear. "It is in and through the extended character of the transcendent in-itself that the for-itself makes known to itself and realizes its own unextended-ness."[49]

The errors of idealism, realism, and separatist dualism are evident here. The first would constitute the extended by starting from the unextended; the second would introduce the double of the extended object "into" consciousness; the last, as we have seen, would juxtapose two natures that had been constituted in advance as the inverse of each other. Bergson makes this last mistake, both in opposing pure perception of the object to pure unlocated memory, and in describing the duration as being a purely qualitative hetero-geneity—prior to its contamination by space in the artificializing processes of intelligence. Such a duration is in fact nothing at all, since it is not a function. Bergson presents it as a being, indeed the very being and nature of consciousness itself; but as such it is incapable of appearing to itself. Regarding Berg-sonian intuition—a sort of prospecting in the depths of mental life far below its superficial appearances—Pradines remarks:

> One may ask whether it has simply replaced *the superficial* with the *artificial* and whether it is not at the expense of our actual mental life that one obtains this concentrated essence of so-called spirituality, which has been emptied of every element of objectivity, quantity, and space. To speak of *states of con-sciousness* without indicating *what it is* that they are conscious of . . . is to speak not of psychic phenomena, which have a meaning . . . but of *natural phe-*

48. *EN,* p. 228; *BN,* p. 249.
49. *EN,* p. 228; *BN,* p. 248.

nomena, which simply are because they are, and not because of any meaning they carry. The sole significance of states of consciousness is to enable us to understand *things.* Thus such interpenetration of subject and object, of quality and quantity, of duration and space, is not an impurity lying in the way of understanding spiritual life but the very condition without which that life would not even merit being called spiritual.[50]

This may enable us to better grasp the in-itself in Sartre's ontology, which has been reproached for using this notion to unjustifiably run together being that is transcendent to consciousness and consciousness's own past. Indeed, this example touches on a central point in Sartre's philosophy. Let us try to see it clearly.

We have just noted that the relation of consciousness to being could only be an internal one that is constitutive of consciousness. Consciousness *by itself* must be a relation of the for-itself to the in-itself, or else it could never be related to the in-itself. That is also why we defined consciousness as a nothingness that maintains itself only at the price of a perpetual nihilation. In more direct terms, consciousness is the perpetual maintenance of tension against the perpetual risk of slackening, and this internal tension, which substantially is *nothing,* grounds every particular intention of consciousness toward the world. This or that intentionality—whether it be directed toward an object in the world, a past consciousness, or an absent object, and whether it be perception, memory, or imagination—rests, if you will, on a foundation of tension that negates all that *is.* From the perspective of consciousness, the in-itself is everything against which this tension sets itself (the being of the phenomenon, one's personal past, etc.). The particular nihilations, which realize the real by positing it as opposite to consciousness, imply a foundational nihilation that makes a nothingness of consciousness itself, thereby allowing consciousness to oppose all that is. In a parallel manner, all realizations, all particular materializations that appear to consciousness by revealing it to itself, imply a foundational in-itself—that is, being in its absolutely transcendent mode—which concentrates in itself every possible refusal that emanates from consciousness.

There is little that is truly original in this. Bergson himself described psyche and matter as the opposition between a tension and a slackening. If one accepts the preceding remarks, his only error was to have substantialized this tension in a "vital impulse" ["*élan vital*"], making it into the absolute reality. Matter is thereby conceived as a degradation, the *result* of a "relapse" of that impulse.

For Sartre, however, matter is an opposite pole which constantly solicits this relapse. The tension of consciousness is for him a true act: *considered as a thing it is nothing.* This tension is constantly struggling to keep from being

50. Maurice Pradines, *Traité de psychologie générale,* vol. 1 (Paris: Presses Universitaires de France, 1943), pp. xxiii and xxiv.

caught, snatched up, or stuck by the solicitation of matter, that is, by its own fascination with being which is what it is.

To anticipate our junction with the moral perspective, it would be vain to demand of being some effort regarding itself. It would be equally vain to speak of moral consciousness if one had begun by making consciousness in general *a being* and then expected it to exhibit the features of *an act*. All things that have being *within* consciousness are precisely what consciousness itself is not: they issue from the various realizations by which consciousness opposes itself to the in-itself in order to constitute the latter in phenomena. It is therefore inevitable that the nihilating power of consciousness, unable to indefinitely sustain everything and remain present to everything, will allow phenomena to be reabsorbed one by one into the in-itself from which consciousness had made them emerge *for itself*.

Thus "the letter" is frequently opposed to "the spirit" that gives it meaning, like a diminution of that spirit that threatens to extinguish it. We are compelled to constantly *deny* the letter by means of the spirit: negating it as letter and surpassing it toward its meaning.

The Known

If knowledge is realization we must specify that of which it is the realization. We have seen that the for-itself is presence to being inasmuch as it must constitute itself as not being this being. But we do not yet understand how it can be present to *such* being, that is, to this rather than that. This must be grasped through features of the for-itself that we have already recognized.

First, the for-itself, having to be its own totality, makes a sort of rendezvous with its own possibles on the other side of being. It thereby makes being a totality that it must surpass toward itself. Consequently, *there must be*, for it, *the whole of being* in the form of *a world*.

Only on the foundation of the totality of being can there be *this* or *that* being for the for-itself. It is always present only to this or that, but this is because it has made itself present to the world. All perception must situate itself on an ontological foundation of presence to the world, and, conversely, the world is revealed with respect to each singular perception as its foundation.

What can this mean if not that human reality must surpass its own original and radical negation of being? If human reality confined itself to not being the in-itself, it would be no more than this negation. It would be nothingness, whereas we know that "nothingness *is* not." Its not-being the in-itself must therefore be a negative form of that total negation; that is, it must not be this or that. The total negation must constitute itself as partial and differentiated negations in surpassing its fundamental negation. It is a certain concrete reality that the negation must at present *not be*. "The being that *I am not* presently, insofar as it appears on the basis of the totality of being, is the *this*. It is what I am not at present insofar as I must in no way be being. . . ."[51]

The *this* becomes diluted with the undifferentiated totality of being and dissolves back into its ground at the very moment that the partial negation dissolves back into *its* "fundamental negation"—in order to allow for a new negative structure and a new "this."

The world is therefore the undifferentiated correlate of my fundamental negation of being. Yet it is also realized in successive concrete realities and appears as their ideal totality—which seems to contain them in advance. In the same way,

> . . . when progressively approaching a landscape that had been given in large groupings, we see objects appear that are given as already being there as elements in a discontinuous collection of *this*es. . . . "[52]

The relation between the *this* and the totality must evidently be external. It must change nothing and leave the *this* intact insofar as it is being-in-itself. The totality, which constantly perishes as such, never *appearing* as a totality, is the ground against which the "this" appears. And this vanishing of the continuous in the direction of the discontinuous, this essential instability which fosters disintegration of the continuous into external multiplicity, is called *space*. Space is therefore the necessity for the world to appear to me here or there while it disappears qua world. I can never thematize the world in my perception or have a thetic consciousness *of* the world. This is why, in studying the imagination, the imagined object, which is stable and closed in on itself, was found to be contrasted with the perceived object, with its perpetual "hemorrhaging." Merleau-Ponty also finds this meaning in perception of an object. I can grasp an object as a plenum only if I have perceived the totality of the world, if—wherever I see the object—it continues to sustain this exterior relation to the whole world. Thus I form the imaged object apart, outside of relations with perceived objects and objective space. But the perceived object can be closed in on itself only at the cost of a synthesis of all possible perspectives, and I can never hold the world in hand in this way. The perceived object always appears to me on a horizon that leaves it "incomplete and open. . . . Through this opening the substantiality of the object flows away."[53]

Let us briefly review quality, quantity, and potentialities, which are the determinations of being revealed here.

In its surge toward being, the for-itself reveals "things," which are thereby affected by certain structures:

51. *EN,* p. 231; *BN,* p. 252.
52. *EN,* p. 232; *BN,* p. 254.
53. Maurice Merleau-Ponty, *Phénoménologie de la perception* (Paris: Gallimard, 1945), p. 84; *Phenomenology of Perception,* translated by Colin Smith (New York: Humanities Press, 1962), p. 70.

Quality is simply the being of the *this* when considered outside of all external relation with the world or with other *this*es. . . . The lemon actually permeates all of its qualities, and each of its qualities permeates in turn each of the others. It is the lemon's sourness that is yellow; it is the lemon's yellow that is sour. . . . The fluidity, the tepidity, the bluish color, the wavy mobility of a swimming pool's water are all given at once through each other and this total interpenetration is what is called the *this*.[54]

Quantity, on the other hand,

is pure exteriority; it does not depend on the terms added and is only the affirmation of their independence. To count is to make an ideal discrimination within an already given totality that is capable of disintegration. The number obtained through addition belongs neither to any of the various *this*es counted nor to the totality capable of disintegration—insofar as this is revealed as a totality.[55]

These structures are linked to "potentialities." The future is the meaning of the present. The present for-itself is haunted by the lack of that solidity which it seeks through coincidence with a possible, complementary for-itself. Consequently, all present negation of the for-itself is itself in the future. The present is concerned with its own possibility, which is beyond the present. Within the instant, the present is meaningless; it is meaningful only as prolonged and projected—if only "provisionally"—toward a future. In the first instance, of course, the present negation appears as simply capable of being maintained; the *this* it constitutes reveals itself, correspondingly, as capable of being what it is. Thus the first "potentiality" of the object is *permanence*. This is simply the object's essence inasmuch as, by maintaining the negation that makes the object appear, one tends increasingly to specify the qualities of that object. As my negation is continued, it tends to contract insofar as it starts out as a negation of pure qualities. In effect, "the green *never is* green"; pure green, the essence "green," "comes from the ground of the future to the existent, like a meaning that is never given and that forever haunts it."[56] Quality always presents itself as a call for quality, which is the correlate of the fact that negation always presents itself as the demand to pursue it. So long as either endures, the realization that it effects is resumed and indefinitely specified. If I have never encountered pure green, it is because none of the partial negations that give me green objects was able to make itself a negation in-itself. As negations, they were insufficient for giving me green as green. Lastly, among the remaining potentialities, there is *beauty*: "the impossible and perpetually indicated fusion of essence and existence."[57] An ideal state of the world, it is the correlate of the for-itself's ideal realization. It points to what we have called "value." "To

54. *EN*, pp. 235–236; *BN*, p. 257.
55. [*EN*, p. 240; *BN*, p. 263.]
56. *EN*, p. 243; *BN*, pp. 266–267.
57. *EN*, p. 244; *BN*, p. 268.

the extent man *realizes* the beautiful in the world, he does so in the imaginary mode."[58]

In a general way, "from the mere fact that I am my own future, the *this* is revealed as provided with potentialities. . . . Except that the *this* has various potentialities which are its *equivalents*."[59] These potentialities bear this relation to the *this* in that they do not affect it; that is, the *this* does not *have to be* these potentialities whereas it does have to be others. Thus all potentialities and probabilities present themselves as meanings, each a pure nothingness in-itself (the famous "casing of nothingness").[60] They define themselves

> as that which the being *is not yet*, without ever truly having *to be them*. Here again knowledge neither adds to nor detracts from being; it confers no new quality. It causes being to-be-there by surpassing it toward a nothingness that sustains only negative relations of exteriority with being. . . . [61]

OBJECTIVITY AND TRUTH

We can now understand, given the above, why the for-itself cannot *know* through contemplation.

> A being that constitutes itself as a lack can determine itself only yonder, by *that* which it lacks and which it *is*, in short, by a perpetual tearing away of oneself toward the self one has to be. . . . Thus the world is revealed to one as haunted by absences that are to be realized, and each *this* appears with a retinue of absences that indicate and determine it. . . . These are pure demands that present themselves as "voids to be filled" ["*vides à remplir*"]. . . . They are *tasks*, and this world is a world of *tasks*.[62]

A thing in this world points beyond itself to tasks to be completed [*tâches à remplir*]. It is therefore an instrument or *implement*. From its very appearance, the thing is a thing-implement. On the foundation of the quantitative relation of exteriority between *this*es, the original relation among things appears and this is the relation of implementality [*ustensilité*]. "The totality of implements is the exact correlate of my possibilities. . . . the order of implements in the world is the image of my possibilities projected in the in-itself."[63] The implement is therefore the thing-towards—that is, the thing not in its capacity as surpassing but in its capacity as being surpassed by that project of the for-itself to which it is given.

This analysis, perhaps barren by itself, covers an important point. The con-

58. *EN*, p. 245; *BN*, p. 268.
59. *EN*, pp. 246–247; *BN*, p. 270.
60. *EN*, p. 247; *BN*, p. 271.
61. *Ibid*.
62. *EN*, pp. 248–249, 250; *BN*, pp. 272–273, 274.
63. *EN*, p. 251; *BN*, p. 275.

cept of implementality is central in Sartre's work. One could even say that the
objectivity of *this* world in which we live rests on implementality. This is because an "objectivity" severed from the human would be unthinkable from
the standpoint of determinability and knowledge: to be objective means to be
determinable, and all knowledge is realization. There is a sort of natural
objectivity in the appearance of a world inasmuch as it appears only through
our own nihilating activity. This activity projects us at a distance from ourselves while it constitutes things as implements that correlate with those possibilities which, across that distance, we have-to-be. As for scientific objectivity,
Sartre says,

> (the thing-implement) will reveal itself to the subsequent inquiry of the scientist
> purely as a *thing*, that is, as deprived of all implementality. But this is because
> the scientist wishes to establish only pure relations of exteriority. Moreover, the
> result of this scientific inquiry is that the thing itself, stripped of all instru-
> mentality, finally evaporates into absolute exteriority.[64]

Science grew on the basis of the Cartesian revolution. Opposing Aristotelian
and medieval pseudoscience, for which objects were penetrated by a sort of
natural psychism, this revolution consisted above all in washing all human
contamination from objects and conferring on them the indifference and
transparency of geometrical space. Modern science followed this same road
further when it renounced even the Cartesian "figures" and reabsorbed the
object into the phenomenon, thereby conceiving the phenomenon as a sort of
resistance encountered by the "physicist-mathematician" in the course of his
calculations, that is, as a purely mathematical substance. However, by exhausting this purely theoretical tendency, the modern scientist has become aware of
the active role he played in the definition of objectivity. Deprived of all metaphysical support (like the notion of extension or "*res extensa*," which is the
correlate of thinking substance or "*res cogitans*" for Descartes), objectivity
could no longer pass for a property of things or matter, since the notion of
matter itself lost all internal consistency. Thus Bachelard, who also believes
that the real is always the termination of a realization, was able to conclude:
"the primary source of objectivity is not the object but the objective method."[65]

Speaking generally, we encounter only what we are looking for, that is, what
we make appear under this or that modality. And this is conceivable, even
at the level of science, only to the extent the natural object is itself constituted
according to our most fundamental needs.

Thus scientific objectivity is sustained by a natural objectivity. Scientific
objectivity dismembers the latter in order to reapprehend it in a context whose
determination is more developed. The distance between them is therefore

---

64. *EN*, pp. 250–251; *BN*, p. 275.
65. Gaston Bachelard, *L'Expérience de l'espace dans la physique contemporaine*
(Paris: Félix Alcan, 1937), p. 85.

merely that between (1) a reflective methodological realization and (2) a non-thetic spontaneous realization in which the world appears "as an organized complex of implements."[66]

If we observe that in the natural attitude thing-implements always refer us to other thing-implements and ultimately to the possibilities that we ourselves are on the horizon of these things, then we shall understand the analogy which many have claimed is the furthest point reached by Sartre's philosophy:

> remember the donkey who draws behind him a cart and who tries to catch a carrot strung on the end of a stick that is attached to the same cart. . . . We run in this manner after a possibility that our running itself makes appear, which is nothing but our running itself and which thereby is by definition beyond reach. We run toward ourselves, and because of this very fact we are the being who can never be reunited with itself.[67]

Again we encounter that failure of human reality which consists in ensnaring itself in a natural attitude—whether fundamental or derived—that no purifying reflection is able to grasp at the reflective level in such a way as to extricate it from itself. We can now see that there is no synonymy between "fundamental attitude" and "necessary attitude," that human reality can fail to coincide with itself either at the level of being or at the level of doing because it never ceases to surpass its facticity. The very fact that human reality is able to describe its own natural attitudes is enough indication that it is not necessarily shut up within them. The failure involved therefore lacks any trace of inevitability. It results from a purpose, namely, that of rejoining oneself, and we have seen that—even taking account of the qualifications that the for-itself's past places upon its present negations[68]—any purpose can be given up in favor of a new one. Thus, again, there is no reason to be distressed by an ontological perspective that situates all endeavor on the ground of failure, since the latent, spontaneous possibility of trying to master the dimension of human meaning is thereby set in relief and made manifest.

One last observation: the world as known possesses an *objective* temporality that is like the projection of the temporality of the for-itself onto being. At the unreflective level the for-itself is incapable of consciousness *of* its own temporality; it must discover it in the world.

THE ABSOLUTELY HUMAN CHARACTER OF KNOWLEDGE

We can now see the position on knowledge to which we have been driven: knowledge is one of the fundamental relationships between being-for-itself and being-in-itself.

66. J.-P. Sartre, *Esquisse d'une théorie des émotions* (Paris: Hermann, 1939), p. 48; *The Emotions: Outline of a Theory*, translated by Bernard Frechtman (New York: Philosophical Library, 1948), p. 89.
67. *EN*, p. 253; *BN*, pp. 277–278.
68. *EN*, p. 269; *BN*, p. 295.

Contrary to idealism, the in-itself is *really* present to the for-itself: ". . . it is outside, upon being, that a world is revealed to me."[69] Knowledge is affirmation. But there can be affirmation only of a being that is not the same as the affirming being and only *by* a being that is a negation of itself. "Intentional affirmation is like the reverse of internal negation"; the in-itself alone is unable to affirm itself but instead undergoes "the adventure . . . of *being affirmed*."[70] In other words, one can affirm only that which *is* but which the affirmant *is not*. Were there no *being* one would have nothing to affirm, and, if one were *himself* being, one would be content merely to be, without any affirmation. To affirm something is always to hold at a distance the being that is revealed and that one is threatened with becoming. The being who affirms must for his part be his own nothingness in order to avoid confounding himself with the being he affirms.

Thus, contrary to realism, the in-itself is never present to the for-itself except at a distance. The in-itself does not *represent* itself to a for-itself that is contained *within* the in-itself. Instead: ". . . from this being that 'invests me' ["*m'investit*"] from everywhere and from which *nothing* [*rien*] separates me, I am separated precisely by *nothing*. And because it is nothingness [*néant*], it is impenetrable."[71]

All the conditions that we have seen accrue to being because it is negated by the for-itself ultimately add nothing to the in-itself.

> They merely serve to realize the *there is*. But those conditions which *are nothing* separate me even more radically from being than would any prismatic distortion, through which I might still hope to discover being. . . . Thus I again find myself everywhere between myself and being as the nothing that *is not* being. The world is human."[72]

All that is there is being. Beyond that, there is *nothing*. But I can no more lay hold of this being than I can ignore its presence. Either I am referred to myself, who is not this being, or—if I try to do without being and reduce everything to myself—I am referred to being, which does not depend on me.

This latter error is committed by idealism, as we have already pointed out. The former is committed by realism. All realism is a "nominalism" according to which conceptual knowledge distorts Reality. The latter is *already there* as *being* and thus does not need to be realized. Anything one might say, all "theories" on the subject, run the risk of distorting it. Reality must be allowed to come forth *as it is*. One must open oneself to it, abandon oneself to possession by it, and live at its same rhythm in order not to disturb its presence, thereby also tying oneself "intuitively" to its pulsations and ultimately confounding oneself with it. But under the pretext of acceding in this way to a

69. *EN*, p. 269; *BN*, p. 296.
70. *EN*, p. 269; *BN*, p. 295.
71. *EN*, p. 269; *BN*, p. 296.
72. *EN*, p. 270; *BN*, pp. 296–297.

knowledge that is rigorously faithful to its object, the subject has deprived himself of the capacity to know, for the world can not appear to him when he is in such a state and thus it can not appear to him at all. The reabsorption is total. There is no longer any danger of error because the truth of being's presence is lacking: there is no longer anything but being.

This error turns out to be altogether symmetrical with the idealistic error of believing the world is *realized* in advance in the form of Ideas, relations, and categories in a transcendental consciousness that communicates with every individual consciousness. In both cases there is a surpassing of the knower's situation, either toward the total absence of situation (the realist's fusion with the world as seen from nowhere in particular) or toward an omnipresent situation (the idealist's production of the world as seen from everywhere at once). The latter dreams of assimilating the object in order to confer an absolute transparency on it, the former dreams of assimilating himself to the object in its absolute opacity.

If, instead, we return to the perspective of realizing knowledge, we shall understand that

> knowledge places us in the presence of the absolute and [that] there is a truth of knowledge. But this truth, although yielding to us no more and no less than the absolute, remains strictly human.[73]

73. *EN*, p. 270; *BN*, p. 297.

Chapter 5

Relations with Others

In dealing with the problem of knowledge we passed over a factor that ordinarily plays a crucial role in the very statement of that problem: the existence of the body. This omission is easily explained. We were describing that fundamental relation of the for-itself to the in-itself called knowledge: in this perspective the body, whatever its function in knowledge may be, constitutes part of the known, insofar as our body appears to us. Far from explaining knowledge, the body can itself be conceived only through the fundamental structure of knowing. This knowledge I have of my own body depends in turn both on the way the body of others [*le corps des autres*] appears to me and on the way others view my body.

Consequently, the nature of *my* body refers me to the existence of another and to my own being-for-another. When I am with another, I discover an additional mode of existence of human reality, as fundamental as being-for-oneself, which I shall name being-for-another [*l'être-pour-autrui*]. If I wish to exhaustively describe man's relation with being, I must now embark upon the study of this new structure of my being: the "For-another."[1]

We start again with a feeling and develop its implications. My *shame*, for example, is a consciousness (of) shame, but it is also consciousness *of* myself as vulgar, maladroit, etc. Therefore, like other forms of consciousness described above, it is intentional: it aims at an object. Also like the others it is

---

1. *EN*, p. 271; *BN*, p. 298. [In his use of the untranslatable indefinite pronoun "autrui"—meaning 'others', or better, 'another', as in "to covet another's property"—Sartre *deliberately* equivocates on two issues: (1) whether there is one or more than one "other" referred to and (2) whether this (or these) other(s) are persons, in addition to being consciousnesses. The "person" arises, for Sartre, only when human reality individuates itself through a project. Cf. below, p. 191. Consistently rendering "autrui" as "the other" overlooks the fact that the same English is conveyed by Sartre's use of "l'Autre." In the latter case, "the" conveys a singularity absent from "autrui," which does not require the definite article "le." I have translated "autrui" as "another" where possible and as "the other" where necessary. Also: "the Other" could embrace nonhuman reality as well as human reality, as in Plato's usage (Cf. Hazel E. Barnes's introduction to *Being and Nothingness* [New York: Washington Square Press, 1966], pp. xxvii–xxviii). In addition, the plural "others" conveys an externality that negates "alterity," that is, potential internal relations, which Sartre always wishes to preserve.]

accessible to reflection, even though originally it is in no way a phenomenon of reflection. I may well *make myself* ashamed, but this is ultimately because I am ashamed without observing myself or tormenting myself. And yet this unreflective moment suddenly provokes, without a trace of reflection, an immediate shudder that runs through me from head to foot. I feel nailed to the spot, emptied of energy, paralyzed, as if my whole existence flowed back over me, as if the impulse that carried me and with which I coincided had recoiled upon me, as the liquid mass of the sea's undertow beats on itself with the same force that led it to the beach.

What has happened here? Clearly, I have apprehended my own movements in a new consciousness, an ashamed consciousness. But I have done so without doubling back on myself. This new consciousness cannot have been motivated either by a reflective thought or by my movements themselves, which tend toward self-perpetuation. I must conclude that the look I experience as directed upon me cannot be my own. I must have seen or imagined *someone who saw me*. I am thus forced, by someone other than myself, to see myself as I am, that is, as the object which I am *for him* and which I also recognize myself as *being*.

It seems that

> shame, in its primary structure, is shame *before someone*. . . . The other [*autrui*] is the indispensable mediator between me and myself: I am ashamed of myself *as I appeared* to another [*à autrui*]. . . . One is never vulgar all by himself. Thus, not only has the other revealed to me what I was, he has constituted me on the basis of a new type of being that supports new qualifications. This being was not in me potentially before the appearance of the other person. . . . But this new being that appears *for* others does not reside *in* others; I am responsible for it. . . . Shame is shame *of oneself before another*; these two structures are inseparable. But at the same time, I need the other to fully grasp all the structures of my being. The For-itself refers to the For-another.[2]

We shall limit ourselves here to indicating (a) the spirit in which Sartre approaches this new problem and (b) the significance of the essential results of his research, which, though already well known, are often misinterpreted.

At the start we should repeat that this discussion is at the level of ontology. It involves descriptions, and, to be comprehensive, these must start out from the interiority of the *cogito*. We are not attempting an explanation of consciousness's being based on an already realized knowledge, because such realization presupposes an original consciousness that has already been understood. Our hasty phenomenology of shame has this immediate import: since my relation to another is a structure of my being it must be approached as a fundamental relation of being to being, not of knowing to knowing. I should not try to grasp my own and others' being as two objects of knowledge with

2. *EN*, pp. 275–277; *BN*, p. 298.

equivalent statuses; "on the contrary, I must establish myself *in my being* and pose the problem of another, starting with my being."[3]

In that case, however, the multiplicity of consciousnesses is an insurmountable problem for me, since I would have to depart from myself and establish a viewpoint in some Totality from which I could contemplate both myself and the other.

> Therefore no logical or epistemological optimism can arrest the scandal of the plurality of consciousnesses. . . . An ontology may undertake to describe this scandal and to ground it in the very nature of being; but it is powerless to overcome it. . . . The dispersion of consciousnesses and the struggle among them shall remain what they are; we shall simply have discovered their foundation and their true terrain.[4]

In short, "the existence of another has the character of a contingent and irreducible fact. One *encounters* another, one does not constitute him."[5] This makes the problem of others' *existence* a false problem and explains why few thinkers have attempted to resolve it by way of "solipsism," that is, the affirmation of my ontological solitude. The only certainty is my relation to others. And this relation is constitutive of my being-for-another. Now we might derive a basis for treating this problem from the following two-sided preliminary observation: (a) the other is not added to myself, as one object is to another in a collection—our relation is internal and indicates a Totality; yet (b) "this Totality is such that it is in principle impossible for us to take up 'the viewpoint of the whole.' . . . since existence-for-another is the radical refusal of the other, no totalitarian and unifying synthesis of 'anothers' [*des 'autrui'*] is possible."[6]

The other is a scandal for me precisely insofar as I am inherently unable either to assimilate him to myself or to take him as a pure object and insofar as he congeals me (in my shame, but also in my pride) into a being that *I am.* Yet, *what* it is that I am for him, what he has made of this being, what possibilities he attributes to it: all this I am powerless to determine. The other is not only this existent who robs me of the world, who de-centers the world of which I was the center and reorganizes it from his viewpoint; nor is he simply a being that I see and that simultaneously sees the same objects I do, thereby conferring on those objects a sort of absence with regard to myself; he is, above all, *the one who looks at me,* the one who renders me vulnerable because he makes me what I am. Through him I *unreflectively apprehend myself.* Inserted between that solitary consciousness (of) myself which is spread out in the world and is indistinguishable from my consciousness *of* the world, and that reflective positing of myself as an object—as in the

3. [*EN*, p. 300; *BN*, p. 329.]
4. Ibid.
5. *EN*, p. 307; *BN*, p. 336.
6. *EN*, pp. 309–310; *BN*, p. 339.

Cartesian *cogito*—we find the presence of this me, of this person that I am. But I am this person in a new mode: as escaping myself qua *object for another*. My presence escapes me here as it did in solitary unreflective consciousness, where I had no need to refer to myself explicitly; in this case, however, my presence reveals itself as it might to a reflective consciousness pursuing its object but unable to grasp it. My self escapes me "not because I am the foundation of my own nothingness, but because I have my foundation outside myself."[7]

Because the other's freedom surpasses my being as an object, that being retains an indeterminate character that I cannot make determinate as I can my possibilities. I have become my possibility for another, a probability in his eyes. Thus

> . . . each of my free conducts engages me in a new context where the very stuff of my being is the unforeseeable freedom of another. And yet through my very shame I assume this freedom of another as my own, I affirm a deep unity of consciousness, . . . a unity of being, since I consent and will that others confer on me a being which I recognize.[8]

"If there is an Other [*un Autre*], whatever or wherever he may be and whatever his relations with me may be, . . . it follows that I have an outside, a *nature*. My original fall is the existence of the other [*l'autre*]. . . . "[9]

This is the central theme of *No Exit*. It emerges forcefully in the final dialogue when Garcin realizes he cannot love Estelle—and thereby forget his cowardice—under the too lucid glance of Inès:

> ESTELLE. Don't listen to her. Press your lips to my mouth; I am yours completely.
> INÈS. Well, what are you waiting for? Do what you're told. Garcin the coward embraces Estelle the baby-killer. The betting is now open. Will Garcin the coward kiss her or not? I'm watching, I'm watching—I alone am a crowd. The crowd, Garcin, do you hear the crowd? . . .
> GARCIN. It will never be night?
> INÈS. Never.
> GARCIN. You will always see me?
> INÈS. Always.
> GARCIN. . . . All right! Now's the moment. . . . I understand that I am in Hell. I tell you everything has been foreseen. They foresaw that I would stand before this fireplace, . . . with all these looks directed at me. All these looks that devour me . . . (*He turns around abruptly.*) What! There are only two of you? I thought there were many more. (*He laughs.*) So this is Hell. I'd never have believed it . . . Don't you remember: the brimstone, the stake, the rack . . . What a laugh! There's no need for a rack, Hell is other people.[10]

---

7. *EN*, p. 318; *BN*, p. 349.
8. *EN*, p. 320; *BN*, p. 351.
9. *EN*, p. 321; *BN*, p. 352.
10. *Huis Clos*, in *Théâtre*, pp. 167–168 (scene 5); *No Exit*, pp. 46–47.

Thus

> Through another's look [*le regard d'autrui*] I *see* myself as congealed in the midst of the world, as endangered, as irremediably lost. But I do not *know* which one I am, or what my place is in the world, or which side of this world where I am situated is turned toward him.[11]

I apprehend *myself* as being an object, but *not for myself*. Since this other is never given as an object, I can defend myself against him only by *summoning* his appearance [*faisant comparaître*] before me as an object; I thereby rid myself of him and escape him. However, this "object" remains

> an explosive instrument that I handle with care because I sense it has about it the permanent possibility that *they* will make it blow up and that, with this bursting, I would suddenly experience the flight of the world away from me and the alienation of my being. My constant wish is therefore to contain another in his objectivity. My relations with another-as-object are composed essentially of ruses designed to make him remain an object. But one glance from him is enough to collapse these artifices and to cause me to again experience the transfiguration he occasions.[12]

This is why I can never feel secure in my objectivisation of another. I remain in an atmosphere of *conflict* with regard to him. "Conflict is the original meaning of being-for-another."[13]

THE BODY

What, then, is another insofar as he is an object? As such, he is a *body*. But what does being this body entail? This question answered, we shall be able to specify the meaning of concrete relations with another as they occur in the context of the "conflict" we have just set in relief.

The sole problem of the body is its relation to consciousness, and correctly posing it requires giving up the traditional scientific conception of the body. On that view, the body is above all "a certain kind of *thing* that operates according to its own laws and that is capable of being defined from without. . . . ";[14] consciousness is of course the object of its own intimate intuition. Such a conception is faulty in wishing to unite *my* consciousness "not to *my* body but to the bodies *of others*."[15] My own body is just what I cannot set before myself like an object or contemplate from a global viewpoint. In one sense I am my body: "The body is the instrument which I am."[16] In another sense it is a worldly object. But it is the latter only for another or for myself

11. *EN*, p. 327; *BN*, p. 359.
12. *EN*, p. 358; *BN*, p. 394.
13. *EN*, p. 431; *BN*, p. 475.
14. [*EN*, p. 365; *BN*, p. 401.]
15. *EN*, p. 365; *BN*, p. 401.
16. *EN*, p. 427; *BN*, p. 470.

through reference to the viewpoint of another. "Either it is one thing among others, or else it is that by which things are revealed to me. But it cannot be both at once."[17]

It follows that I cannot demarcate within myself the psychical and the physiological as two realities capable of acting upon each other. "Being-for-itself must be wholly body and it must be wholly consciousness; it cannot be *united* to a body. . . . the body is entirely 'psychical.' "[18]

It will perhaps be useful at this point to head off a mistake whose innocence—in light of the texts just cited—is suspect. Though it is also committed by other authors, Lucien Fabre's version of the error is the most striking. Fabre attempts—as one among several urgent tasks—to assimilate Sartre's outlook to that of materialism. This tour de force rests, however, on an odd mistake in quoting from *Being and Nothingness*. Fabre quotes Sartre as writing: "Consciousness is the body, it is not even anything substantial, but is instead a pure 'appearance' in the sense that it exists only to the extent that it appears to itself."[19] The passage in question is on page 23 of Sartre's work [*BN*, p. 17]. But the reader will find that Sartre's text does not contain the first four words in Fabre's quotation. We can understand what follows from this passage, and Fabre's readers could have also, if they had had before them the qualification that Sartre immediately adds to it: "But it is precisely because consciousness is pure appearance, a total emptiness (since the entire world is outside of it)—it is because appearing and existing are thus identical in it that it can be considered as the absolute."[20] In other words, it is to the extent that consciousness is nothing *substantially*, nothing so far as material being is concerned, that it may be "a fullness of existence"[21] *as consciousness*.

The charge thus reveals its inconsistency on precisely those points on which it was supposedly based. This "mistake" interests us more than others only as occasion to better outline a central stage in our progressive definition of human reality.

Indeed consciousness *is* the body—insofar as there is a *facticity* proper to the for-itself. The body

> is none other than the for-itself; it is not an in-itself *within* the for-itself, for then it would congeal everything. It is rather the fact that the for-itself is not its own foundation, inasmuch as this fact is expressed by the necessity of existing as a contingent being engaged with other contingent beings.[22]

The body is the contingent aspect of my situation. It is my fundamental point of view beyond which I cannot further retreat. It is an implement among

17. *EN*, p. 366; *BN*, p. 402.
18. *EN*, p. 368; *BN*, p. 404.
19. Lucien Fabre, "Essentialisme et existentialisme," *Revue de Paris* 54 (April 1947): 107.
20. *EN*, p. 23; *BN*, p. 17. [Sartre's parentheses.]
21. *EN*, p. 22, *BN*, p. 16.
22. *EN*, pp. 371–372; *BN*, p. 408.

implements; yet it is only on the basis of the body that the world can order itself as a complex of implementality in the first place. The body situates this complex by its own situation.

These points confirm our previous observations on knowledge. The objectivity of knowledge is *human* because knowing is not contemplation but *experience*, which implies "a first opening upon things without which there could be no objective knowledge."[23] This primary openness, this subject of experience, *is* the body, and it is a consciousness inasmuch as consciousness *has* a body. And if contemporary science has itself been led to define objectivity through the method of objectivisation, that is because it ended up reformulating its notion of experience as "a system of univocal relations from which the observer is not excluded."[24] Knowledge, then—even under the form of "Relativity"—is not at all relativistic; it simply aims at a being that *is* a relation, a being that is given to the observer only as the orientation of his own various relationships toward himself. One can speak of relativism only to the extent one has already formed the contrary concept of "pure knowledge." But if one sees that all knowledge requires a point of view, that all knowledge is *engaged* and refers to an action as its inverse side, then one will have no difficulty admitting the absolute character of the object put forth by human knowledge.

Since it follows that the body is "that instrument which I cannot use by means of another instrument, that point of view upon which I cannot achieve a point of view," it is now legitimate to say of spontaneous, unreflective consciousness, "using 'exist' as a transitive verb, that [such consciousness] *exists its body*."[25]

This brings out the fact that consciousness *is not* its body, meaning that consciousness does not identify itself with it. Instead, it is with its body in an existential relationship. So long as consciousness is unreflective, the body is one of its structures. More precisely: such consciousness

> is consciousness (of) the body as something it surmounts and nihilates in making itself consciousness, that is, as something which consciousness *is* without having to be it and *over which consciousness passes* in order to be what it has to be.[26]

To conclude: consciousness is its body in the specific sense that if it were *only* its body it would not be consciousness. This is because the very vocation of consciousness is to nihilate this corporal structure, to surpass it, to "neglect" it, to "pass over it in silence."[27]

23. Merleau-Ponty, *Phénoménologie de la perception*, p. 113; *Phenomenology of Perception*, p. 96.
24. *EN*, p. 369; *BN*, p. 406.
25. *EN*, p. 394; *BN*, p. 434.
26. *EN*, p. 395; *BN*, p. 434.
27. Ibid.

The body is, then, *"that contingency which the for-itself exists. . . ."*[28] It is the contingency which the for-itself *is* as a facticity and which it must surpass.

"Nausea" is precisely consciousness's lived apprehension of its own contingency, of its own factual existence. "Consciousness never ceases 'to have' a body."[29]

This same body also exists *for-another*. Such, for example, is Pierre's body as seen by me or mine as seen by Pierre. The body of another is his facticity and the contingency of his being. This contingency is felt by the other as a sort of taste of himself expressed in the discomfort of "nausea." It is apprehended by me as *his flesh* [*chair*].

This flesh is never a simple object for me, except when I am before a cadaver.

> . . . the other is originally given to me as *a body in a situation*. . . . Another's body as flesh cannot be *inserted* in a predefined situation. Rather, it is precisely that starting with which *there is* a situation. Here again it can exist only in and through a transcendence. . . . In this way the body of another *signifies* or confers meaning.[30]

We apprehend another's psyche on his body. There is nothing surprising in this so long as we remember that we perceive another's gestures, not like fragments of worldly objects, but on the basis of the other in his entirety, as existing in his particular situation. All the "signs" of anger that another gives to us

> do not *express* the anger, they *are* the anger. We must avoid misunderstanding here. In itself a clenched fist is nothing and means nothing. But also we never perceive *a clenched fist*; we perceive a man who, in a certain situation, clenches his fist.[31]

Another's body always indicates something beyond itself. This holds both for space, where his body indicates a situation, and for time, where it indicates his freedom in an objective form. "Thus the other person's body is always 'a body-more-than-body' because the other person is given to me without intermediary, totally, in the perpetual surpassing of his facticity."[32]

Let us add that if "I exist my body" and if my body is used and known by another, it is because even more fundamentally "I exist for myself as known by another, specifically in my very facticity . . . as a body." This is the same essential relation we caught sight of at the start, in which "the other is revealed to me as the subject for which I am an object." Thus, Sartre continues, my body escapes me at every point: "My body's being for me is, at its deepest level, this perpetual 'outside' of my most intimate 'inside.' "[33]

28. [*EN*, p. 405; *BN*, p. 445.]
29. *EN*, p. 404; *BN*, p. 444.
30. *EN*, pp. 410–411; *BN*, pp. 451–452.
31. *EN*, p. 413; *BN*, 455.
32. *EN*, p. 418; *BN*, p. 460.
33. *EN*, pp. 418–419; *BN*, pp. 460–461.

Concrete Relations with Others

We can now specify the modes of conflict that are created by the existence of others. We shall recall well-known positions, but with the aim of understanding the significance Sartre attributes to them.

Since the other endangers my free project of attaining the being of a "self" [*soi*] by robbing me in advance of any foundation I might give myself, I am compelled either (a) to require that the other use his freedom to justify (rather than undermine) my being or (b) to desire the simple suppression of the other's freedom and hence of any further danger to me from it.

In the first case, I address myself to another insofar as he is a subject: I seek to seduce him in his transcendence, to obtain his free choice of me as a limitation of his own freedom. I strive to be loved by him. He will thereby found me as a sort of absolute, as a supreme value. In the second case, I address myself to the other insofar as he is an object. I seek to lay hold of him, to imprison him in his facticity—in his body. I wish to appropriate his freedom through a total appropriation of his body.

I am haunted by the sense of being "alienated" by another, the sense of a lack of control over this "outside" that I am for him. My goal is consequently either (a) to endow my existence with value through another, fascinating him in his freedom so as to obtain his willing collaboration, or (b) to recover my being-for-another by constraining his freedom—through desire or violence—to admit it has been conquered.

In love, my existence seems indeed to take its foundation from another. It is "because it is *given a name* [*appelée*]."[34] It is no longer "in the way," it feels justified. But, precisely because love is my demand to be loved freely by another, it must be rigorously reciprocal, and so the other's freedom must address itself to my own. I seek a foundation in the other's subjectivity as its absolute object; what I in fact achieve is a referring of his freedom back to my own subjectivity. Scarcely have I obtained love when the being who loves me loses all power to justify or found me in virtue of experiencing me as a subjectivity; I am thrown back on my duty to make myself exist for myself. "It is therefore in vain that I will have tried to lose myself in objectivity; my passion will have been pointless. The other has inevitably brought me back . . . to my own unjustifiable subjectivity."[35]

The *masochistic* attitude may present itself at this point. In it I give up trying to ground my own value in another. I ask no more of his freedom than that it found me as object, no longer as a "self," but simply as a "being-in-itself." I leave to him the worry of making me exist.

34. *EN*, p. 438; *BN*, p. 483. [Sartre here plays on ambiguities in *"appelée,"* among whose meanings are: 'to be given a name' and 'to be called or destined for something'.]

35. *EN*, p. 445; *BN*, p. 491.

Baudelaire's existence was "fractured" by the second marriage of the mother he adored. The effect, Sartre notes, was to cast him "without transition into personal existence."[36]

> The child takes his parents for gods. . . . When these divine beings direct their glance at him, their look is enough to justify him at once to the very roots of his existence. It confers on him a definite, sacred character. Since they cannot be mistaken, it follows that he really *is* as they *see* him. . . . It was for the absolute security of childhood that Baudelaire yearned. . . . Unjustified and unjustifiable, he suddenly becomes aware of his terrible freedom. Everything has yet to be initiated. He suddenly emerges into solitude and nothingness. This is just what Baudelaire had wished to avoid, whatever the cost. His parents remained detestable idols for him, but idols all the same. . . . He complains of being *another*, to be sure, but *another among others*. His disdainful otherness remains a social tie with those whom he despised. They had to be there in order to recognize his otherness. . . . What he wanted was not friendship, or love, or relationships among equals. He had no friends, only a few rascally confidants at best. He sought judges—beings he could deliberately place outside of original contingency, who exist simply because they have the right to exist and whose decrees conferred on him a stable and sacred "nature." Baudelaire was willing to pass as guilty in their eyes; and "guilty in their eyes" meant, of course, absolutely guilty. . . .

> > *I would like to live at the feet of a young giantess*
> > *Like a voluptuous cat at the feet of a queen.*

> To attract the attention of a giantess; to see himself through her eyes as a domestic animal; to lead the nonchalant, sensual, perverse existence of a cat in a society of aristocrats or giants; to have man-gods decide for him and without consulting him what is to be the meaning of the universe and the ultimate end of his life: such were his dearest wishes. He wanted to enjoy the limited independence of a *bête de luxe*, idle and useless, whose little games are protected by the seriousness of its masters. . . . Was he not necessarily masochistic to the extent his need for consecration led him to turn himself into an *object* for these great stern consciousnesses?[37]

Just because it is an attitude, though, masochism is a failure: I may succeed in becoming another's object, but I can never become that object for myself. I can *undergo* my presence-as-an-object to another, but I am obliged to *give* it to myself and, moreover, I use the other as an instrument for my ends, which, again, opposes me to him as subject to object. Sartre concludes: "Masochism is therefore in principle a failure. This should not surprise us if we consider that masochism is a 'vice' and vice is, in principle, the love of failure."[38]

So far described, masochism might appear from an ontological viewpoint to

---

36. [Introduction to *Ecrits intimes de Baudelaire*, p. 3; *Baudelaire*, p. 17.]
37. Introduction to *Ecrits intimes de Baudelaire*, pp. 38–43; *Baudelaire*, pp. 52–57.
38. *EN*, p. 447; *BN*, p. 493.

be less ambitious than love, entailing as it does only the subject's *denial* of his own subjectivity, whereas in love the subject aspires to justification *as* subjectivity through an objectivisation of himself on the part of another. But this is appearance only. Both endeavors are equally destined to fail, one no more than the other.

When Sartre speaks of "the vice of masochism" or "love of failure," should we not consider that in love, as described above, man appears to Sartre to be on the verge of masochism? For Sartre, isn't the failure of love close to becoming the love of failure? Certainly on the unreflective level, man throws himself into his enterprises and seeks their success one after another without asking himself about their fundamental significance. He is never conscious, on this plane, of desiring to fail. Thus the masochist takes pleasure in his effort without saying so. The lover, however, is always apprehensive about his love. Yet we must be careful here: what the lover fears and deplores is this or that particular failure. Perhaps another's love is insufficient to justify him, or it is too great, restraining the other's freedom and hence his capacity to infuse the beloved with value. The world may possibly contain a perfect being with whom success would occur on first encounter. Consequently, Don Juan went from woman to woman. Along with the Comedian, the Conqueror, and, above all, the Artist, Don Juan exemplifies one of the heroic forms of absurdism for which we are indebted to Camus.[39] Equally absurd is the behavior of the souls of ancient tyrants which, in one of the most beautiful of the Platonic myths,[40] constantly rechoose the destinies of tyrants at the start of each new life, convinced that changes in exterior conditions will make their renunciation of self-change harmless. We shall return to this myth when we discuss destiny. In passing, let us note Alain's illuminating remarks on this topic:

> The disappointed go-getter decides that he was caught off guard. . . . The miser who is robbed complains of being robbed, not of being miserly. . . . The defeated tyrant raises a new army. Upon being humiliated, the vain person dreams of a triumphant vanity. . . . These souls are extremely enthusiastic over the idea of choosing, of beginning anew, of changing everything, but without changing themselves! . . . Every instant (is) a death and a revival. At each instant a new life is offered to us. . . . Our flaw is to try, just once more, the same old ruse, hoping that God will change things. . . .[41]

The attitude Sartre describes as love is similarly absurd. It is the attitude of one guided by a fundamental wish. He confines himself, completely in bad

39. Cf. Albert Camus, *Le Mythe de Sisyphe* (Paris: Gallimard, 1942), esp. pp. 97–106; *The Myth of Sisyphus and Other Essays*, translated by Justin O'Brien (New York: Knopf, 1955), pp. 69–77.
40. Plato, *Le République*, Book X, pp. 614a, *ad finum*; *The Republic*, translated by Paul Shovy, in *The Collected Dialogues of Plato*, edited by Edith Hamilton and Huntington Cairns (Princeton: Princeton University Press, 1961), pp. 838–844.
41. Emile Chartier [Alain], *Idées: Platon, Descartes, Hegel* (Paris: Paul Hartmann Editeur, 1932), pp. 95–103.

faith, either to the unreflective use of means or to "accessory" reflection on the obstacles created by his own passionate search. Sartre states explicitly:

> Man searches blindly for being by hiding from himself the free project which is this search. He makes himself such that he may be *awaited* by the tasks placed in his path. Objects are mute demands and he is nothing in himself beside the passive obedience to these demands.[42]

This attitude is aimed only at avoiding the anguish of finding oneself face to face with oneself, free and unjustifiable.

Taken at this level, human life appears radically absurd, and absurdism consists in *holding it at this level*. Alternatively, however, we may envisage the intervention of a purifying reflection that is beyond both the unreflective attitude and the accessory reflection. The role of such a reflection can only be to reveal the absurdity of our spontaneous existence by exposing our bad faith as a project of *passion*, a result of our anguish over free action. Such a "love of failure" is the direct consequence of declining all personal endeavor.

We should remember that such ontological descriptions are on the plane of generality. As we saw with Merleau-Ponty, this is the level at which we find the hypocrisy of a self to itself.[43] It is the realm of the anonymous and inauthentic. In this domain our tasks seem inscribed upon the world like the tasks of others, since they issue from a spontaneous valuation common to all men. Our failures are objective failures based on generalized existence and types of situations, a foundation from which our individual existence could scarcely emerge. Love is no more than the encounter between the tendency impelling man in general to realize himself as a plenitude of being, and the contingent existence of the other, which threatens to frustrate this wish.

Should one stop being taken in by this generality, uncovering for himself his fundamental project beyond the particular situation, and should he thereby realize, not only the vanity of his efforts in general, but also the vanity of this very project, he can then choose himself either (a) as freely assuming this failure or (b) as surpassing it toward a specifically human use of his freedom. In the first case, his anonymous passion, which is in bad faith, can become a personal action—in the form of an unconditioned resurgence of self, partly because conflict with others loses meaning once one grasps the vanity of the project underlying it and partly because a person who realizes that he himself lies at the origin of the difficulties he encounters, far from thinking of transferring those difficulties onto others, accepts them with joy, confirming his freedom through such generosity. In the second case, the person sees he must renounce all surpassing of the human dimension toward some dimension beyond it and must manifest his choice of the human dimension in a free

---

42. *EN*, p. 721; *BN*, p. 796.
43. See *Phénoménologie de la perception*, p. 190; *Phenomenology of Perception*, pp. 162–163.

commitment that will no longer be split apart by his primitive wish for coincidence with himself.

These two attitudes must be set in greater relief. In either case, the cause of the failure has disappeared, along with all of its repercussions in the various areas of conduct.

Philosophy, we should note, is by nature situated on the plane of purifying reflection, which is its very raison d'être. It would be contradictory for philosophy to characterize the human domain as already purified. If there is a philosophical urge, it is because there is a need to purify existence in its primitive form and a possibility of doing so. Thus the two basic philosophical mistakes are optimism, which considers the Good to be existent and ingredient in reality, and pessimism, which considers the Good to be inaccessible. In either case one admits that nothing can be changed, that human reality is what it is and no more, and, simultaneously, one advances the same absurdities as the materialist who would demonstrate that consciousness does not exist. To philosophize is always to evince some capacity for self-transformation. It is to introduce into the world—which is already infused with value by the very fact of human existence—an authentic value situated not on the plane of fact and spontaneity but on that of right and freedom.

The cause of love is badly served by attributing to it an arbitrary and universal value more or less present in particular cases. Who would fail to see that such a "value" lacks any value, so to speak? We should therefore recall how our moralists of the seventeenth century—the century of "the honest man"—spoke of love. Didn't La Rochefoucauld give the key to the description of all natural attitudes when he spoke of self-respect [amour-propre]?[44]

Self-respect is love of self or the wish to coincide with oneself. Spinoza characterized it as "the tendency of a being to continue in being." However, La Rochefoucauld provides no means for breaking the circle of self-interest, and Spinoza proposes only a deterministic "ethics" for which our liberation consists in joyous adherence to universal necessity. Absurdism's seed is already in such descriptions that erect inauthentic existence into systems. It therefore seems inappropriate to reproach Sartre for describing the absurd, thereby avoiding absurdism.

Regarding the second tendency in our relations with others—the endeavor to appropriate another's freedom by a total appropriation of his body—Sartre's descriptions of desire, sadism, and hate contain certain pointed remarks:

44. [Françoise VI Duc de la Rochefoucauld, "Réflexions morales," *Maximes de la Rochefoucauld* (Paris: Bibliotheque Larousse, 1924), pp. 33, 35, 139–142: *The Maxims of La Rochefoucauld*, translated by Louis Kronenberger (New York: Random House, 1959), pp. 33, 35, 139–142. La Rochefoucauld plays on the ambiguities of *"amour-propre,"* and his usages may be variously translated by "self-respect," "self-interest," "self-love" and "vanity." Typical of his outlook is Maxim #1: "What we consider virtues are often merely a group of actions and personal promptings displayed with care or the help of luck; and it is not always through valor and chastity that men are valiant and women, chaste." Ibid., p. 33.]

We have not thought by these few observations to exhaust the question of sex, still less that of possible attitudes toward Another. We have wished merely to show that the sexual attitude is a primitive behavior [*comportement primitif*] toward Another.[45]

And:

These considerations do not exclude the possibility of a morality of deliverance and salvation [*salut.*] But such a morality can be reached only after [*au terme d'une*] a radical conversion, which we cannot discuss here.[46]

And so forth. These remarks suggest the meaning of the so-called scandal, namely, preserving in the form of a value that by which a human being may, if he chooses, tear himself away from the blindness of the species—that value being the free invention of *his* humanity.

Let us draw a point from Sartre's description of sadism, based on his extreme example of a manner of being proper to all consciousness insofar as it has not yet arrived at authentic existence.

One scene in *Men without Shadows* shows a militiaman who attempts to prove to a victim, as he tortures him, that he is cowardly.[47] His aim is not only to obtain information but also to justify the punishment by rendering the Resistance fighter absolutely contemptible. Of course, he will not be truly convinced he is justified unless he can make his victim confess his contemptible character. It is not enough for the militiaman to *think* his victim is cowardly, the latter must confirm it by an avowal. The more he tortures, the more he burdens himself with this terrible weight, and, thus, the more he needs justification. As his failure becomes increasingly evident his culpability is aggravated and it pushes him to more desperate efforts. Guilty of not having obtained a spontaneous avowal, he pushes the impossible project of synthesizing persuasion and violence to its outer limit.

. . . the spectacle offered to the sadist is that of a freedom that struggles against the blossoming of the flesh and that finally chooses freely to be submerged in the flesh. At the moment of betrayal, the sought-for result is achieved. . . .[48]

The gasping body, bound by ropes,

has ceased to be an object that stirs spontaneously. Through betrayal a freedom chooses to wholly identify itself with just such a body. Indeed, this disfigured and panting body is the very image of a broken and enslaved freedom.[49]

45. *EN*, p. 477; *BN*, p. 527.
46. *EN*, p. 484n; *BN*, p. 534n.
47. [*Morts sans sépultures*, in *Théâtre* (Paris: Gallimard, 1947), pp. 204–207 (act 1, tableau 2, scene 3); *The Victors*, in *Three Plays* by Jean-Paul Sartre, translated by Lionel Abel (New York: Knopf, 1949), pp. 228–231 (act 2). A "tableau" is a scene or group of scenes that take place in one setting. The translator has elected to treat the four tableaux as four acts in this case.]
48. [*EN*, p. 474; *BN*, p. 524.]
49. *EN*, p. 474; *BN*, p. 524.

The point is to *grasp* another's freedom, which, paradoxically, must be constrained. This grasping is possible only by inviting that freedom to *incarnate itself*. But at this point in the scene the torturer apprehends his failure. "The sadist discovers his error when his victim *looks* at him. . . ."[50] His victim sees him as "sadistic," as "torturer," thereby congealing into inherent traits what he thought was a free activity that would justify him.

Self-examination can discern the seeds of the sadistic and masochistic attitudes in some apparently mild behaviors. Anger, we saw, is the defeatist behavior of one person who rejects the effort to convince another through an understanding between two freedoms, resorting instead to magical procedures. We can now push this analysis further: through his anger, the angry one attempts to remedy the ineffectiveness of his own argumentation by upsetting his interlocutor. He seeks to make his interlocutor enter a terrain where arguments no longer count. Perhaps the latter will consent to reduce himself to a corporal presence, assuming a posture whose effect will be to make him live in fear for his very being. One need not wield pincers or close vises in every case in order to play sadist or torturer. Who can say he has never enjoyed—if only in imagination—the prodigious efforts a fit of anger allows him to exact from others? Equally, what man is ignorant of the unreflective "procedure," usually following a vain argument with the woman he loves, of enveloping her in physical tenderness, creating an uneasiness of the flesh to obtain an assent, a justification, a pardon, that would not have been granted in the context of a relationship between equals? The wheedling child is already a tyrant. The sweetness of a glance is first of all a spell, a piece of sorcery. Idealism triumphs easily when faced with those who say "men are dogs to each other." It is more difficult to break down that better formula for the ambiguous reality of intersubjective relationships, namely: "men are sorcerers to each other."[51]

If reaching out toward another was already valid in the natural attitude and carried its own value in itself, the problem of morality would never arise. What matters is not the desire for communion but the deeper significance of this desire. Nobody would think of placing the "purity" of a child reaching for its mother on the same plane with the purity of a Charles de Foucauld receptive to the suffering of his fellow man.[52] One is natural and spontaneous; the other is a hard won reconquest against all the temptations of false tenderness. The first maxim of morality could be: "Beware of tenderness."

50. [*EN*, p. 476; *BN*, p. 525.]
51. [*Esquisse*, p. 46; *Emotions*, p. 86.]
52. [A Trappist who founded a hermitage in the Moroccan Sahara at Beni-Abbès in 1901, dying there in 1916. Shocked by the colonials' willing ignorance of indigenous culture, he wrote a Tuareg grammar and argued—in letters that were later collected and published—for fairer treatment of colonized peoples. See *Spiritual Autobiography of Charles de Foucauld*, edited by J.-F. Six, translated by J. H. Smith (New York: P. J. Kennedy and Sons, 1964), especially p. 94.]

PART THREE

Toward the Morality of Ambiguity: The Conditional Realization of the Human

"He didn't have the life he deserved." Baudelaire's life seems an excellent illustration of this reassuring maxim. . . . And what if he had deserved his life? What if, despite popular ideas to the contrary, men always had precisely the lives they deserved? The issue must be examined closely.

—J.–P. Sartre, *Baudelaire*

Chapter 1

Action and Freedom

ACCESSORY REFLECTION

The fourth and final part of *Being and Nothingness* is perhaps the easiest and most interesting, particularly for readers who have little desire to master technical difficulties. On the basis of points that were implicit in the three preceding parts the fourth part develops, in a much more accessible manner, a theory of action in general. To *act*, for human reality, is to enter into the most fundamental possible relationship with the world: one surpasses the world's merely static configuration and modifies its materiality.

This is most immediately evident in the intentional character of action— "intentional" in the fullest sense. Action is not mere movement: one must be pursuing some goal. And this means that action's prime condition is *freedom*. Owing to its freedom, consciousness can withdraw simultaneously from the full world of which it is conscious and from its own past and consider both "in the light of a non-being."[1] This withdrawal enables consciousness to imagine something other than what is. We know that "man is free because he is not himself, but rather presence to himself."[2] Freedom is precisely the nothingness at the heart of human reality which constrains it "to *make itself*, rather than to *be*."[3]

In one sense this freedom is absolute. It is not pressured by any "motive" or "impulse" or "passion"—being itself the source of the meanings such "determinations" appear to bring it from the outside or from its past. In projecting itself toward an end it freely chooses, freedom encounters supports or obstacles whose value or disvalue is due entirely to its initial choice. Consequently, freedom is beyond the realm of voluntary deliberation. Such deliberation is itself the outcome of a certain intention, namely, the subject's prior decision to place himself, for purposes of action, on a reflective plane.

Liberty's absolute character in no way entails that it be mere caprice or that

---

1. Jean-Paul Sartre, *L'Etre et le néant: essai d'ontologie phénoménologique* (Paris: Gallimard, 1943), p. 511; *Being and Nothingness: An Essay in Phenomenological Ontology*, translated by Hazel E. Barnes (New York: Washington Square Press, 1966), p. 563.
2. [*EN*, p. 516; *BN*, p. 568.]
3. *EN*, p. 516; *BN*, p. 568.

action be arbitrary, perpetual agitation. "To be sure, each of my acts, even the most trivial, is completely free . . . but this does not mean that it might be *anything whatever* or even that it is unforseeable."[4] Each of my particular possibilities is encompassed within the ensemble of projects that I am. This ensemble is an organic totality, a unitary synthesis that represents my ultimate possibility, which is my fundamental choice of myself. I can obviously return to this choice and disengage myself from it. And anguish is just the apprehension of this perpetual possibility of radical self-transformation. But so long as I remain within the framework of this fundamental choice, then my particular projects, though not logically entailed by that choice, will become articulated along with it in a pliant continuum. If momentarily I abandon the unreflective plane, I can in reflection attempt by sheer force of will to impose upon myself projects that contradict my original project. This has a curious consequence. Since my will in this case really modifies only secondary projects, while leaving untouched the original choice I have made of myself, it is in bad faith and incapable of valid results.

> Thus, for example, if my initial project aims at choosing myself as inferior amidst others (which is called the "inferiority complex") and if stuttering, for example, is behavior that apprehends and interprets itself by means of this primary project, then I can, for social reasons and through a misunderstanding of my own choice of inferiority, decide to break myself of stuttering. I can even *attain this end*, yet without having ceased to feel and to will myself as inferior. To obtain a particular result, technical means will suffice. This is what is usually called voluntary self-improvement. But these results will only *displace* the infirmity from which I suffer and another will arise in its stead, expressing in its own way the total aim of my pursuits.[5]

Here we have perhaps the most important result of Sartre's ontology, and as such we should focus on it briefly. It looks dangerously paradoxical. Those who strive to live morally may be distressed by the limits to voluntary or willful action just described, for such action seems to be essential to moral striving.

Nevertheless, a theory that erects will into an all-powerful faculty of soul, an unconditioned power of decision, is bound to fall into confusion. Although the voluntary attitude is often admitted to be reflective, the difficulty is due to identifying this reflective voluntariness with absolute freedom. Thus the will as reflective is said both to have motives which explain its decisions, and also to be an absolute driving power—an act that decides itself, a power of self-movement quite beyond motives and reflection. It is described *both* as something squarely within the context of constituted thought *and* as the spontaneous constitution of thought. This leads to an irreducible antinomy. Avoiding it re-

---

4. *EN*, p. 530; *BN*, p. 584.
5. *EN*, p. 550; *BN*, p. 606–607.

quires recognizing that the will, as reflective effort, would be unintelligible to itself if there were not a background of unreflective life for it to take account of, an unreflective life oriented around the fundamental choice by which consciousness—at this level of free spontaneity—defines itself.

Far from being suspended in a void, then, the will acquires meaning only within the original project of an intentional, oriented freedom. And while the will may attempt to contravene this original project, it cannot basically modify it through secondary projects that depend on itself alone. The original project is "totalitarian"; it cannot be weakened by any failure of the partial structures to which it gives rise in action. On the contrary, it may consist in the very choice to fail, as in the example we cited. In such a case the will intervenes only to reinforce the choice that inspires it. In effect, "the choice of inferiority implies constantly bringing about a *gap* between the end which the will pursues and the end which it obtains."[6] In order *to confirm itself*, such a choice must employ an overextended will that is in bad faith, that avoids recognition of its own ends, namely, shame and suffering. The fundamental choice of consciousness here is to make more palpable the inferiority on which it has already decided, inventing voluntary "remedies" that are all later seen as leading to so many failures.

To "have" an inferiority complex means, therefore, to choose oneself as inferior. Difficulties presented by the existence of others are immediately resolved through a kind of hemorrhaging of one's being-for-oneself insofar as this is also a being-for-others, insofar as it has "an outside," and insofar as its freedom plays the part of an object in the world. Garcin, in *No Exit*, is remorseful over having been a coward. He can choose among a variety of fundamental attitudes for encountering the two "others" whose presence is forever imposed on him. He decides to try a sort of *recovery* of his being, and from then on his sole project is to convince the all-too-perceptive Inès that he *is not* a coward. He could have chosen to be indifferent to Inès's opinion, and then his project would have amounted to denying or ignoring—also in bad faith—his being-for-others. This would call for convincing himself of his absolute *strangeness* in relation to Inès, pretending to be in a world apart from hers with no possible communication between them, like Camus's Stranger, who is similarly indifferent to others. Finally, he might just as well have chosen himself as cowardly once and for all, trying thereby to elude (again in bad faith) the responsibility he must assume for his being-for-others. But clearly this last alternative, no less than the others, could not be reflective, and it would be pointless to express it in speech. On the contrary, the choice of cowardice would have to be a constitutive one, made at the root of his freedom and confirmed by the repeated failure of willful attempts at heroism. This cowardice would have to be constantly realized, regularly lived and proved. This is just what happens in an

6. *EN*, p. 551; *BN*, p. 608.

inferiority complex. Declaring oneself inferior is not enough, for one would not believe it oneself, and if one is to effectively resign oneself to inferiority the first person to convince of it is oneself. One must perpetually *make* oneself inferior by deliberate attempts at some form of superiority. We know that, at this level, the will is capable only of passing inclinations.

This is the level of "*accessory* reflection." Such reflection bears only on the secondary structures of action, as in deliberation over the means to attain a certain end. While engaging in it, one refuses to ask oneself about the existence or significance of a supreme end or of a fundamental choice. Accessory reflection permeates day-to-day living, living which thinks of itself only to justify itself, which finds itself in the wrong only with regard to the use of this or that procedure, which finds one's basic failure not in a choice—which, being fundamental, it prefers to ignore—but in the unavoidable disappointments of "destiny."

Of course even this "destiny" would be willed as such by the subject. His single though inexplicit wish is to constitute himself an essence that is fully achieved but still self-conscious. He wants to be done with the exhaustions of existence, an existence which constantly defeats itself and which at every point lacks coherence and security.

Few persons are content not to *be*, but many are content simply to be this or that. They prefer to resign themselves, giving up one or another ambition instead of giving up the deep self-falsification by which they seek to escape the freedom that oppresses them. They are like sleepwalkers, choosing never to awake from their basic project of constant sleep. Within oneself and through one's dealings with the world, one confirms one's choice of oneself. There is no deliverance from one's fundamental project in turning one's back on it, getting immersed in the secondary behaviors that flow from it. To stop oneself from stammering will no more cure an inferiority complex than sponging the floor will stem a flood.

Schemes for educating the will, themselves blind to the will's dependence upon a fundamental choice, only make the will a party to their blindness. This is why Alain's well-known remark—"To appear is itself one way to be, and it may be the only way"—also characterizes the level of accessory reflection. This proposes being as an ideal without inquiring about the significance of that ideal. It also implies that one must use means that are purely external to the end one wishes to achieve.

Purifying Reflection

So it seems that a pedagogy not founded on *purifying reflection* is without value. Only by such reflection can a being discover himself, no longer as constituted and governed by Destiny, but as an initial choice of himself which is altogether contingent and unjustifiable. This choice is "absurd" in that no reason can be given for it, since it is through the choice itself that reasons come to be. Indeed it is through such choice that the very notion of absurdity receives a meaning. Made without any basis, determining its own motives, the choice is also compulsory, for it is impossible to avoid. It implies the simultaneous arising of both the world and time. It implies the former because no choice could start from nothing and be related to nothing. It implies the latter because it is necessarily intentional, and therefore it brings to light a temporal present by one or another self-projected future. Choice therefore develops within both the world and the enduring moment, and accessory reflection tries to keep it there (a being's tendency is to persevere in being).

Accessory reflection dreads the appearance of the *instant*. In dislocating the enduring moment, the instant keeps consciousness from narrowly focusing upon actions by which a subject can lose himself in the world. As a fissure terminating the initial project, the instant facilitates a new choice of oneself, a conversion. Any fundamental project, insofar as it is an intention and not a state, is at the mercy of the instant. Although an intention tends to extend itself into its manifestations, it must always be in some way aware (of) itself. "At each moment I am still initiating any undertaking," and thus I may always examine and reject my initial choice.

> Consequently, I am in anguish, in fear of sudden dispossession, that is, of becoming radically other. But it therefore also happens that there are frequent "conversions," which make me totally metamorphose my original project. While these conversions have not been studied by philosophers, they have often inspired writers of fiction. Recall that *instant* at which Gide's Philoctetes casts off his hate, his fundamental project, his raison d'être and his being. One may recall that *instant* in which Raskolnikov decides to turn himself in. These extraordinary and marvelous instants in which the previous project collapses into the past in light of a new one that arises—still only in outline—on its ruins, in which humiliation, anguish, joy, and hope are closely married, in which we let go in order to grasp and grasp in order to let go—these instants have often seemed to provide the clearest and most inspiring image of our freedom. But in fact they are just one manifestation of it.[7]

This last remark is worth close attention as it brings up a couple of additional points.

First, it implies that we do not *become* free in movements of conversion, since after all our prior choice was itself free. We *are* freedom, in relation to every form of being, and in this sense we are the *nothingness* of being. Because we are the *project* of being, we *are not* the being toward which we strive. Such is our freedom, in an ontological sense. It is a factual freedom, contingent, irreducible, absurd. Human reality is condemned never to coincide with itself, to be a perpetual flight toward selfhood by a being that can never "be itself." Hence freedom seems a kind of fatal impotence. It fascinates man

7. *EN*, p. 555; *BN*, p. 612.

by proffering him a value without value, inviting him to fail utterly, making him "a useless passion."[8]

Second, Sartre's remark also points to a fundamental deficiency in such "conversions." Supposedly they produce more than the subject contributes to them. Remember the dense, laconic sentences we cited earlier: "These considerations do not exclude the possibility of a morality of deliverance and salvation [*salut*]. But such a morality can be reached only *after* [*au terme d'une*] *a radical conversion*, which we cannot discuss here."[9] Notice, however, that different sorts of conversion are involved in the two cases. One is immediate, gratuitous, and itself "absurd." The other is laborious and puts into play a moral effort at *deliverance*. It evinces a new attitude toward freedom. Instead of simply being lived, and used for disowning oneself so as to avoid anguish over one's lack of justification, freedom must be *assumed* as the stuff of one's person. So valued, freedom becomes a project—a project which is content with this freedom itself as its only foundation and which forsakes reassurance by justifications in bad faith.

> This particular type of project, which has freedom as both its foundation and its goal, deserves a special study. It is radically different from all other projects because it aims toward a type of being that is radically different. It would be necessary to explain in detail the relations between this and the project of being God (the absolute who is self-conscious and self-caused), a project which we have found is the deep-seated structure of human reality. But we cannot undertake this here: it leads to an *Ethics* [*une Ethique*], and it supposes that one has previously defined the nature and role of purifying reflection, whereas our descriptions to this point consider only an "accessory" reflection. It also supposes taking a position that can only be *moral* in the face of the values that haunt the For-itself.[10]

What information do we have at our disposal for developing the idea of purifying reflection?

We have often encountered this idea, starting with the psychology of emotion. There we saw that consciousness is caught in its own trap.

> Emotional consciousness is captive, but this must not be taken to imply that it has been imprisoned by some exterior existence. It is its own captive, inasmuch as it never gains control of the belief which it tries to live. It is captive precisely because it does live it, because it is absorbed in living it. . . . Liberation can come only from a purifying reflection or from a complete disappearance of the emotional situation.[11]

8. [*EN*, p. 708; *BN*, p. 784.]
9. *EN*, p. 484n; *BN*, p. 534n. [Jeanson's emphasis.]
10. *EN*, p. 670; *BN*, p. 742. [The phrase in parentheses is Jeanson's addition.]
11. J.-P. Sartre, *Esquisse d'une théorie des émotions* (Paris: Hermann, 1939), p. 43; *The Emotions: Outline of a Theory*, translated by Bernard Frechtman (New York: Philosophical Library, 1948), pp. 78–79.

And, further along:

> The purifying reflection of the phenomenological reduction can grasp the emotion in the very act of constituting the world under the aspect of magic, as when we reflect: "I find him hateful *because* I am angry." But this reflection is rare and requires special motivations. Ordinarily we direct an accessory reflection on the emotional consciousness. While it does grasp the consciousness as a consciousness, it grasps it only insofar as it is motivated by the object: "I am angry *because* he is hateful." Passion structures itself, starting with this reflection.[12]

This passage is valuable because it effects the identification between the phenomenological attitude and the ethical attitude—an identification which carries in itself the conversion required by a moral action. Thus it seems that phenomenology, in describing the planes of unreflectivity and accessory reflection, makes use of a purifying reflection that is none other than Husserl's famous "reduction." And from Sartre's viewpoint, this is the return to consciousness, the initial stance of the pre-reflective *cogito*. It is now clear that one cannot describe the unreflective so long as one remains on the same unreflective plane—a difficulty we have already encountered. Except that the thing to avoid, in passing to the reflective plane, is cutting oneself off from the unreflectivity one wishes to describe. One has to remain in some sort of continuity with it. And the possibility of this depends precisely on there being in fact two sorts of reflection:

> Pure reflection, simple presence of the reflective for-itself to the for-itself reflected-on (that is, to the unreflective, which thereby finds itself "reflected"), is at once the original form of reflection and its ideal form. It is that on whose foundation impure reflection appears. It is also that which is never initially *given* but must be won by means of a sort of katharsis (purification). Impure or accessory reflection . . . includes pure reflection but surpasses it because it makes further claims.[13]

Here, notice, are reverberations of the ambiguity we have regularly pointed out: when it first arises, reflection is "pure," but all the same it must be "purified." *In fact*, it *is* pure; but, to repeat a question Valéry asked of historical method: "What should we make of a fact?"[14] A fact is never "given" to us, rather the recognition of it is proposed to us, which is never more than an occasion for us to grasp it. Thus, freedom is no more than an appeal from within, which we are free to disregard. And since at the outset we always disregard it, denying (freely) our own freedom, we should then try to liberate ourselves. Now impure or accessory reflection is just this effort by the for-itself

12. *Esquisse*, p. 49; *Emotions*, p. 91.
13. *EN*, p. 201, cf. equally p. 206; *BN*, pp. 218 and 224. [The phrases in parentheses are Jeanson's additions.]
14. [Paul Valéry, "Le Fait historique," in *Variété I* (Paris: Editions de La N.R.F., 1934), p. 159.]

again to apprehend its being, to be entirely *for itself*: "a reflection that seeks to determine the being I am. . . ."[15] This attempt at self-recovery, at founding oneself, is doomed to fail. Squarely within the for-itself it introduces an absolute reflective distance, unbridgeable insofar as recovery of the for-itself first involves a tearing away from itself without reassembling itself as a new for-itself. "Impure reflection is an abortive effort by the for-itself to *be another* while *remaining itself*."[16]

Consequently, reflection must be purified so that it forgoes this kind of recovery, going back to an original presence to self which, if one may say so, is at the same time both naïve and deeply cognizant of itself.

At the level of accessory reflection, a person sometimes seems hard on himself. Perhaps he is bitter about life, fixing on the general and anonymous aspects of its shortcomings. But this prevents his reaching a personal foundation, an ultimate project, which sometimes he may apprehend anxiously as still an issue he will have to confront. And it is on just this level of hypocrisy that we see arising, in impure reflection, both psychical temporality and the succession of *psychic facts*. As already noted, psychical temporality is a weighing down and substantializing of original temporality. The will, for example, desiring to avoid the initial choice, "constitutes false psychic objects as *drives*, the better to deliberate on these drives (love of glory, beauty, etc.) and to determine itself in terms of them."[17] But we know that "voluntary deliberation is always faked. How can I appraise motives and drives whose entire value I confer before any deliberation by the choice I make of myself?"[18] In themselves these motives and drives are nothing. They are not independent, qualitatively determinate objects; they are sustained before consciousness only in the indissoluble unity which my free project gives them.

In contrast, the weighing down of consciousness which typifies psychism is absent at the level of pure reflection. Here one has stopped trying to give himself motives, drives, supports, or justifications. Instead, all needs and exigencies are referred back to the choice of oneself that constitutes one's fundamental project.

THE HUMAN CONDITION AND FREEDOM

We shall not consider all of Sartre's remarks about one's *situation*. As is plain from everything we have so far considered, when Sartre refers to freedom he means freedom *within a condition*. The for-itself is free only in a situation, that is, free in relation to its condition. This condition involves such factors as the place occupied by the for-itself, its past, and what it can do with the things

15. *EN,* p. 218; *BN,* p. 237.
16. *EN,* p. 208; *BN,* p. 226.
17. *EN,* p. 552; *BN,* p. 608.
18. *EN,* p. 527; *BN,* p. 581.

around it (the manipulability, so to speak, of the implements found in its environing world). Sartre shows that none of these external factors can actually limit freedom: ". . . a freedom encounters no limits but those within itself."[19] Now it does encounter limits in an alienated situation, that is, one on which an "outside" is imposed by virtue of the simultaneous existence of that situation for others. But limits of this kind are always freely chosen, for inasmuch as the experience of this alienation means recognizing the other as freedom, I already freely *assume* the being that I am for him. I remain perfectly free not to assume it, as when I choose to ignore my being-for-others, disowning the "hyphen" uniting me with the other, and thus see him as an object. In this respect, even the torturer fails to limit his victim's freedom. But when we recall that all freedom is contingent, that on its reverse side it is *facticity*, that there is a fact which consists in the flight from fact, then we may also observe that the torturer determines this facticity as completely as possible, he situates it with exactitude, he *conditions* it totally. What he controls, however, is not his victim's freedom or power to escape facts, but rather the contingent circumstances in which his victim retains the freedom to escape the fact of torture. If the victim gives in to the torturer, he does so freely. His freedom then identifies itself with the facticity of his battered body, which, since he no longer strives to surpass it, is given over into the torturer's possession.

As for death itself, it does not concern human reality in any way. Since death arrests the activity of meaning-giving, it cannot be what gives meaning to life. Even suicide

> should not be considered as a self-founded termination of life. As an act of my life, it requires a significance that the future alone can confer upon it; but since it is the *final* act of my life, it rejects this future. . . . Suicide is an absurdity which sinks my life into the absurd.[20]

In general, death is not one of my possibilities. " . . . because the for-itself always claims an 'afterwards,' there is no place for death in that being which is for-itself."[21] I can project this or that death (by suicide, martyrdom, combat, etc.), but I cannot project *my* death, except in an illusory manner, since this would be to project the impossibility of all projects. It would ultimately entail observing myself from the outside, so as to grasp a semblance of meaning. But even in this I give advance notice of the triumph of the viewpoint the other has on me over that viewpoint on myself *that I am*. In *The Wall*, Tom, one of the three men condemned to death, tries to understand what will happen to him:

19. *EN*, p. 608; *BN*, p. 673.
20. *EN*, p. 624; *BN*, p. 690.
21. *EN*, p. 624; *BN*, p. 691.

It's like a nightmare . . . [;] you want to think about something, and all the while you have the impression that there it is, that you're going to get it, and then it slides off, it escapes you and falls away. I tell myself: afterwards there will no longer be anything. But I don't understand what that means. There are moments when I almost succeed . . . and then that too falls away and again I think of pains, of bullets, of explosions. Believe me, I'm a materialist; I'm not going to go crazy. But some things don't make any sense. I see my dead body; that's easy, but it is *I* who see it, with *my* eyes. I must try somehow to think . . . to think that I will no longer see anything, will no longer hear anything, and that the world will continue for others. We aren't made to think such thoughts, Pablo. Believe me, I have already stayed up a whole night waiting for something. But this thing is different: it will take us from behind, Pablo, and we won't be able to prepare for it.[22]

To conclude: death

cannot therefore belong to the ontological structure of the for-itself. . . . it is *a contingent fact* which as such escapes me in principle and is fundamentally a feature of my facticity. . . . it is a situation-limit. . . . Since death escapes my projects because it is unrealizable, I myself escape death in my very project.[23]

In this way human reality, as a being in a situation, confirms itself for us as "responsible for its manner of being without being the foundation of its being."[24]

The obstacles that human reality encounters appear to it as obstacles only in virtue of its free project. And this project excludes death by making it, as Epicurus said, the moment of life that is never ours to live.

Finally,

I am responsible for everything, in fact, except my responsibility itself, for I am not the foundation of my being. Thus everything takes place as if I were required to be responsible. . . . I never encounter anything except myself and my projects, such that ultimately my abandonment, that is, my facticity, consists simply in my being condemned to be wholly [*intégralement*] responsible for myself.[25]

The Practical Meaning of Freedom

Obviously we have departed from consciousness in its purest form. The successive descriptions of it inspired by the initial *cogito* have progressively revealed, though still only schematically, both the complexity of human reality

---

22. Jean-Paul Sartre, "Le Mur," in *Le Mur* (Paris: Gallimard, 1939), pp. 21–22; "The Wall," in *Intimacy and Other Stories*, translated by Lloyd Alexander (New York: Berkley Medallion, 1956), pp. 68–69.
23. *EN*, pp. 629–630, 632; *BN*, pp. 697, 700.
24. *EN*, p. 633; *BN*, p. 701.
25. *EN*, pp. 641–642; *BN*, p. 710.

and the threats of engulfment presented to it by the world, by its own past, by its body, and by the existence of others. These threats come together as a web, a tangle. So constrained is human reality that it may lose sight of its fundamental project by losing itself. It bogs down in a crush of secondary projects that throng about one's situation in precise proportion as one fails to choose among them.

In this connection Sartre's views on freedom have been criticized by Merleau-Ponty. The following is representative of these objections:

> The real choice is that of our whole character and of our manner of being toward the world [*être au monde*]. Now if, on the one hand, this total choice is never made explicitly, being the silent assertion of our being toward the world, then it is hard to see how it could be called our own, since such a freedom glides over itself and amounts to a destiny. On the other hand, the choice we make of ourselves may be a true choice, that is, a conversion of our existence, but then it necessarily presupposes a previous accomplishment [*un acquis préalable*] which this choice sets about modifying and it founds a new tradition. . . . For . . . there could be no uprooting if freedom had not first installed itself somewhere and was preparing to settle elsewhere. . . . choice presupposes some previous involvement [*engagement*] and the idea of a first choice is self-contradictory.[26]

Merleau-Ponty is asserting the primacy of concrete experience in this passage, where he also accuses Sartre of searching for "the conditions of possibility while neglecting the conditions of reality." As we have just seen, *Being and Nothingness* takes frequent note of facticity and contingency, describing the various circumstances by which freedom is inevitably conditioned. But Sartre does indeed maintain that freedom has no external limitations, that it consists in a perpetual capacity to remake one's original choice, hence, to make an original choice—all of which is at odds with Merleau-Ponty. For Merleau-Ponty all choice presupposes an initial diversity, all negation intervenes against a previous natural affirmation. He reminds us that young children are not concerned with tearing themselves away from their world and situation, that they can hardly be said to make choices of themselves. To suppose they could would be like supposing that Valéry could have written his poems on the slender resources of that vague denial and seductive negativism that permeate his work. It might be further asserted that inspiration, which is received by the poet *before* it is chosen, is necessary for poetry. So it was that Morgan, in *Sparkenbroke*, described poetry without inspiration as "a labour not of choice among riches but of struggle with poverty."[27]

26. Maurice Merleau-Ponty, *Phénoménologie de la perception* (Paris: Gallimard, 1945), pp. 500–501; *Phenomenology of Perception*, translated by Colin Smith (New York: Humanities Press, 1962), pp. 438–439. [Jeanson has reversed the order of the two segments of this quotation from Merleau-Ponty's text.]

27. Charles Morgan, *Sparkenbroke* (New York: Macmillan Co., 1936), p. 210.

Nevertheless, we should be careful. First of all, by rejecting in this way the free choice that operates after experiences which demand action, we risk making the very possibility of such action incomprehensible. We have here a paradox that is found more than once in the history of philosophy: one's morality requires a kind of personal conversion which one's psychology completely disallows. Worse still, this paradox arises in this case in the unique context of phenomenological description, which is sometimes used to reveal the progressive and natural formation of our character, our manner, our style of life, and sometimes to show the free conscious choice that starts with this "given." But human reality is thereby left with the alternative of a *destiny* undergone or a *destiny* resumed and modified as it proceeds. Conversion here would amount to passing from an alienation that is total and primitive to a possession of self that is secondary. Poetic or musical composition, for example, would be just a matter of taking dictation from a muse ("One does not work; one listens. It's like a stranger who speaks in your ear."), followed perhaps by a certain amount of editing and rewriting. In short, the activity would take root only on the foundation of passivity; consciousness, in the full sense, would intervene only against an unconscious background.

Clearly, Merleau-Ponty does not hold these views. His *Phenomenology of Perception*, which many will agree with Alphonse de Waehlens[28] in calling "admirable," is entirely devoted to revealing the meaning-giving activity [*l'activité signifiante*] of consciousness, even in the last recesses of unreflective human behavior. Thus, for example, the child *acquires* only what he understands and what he understands is that to which his own activity attributes a meaning, appearing to him as filled with a significance which, for good or ill, he may consider as his own doing. This accounts for the surprises that sometimes occur when he tries to use this acquisition. Having spontaneously *rejected* it as a pure *given*, it truly becomes his own; he has made of it something valuable to him, whether an exciting mystery or a precious oddity. The subject achieves, perhaps inexplicitly, a certain subjective orientation. Of this Merleau-Ponty says: ". . . the acquisition is truly acquired only if it is taken up again in a new movement of thought, and a thought is situated only if it takes its situation upon itself."[29]

Accordingly, the debate must be carried to a deeper level, and for this we believe we have assembled all the elements necessary.

To start with, the issue as we see it turns on equivocations in the use of the words "choice" and "freedom." We have dwelt upon the negative character of freedom at the level of the natural attitude and accessory reflection. Similarly, at this level choice must also be viewed as an elimination effected by the subject—one by which he progressively appears to himself through making one

28. Alphonse de Waehlens, "Heidegger et Sartre," in *Deucalion I* (Paris: Editions de le Revue Fontaine, 1946), p. 22.

29. *Phénoménologie de la perception*, p. 151; *Phenomenology of Perception*, p. 130.

or another kind of world appear. To say he is absolutely responsible for such a choice simply means no one else would have chosen the same, not even if he were in exactly the same objective circumstances. And this entails that these objective conditions show themselves as such only through the subject's intervention. One is reminded in this connection of Bergson's remark that "consciousness . . . consists of . . . choice."[30] But the resemblance is far from complete, since in the first chapter of *Matter and Memory* Bergson makes this "choice" rest entirely on one's physical activity in dealing with the objects of the world. This is because for Bergson concrete consciousness can do nothing but flow along in its deep spontaneity. This point indicates again the necessity of attributing to consciousness itself an original power of discrimination. Only on the basis of this power shall we later be able to understand even a modest attempt at free conversion.

Like correlative notions, choice is ambiguous. A power of discrimination exists; insofar as it contains a power of refusal, it is the most fundamental structure of consciousness. But this power exhausts itself in its actual operations upon the world, and it can become "genuine" choice only after a purifying reflection which takes it on as its own. *In fact* it is already a free choice, and it is mine; but paradoxically I must still *make* it into my free choice of myself. I am already myself before I apprehend myself—but I am such in the mode of having-to-be myself, and this is why, even though I am already constantly choosing what is to constitute myself, I must still also choose myself. It is therefore preferable not to speak of "genuine" choice so long as it is no more than "the silent assertion of our being toward the world." All the same, we continue to hold that this too involves choice. That it does is confirmed by the observation that, in conversion, it permits the emergence of an authentic choice. It is also confirmed by a feeling all of us have experienced to some degree: whatever our birth, whatever our past, we choose them in proportion as we explicitly relate them to ourselves, as we assume them, as we consent to live the life initiated by them. What is self-contradictory is therefore only the idea of an *authentic* first choice.

By the same token, when Merleau-Ponty describes as "ready-made freedom"[31] the freedom of which Sartre speaks, we would like to add that it has this character only from the negative perspective in which it has not yet grasped itself. From this angle freedom does indeed resemble a destiny. Sartre calls this its facticity: we undergo it, we are condemned to it. But if it were a true destiny, if it were simply an entanglement, one cannot see how a subsequent disentanglement could be accomplished. Sartre certainly does assert that all

30. [Henri Bergson, *Matière et mémoire* (Paris: Félix Alcan, 1929), p. 26; *Matter and Memory*, translated by Nancy Margaret Paul and W. Scott Palmer (London: Allen and Unwin, 1919), p. 31. Bergson's full sentence reads: "Consciousness—in regard to external perception—consists in just this choice."]
31. [*Phénoménologie de la perception*, p. 501; *Phenomenology of Perception*, p. 439.]

freedom is engaged. But he also shows that if this engagement does not place itself in question at the very moment it occurs, no return to it later would be conceivable.

This brings us to the heart of the debate. It is inaccurate to depict freedom as at first a *response* to oneself. Instead it is a question, yet an unformulated one, an interrogative atmosphere that is implied in each attitude of consciousness. What Sartre does when he reascends from this to negation amounts to furnishing "the conditions for the possibility" of all interrogation and so of freedom itself. But inasmuch as we *remain* on the level of interrogation we are concerned with "the conditions for reality." Freedom exists as the impossibility of an absolute affirmation of that reality, of a totally convinced posture; choice exists as a constant risk of sliding toward negation and refusal.

I *am* free, in this sense, insofar as I cannot act in any way without also apprehending—albeit without precision or attention to means—the possibility of acting differently. Despite Merleau-Ponty's criticism, Sartre nowhere speaks of the possibility of real freedom, but of the reality of that possibility which continually preserves freedom. This is why Sartre thinks it inappropriate to speak of a freedom "that has nothing to accomplish because it is already acquired."[32] In fact it has not been acquired, it simply *is*; but it is such that it *must be* accomplished and conquered. It is engaged *in* itself and it must be engaged *by* itself. It is choice, but it must choose itself.

We should emphasize the difference between these two approaches. Merleau-Ponty declares that freedom as conceived by Sartre cannot put itself into effect or engage itself. We, on the other hand, believe that *Being and Nothingness* adequately brings out the *intentional* character of all freedom. However, the freedom of consciousness derives from its being exhaustively manifested in the totality of its own intentions, such that these may try to prolong themselves and thereby enmire consciousness in its own products. If consciousness were able to engage itself in things themselves, it could never again disengage itself from them, and it would no longer be consciousness. And yet it never grasps itself except through its attitudes regarding things. Thus consciousness is never a victim, except of its own projects; its freedom knows only those prisons that it builds out of its own impulses.

Continuing his discussion of Sartre's conception of freedom, Merleau-Ponty writes:

> . . . the result of this initial reflection on freedom would be to make it impossible. If in fact freedom is equal in all of our actions and even in our passions, if it lacks common measure with our conduct, and if the slave evinces as much freedom in living fearfully as in breaking his irons, then one cannot say there may be *free action*, for freedom has been forever placed on the antecedent side of all action. In no instance could it be said, "Here is where freedom appears,"

32. *Phénoménologie de la perception*, p. 499; *Phenomenology of Perception*, p. 437.

since for free action to be detected it must stand out against a ground of life that is either not free or less free. It is, so to speak, both everywhere and nowhere.[33]

On this point we can only set in relief a misunderstanding we have hinted at. It consists in conflating two senses of freedom which Sartre keeps distinct. They are the two freedoms concerning which Sartre holds that passage from one to the other requires a "radical conversion." It must be granted that, in one sense of "free," the slave who lives in fear is just as free as the slave who breaks his chains. That is, the two slaves are equally responsible and resignation is an attitude which puts itself in question the more it develops. But freedom in the second sense is something beyond this negative or factual freedom. Freedom in the first sense is a structure of our being and almost a "state of nature,"[34] but freedom in the second sense is freedom-as-valued; it enjoins one to assess the value of the various uses to which it may be put. It is on this basis that the differences between persons arise in the first place. A slave who undertakes an authentic act does not initiate a novel intention that stands out incomprehensibly against a life that is more or less determined. Such an act is rather the secondary or reflective assumption of that life, together with a conscious conversion of the perspective through which the situation had at first inclined him toward resignation.[35] This is why the notion of free action is equivocal: there are no unfree acts, but some have a freeing effect when undertaken—that is, they consolidate their factual freedom in an authentic freedom. The latter is never *given*, but the former is never absent, since it points toward and solicits its metamorphosis into the other.

Thus the moral aspects of Sartre's ontology, far from rendering freedom impossible, should be seen as incomprehensible apart from reapprehension of the natural freedom that is essential to human consciousness. Curiously enough, Merleau-Ponty also puts forth the inverse of the above criticism. According to this reproach, freedom in *Being and Nothingness* is *so* efficacious that we cannot take account of certain improbable occurrences, for example: ". . . if one has for twenty years constructed his daily life on a continually sustained inferiority complex, [Sartre could scarcely deny that] it is not very *probable* that one will change." Moreover, Merleau-Ponty explains,

> if freedom allows itself to be touched by no motives, then my habitual being toward the world is always fragile, the complexes I have complacently nourished

33. *Phénoménologie de la perception*, p. 499; *Phenomenology of Perception*, pp. 436–437.
34. *Phénoménologie de la perception*, p. 499; *Phenomenology of Perception*, p. 437.
35. "When we state that the slave is as free in his chains as his master, we do not wish to speak of a freedom that would remain indeterminate. The slave in his chains is free *to break them* . . . "; see also the remainder of the passage. *EN*, pp. 634–635; *BN*, p. 703.

over the years always remain equally harmless, and an effortless gesture of my freedom can instantly blow them all to bits.[36]

Of course this is not what happens, but Sartre is not committed to saying it is. Even if my free project of transforming myself were really able thus to introduce itself in an instant, in such a break in temporality, it would still not follow that I could actually effect this self-transformation all at once in that same instant throughout all my relationships. It is one thing to contemplate motives; it is quite another to be motivated by them. In the first case, consciousness is inevitably passive when it encounters constituted motives: it submits to their mechanical interplay, which determines the result. In the second case consciousness is active, but its activity is ambiguous, consisting in meaning-giving projects, which, as they achieve results in the world, are perpetually confirmed in their existing direction, becoming weighed down by a sort of active inertia. In the latter case, however, it is not our factual freedom, freedom as a structure of consciousness, that becomes less probable. Instead the threat is to the reapprehension of this freedom on the plane of authenticity, which would enable it to effect a conversion. Still, an unexpected conversion is always possible; it would then open up the various routes to a purifying reflection that could confirm or invalidate the new choice.

Sartre once remarked that it is false to assert that if man is free, his liberation becomes meaningless.[37] On the contrary, he said, this liberation will be incomprehensible if man is not free at the start. Only a being who is in essence free can envisage its own liberation.

This is really the chief point of contention. The passage to ontology requires that the ambiguity of human reality be defined in its essence before its manifestations may be described. Failing this, the ambiguity is likely to be conceived as the mere coexistence within man of a subjugation to, and a freedom to surpass, the motivations of the world. In that case, however, the motivations would be causes and the freedom would be ineffectual. To understand a situation is nothing if it is not the ability to make it appear as something different, and hence the ability to resituate oneself at the origin of what is.

---

36. *Phénoménologie de la perception*, p. 504; *Phenomenology of Perception*, pp. 441–442.

37. [For example: "But, the Marxists will say, if you teach man that he *is* free you betray him for he then has no need to *become* free; can you conceive of a man free from birth who lays claim to being liberated? To which I answer that if man is not originally free, but determined once and for all, one cannot even conceive what his liberation might be. . . . It's precisely by becoming revolutionaries, that is to say organizing with other members of their class to throw off the tyranny of their masters, that they best demonstrate their freedom: oppression leaves them no choices besides resignation or revolution. But in either case they show their freedom to choose." "Materialisme et révolution," in *Situations, III* (Paris: Gallimard, 1949), pp. 208–209; "Materialism and Revolution," in *Literary and Philosophical Essays*, translated by Annette Michelson (New York: Philosophical Library, 1955), pp. 184–185.]

But clearly such a power is incompatible with an engagement that one merely undergoes. *To live is not to undergo one's situation; it is to consent to undergo it.*

An odd divergence becomes evident at this point. Merleau-Ponty, concerned to remain in the concrete, runs the risk of seeing his unitary description fall apart into an irreducible duality, the two terms of which are incompatible. Sartre, on the other hand, having started from an elucidation of the essential structures of consciousness in its relations to the world and itself, later rediscovers the concrete. But he sees this as penetrated through and through *by a factual or real freedom [une liberté de fait], without which moral freedom would be an empty phrase,* behind which we would have to imagine some sort of passive conversion of the subject by a kind of divine grace. Thus we could say that Merleau-Ponty describes a "moral situation,"[38] while Sartre "loads" his description of the situation by moralizing it.

All of which is to say that human ambiguity does not arise in regard to any relation between freedom and what freedom opposes. Instead it lies at the heart of freedom, between its impulse and its reassumption of the impulse, in a purifying reflection on its own ends. We believe, for our part, that what is needed here is an essentialist phenomenology in which a primitive duality of being and nothingness is defined and determined. Such a duality, in which being is both sought and rejected, holds the key to the deepest meaning of human behavior.

This is why we would define *Being and Nothingness* as an ontology of freedom. Basically this work is not a study of Being after the manner of metaphysics. Instead it is a study of human reality's free attitude toward every "in-itself" which is capable of attracting that freedom and tempting it to bog down. Thus, for example, Sartre does not hesitate to assimilate the body and the past of consciousness to the mode of existence of things. Even though the body is not an object and even though the past can be reapprehended in a present that is oriented toward a future, they nevertheless represent, for the for-itself, the threat of *being* this or that, finally and contingently, that is, they invite the for-itself to abdicate its free power of renewal. The body and the past penetrate consciousness neither more nor less than they penetrate the objects of the world, which in any case are always transcended. Yet, like the objects of the world, the body and the past constitute a pole of being whose irreducibility perpetually solicits the intentions of consciousness, thereby justifying the rule that consciousness, unless it is vigilant, will succumb to a growing inertia.

To conclude, we think it a mistake to describe the moral attitude and the natural attitude as if they were parts of a greater whole, as if they entered into an "exchange" that always tended toward equilibrium between the "pro-

38. *Phénoménologie de la perception,* p. 158; *Phenomenology of Perception,* p. 136.

posals of the world" and the "power of initiative" of man.[39] Either the moral attitude is an evolved character of the species—in which case it loses all peculiarly moral value—or it is a conquest by the individual. If the latter, analogies from hydrodynamics are not apt, since it involves a potential for explosion and rupture, an energy that is best liberated only when it is pointed in the most efficacious direction.

The description of such an oriented freedom is precisely the role of an Ethics [*une Ethique*]. But it cannot be accomplished without a thorough examination of the objects for which human reality strives.

39. Cf. *Phénoménologie de la perception*, p. 501; *Phenomenology of Perception*, p. 439.

Chapter 2

Existential Psychoanalysis

IT IS NOT enough to show that human reality is always impelled by a freely chosen fundamental project. It remains to determine the type of relation to being which this project posits as its end. Existential psychoanalysis intervenes at this point. We have had several glimpses of it in our references to Sartre's study of Baudelaire, a work that helps clarify *Being and Nothingness*.[1]

In this chapter we shall merely underline certain essential features that help us define this method from our viewpoint.

It is, first of all, a "phenomenological method."[2] These principles are now familiar enough to allow us to forego repeating them here; what differs in the present case is the field to which they are applied. Up to now we have remained on a general plane, whether our concern was with psychology or with incorporating psychology into ontology. We have described human reality, the human condition, and the fundamentals of consciousness itself, which we have called a freedom in situation.

Everything said so far about the passage from ontology to ethics points toward *moral description*.[3] Such description is characteristic of existential psychoanalysis, a psychoanalysis whose aim is precisely to effect the transition from ontology to ethics. This transition entails an important correlative movement from the general to the singular. Let us examine these points more closely.

We have seen that the fundamental project of human reality is its desire to attain being-in-itself. But we also know that this desire does not have as its desideratum "the pure in-itself, contingent and absurd, corresponding at every point to what it encounters and nihilates."[4] Instead, human reality wishes to be an in-itself that would also be for-itself, that is, an in-itself that would be its own foundation and yet would continue to exist for-itself. The fundamental value presiding over this project is therefore

1. [See in this regard pp. 140–141, 145 above.]
2. *EN*, p. 559; *BN*, p. 617.
3. *EN*, p. 720; *BN*, p. 796.
4. [*EN*, p. 653; *BN*, p. 723.]

the in-itself-for-itself, that is, the ideal of a consciousness that would found its own being-in-itself through the pure consciousness that it would have of itself. It is this ideal which may be called God. Thus the best way to conceive of the fundamental project of human reality is to say that man is the being whose project is to be God.[5]

But, if this is true, does it not then seem that freedom has been replaced by a human "nature" or "essence"?

To this we would reply that although the *meaning* of this desire is ultimately the project of being God, the desire is never itself *constituted by* this meaning; on the contrary, the desire is always itself a *particular invention* of these ends. Such ends are pursued from within a particular empirical situation, and it is this very pursuit that constitutes the surroundings as a *situation*. The desire to be is always realized as the desire for a way of being. And this desire for a way of being is in turn expressed as the meaning of the myriads of concrete desires which make up the fabric of our conscious life.[6]

We now have the elements needed to situate existential psychoanalysis. Insofar as freedom is an abstract structure of human existence it can be described by phenomenological ontology. At the other extreme, classification of various empirical desires must be the object of strictly psychological research. Between the two domains are the fundamental desires by which freedom manifests existentially its abstract structure. It is in this middle region that we encounter the *person*, and this is the terrain investigated by existential psychoanalysis.

The overall direction of Sartre's work can now be more satisfyingly illuminated than was hitherto possible: starting from psychology, we saw the movement of his thinking consolidated in an ontology; we now observe its passage toward an ethics. It was essential to begin with concrete experience. Aiming to describe such experience comprehensively, Sartre started with an empirical nomenclature, though even then he had recourse to the essences which bring out for human reality the meaning of its own behaviors. It then became possible to set in relief the essence of these essences, that is, the abstract structure of consciousness itself—the intentional character of its freedom. Finally, our grasp of this abstract structure assured us that all human being is in principle accessible through an inquiry into the fundamental choice by which it is freely lived and oriented. Ontology thus establishes the underpinnings and principles of an existential psychoanalysis, even though it cannot itself conduct it, since the latter is already situated in a moral context. Our use of "essence" above cannot be interpreted in a Platonic manner because the essences that concern empirical psychology are not pure Ideas subsisting independently of their existential realizations but meanings [*significations*] that are understood only insofar as they are lived. And although it is convenient to speak of the es-

5. *EN*, p. 653; *BN*, pp. 723–724.
6. *EN*, p. 654; *BN*, p. 724.

sence of consciousness, we must remember that freedom, which is the structure of consciousness, "is (an) immediately concrete surging-forth"; it *is* existence, or, as Sartre puts it, "in freedom, existence precedes essence."[7]

To conclude: in any inquiry into human reality, describing the "essence" designates that phase whose aim is to bring out and conceptualize the spontaneous understanding that human reality already has of its own attitudes. This entails an "eidetic reflection," and what we have called Sartre's essentialist method rests on it. Phenomenology is therefore a method for investigating the concrete. Its concepts possess a strictly methodological and inclusive value and are never to be confused with any "realities" beyond the concrete postulated to explain or account for it, and it is in this light that Sartre warns against confusing ontology with metaphysics.

Existential psychoanalysis will therefore in turn start with an empirical classification of human behaviors from the angle of desires, tendencies, and inclinations. Like psychology, it will be guided by the principle that man "expresses himself as a whole in his most insignificant and superficial behaviors. In other words, there is no whim, no mannerism, no human act that is not *revelatory*."[8] On this point existential psychoanalysis converges with Freudian psychoanalysis. The goal of the former will be to "*decipher* man's empirical behaviors, that is, to bring to full light the revelations contained in each such behavior and to grasp it with concepts."[9] Its method will be to compare behaviors in order to separate out those accidental features which mask the fundamental choice that is distinctively symbolized in each behavior. This will lead to the "springing forth of the unique revelation"[10] which each of the particular behaviors expresses differently—another convergence with Freudian psychoanalysis. We already know how the two methods differ. As we have seen, Sartre rejects the notion of an unconscious psychism.[11] However, since "lived consciousness" is not the same as "explicit knowledge" for existential psychoanalysis, the latter—like Freudian psychoanalysis—must be a strictly objective method in which the analytic subject no longer possesses any privileged position. Thus, when one directs the inquiry upon himself, the subject must treat himself "exactly as though he were another."[12]

The essential distinguishing character of existential psychoanalysis is that it is based, not on secondary tendencies like sexuality or the will to power, but on human reality's fundamental relation to being and its way of living this relation. Our passage through ontology is clearly what allows us to consider the one secondary and the other fundamental. Whereas psychology appeals to

7. *EN*, p. 655; *BN*, p. 725.
8. *EN*, p. 656; *BN*, p. 726.
9. Ibid.
10. [*EN*, p. 656; *BN*, p. 727.]
11. [*EN*, pp. 88–91; *BN*, pp. 90–95.]
12. [*EN*, p. 658; *BN*, p. 728.]

the idea of a totality that is human, ontology places it on the terrain of a "totalitarian" [*totalitair*] knowledge of man.[13]

> What ontology can teach psychoanalysis . . . is first of all the *true* origin of the meaning of things and their *true* relation to human reality. Ontology alone can place itself at the level of transcendence and grasp in a single view the two terms of being-in-the-world, because it alone originally situates itself in the perspective of the *cogito*.[14]

We should note in passing the perfect definition of an essentialist grasp of human ambiguity that Sartre gives us in the above passage: "a single view (with) two terms." This perspective falls between Merleau-Ponty, who declines to distinguish the two terms, and dualistic metaphysics, which effects a separation at the start and then claims impotence in restoring any relationship, except through arbitrary monisms of Matter or of Mind. In either case the possibility of a Morality seems compromised. If (as we have suggested above)[15] an attitude is moral only (a) if it is discontinuous with the natural attitude, that is, if it requires a revolution beyond any evolution, and (b) if this revolution, to preserve its value, is accomplished by the same subject who evolves— then, only an ontology that preserves the ambiguity at the very heart of the subject's action (and that shuns reabsorbing that ambiguity into an artificial unity, just as it shuns splitting it into a duality of independent substances) can furnish Morality with a nonillusory point of departure.

The appearance of the moral attitude is not an episode in the evolution of the human species. It is no more assimilable to biological facts than it is to social ones: no natural "mutation," no objective transformation of human relations, can account for it. It is not situated on the plane of generality but always refers back to the singular act of an individual conversion. Whatever its degree of success, it always proceeds from an absolute advent. Only from an exterior viewpoint, the viewpoint of others, does it appear as a simple event imbedded in the continuity of an existence.

This implies no disregard for the influence of society on the individual, but the strictly social character of this influence must not be overlooked. The subject does not invent social contexts; they present themselves enveloped in generality and anonymity. With Merleau-Ponty

---

13. Cf. *EN*, p. 663; *BN*, p. 735. [This was later to be specified as a study of "totalizations" or the developing syntheses inherent in historical praxis. See Sartre's *Critique de la raison dialectique*, vol. 1, *Théorie des ensembles pratiques* (Paris: Gallimard, 1960), pp. 139–140; *Critique of Dialectical Reason,* vol. 1, *Theory of Practical Ensembles*, translated by Alan Sheridan-Smith, edited by Jonathan Rée (London: New Left Books, 1976), pp. 46–47. It is central to Sartre's huge study of Flaubert, alluded to as a future project on the same page of *Being and Nothingness* cited here.]

14. *EN*, p. 694; *BN*, p. 769.

15. [See pp. 183 et seq. above.]

we therefore recognize, surrounding our initiatives and the rigorously individual project that is ourselves, a zone of generalized existence and of already accomplished projects, of meanings that linger between ourselves and things. . . .[16]

We even admit that each person is "in a moral situation," in that history and his age always compel him to discover others, either predecessors or distant contemporaries, who have brought off acts of liberation and made efforts at authenticity. But then either he uses these acts and efforts as guides by objectifying them as "values" or examples to "imitate" or he resolutely tries to go beyond such inert and chilled significations by reinventing them from within his own situation, as something called into question.

Strictly speaking, we do not *invent.* Discoveries of others' acts of liberation can either be oriented by us according to that other orientation which has already been spontaneously adopted by our natural attitude or be grasped expressly in a liberating conversion of that "free" spontaneous orientation. A world of difference separates these two attitudes: the latter, which is a reinvention, is not a continuous temporal progression but instead requires an absolute act in which this course is dislocated, giving way to the "nothingness" of the instant. This is implicit in the feeling, familiar to us all, that it sometimes takes a mere "nothing"—like pressing a button or flipping a catch— to utterly overturn the meaning of a situation. My laziness, for example, being an anonymous deficiency, is easily confessed, so long as I remain on the plane of generality. I know a simple decision is sufficient to renounce it; but that is precisely why I hesitate to make it. And, if I finally make the decision, I shall certainly encounter several obstacles to execution which I shall have to skirt, "fake out," pretend to ignore, or, inversely, approach with a tentative free-and-easiness. However, despite the objective appearance of imperceptible sliding, of naturalness and continuity in my behavior, the simple making of the decision either way will have radically transformed me. If I choose to be energetic, my lazy moments will appear no longer as manifestations of my lazy "nature" but as lapses for which I alone am accountable in light of my project of being energetic. And that explains my hesitation in deciding. It is not that I love my laziness itself, but, by denying its objectivity, by dissolving its impersonal solidity in a single free act, I withdraw from it what I had valued most: the possibility of always offering an excuse for my conduct. I fear being suddenly in my own hands rather than those of laziness, having exchanged servitude for responsibility.

In this connection Merleau-Ponty seems to draw alongside Sartre's thesis when he states:

16. [*Phénoménologie de la perception*, p. 513; *Phenomenology of Perception*, p. 450. The sentence ends as follows: ". . . and which qualify us as man, as bourgeois, or as worker."]

I can no longer pretend to be a nothingness and to continually choose myself on the basis of nothing. . . . It is true that I can at any moment interrupt my projects. But what is this power? It is the power to begin something else, for we never remain suspended in nothingness. . . . I can defy all established procedures, I can laugh at everything, I may be nowhere occupied entirely: but this is not because I withdraw into my freedom; rather, it is because I am engaged elsewhere.[17]

Sartre expresses himself similarly. It is not a question, for him, of remaining suspended in nothingness. Only in time's instant one can disengage himself from his temporal situations, whereas, living in the enduring moment, one is always in some way engaged, since one's temporality is then already deployed according to one's project. The central point here, though, is Sartre's insistence on accenting the instantaneous nihilation at the origin of every reengagement. Without this we could not speak of intentions or of attitudes within the natural attitude that differ from it or, especially, of conversions that have moral value.

Purifying reflection cannot enable us to reject everything; no one can enclose himself in a freedom of indifference. Freedom is action and even negative action requires something to negate. This is why Sartre upholds the ontological primacy of being over nothingness.[18] In *The Age of Reason*, Mathieu is in bad faith in wishing to detach himself from everything. But it does not follow that "the roads to freedom" can be opened to a being who remains within the fullness of being.

We often consent to being carried away by generality—all the more willingly if it appears to be validated in advance. We ask it to progressively humanize us, to make us blossom in the cultural world. The result is conflation of morality with civilization. Yet we cannot smother the calls of doubt, of negation, of revolt, and of challenge that rise within us. Among those who do not resign themselves, some choose to be rebels and nihilists, others choose to be "revolutionaries," that is, human beings who live their liberation instead of tethering themselves to their original negation.

The role of existential psychoanalysis is precisely to uncover the moral sense of various human projects and to keep the spontaneous freedom that is thereby put into play from returning against itself. By disengaging from its background of generality that singular choice of self that all persons *live,* but which each is also "called" *to bring about* by resuming it himself, this psychoanalysis prepares for the infusion of all conduct with moral meaning.

The reader—if he has followed us this far—is now referred to the passages where Sartre lays out the first elements of existential psychoanalysis. The

---

17. *Phénoménologie de la perception*, pp. 515–516; *Phenomenology of Perception*, p. 452.
18. Cf. *EN*, pp. 711–720, esp. p. 713; *BN*, pp. 785–795, esp. pp. 787–788.

reader is asked to see in them neither a burlesque fantasy nor a piece of bad taste on the horror of the viscous, neither a desire to fill up hopes nor a desire to go bicycling, but, instead, an attempt to elucidate the meaning of human action in the natural attitude. To *do* is always the *effort* to *be* or to *have*; to do is to endeavor to realize oneself or to appropriate some object. The problem this endeavor poses for ontology is in the relationship between the desire for possession and the desire for being. Sartre points to the following solution: free choice in the primary sense (that is, prior to purifying reflection, a choice we have seen must be understood ontologically)

> is a choice of being. This choice may be made directly, or indirectly via appropriation of the world, or, more likely still, both at once. It is in this sense that my freedom is a choice to be God. All my acts and projects are translations of this project, reflecting it in thousands of ways, for my freedom is itself an infinity of ways of being and ways of having. The aim of existential psychoanalysis is to rediscover—through these empirical, concrete projects—the original manner in which each person chooses his being.[19]

This project of possessing being manifests itself through tastes: the feelings of attraction and revulsion that we have toward the *qualities* under which particular objects are present to us. "Existential psychoanalysis must set in relief the *ontological meaning* of qualities,"[20] since these meanings express, beyond our tastes themselves, the aspects under which we choose to discover and to possess being.

In conclusion: psychology is already "ethics" inasmuch as it must appeal to the unity of the subject in order to understand phenomena. There are no irreducible psychic elements. Human reality qua consciousness is a single center of intentions. Yet this very unity in turn implies that the subject spontaneously chooses his being. This choice is not closed in on itself, it is not absurd; rather, it surpasses itself toward a meaning, just as its empirical manifestations surpass themselves toward the meaning the subject confers on them. Here ontology can elucidate the possible relations of human reality to being. By bringing out the variety in such relations, ontology allows existential psychoanalysis both to interpret a person's behavior according to one of them and to render understandable the conversion of his spontaneous initial choice into an authentic choice. This conversion allows a person to attain a true grasp of himself, but it also accounts for the *moral* character of any genuine self-knowledge. Such a self-knowledge calls for a constant exchange between reflection and action. To know oneself one must make oneself—but to authentically make oneself, one must be attempting to know oneself. No paradox or vicious circle is involved. We are quite aware that all knowledge is action. The noncircular

19. *EN*, p. 689; *BN*, p. 764.
20. *EN*, p. 690; *BN*, p. 764.

exchange is therefore between an active purifying reflection and an action upon the world which is necessarily unreflective in its concern with technical questions of means rather than with ends.

Each person represents a certain ideal that has been translated into a certain style of life. This style is manifested and exercised in that person's action upon the world. Thus a person can be understood by others only by reascending to his choice of style. And that person is for his own part able to imbue his acts with value [*valoriser*] only if he assumes total responsibility for this choice.

Chapter 3

Moral Perspectives

Morality and Faith

Ontology itself cannot formulate moral prescriptions. It is solely concerned with what is, and imperatives cannot be extruded from its indicatives. Nevertheless, ontology allows us to catch a glimpse of what an ethics may be that will assume its responsibilities before a *human reality in situation*.[1]

Such is the start of the final brief section of *Being and Nothingness*. In it Sartre begins to answer the question we have been raising since our Introduction. Even though the lines above and those that follow them in Sartre's text are unequivocal, they must still be read—and not with the advance plan of extracting passages from which to generate one last bit of scandal.

So let us reexamine this section, drawing as much clear meaning as possible from the text. This will serve as a basis on which to decipher more distant and indirect implications, a procedure for which we shall have to assume sole responsibility.

Ontology has shown that "the for-itself's various enterprises can be made the object of an existential psychoanalysis because they all aim to produce the desired synthesis of consciousness with being which takes the form of value or self-cause."[2] From the human angle, which is the only one philosophy can have, a being that is its own foundation, that exhibits perfect coincidence of consciousness with itself, is absolutely contradictory and therefore inconceivable. Religious faith, not philosophy, can say with Tertullian: *credo quia absurdum*, "I believe because it is absurd." Or again:

The Son of God was crucified—this is not shameful because it is shameful; and the Son of God is dead—this is all the more believable because it is idiotic; after burial he was resurrected—this is certain because it is impossible.[3]

1. *EN*, p. 720; *BN*, p. 795.
2. [*EN*, p. 720; *BN*, p. 796.]
3. Cf. Lev Isakovich Shvartzmann [Léon Shestov], *Kierkegaard et la philosophie existentielle*, translated from the Russian by T. Rageot and B. de Schloezer (Paris: Les Amis de Léon Chestov and Librarie Philosophique, 1936), p. 152; *Kierkegaard and Existential Philosophy*, translated from the Russian by Elinor Hewitt (Athens: Ohio University Press, 1969), p. 125. Cited by Emmanuel Mounier, *Introduction aux existentialismes* (Paris: Denoel, 1947), p. 39.

But faith may assert this only if it can regenerate men and transcend speculative contradiction by declining to remain on the speculative plane. Because faith establishes itself on a level at which it breaks with the laws of thought, it can sustain itself through its own acts. Yet even here the problem of the orientation of action recurs. There is again no alternative to attempting a solution on the human plane, the only plane where human action can take place. The problem cannot be eluded by arguing that faith moves mountains; this artificially dissolves all real problems so that only mysteries remain. A person can act only by starting with his situation, and the manner in which he acts always refers back to the choice he makes of himself.

There are many alternatives even within religious faith, but choices among them are made too quickly to be submitted to God in advance. The road that ought to lead to Him has few signposts. There are no specialized agencies that can provide even authentic believers with itineraries for such a voyage. For the others, there are only tourist *circuits* leading back to their point of departure, a journey they easily find satisfying. In these ways, man is thrown back on himself, abandoned, alone, free, and unjustifiable. Even if he believes grace will illuminate his groping way, he has no right to rest under a tree until it comes. He must strive amidst realities, unmindful of eventual miracles. To thus invent his route is to invent himself and to freely choose himself. But does this mean all choices are equally valid and that there are a thousand and one ways to serve God?

It does indeed mean that. It must be added, though, that it is at least necessary to serve *authentically*. Indifference to the absurd is no longer possible here.

Thus nothing, not even the religious choice, exempts man from moral choice, whose sole criterion lies in "the degree of consciousness that (he) possesses of his ideal goal."[4] God is *real* only for the theologian. The believer may defer to the theologian but his faith then founders in the absurdity of sterile metaphysics, a fate worse than doubt. Belief is always solitary; it is always the free choice of an ideal. This ideal is imbued with value, not by naming it God, but by the perpetual tendency toward authenticity in the practical definition of that ideal which inevitably results from serving it. Such is the profound truth behind the scientistic excesses of those who attempt to demonstrate God's nonexistence by the anthropomorphic character of the concept of God. Each believer's God is the God whom that person has chosen to serve. If man could reach God and coincide with him, the question would perhaps be resolved, for there would then be no more choices. But for human beings this goal is unreachable; man is therefore restricted to serving God and defining him only through that service. I may choose to abandon all concern for this world and spend twenty years on a pallet without rising; or to struggle to guarantee my coreligionists' freedom of conscience in all circumstances;

4. [*EN*, p. 721; *BN*, 797.]

or to evangelize my fellow man; or to nurse the leprous; or to devote myself to infinite orisons and macerations; or to lead a worldly existence in order to show skeptics that a believer is not an inhuman person.

Whatever my choice, can I be sure of its value if I do not inquire into its deep meaning, if I refuse to question it, if I blindly risk accepting—under color of ardent faith—some form of self-abandonment, renunciation, or premature salvation, in short, some immediate but false justification—just in order to cease feeling unjustified?

THE CHOICE OF FREEDOM

To approach this issue in a different light, let us note that Descartes's "*cogito*," though it cannot be our ontological starting point, may yet serve—in virtue of its reflexive character—as a point of reference for posing the problem of morality. Descartes's "*cogito*" is originally a "*dubito*," an "I doubt." It is not situated on the same level as my existence, which is already confirmed and present to itself through what, with Sartre, we have called "the pre-reflective *cogito*." Thus the "*dubito*" or act of reflection cannot doubt my existence but only its meaning. In other words: at the level of the natural attitude I am in question in each of my actions upon the world and this is the initial form my freedom takes; at the level of philosophical reflection I question my own value, inasmuch as I discover that I am responsible for those actions. The problem of morality can therefore appear only in a moment of hesitation, when I catch sight of the possibility that I shall deny myself any moral value. Starting with this hesitation, the problem of morality appears as both inescapable—in that even in denying I am of value I evince an attitude that engages me morally—and as indeterminate—in that merely posing this problem in no way prefigures any solution.

By contrast, we know how Descartes goes on to prove God's existence: I doubt; therefore, I am an imperfect being who has the idea of perfection—an idea that cannot have been put in me except by a being who is himself perfect. However, on this last note the likelihood of a moral attitude collapses because all possibility of future doubt or denial of self-worth becomes illusory. For consider the following dilemma. On the one hand, I may be conceiving God as utterly "transcendent"; but in this case his existence is henceforth an absolute without any effect upon me, and I am reminded of my own nothingness precisely because I have made God the total being. On the other hand, God may be conceived as in some way immanent in me such that I participate in his perfection. However, since this perfection is already realized in him, it must also govern and realize me according to Truth and Goodness. All doubt is therefore froth and ridiculous epiphenomenon. In this way Descartes's rationalism led equally to the eighteenth-century atheism which suppressed a transcendent God who was indifferent to everything human and to the pantheism of necessity formulated by Spinoza with merciless logic. The error behind the dilemma lies in the fact that Perfection is *realized*, whether outside of man or within man. What is ignored in both cases is that value is always valorization [*valorisation*].

The perfect does not grant itself to us except by refusing itself. For us it exists solely as having-to-be-realized. In the idea of the perfect we do find, not the obviousness of a being, but, instead, the experience of a vocation. "God exists," as a *proposition*, is impossible, just as it would be if it were a theoretical *supposition*. It can have worth only as an active *positing* and a practical valorizing. Only that believer who engages himself with all his faith in the supposition that God exists can draw profit from it. But in that case he is the person who makes God exist for him. The idea of God is not a possession of ours; it does not fall to us to encounter it once and for all; we never *have* the idea. We must constantly give it to ourselves in the choice we make of this or that moral pathway.

The point is therefore not to deny God's existence but to reject it as a proposition that is valid in itself. God exists to the extent my action lays claim to that existence, causing it to exist for me. When the believer doubts God he doubts himself and his own power to maintain in himself this practical orientation with its intimate agency.

A God that exists *despite* man is a culpable God who is responsible for all Evil. Man is then innocent, for he is situated on the near side of all problems and all morality. But our experience of doubt is understandable only within a human world in which man is at least capable of a self-transcendence; when this capacity is realized in action, it is the only authentic positing of God.

God gives himself only to those who search for him. To say that God exists is to speak only for oneself. It is to affirm a faith that is sufficiently active to continually promote that existence. In short, either the Cartesian "*dubito*" is a mere metaphysical artifice or it must mean: "I hesitate; therefore, I can will that God exists."

Hesitation, once it is apprehended as such, evinces moral freedom. The antipode of the distraction through which animals are enslaved to external determination is precisely the doubt that consecrates spiritual power to posing a problem and to imposing, upon oneself, its solution. Even if I deny this power or explain it by God's existence, I have adopted an attitude, thereby demonstrating an ability to intervene in my own orientation and to make my life a vocation.

This is the point to which we must always return, because it is the only one from which we can take our departure. We have just seen the extent to which an authentic humanism can call itself "atheistic." All philosophy is a humanism, because the philosophical attitude itself is ultimately never more than the questioning of the human by man. And it is solely at the level of a human vocation that invocation of God can have meaning.

Yet most philosophies seem to forget that their role is to frame a question whose sole answer is existence itself. We should reread Merleau-Ponty's beautiful conclusion:

> Shall I make this promise? Shall I risk my life for so little? Shall I give up my freedom in order to save freedom? There is no theoretical reply to these questions. But there are these *things* that unquestionably present themselves, there is this beloved person before you [*toi*], there are these men who exist as slaves around you, and *your* freedom cannot be willed without going out of its singularity and willing *freedom itself*. . . . But this is where silence is called for: only the hero lives to the hilt his relation with others and with the world, and it is improper for another to speak in his name. [Saint-Exupéry:] "Your son is caught in the fire? You will save him! . . . If there is an obstacle, you would sacrifice your shoulder, provided only that you can batter that obstacle with it! You reside in your act. Your act is yourself. . . . You give yourself in exchange. . . . Your significance shows itself, effulgent. It is your duty, it is your hatred, it is your love, it is your loyalty, it is your inventiveness. . . . Man is but a knot of relationships. Relationships alone matter to him."[5]

Now let us go back to what Sartre tells us. "Man makes himself man in order to be God. . . . "; but this does not entail accusing man of egoism. We must give up utilitarian interpretations of human behaviors in order to reascend to their *ideal* meaning:

> . . . for the very reason that there is no common measure between human reality and the self-cause that it wishes to be, one can just as well say that man loses himself in order that the self-cause may exist. We therefore consider that all human existence is a passion. The all too famous concept of "self-interest" ["*amour-propre*"] merely represents one freely chosen means among others for realizing this passion.[6]

Insofar as purifying reflection has not yet intervened, insofar as man continues to imagine that his mission, however conceived, is inscribed in things, all human activities are equivalent and all are destined to fail.

> Thus [in this perspective] it comes to the same thing whether one gets drunk in solitude or leads the people. If one of these activities takes precedence over the other, it will be due, not to its real goal, but to the degree of consciousness it possesses of its ideal goal. And in that case the quietism of the solitary drunk will take precedence over the vain agitation of a leader of the people.[7]

5. *Phénoménologie de la perception*, p. 520; *Phenomenology of Perception*, p. 456. The quotation in this passage is from Antoine de Saint-Exupéry, *Pilote de guerre*, in *Oeuvres* (Paris: Gallimard, Bibliothèque de la Pléiade, 1953), pp. 345–347; *Flight to Arras*, translated by Louis Galantière (New York: Reynal and Hitchcock, 1942), pp. 177, 181, and 183.
6. [*EN*, pp. 720–721; *BN*, p. 796.]
7. [*EN*, p. 721; *BN*, p. 797.]

"Pure, non-accessory reflection" must therefore intervene. Its role will be to reveal to man—by giving him access to the moral plane of authenticity—that his quest of being and his wish to appropriate the in-itself *are merely possibilities among other possibilities*. Pure reflection allows him to stop taking as irreducible the basic value that orients all his choices; it ceases to be the ideal presence of the self-caused being. He is then in a position to *choose* this value himself; to imbue it with value [*valoriser*] or to reject it. Each of these two attitudes is possible only if the other is equally possible. Pascal said, in effect, that it is because God exists that he is not certain. This formula implies its own reversal: it is because God is not certain that there can be an authentic value in actively taking him as existent. The believer's choice is authentic only when he stops conceiving his faith as a pole that stands face to face with a manifest God and instead reassumes that faith as his own, a "wager" that unreservedly involves him.

However, not everyone is a believer. There are many more atheists than is commonly thought. Clearly the same question remains for atheists as for believers. Some atheists try to ignore their own atheism, covering over with a word what their acts have long since ratified. Others cynically flaunt it, demonstrating an uneasy conscience which is fed by this flaunting rather than remedied. Still others believe they can remain neutral. Finally, a small number may have brought themselves to the authentic choice of the total absence of belief. With genuine believers they have arrived at that absolute simplicity from which one can invoke either Presence or Absence, Being or Nothingness —in short, where one can invoke or choose not to invoke—with equal validity. These few have opted for an existence whose constant self-surpassing is not polarized by any end exterior to itself. They have chosen a freedom that grasps itself as its own value and its own end.

It is tempting to oppose the atheistic to the believing attitude as one would oppose moral autonomy to heteronomy. This temptation should be resisted. For a person who has mastered the factual value that orients his choices, it matters little whether he chooses for or against this value, since in either case he has already disengaged himself from what he was in order to choose what he must be. The authentic attitude is beyond autonomy because it founds both autonomy and heteronomy through its initial effort to surpass illusory justifications of conduct through laws pretending to render it consistent in advance.

Whatever one may think of this last point, we can at least apprehend the meaning of moral conversion. Regardless of the choice that can follow from it, this consists in reaching a plane where freedom ceases to be the free pursuit of its preset goal in order that this goal may itself be placed in question. We have argued from the start of this work that morality consists in the "moralization" of the moral being; we might have anticipated that "value"—itself merely indicative of the self-surpassing constitutive of human reality—would turn back on itself in order to valorize itself [*se valoriser*]. Man would thereby give up pursuing the impossible coincidence with himself, the inaccessible justification of himself, in order to accept both this distance from self which constitutes his humanity and the absolute responsibility which guarantees its humanization.

We seem distant from the Roquentin of *Nausea* who sought the best way to justify his existence. Yet Roquentin also observed that it is a mistake to wish to *be*, because sooner or later one must remember that one *exists*. And this existence that flows back over you is ambiguous: it is revealed in Nausea, but also in Anguish. Freedom can never end up merely with itself. Up to his final moment man must bear the burden of his initiatives.

Thus we have passed from bad faith—which rests on the fact of one's non-coincidence with himself—to a new, more fundamental attitude that rests on the valorization of this non-coincidence, that is, imbuing it with value through the subject's free choice of it. We have passed beyond the moral *existent* toward the moral *agent*. The latter initially manifests itself in the recognition that the ambiguity which defines human existence is the sole source of values.

THE HUMAN AND THE SOCIAL

Such, in principle, is the perspective at which we have arrived. However, the problem remains whether man can in fact "*live* this new aspect of being." Only an Ethics can formulate this problem precisely and attempt its solution by indicating the conditions for the possibility of realizing such a choice.

> In particular, by taking itself as its end, will freedom escape all *situation*? Or, on the contrary, will it remain situated? Or, again, will it situate itself all the more precisely and all the more individually as it projects itself further in anguish as a conditioned freedom, further assuming its responsibility as an existent by which the world comes to be? All these questions, which refer us to a pure and not an accessory reflection, can find their answers only on the moral plane. We shall devote a future work [*un prochain ouvrage*] to them.[8]

The very formulation of these questions suggests the direction in which Sartre intends to answer them. Of the three alternatives put forth, he will clearly favor the last two in his future work. Quite explicit confirmations of this may be found in Sartre's known works. To bring it out let us review certain essential themes. We shall indicate for each theme the practical perspectives that now open up beyond the discouraging walls erected, as if with relish, by ontology.

We must return to that man we left on a beach. The worlds before him and behind him appeared hostile. All horizons seemed blocked and all acts foredoomed to failure. Yet, if the purifying reflection which reveals the structures and implications of the natural attitude is valid, this man must have the

8. [*EN*, p. 722; *BN*, p. 798.]

possibility of liberation starting from his freedom itself. There must be "roads to freedom."

The first two volumes of Sartre's novel with this hopeful title scarcely furnish practical indications except negatively. As such, they are nevertheless clear. From the beginning of *The Age of Reason*, Mathieu appears to us as a man who has lost his freedom as a consequence of having wished to escape all situations.

> Your life is full of missed opportunities," Marcelle said to him. . . . "Nowadays you are very seldom in the mood. . . . It's always that lucidity you make so much of. . . . you have such a fear of being your own dupe that you would reject the world's finest adventure rather than risk lying to yourself. . . . Do you know what I think? That you are sterilizing yourself a bit. . . . Of course everything is neat and tidy in your mind; it smells of clean laundry; it's as though you had just come from the drying room. All that's missing is shadow. There is nothing unnecessary, nothing hesitant or shifty. It's all high noon. . . . you have a taste for self-analysis. . . . It helps you to liberate you from yourself; to look at yourself, to judge yourself; that's the attitude you prefer. When you look at yourself you seem not to be what you are looking at, you seem to be nothing. At bottom that's your ideal: to be nothing."[9]

And Mathieu tries to rectify this:

> To be nothing? . . . No, it's not that. Listen: I—I want to recognize no allegiance except to myself. . . . If I didn't try to assume responsibility for my own existence, it would seem utterly absurd to go on existing.[10]

We recognize in this the classic "freedom of indifference" the empty notion of a total availability, the vain attempt by personal consciousness to withdraw to the level of transcendental consciousness in order to assume "God's point of view" on the world. Having been confused with detachment, Mathieu's freedom, like that of Orestes in *The Flies*, makes him a floating being estranged from everything, alone among other persons and nonexistent for himself. This is in no way equivalent to the feeling of strangeness described by Camus: Mathieu had himself willed this self-nullifying freedom. He sought to *be* free, which means to be nothing. He wanted to "recover" his freedom, having misinterpreted the essential aspect of human reality that ontology uncovered. His freedom is that being that has to be what it is. This entails that it not be what it is, but also that it be what it is not. Mathieu had only sought not to be what he is. He disengaged himself from himself, forgetting that such disengagement is meaningful only if it allows for an engagement which endows it with value. He forgets that to be free is to choose and to act.

9. [Jean-Paul Sartre, *L'Age de raison* (Paris: Gallimard, 1945), pp. 15–17; *The Age of Reason*, translated by Eric Sutton (New York: Knopf, 1947), pp. 12–14.]
10. *L'Age de raison*, p. 18; *The Age of Reason*, pp. 14–15.

Brunet is Mathieu's antithesis. He adheres unquestioningly to the direction life proposes. He engages himself once and for all. He exemplifies the spirit of seriousness: "he makes himself such that he may be *awaited* by all the tasks placed in his path."[11] His life is for him a destiny, a mission inscribed in things. His existence is justified by the objective values to which his freedom submits. Unlike Mathieu, Brunet wishes to *be* engaged, to be something. Seeking to "recover" his project, Brunet wants to coincide with it, to be what he is not. He too misses his freedom.

The remaining characters in the first two volumes also missed their freedom. Up to the end of *The Reprieve*, we are on the plane of ontological failure. This is also the plane of solitude, and there one must no doubt see an indication that has positive value. This recalls Roquentin's solitude in *Nausea*. That novel never frontally approached the theme of other persons. Roquentin always imagines he must save himself alone, act alone, even if only to impress others so that they will talk about him. Never does he arrive at the frame of mind in which he could act *with* others. And the only action that strikes him as possible is ultimately action by means of imagination and artistic creation.

Yet a single passage in Roquentin's journal outlines the presentiment of the falsity of this solitary search.

> I am alone, but I walk like a regiment descending on a city. At this very instant there are ships at sea resounding with music, lights blazing in all the cities of Europe, Communists and Nazis shooting it out in the streets of Berlin, unemployed workers pounding the pavements in New York, women at dressing tables in hot rooms putting mascara on their lashes. And I am there, in this deserted street, and each shot that comes from a window in Neukölln, each bloody gasp of the wounded that are carried off, each precise little gesture of the women at their dressing tables resonates with each of my steps and with each beat of my heart.[12]

This passage is also the only one in the course of which Roquentin experiences genuine anguish, not merely the fear of a return of Nausea but the crushing weight of his freedom. "I am filled with anguish: the smallest gesture involves me. I cannot figure out what is wanted of me. Yet I must choose. . . . " But he then commits the error of considering himself "awaited" by something, by an "adventure." Scarcely has he caught a glimpse of his freedom when it turns into a mockery.

It does not matter that we can follow this theme no further in *Nausea* itself: we have already recognized in the above passage the central theme of *The Reprieve*.

11. [*EN*, p. 721; *BN*, p. 796.]

12. J.-P. Sartre, *La Nausée* (Paris: Gallimard, 1938), p. 77; *Nausea*, translated by Lloyd Alexander (Norfolk, Conn.: New Directions, 1959), p. 77.

This work provides an imposing counterpoint that raises in its full breadth the problem of the relations of persons with other persons. From a social viewpoint, if freedom is to retain the value we have progressively recognized in it, this can only be in the bosom of human groups that are neither indifferent collectivities in which each lives in solitude nor tribes in which the individual is engulfed by participation in the "collective soul." From the primitive person who *is* his totem, to the civilized person who encloses himself in an exasperated individualism, no progress toward authenticity seems to have been made; the one *is* his engagement, the other refuses to engage himself.

But the moment of Munich, with its haunting memory of war, forces men to surpass simultaneously the notion of society and the notion of the individual. War is not a "social" fact, since it is unthinkable in its totality, but neither is it an "individual" fact, since each person feels suddenly tied up with all other persons. We can say at least that it is neither an object that is all at once determined for everyone nor a personal project of each; it is neither a common destiny nor an individual vocation. Such is the ambiguous character of everything that goes to make up the presence about us of a human world. We initially undergo this presence with a mixture of voluntary abasement and distrust or hostility; later we imagine we can disengage ourselves from it through indifference and contempt. Obviously both of these social attitudes are inauthentic. We cannot will our own freedom without also willing to pass beyond these attitudes toward free relationships with the freedoms of others, that is, toward an interhuman communication which would reapprehend on the moral plane the ambiguous fact of the existence of other persons.

Again it is a mistake to reproach Sartre's ontology or the first volumes of *The Roads to Freedom* for considering only this fact without showing its valorization. If the two had been thus compressed together, no efforts would have to be made, everything would be given, and nothing would have value. But neither genuine community nor our authentic humanity—and we have just seen these two values are essentially connected—awaits our birth in order to deliver themselves to us ready-made. We must invent them. Man must make himself man, in himself and with other men.

Sartre's remarks on literature, and particularly on the responsibility of the writer, have their proper place in this framework.

> . . . every literary work is an appeal. . . . the writer appeals to the reader's freedom to collaborate in the production of his work. . . .
>
> . . . if the writer accepts being the creator of injustices, it is within a movement that points beyond them to their abolition. As for me, the one who reads, if I create and maintain an unjust world, I can do nothing without rendering myself responsible for it. . . . The two of us thus carry the responsibility for the universe. . . . And if someone gives me this world with its injustices, it is not so that I may coolly contemplate them but so that I may animate them by my indignation, expose them and show their nature as injustices, that is, as

abuses to be suppressed. Thus the writer's universe will reveal itself in all its depth only to the reader's examination, admiration, and indignation. The reader's generous love is a vow to abide, his generous indignation is a vow to change, and his admiration is a vow to imitate. Though literature is one thing and morality another, at the root of the aesthetic imperative we discern the moral imperative. For since he who writes recognizes the freedom of his readers by the very fact that he troubles himself to write, and since he who reads recognizes the freedom of the writer by the simple fact that he opens a book, the work of art, from whichever side one approaches it, is an act of confidence in man's freedom.[13]

WHAT IS EXISTENTIALISM?

In the course of the preceding chapters, the reader may have grasped the full distance that separates Sartre's thought from classical philosophies. The criteria suitable for the latter do not apply to him. For this reason Sartre's philosophy, more than any other, must first be penetrated in spirit before being criticized in its formulation. Perhaps that is why it is almost impossible to give a conversational answer to the question that has become a ritual: "What is existentialism?" Of course one must take care to emphasize that there are several quite distinct existentialisms; that Sartre's existentialism, the focus of the question, is not complete and that perhaps it asks never to be completed; and that Sartre himself deplores the use of this expression, which has gradually become meaningless.[14] But one must nevertheless endeavor to somehow characterize a philosophy whose repercussions are all the more unforeseeable because our minds seem quite unprepared to accept it at the level of its most fundamental rhythm.

We shall retain its baptismal name. Let us get a firm grip on the conducting thread that has guided us the length of our study. By means of successive interlacings, we shall make one last effort to capture this troublesome monster in our nets, a monster who sometimes envelopes himself in clarity the better to escape our view.

13. J.-P. Sartre, "Qu'est-ce que la littérature?" *Les Temps modernes*, no. 17 (February 1947), pp. 793, 803–804; *Situations, II* (Paris: Gallimard, 1948), pp. 96–97, 110–111; *What is Literature?* translated by Bernard Frechtman (London: Methuen, 1950), pp. 32, 44–45.

14. [The word "existentialism" was invented in 1943 by Gabriel Marcel. Recently Sartre said he still believed "existentialism" is autonomous within Marxism but added, "The word is ridiculous. Besides, as you know, it wasn't I who chose it: they stuck it on me and I accepted it. These days I wouldn't. But no one calls me 'existentialist' any more except in textbooks, where it doesn't mean anything." Asked if he preferred the label "existentialist" to "Marxist," he said, "If a label is absolutely necessary, I would like 'existentialist' better." "Autoportrait à soixante-dix ans," interview with Michel Contat, in *Situations, X* (Paris: Gallimard, 1976), p. 192; "Self-Portrait at Seventy," in *Life/Situations*, translated by Paul Auster and Lydia Davis (New York: Pantheon, 1977), p. 60.]

Existentialism is the philosophy of human ambiguity. Recognition of this ambiguity may not be new in the history of ideas. What is more novel, what first appeared "strange to every Mediterranean mind"—in the words of a writer for whom they constitute a decisive condemnation[15]—is a philosophy which tries to make itself sufficiently objective to adapt to its object: human subjectivity. That a being can question itself about itself is a fact that demands separate consideration, since it immediately implies a special method. This method must start with an attempt at definition in which being is attributed only with reservations and in a quite special sense. Such "attribution with reservations" seems necessarily to characterize the primordial step of the philosopher. Descartes missed it, committing the error of doubting all existent things while at the same time taking himself—the one who doubts—as a thinking *thing*. This results from the exaggerated character of any doubt addressed to the whole world: one can in fact doubt only this or that particular thing. And the doubt one directs at himself cannot be of the same type as the doubt one directs at a determinate thing. More precisely, I cannot "doubt" my own existence at all and in this sense the question can not even be posed. But although doubting *that* I exist is meaningless, I can doubt *what* I am. I then perceive that the characteristic of my "being" is not to be what it is, since my being places itself in question with regard to itself. Thus, whereas my existence has an obviousness that no subsequent reflection can threaten, my essence is a problem which reflection in bad faith wishes to disregard but which purifying reflection makes manifest.

Let us go further: my essence is only that, a problem. *To exist is to be a problem for oneself.* And since I shall never cease existing until death, any effort by me to cease being this living problem will show a desire for blindness, a resignation vis-à-vis myself. We are left with two relationships which, according to the viewpoint adopted, can be validly established between essence and existence. In the one alternative, I consider my essence is the completion and fixation of myself by death; I must then say that existence precedes essence. In the other alternative, I designate as my "essence" what defines me as human subjectivity—the fact of being my own problem—but I shall then have to say that essence and existence are contemporaries within me, since my essence is merely the fundamental character of my mode of being, namely, existence, which differs absolutely from the mode of being of things.

This way of seeing things totally escapes the classical philosopher. Even if he is aware of the philosophical problem raised by the mere existence of the philosophical attitude, he does not hesitate to treat this originary "problem" essentially like those that present themselves in the sciences. It becomes merely a problem *to be solved* rather than the inescapably problematic origin of all

15. Lucien Fabre, "Essentialisme et existentialisme," *Revue de Paris* 54 (April 1947): 92.

problems. Although he is constrained to exist in order to explain the world, such a philosopher nevertheless tries to explain his own existence—and by the very methods he invents with regard to the world. Caught within his attitude of objectivation of things, he comes to objectivate this attitude itself, thereby renouncing all positivity and yielding to the imaginary. Because he seeks to take up God's viewpoint with regard to himself, his attitude involves a contradiction, since such a God-like viewpoint excludes all situation and, consequently, all attitude. In this way he suppresses himself in order to know himself, forming—even if he is an atheist—the fiction of a superexistence charged with defining his own human existence. The probelm is resolved but at the cost of passing over it in silence. If I confer on an absolute consciousness the role of foundation for both myself and the world, I then make myself a part of the world for this consciousness, becoming merely one object among others. My essence is then my passive being; it is made in order to be known. The result is that I shall know myself only through the intermediary of a fictive existence capable of conceiving (meaning both to create and to know) my essence.

The contradiction here lies in unreservedly attributing to myself the characters essential to all being, while also presuming I retain the benefits of my self-knowledge. This is why philosophy in its traditional form rests on an accessory reflection in which human reality enslaves itself to its desire to *be*. Various consequences which we have already encountered flow from this, including: an avowed or more or less dissimulated theory of psychological determinism and a mystification of morality—which is metamorphosed either into a sterile idealism or into a science of customs. The philosopher thereby becomes a mechanic and a "moralist," that is, a rationalist in theory and a "politician" in practice, convinced that it's all a matter of pulling strings.

But to reconstruct human beings (which is to reconstruct oneself) with "faults" and "qualities," and then to judge or maneuver them, is to contradict oneself. It amounts to concealing from oneself that one's principles are called into question just by formulating them. I may assert Paul is a sort of machine whose levers I can operate. But this means Paul has previously adopted an attitude of self-suppression through which he constitutes himself an object, repudiates his freedom, and becomes like a mechanism with foreseeable reactions. However, if I pretend that all men are similar machines, I then also affirm this of myself, and, in doing so, I withdraw all meaning from my affirmation.

To declare human reality ambiguous is therefore meaningless, if in practice one disregards this ambiguity's essential character by treating it the way one treats things which are what they are. Psychology becomes mere inventory and the moralization of the self becomes training—of someone else. If one truly understands that man is the "being" who remains perpetually in question for himself, one must ultimately give up all attempts to *account for* what is human. Philosophy then appears as our thinking's perpetual *challenge* of itself.

The point of departure is the fact that the world appears. This is indissolubly linked to my own appearance to myself. And this presence to myself assumes with equal ease either the character of fact or the character of duty. *I am* this presence to myself—and it is only as such that I can progressively attain a personality. Yet equally, *I have to be* that presence, and this is why my "personalization" is not a natural evolution but a moral activity. Subjectivity is given to me, but I must still conquer it in a process of subjectivation. I exist, but I can attain this existence only by assuming it. Scarcely having posed that question which I am, I discover myself tied to myself, responsible for myself, entwined suddenly in the act of the very "I" who poses the question. To know oneself and to make oneself are the same, since one cannot know oneself without also positing oneself as subject, thereby challenging the objectivation toward which the act of knowing reaches.

I exist. This declaration should not be confused with the claim made in saying *there is* a scratch pad before me, even though the latter claim also implies that I exist. All classical philosophies speak of the subject, the me, the person, but only in order to reinsert them in the category of existence, which amounts to omitting the "I" in "I exist." This omission has weighty consequences, for the me is henceforth only an object of knowledge, an essence, while the knowing subject is cast into the impersonality of some "transcendental consciousness."

Existential philosophy's first point of dispute bears on the unreality of such a non-existent consciousness. This "metaphysical error" consists in presuming to explain my consciousness by the products of its activity. I can strive toward depersonalization, but I cannot situate myself in the impersonal, outside of all situations. In short, I cannot leave myself; I always carry myself with me. Moreover, there is no attainable terrain from which I can account for this "I" that I cannot cease being.

This classical philosophical illusion results from sundering the ambiguity. In its place we find, on the one hand, a natural behavior imbedded in the world and, on the other, a moral behavior of self-realization. But if the natural behavior were merely natural, if it were a behavior in the same sense that we say a ball behaves a certain way on an inclined plane, then the transition to men's moral behavior would be incomprehensible. Philosophers who have spotted this illusion have simply suppressed it. Once set forth though, the moral problem is not so easily dismissed; it is implied through the sole fact that man can *attribute to himself* a natural behavior. Such attribution constitutes an *attitude* on the part of the person who effects it and, as such, is therefore open either to a more extended naturalization or to a challenge—as implied in the very definition of an attitude. Consider: "I am a brute beast."

Above all, this means that I *am* not a beast and that for me the issue is whether to sink myself deeper into such a way of being or to disengage myself further from it, as I already had to do to some degree in order to become aware of it.

Thus to become aware does not mean to note that one *is* this or that. I exist; that is, I carry within me my own self-understanding, my own relation to myself. When I picture the face of my girl friend, I need not also reflect in order to understand that she is absent. I do not confuse this face with the objects surrounding me. In short, I cannot imagine without being conscious that I imagine; merely to exist implies becoming consciously aware. But what is generally taken for such conscious awareness is in fact the revival of this spontaneous consciousness in the reflective effort to *recover* it. Classical philosophies assimilate consciousness to knowledge, perception to representation, self-presence to reflection on oneself. They deliberately omit *consciousness as consciousness*. They end up wanting to explain consciousness by what can only be understood through consciousness. This commits the error of accounting for man by the material results of his labor, explaining the pioneer by the gold seam and the gold ingot by the wad of bank notes.

I exist; that is, I am a perpetual signification for myself. Even in the heart of the most extreme conformism, I cannot forget myself altogether. I cannot cease to be present to myself, except at the cost of adopting a general attitude of blindness. In emotion, for example, I try to ignore the choice that the situation demands of me. But however spontaneous such an attempt may be, it is still another choice that I make and I implicitly understand it as such. I persist in taking refuge in it even after reflection has demanded of me some "voluntary" act of self-control. And if, in doing the psychology of emotion, I later declare there is an "essence" of emotion, it is clearly a lived essence, an "existential essence," an implicit understanding of my own attitude. Although such an essence can be disengaged, described and fixed in concepts, it has no relation to the traditional "essences" philosophers posit in imagination as pre-existing all existence. Essences of the latter kind are made to be known. They are objects of knowledge, fully realized as conceptions before any act of conceptualization. Indeed their mode of being consists in an appeal toward their own *essentialization*.

In sum, my attitude, whatever it may be on any occasion, always *means* something. However, this signification is itself ambiguous just because it must not be confused with a sign. A reference to Kafka's work will help clarify the full difference. In Kafka's universe there are signs everywhere that objectively offer themselves. If this universe appears absurd, it is because the persons in it are always encountering the absolute emptiness of these signs, each of which demands that a signification be resolutely conferred upon it by a subject who involves himself with it. Thus there is a door standing open before a man who needs to pass through it. The guardian in front of the door speaks firmly.

These are so many signs which, objectively, are what they are. The man chooses to interpret them as representing an impossibility. He waits, resigned, before the door—only to learn, at the moment of his death, that this door had been made for him, and for him alone.

In this regard Camus is at antipodes with Kafka. Sartre's existentialism opposes the absurdist dictum—"One must maintain the absurd"—with a theme that is undoubtedly more fruitful: *"One must maintain the ambiguity."*

Existentialism is not compelled to choose between a rigid consciousness that tends to suppress itself in its respect for objective values, for signs without signification, and a consciousness in revolt that renounces all signification. Instead it draws lessons from each such *attitude* and describes consciousness as presence to self, as non-coincidence with oneself, as absolute origin of all meaning and valorization. No existing consciousness can ever totally rejoin itself in order to *be*; nor can it break with itself in order to be quits with its responsibility. It can *strive* in one of these directions, but the effort alone manifests the bad faith involved in such a choice.

This is the point of departure. The whole of existentialism flows from it—insofar as it remains faithful to it. As a system of challenges it must challenge itself. And its greatest constant risk will be that of repudiating ambiguity by passing from descriptions to moral imperative. Having recognized the problem of morality within human existence, existentialism would have to forego all solutions, since in suppressing ambiguity it suppresses human existence itself. For existentialism the moral attitude cannot be a passage from the natural world to a universe of values, a suppression of the human dimension. This is why it asserts itself as an authentic humanism.

Authenticity, however, cannot be taken as a *state* attainable by man, a level on which he might succeed in situating himself. Nothing concerning oneself is ever finished. To say that freedom is ambiguous because it must liberate itself is still to say too little; it should be added that freedom must will itself as ambiguous in the knowledge that this liberation will never be total. No "authentification" of myself can deliver me from the incessant problem of my situation, that is, my relation to the world and to other persons. I cannot exist without engaging myself, and my engagement cannot rest content with attaining lucidity once and for all. The authentic choice that I make of myself is not a solution but a point of departure for new problems. I may well claim in a particular situation that the style I adopted following a moral conversion "sets the rules aside"; however, without me, this style alone is unable to guide my future conduct. Just as with the natural attitude, any such style carries its own challenge within itself. Indeed from this perspective the only difference between them which distinguishes the genuine result of such conversion is that what had been a spontaneous challenge changes henceforth into a duty to challenge.

In this sense existentialism's sole moral recommendation would be a simple transposition of its description of the human: "live with the rent in consciousness." This involves maintaining a perpetually invented and perpetually unstable equilibrium between action that calls for a coherent engagement and reflection that calls for an explicit distancing or ratification of the rent, which usually lies latent in one's presence to self. The effort at authenticity is therefore not an evasion of action since the disengagement it entails as means need not be its end. The human condition may be either ignored in bad faith or understood and lived in such an effort at authenticity; but in no case can one take leave of it. The conversion that starts with natural bad faith is not inscribed in the unfolding of any necessary dialectic; but neither is there any room for individualistic suppression of that problem which everyone always constitutes in his own eyes to the extent his existence is inevitably situated. Each person is tied to himself from the moment he accepts this situation as his own by formulating this implicit relation to himself that already constituted him in his presence to the world.

The first consequence of these observations is that every solution is at once provisional, individual, and practical. This means that: (a) its author cannot rest on the choice of solution that he has made, (b) he cannot ask others to make that choice for him, and (c) that choice will attain consistency with itself only through deploying its effects in the world. I cannot be said to choose liberty without engaging myself in a liberating enterprise. The approach of a consciousness to authenticity would itself be inauthentic if this consciousness— in order to reach authenticity more quickly—were to forget that it is situated. Freedom cannot be immediately salvaged by abstracting itself from a situation; rather, it is the situation that must be progressively penetrated by freedom. Thus choosing my own freedom entails choosing some mode of free relationship with other persons. And since my own freedom needs the freedom of the other in order not to deny itself, I may, for instance, will the emancipation of women. But if I happen to be in a country where the right to vote is not accorded to women and if I struggle to help them obtain it, I must not forget that this right will be theirs as women—a situation that no passage to the universal plane can ever suppress. Moreover, I must take account of women's aptitude, in that country, for making use of such an emancipation. This is to say, my enterprise must be not political but, above all, moral, since the political attitude aims to create a new situation in the name of certain principles, whereas the moral attitude aims to transform an existing situation to make it accessible to these principles.

The error in all artificiality appears at this point: the conservative wishes to artificially maintain a state of affairs and the revolutionary wishes to artificially impose some ideal norm on concrete individuals with differing situations. The former believes in the absolute value of fact, the latter in the absolute value of the ideal. But positivism and idealism are equally incorrect. They disregard the ambiguity of the human fact, which carries its own ideal within itself in the form of the choice each of us makes of himself within his situation. Artificiality is in general the attempt to impose a solution from without before ascertaining whether it can be effectively lived as a point of departure for authentic problems. Emotion is an artificial solution that consists in rejecting the real problem; the same holds for the act of imagining to the extent it pretends it can obtain satisfaction. The political attitude also wishes for immediate solutions; it dodges what is human, refusing to recognize that progress for man is not technical transformation but subjective conversion and conscious awakening from within the natural attitude.

Here existentialism finds itself at a dangerous crossing. It is tempted to capitulate either in the direction of a transcendental philosophy ignorant of individual historical situations or in the direction of exclusive preoccupation with historicity, where the risk is great that one will give up all concern for authenticity. The ambiguity can be maintained to the end only on condition that it establish some synthesis between radical conversion and historical development or, if you will, between the realism of authenticity in Husserl, or even in Heidegger, and the realism of history in Marx.

Such is undoubtedly the method that suggests itself for surmounting the dilemma of individualism and communism. If man were able to make an abstraction of other men, he could accede to authenticity directly from the height of his ivory tower. And, if he could make an abstraction of himself, the question would cease to be raised. But the question remains and man is himself that question. To wish to save oneself all alone is simply to run away from oneself. To wish to save others without their own participation is to retract any value from the salvation imposed on them. Each must decide what means he possesses for working for the liberation of what is human, without either restricting himself to his own case or passing those limits beyond which his action becomes merely a fruitless constraint.

This means that no solution should be left to its own inertia, that no conviction should be exempted from infinite challenge, and yet that one must invent solutions and start off as someone who is convinced. The central point is to understand that conviction must be faith and not belief since belief is addressed to *what is*—whether in facts or in ideas—and it can only be in bad faith. Faith, on the other hand, is concerned with *he who exists*, he who makes his existence his own without pretending that merely assuming it justifies it. To assume it is to carry that existence further, to hollow it out more deeply, and to make the question it poses even more urgent.

As a philosophy of the awakening of consciousness, existentialism entails a mediation of the immediate, a reflexive recoil in relation to the natural attitude that does not go so far as to disengage man from himself. But, since this mediating thinking is a purifying thinking, it cannot fail to challenge itself and to judge as inauthentic any "awakening of consciousness" in which the subject is content to place the world between parentheses and to "roll itself up in itself," according to Montaigne's phrase, which nicely characterizes accessory reflection.

As Alain writes,

> To believe is agreeable. It is a drunkenness from which one should abstain. . . . man is never in a situation where he can offer himself the luxury of believing. Belief means slavery, war, and misery. And in my opinion faith stands opposite to belief. Faith in man is hard for men, for it is faith in living spirit; faith lashes the mind, pierces it, puts it to shame; it is faith that rouses the sleeper.[16]

If you have faith in man, do not believe in any man. If you pretend to exist, do not accept any answers, invent your own. To write is a useless act if it is for those who *expect* answers. The greatest respect one can pay Sartre's work is to perpetually challenge its practical effectiveness; thereby one will have already allowed it to attain its essential goal.

> It is to be hoped that all of literature will become moral and problematic. . . . Moral, but not moralistic, showing simply that man is *also* value and that the questions he raises are always moral ones. Above all, let it show the inventor in man. In this sense each situation is a trap, with walls everywhere. But I express myself poorly: there are no exits to *choose*. An exit is something invented. And each man, by inventing his own exit, invents himself. Man must be invented every day.[17]

But finally, if I do not wish to attach any importance to the humanization of man and if it pleases me to choose myself as resigned, resigned to bogging down, resigned to degradation, resigned to bad faith, then the following is the last and ultimate challenge: "What purpose does it all serve?" The problem of morality, the placing in question of man by himself, thus finds itself in turn placed in question. Even the decision to adopt the moral attitude does not allow a person to take himself seriously. This attitude rests on nothing; it is founded on no absolute sign; nothing guarantees or justifies it from without. The radical invention of man by man lies in it. And if this invention is human it is because it proceeds from the nothingness of that which *is* not, it is because nothing, absolutely nothing, indicates any values to that invention in advance, and, finally, it is because the freedom from which that invention issues is as free to disown itself as it is to conquer itself.

> Through literature . . . the collectivity passes into reflection and mediation, it acquires an uneasy consciousness, an unbalanced image of itself which it seeks constantly to modify and improve. But in the end, the art of writing is not protected by the immutable decrees of Providence; it is what men make it; they choose it in choosing themselves. If it were to turn into pure propaganda or

16. Emile Chartier [Alain], *Minerve, ou de la sagesse* (Paris: Le Club du meilleur livre, 1956), pp. 301–303.

17. J.-P. Sartre, "Qu'est-ce que la littérature?" *Les Temps modernes*, no. 22 (July 1947), p. 112; *Situations, II*, p. 313; *What is Literature?* p. 217.

pure entertainment, society would regress to the nest of immediacy, that is, to the memory-free life of hymenoptera and gasteropods. To be sure, all that is not very important: the world can do quite well without literature. But it can do even better without men.[18]

18. Sartre, "Qu'est-ce que la littérature?" *Les Temps modernes*, no. 22 (July 1947), p. 114; *Situations, II*, p. 316; *What is Literature?* p. 220.

Conclusion

At the close of a work that one intends to submit to the judgment of others, any conclusion is tiresome. Either the author tries belatedly to express what he has not yet been able to say or he reveals pedagogical ambitions by summing up the "lesson" he has given the reader, as in botany or geography manuals.

We cannot cram into a few lines here what would in any case be useful only for evoking an atmosphere of thought or for resuming mutually enriching themes or for further cross-checking their perspectives.

Yet we are compelled to give in to the custom while rejecting its spirit. To put it in a phrase, we have an uneasy conscience. This feeling—which no doubt establishes that we have not reached authentic existence—originates in a painful discovery for the author of a critical work: we have forgotten to "criticize" Sartre's philosophy. We have arrived at the last line of our last chapter without taking the time to reveal an internal fault in his work, a basic paralogism, a disappointing plagiarism of a Hindu philosopher, or some republication from a movement of young intellectuals of the era between the wars. Perhaps this default is due to an alienation of our freedom to the profit of a philosophy whose seductiveness has drawn us in, engaging us in its continuation in spite of ourselves. The author in question may very well have corrupted us with the help of under-the-table subsidies furnished, as everyone knows, by the Communist party and by the "bourgeoisie," for each of whom he has simultaneously made himself the champion.

Also, a certain spirit of contradiction in us may have to assume its part of the guilt. It is difficult to arrive last, after a number of other works, the majority of which seem to have adopted the rule "do not handle too much or you will soil your hands," without having an ardent desire to go see, on the inside, what this buffoonery, this monster, is really like. One obviously runs the risk of being unable to conceal that the buffoonery has a meaning and that the monster is not without attractiveness.

It is not for us to put forth one of these interpretations or some other that we have not yet thought of. Let us simply admit, having imprudently put ourselves in the position of having to conclude, that in gradually plumbing the depths of Sartre's work we have experienced our most intense philosophical satisfactions. One need not be burdened with age to learn that the capacity for enthusiasm tends to blunt with use: when one is enamored of Bergson, one discovers Brunschvieg with a calmer happiness; in turn, Alain suffers from being in the third position; and subsequent encounters may well develop within an intellectuality that continues to be receptive but that is also a bit disillusioned. This phenomenon has not spared us. In addition, neither the war years, which forced one to learn new modes of life, nor preparation for the official competitive examinations—with its daily sacrifices before the idol of intellectual repletion—were calculated to reanimate dampened ardor.

Despite such adverse circumstances—and even though our first contact with *The Roads to Freedom* led us to speak less than warmly of its author—we had ample cause to retract this hasty judgment. We have no hesitation in speaking of a series of revelations, each astonishingly convergent, that progressively brought us to grasp this philosophy.

Yet, paradoxically, we felt a certain familiarity, as though we had encountered it in a previous life. This is the same kind of phenomenon that Merleau-Ponty characterizes in saying, with regard to the phenomenology of Husserl and Heidegger: "several of our contemporaries had less the sense of encountering a new philosophy than of encountering what they were waiting for."[1]

Doesn't this come down to saying we remained inaccessible to the doubts raised here and there, not all of which—one must admit—issued from spite or prejudice? Doesn't the confession we have just made mean that we threw in our lot unreservedly with this philosophy? The latter would have profited little from the kind of impulse it was able to communicate to us, for all valid thinking demands that one surpass it, and one cannot surpass this philosophy without in some way rejecting it.

However, to reject is not necessarily to refute. A range of possible attitudes lies between the desire to retain one's freedom of judgment and the ambition to oppose one body of thought with another that combats it. Sartre brought us a method for understanding human reality that fully satisfies us. That this method results in some dangerous viewpoints, we have not thought of denying: the moral enterprise that every man is called to engage in on his own account and under his full responsibility represents—as Plato has suggested—"a beautiful risk" to run. It is impossible to run such a risk without to some degree affecting others; the adventure cannot remain purely personal. It is important to note that whatever we do we cannot elude this responsibility vis-à-vis other persons. Our silence acts upon the other just as does our utterance, our departure disturbs him as does our presence, our indifferences can destroy him as effectively as our interventions, and our unreflective solicitude is sometimes deadly. Between two roughly equivalent risks, would not the most

1. [Maurice Merleau-Ponty, *Phénoménologie de la perception* (Paris: Gallimard, 1945), p. ii; *Phenomenology of Perception*, translated by Colin Smith (New York: Humanities Press, 1962), p. viii.]

genuinely human person be able to choose the meaningful one, the one that implied recognition of his responsibility, the one that would issue, not from the perpetual intervention of chance, but from the initiation of a definite oriented line of behavior aware of its principles? The most real danger a person runs is to find before and about himself that confusion of attitudes, that wave of amorphous generality, that complex of entreaties in which no one discovers his own true image. The question is whether men should let themselves be shunted about indefinitely on a sea of unforeseeable reactions or whether they should call on all their resources in order to take hold of a determinate current that has some chance of restoring to them the human meaning of their action. A man who "turns bad" for having read Sartre is one who would have made the wrong turn at the first street corner. And street corners are dangerous these days. We are "situated" in an atmosphere of moral disintegration. If Sartre has sometimes seemed to aggravate the ill it is to the extent that all effective thinking can suddenly reveal to one a choice made with the complicity of the spirit of seriousness. Even though it is thereby deprived of its usual protection of hypocrisy, such a choice may still try to find a justification through the very movement that is best suited for discrediting it.

Certainly from the social perspective, hypocrisy is preferable to disorder, if, that is, one considers the social as a sort of anonymous springboard from which each can pursue with maximum security his own half-century of egoistic enterprises. However, there is no want of examples of human societies in whose heart the present generation—for love of order—calmly prepares the most successful catastrophes for those to follow. Does the meaning of the social consist in saying: "After me, the deluge"? Must man settle for the ideal of holding himself in the ostrich posture to the death? In fact it seems that the social must itself issue from a socialization, for which, initially, the moral effort of each individual is required.

There again, we do not consider Sartre can fairly be attacked for the movement he set in motion. For our part we are afraid, not that this movement is too dangerous, but that it lacks effectiveness. And the only "criticism" we would be tempted to make of it is in fact aimed at all human works situated on the intellectual plane: existentialism will teach the meaning of existence only to those who have already chosen not to ignore that meaning but rather to constantly seek it and to those who have assumed in advance the burden of the subsequent discovery.

It is above all for these persons that we have sought to disengage Sartre's philosophy from the atmosphere of confusion which so many others attempt incorrigibly to aggravate.

January–May 1947

Postface 1965

Somebody Called Sartre

EIGHTEEN YEARS separate me from my first meeting with him. I had just written this book. I was about to send it to the publisher when a certain uneasiness began to take hold of me. Daily, before my eyes, the distance grew between my own understanding of Sartre's thought and the various interpretations then circulating. I was twenty-five, an age that inspires little self-doubt. Yet there were so many chieftains ready to condemn me, so many luminaries whose wrath, profane or sacred, would certainly cause my weak candle to flicker. It was too much for me. Having adversaries did not trouble me. But I believed the disavowal that I might get from Sartre would be more worthwhile if administered privately by God himself, than publicly, by those divided apostles who were in the process of reinventing theological assassination in his name.

I therefore hurried to the temple or chapel—as a certain crowd willingly called it—that is, to Les Temps modernes,[1] to tell all. Advanced missionary elements of the review then occupied a key position on "the left bank" of the rue de l'Université, a street they had not yet succeeded in bridging.[2] Duly informed of office days and hours through assiduously reading the first page of the parish bulletin, I arrived as always a few minutes late, in the middle of

1. [A literary and political review established in 1945 in the editorial offices of the Gallimard publishing house, across the rue de l'Université from Julliard publishers. Founders included: Sartre, de Beauvoir, Merleau-Ponty, Raymond Aron, Michel Leiris, Albert Ollivier, and Jean Paulhan. Michel-Antoine Burnier adds: "André Malraux did not want to participate and Camus refused because of his responsibilities at Combat. The first issue of Les Temps modernes appeared in October, 1945." Les Existentialistes et la politique (Paris: Gallimard, 1966), p. 28; Choice of Action: The French Existentialists on the Political Front Line, translated by Bernard Murchland (New York: Random House, 1968), p. 20.]

2. A few years later they were to establish a beachhead on the other "bank" of the street [that is, at Julliard] that was quite solid, for it has held until recent months. But no doubt the essential ambiguity of the Human Condition, together with the Contradictions of the Dialectic, would require that sooner or later a movement in the reverse direction would take place. This has now happened. The saga is "to be continued." [In 1965 Les Temps modernes quietly returned to Gallimard, from which Malraux had chased it in 1947 after Sartre had compared Gaullist posters with Nazi propaganda. Les Temps modernes left Julliard after seventeen years when ownership of the publishing house passed into the hands of a new financial group "from which we could expect the worst," as Jeanson put it to me in 1973.]

227

mass, at the very moment of communion. Praise be to God: He was there amidst the faithful of which at most sixteen or seventeen in file separated me from him. Three minutes later, his Word having filled them each in turn, I found myself in front of him, soul afire and mind in turmoil, but fiercely resolved to take exception to any such miracle in my own case. When piety departs, true faith is not far behind. Before my eyes, by some reverse miracle, this god made himself man.

"I would like to talk with you," I said to him.

"Yes," he answered me.

"But not here," I forced myself to specify. "Anywhere, I don't know, in the next room."

"Good. If you wish."

It was empty, luckily, and I disappeared in there with him, under the less than filial glances of a dozen remaining communicants, whose line extended from the secretarial throne to the temporarily deconsecrated altar. The door closed, we sat facing each other over the corner of a table.

"Let's have at it. What did you want to talk about?"

I undertook to tell him. I had two problems to raise, but he did not let me get to the second:

"That's enough, excuse me. I could not know that you wished to pose serious questions. But we can better discuss them at my place. Tomorrow at noon, is that all right?"

After our conversation the next day, I left him my manuscript. It came back to me in eight days enriched by a short letter which filled me with joy, but which I have just—imprudently—reread today.

Today I feel I have fewer resources than ever for speaking of this man— fewer, certainly, than on that day in January 1947 when I valiantly launched into the first part of a study of Sartre's philosophy with no knowledge of *L'Etre et le néant* besides page 705.[3] That page had been read to me two years previously, during a brief army leave, by a philosopher friend who was amused to be able to reveal to me that a good part of our lives is spent plugging holes. Was my undertaking a bad bet? It may be judged so. After a dispute in which I called him to task for speaking of existentialism without knowledge of it,[4] my friend, a charming old gentleman, a disciple of Bergson

3. Jean-Paul Sartre, *L'Etre et le néant: essai d'ontologie phénoménologique* (Paris: Gallimard, 1943); *Being and Nothingness: An Essay in Phenomenological Ontology*, translated by Hazel E. Barnes (New York: Washington Square Press, 1966), pp. 781–782.

4. I was no doubt boasting, but not as much as it may seem. At that point I had already read *Imagination: A Psychological Critique*; *The Psychology of the Imagination*; *Outline of a Theory of the Emotions*; *Nausea*; *The Wall*; and *No Exit*, not to mention various articles published by *Les Temps modernes*. This body of thought soon struck me as being so coherent, so constantly present to itself in its totality, so "totalitarian" (in the best sense of the term), that I expected to rediscover it upon reading *Being and Nothingness* as I had in these various works.

and a director of a collection with an unknown publisher, generously commissioned me to write a book on this burning subject. He allowed me three months; I took four. Today four years seems insufficient to fully take in this philosophy, even though I am not the least behind in reading Sartre. Premature senility is a possibility. I willingly accept the hypothesis of intellectual decrepitude since I have dreaded it, constantly and spontaneously, for over ten years. But in looking around, must I who keep roughly abreast of what is written on Sartre conclude there is a universal decrepitude? Or should I consider my case aggravated because I have—unlike most commentators—a certain experience of the man himself, including the possibility of going back to him as the source of this philosophy's spirit in order to reinterpret its letter? I acknowledge that I had this advantage; I still have it; I hope it will never be taken away from me. Yet even if I had seen Sartre daily for these eighteen years, I do not believe I would today feel more capable of defining his thought or that I would know him much better personally. I have written twenty or so articles about him, and, on more occasions than that, I have spoken of him in France and abroad, before audiences of every kind. Thus, according to their temper, many people take me for a *disciple* or a *friend* of Sartre's. I shall therefore disappoint them in confessing without any shame my fear that, in truth, I am neither. Still others may say this is not the issue and that I would be better advised, if indeed I have anything to say, to go directly to the heart of it. They fail to see that I am already in it up to my neck.

For there is henceforth for me no other subject, regarding this man, besides our relationship to him and what he reveals to us of the world in which we live.

Sartre's philosophy was then (or seemed to be) only a philosophy—the most satisfying of all. My own thinking was at ease with it, discovering itself through it, and even recognizing itself in it. Philosopher that I was, I needed a philosophy. All evidence indicated this one was made for me and I for it; I learned from it what I had always known but had not known how to say. The idyll was to last nine years, at first in my head, as is fitting, and later extending to incarnation in certain public activities. I was to enter the R.D.R. in Sartre's path, leaving it the same way;[5] I became manager of *Les Temps modernes*;[6] the Henri Martin affair found us in solidarity;[7] and, finally, while directing a

5. [The R.D.R. (*Le Rassemblement Démocratique Révolutionnaire*) was a left political grouping founded in early 1948 by David Rousset, Georges Altman, Gérard Rosenthal, Sartre, and others. Sartre resigned from it in October 1949.]

6. [Jeanson joined the staff of *Les Temps modernes* in 1948 and was manager from January 1951 to November 1956. He returned as a member of the editorial committee in the fall of 1960 and left for the last time in December 1967.]

7. [Henri Martin was a sailor who had been imprisoned in May 1950 for distributing tracts against the war in Indochina—to which he had been sent expecting to fight Japanese but was instead set against an independence movement. He was released in August 1953 as a result of popular pressure and campaigns by the Communist party and *Les Temps modernes*. *L'Affaire Henri Martin*, with commen-

collection called Ecrivains de toujours [Writers for All Time], I was luckily able to commission myself to do *Sartre par lui-même* [*Sartre by Himself*].[8]

That was in 1955. Toward the end of the next year a thunderbolt was to strike Budapest, and one winter evening its echo separated us, on the sidewalk of rue Jacob. I was leaving Editions du Seuil, Sartre was going to see someone in a neighboring apartment house. He told me of a text he had just signed and he asked me to sign also, offering it to me after enumerating the other signatories. Had this detail been absent the matter would have been dispatched quickly, but because of it I suspended my answer, which means that in effect I refused. This was absurd: we had joined together in so many ways already that it was impossible to add to or detract from our solidarity. Moreover, his signature at the foot of a text whose contents I accepted compensated for those two or three declared adversaries of the U.S.S.R. who were a bit too delighted, it seemed to me, by the bloody grist this burnt offering of Hungarian lives brought to their mills. Almost immediately, perhaps the second day later, an article appeared in *L'Express* titled "After Budapest, Sartre Speaks." In it Sartre denounced "twelve years of terror and imbecility" as well as "the complete bankruptcy of socialism as merchandise imported from the U.S.S.R.," and he announced his decision to break with the French Communist party.[9] Again, I was disturbed not by the content of these declarations, but by their vindictive and almost snarling tone and by the bourgeois support he had accepted in making them public. Through various intermediaries who had various intentions my criticisms naturally came back to him in the form of those amiable extrapolations customary in such cases. Everything happened at a distance, in a silence padded by whispers, and yet, to tell the whole story, nothing happened, except that I ceased to be manager of the review[10] and Sartre and I went for two years without seeing one another. This was the cost of my futility, or, which comes to the same thing, of the spirit of seriousness that I demonstrated in this affair. The anti-Soviet attitude appeared to me so monstrous as to ultimately blind me, paralyzing in me any critical response to the U.S.S.R. Radicalized, in addition, by my engagement in the Algerian struggle, my politi-

---

tary by Sartre and articles by Jeanson and others (Paris: Gallimard, 1953), was aimed at defending Martin and opening a new trial.]

8. [Francis Jeanson, *Sartre par lui-même* (Paris: Editions du Seuil, 1955.) A second "edition," extensively rewritten, appeared in 1971. As previously noted, this work is not to be confused with the later film, directed by Alexander Astruc and Michel Contat and the transcript of its soundtrack, whose early impression also carried the title *Sartre par lui-même* (Paris: Gallimard, 1977); *Sartre by Himself*, translated by Richard Seaver (New York: Urizen Books, 1978).]

9. "Après Budapest, Sartre parle," *L'Express*, 9 November 1956; "After Budapest," anonymous translation, *Evergreen Review* 1 (1957): 5–23.

10. Which would have occurred in any case since my clandestine activities were beginning to take shape, making me a rather useless legal respondent should *Les Temps modernes* be cited in the courts. ["Clandestine activities" refers to Jeanson's aid of the cause of Algerian independence. As manager of the review, it was in part his duty to speak for the review in routine legal actions against it.]

cal thinking became paradoxically abstract, schematic, and a bit terroristic. His brutal coming about, his disturbing impulsivity, in which I thought I saw evidence of a purely intellectual attitude (by which I meant: more or less irresponsible): all this was really evidence that he was quite able to maintain his freedom to become indignant and to judge. In the angry outburst he had voiced I soon recognized twenty contrary stirrings of that generosity I had witnessed in him earlier, as well as the caution implicit in his lucidity. Indeed, his analysis following these events was a model of the genre.[11] It was with profound joy that I discovered in it the groundlessness of my complaints and the stupidity of my fears.

In the first months of 1959, I could not stand it any more. I was not masochistic enough to wish to be punished indefinitely and my estrangement had lasted long enough. One morning, in my impatience to find and confront this man again, this fine argument came to me: *I did not have "the right"* to interpose scruples that concerned only myself between the cause we were serving and one of the people who could best support it. We needed Sartre.[12] I had to approach him, and it was just too bad for me if he told me to go to the devil. Accordingly, one of our comrades was sent to find him. She was to speak with him alone and bring him back immediately by explaining that somebody he knew well had to meet with him at any cost. Alone in an apartment near the Hébertot Theatre, I imagined twenty different outcomes for my foolish initiative. When the doorbell finally rang in the agreed rhythm, I was certain I would only be listening to the woebegone explanations of an emissary; but it was Sartre who came into the room and said: "Ah! I was hoping it concerned you. So, how are you?" Without leaving me time to answer he added: "You know, I am one hundred percent in accord with the action you are pursuing. Use me as you can. I also have friends who ask only to be placed at your disposal. Tell me what you need." When he left two hours later, I had completed an interview with him for our clandestine newspaper[13] and secured some addresses that proved quite valuable. He later said that, like us, he would have willingly "carried suitcases,"[14] which I knew. If he did not do it, it was

---

11. J.-P. Sartre, "Le Fantôme de Staline," *Les Temps modernes*, nos. 129–131 (November 1956–January 1957), reprinted in *Situations, VII* (Paris: Gallimard, 1965), pp. 144–307; *The Ghost of Stalin*, translated by Martha H. Fletcher with the assistance of John R. Kleinschmidt (New York: George Braziller, 1968).

12. [The "we" refers to the "Jeanson network" described in the Translator's Introduction.]

13. ["Interview de Sartre" in *Verities pour . . . ,* no. 9 (2 June 1959), pp. 14–17, reprinted in *Les Ecrits de Sartre: chronologie, bibliographie commentée,* by Michel Contat and Michel Rybalka (Paris: Gallimard, 1970), pp. 334, 723–734; *The Writings of Jean-Paul Sartre,* translated by Richard C. McCleary, 2 vols. (Evanston: Northwestern University Press, 1974), vol. 1, *A Bibliographical Life,* pp. 366–367, vol. 2, *Selected Prose,* pp. 229–235.]

14. [Slang for clandestine movement of money contributed by Algerians in metropolitan France who wished to aid the rebellion headquartered in Tunis, as explained in the Translator's Introduction.]

because we did not think we could ask him. This revolution was and was not our own; since we were trying to aid our Algerian comrades in *their* struggle, we owed them a minimum of discipline concerning the rigorous imperatives of security that they imposed on themselves. Had it not been for this concern we would have joyously consented to compromise Sartre to the hilt by making him carry—under the eyes of the guardian angels permanently assigned to him by the police—some real suitcases stuffed with false documents. Sartre indicted, even jailed (with a bit of luck); the cops intoxicated, exhausting themselves pursuing false leads for months: it was quite a picture for us to dream about!

Those were good times. Sartre was Sartre as Yahweh is Yahweh. He fulfilled his function with the same sovereign overabundance as the God of Israel and showed himself no more alien to our human passions. A turbulent people, many of us revered this Guide by whom we felt elected, this Master whose teaching always surprised us even though it seemed to come from within ourselves. He was there, quite near; during certain hours of the day one could even know where he was located: Heaven bowed low, the Ark of the Covenant remained visible in it. And if a secretary-angel nevertheless prevented a direct encounter (the leaders of the cult having put an end to public communion), at least the Word, always familiar and locatable, never stopped reaching those who wanted to hear it.

Turning to the present: for some time this Word, which daily becomes more familiar, is now hardly locatable. It is everywhere and nowhere. It is within us, if you will, but it is also around us; we cannot take a step in the world without meeting it. During a quite determinate period of time, an individual I knew had tried to understand his childhood—and himself as the one who started with it—and had made extensive notes that then seemed transparent to me; ten years later this same individual drew *The Words*[15] from these same notes and yet I no longer knew the man of whom they spoke. Did the use he made of those notes alter their meaning? That is certainly the easiest answer—true, yet also false, as Sartre would say.[16] In a way, he did intervene as editor only to produce one of the genuine masterpieces of world literature. But it must be seen that this too is new for him and that he has more or less transformed himself during these ten years.

It will be said all this is self-evident. Perhaps. There are several ways to transform oneself. I can immediately cite three: either you have become another by the simple changing of contexts (the scene shifts); or you have simultaneously carried out on yourself some transformatory act; or, finally, you have

15. [J.-P. Sartre, *Les Mots* (Paris: Gallimard, 1964); *The Words*, translated by Bernard Frechtman (New York: Braziller, 1964). Sartre showed Jeanson the notes for *Les Mots* in 1954.]

16. [*Les Mots*, p. 54; *The Words*, p. 69.]

changed the context even though you undertook to change yourself. Of course one cannot separate the last two alternatives as radically as I have just done. However little one may wish to act on the world, one cannot act on oneself at all without affecting it in some way. But in this regard, I dare say Sartre has changed our world at least as much as he has changed himself. This adventure is worth pondering. It is also our adventure *since his passes through us*. A man alone who forbids himself any recourse to material power can influence events only by modifying the way his fellow men live those events.

I am well aware: our France has an atomic program but lacks housing, teachers, and professors. Meanwhile, our evasive Left has yet to ask itself who Sartre might be, this Mr. X they were told about jokingly one day. These problems concern me, but the charge of ineffectiveness usually drawn from them leaves me cold. Diderot died in 1784 and d'Alembert a year earlier; was the revolutionary ineffectiveness of the *Encyclopedia* thereby demonstrated? For twenty years we have suffered from such inertia that we can now think only in terms of impatience. When the working class keeps silent the intelligentsia bestirs itself. Professional politicians disdainfully label our erratic agitation "activism" (or, on their good days, "voluntarism"). To them we are little more than leftover romantics. But their taste for maneuvers and their constant desire to master the Apparatus (for lack of mastering its basis) conceal from them the true meaning of our anxiety. Similarly, the obvious impotency in which we are currently vegetating conceals from us the real action that could be our own and that perhaps is ours without our knowledge. We prance with rage within the bourgeoisie, while the residents of Aubervilliers[17] resign themselves, from which we conclude that we are cuckolds. At this rate even if the glowing future does arrive (perhaps a little brighter and less tarnished thanks to us), luck will have it that we shall have died the night before from frustrated apoplexy. These moods supply us with alibis and hide a profound defeatism. We have History under our skin. Unshakably gripped by this hard seductress, we dream either of violating her or of being annihilated in her arms. It matters little, then, whether we are sadists or masochists: faced with history we have chosen to consider ourselves impotent. Of course we are powerless—totally so in certain respects. But in other respects we are not and we are beginning to realize this. The course of events being what it is, this new consciousness certainly could not originate with it. I am therefore asking to whom we owe it.

If all our scarcely formed images of Sartre tend today to come undone before our eyes, it is because he has rejected all such images. And, if our world seems impregnated by his thinking, this can only be because we have looked at it

17. [A working class district of Paris.]

through that thinking. This Traitor introduced himself into our bastardized minds[18] by ruse as much as by affinity, only to expel us from them, just as he undertook to expel himself from his own mind. This fraternal trickster haunts us *by his absence* for we can interiorize him only by following him in his own effort at self-exteriorization. It is at the cost of everywhere escaping us that his thinking never stops incorporating itself in the world as the elusive tonality of our rapport with him.

Each philosophy has its own character and language, its obsessions and passwords. How, then, does it happen that this philosophy is also more personal than any other, becoming so near at hand for each of us that we can no longer distinguish our understanding of the world from that of its author? I do not know of any Sartrean phantasm that I experienced in the precise form described by Sartre, yet my presence to the world is each time a little better revealed by these strange projections.

I have said I did not consider myself a "disciple" of Sartre's. I am afraid the reality is more complex. A *disciple* I have certainly been. How and to what extent I have ceased to be one is what I must try to clarify. During an initial period I was a rather good parrot. The Master had a complex philosophy, sometimes a bit difficult, and more or less misleading because of the extreme diversity of the modes in which it was expressed. The student, trained in the art of exegesis, carefully abstracted the essential themes, then, hopping on his roost, squawked to proclaim them to all comers. If there has been cleavage, where did it occur, and why? Errors aside, my adventure was the same as many others among us: we experienced a *weaning away* from this philosophy to the very extent it came to exercise *a real influence* on us. This did not happen in a day and I can attest that we were tormented at least as much as we tormented ourselves.

To judge by my own case, there were serious resistances in us to this weaning. I have already mentioned our "political" attitude as left *intellectuals*: since Sartre "engaged himself" we expected that espousal of his thought would lead us to take action. Closely linked to this, however, was our *idealistic* attitude as "revolutionaries" of thought: this philosophy suited us because it went beyond preceding ones and gave us the clinching dismissals for thinkers of every temper. I admit falling into this trap "head first"—an apt phrasing—and I do not know if I would have extricated myself by my own means. This must be understood, without either pride or empty humility. If Sartre had disciples, they were in a sense only those he deserved. Our idealism responded to his, to that portion of his original idealism that his thinking retained. And in a polemical perspective this shared fault could be understood through the situation in which we had together been plunged, that is, having to simultaneously face more or less subtle extensions of spiritualism and a materialism that was

18. [Treason and bastardy were themes developed by Jeanson in his *Sartre par lui-même* (Sartre by Himself) (Paris: Seuil, 1971).]

less and less concerned to take itself as dialectical. To each of these parallel aberrations (the one ignoring materiality, the other not bothering with consciousness) we were certainly justified in opposing the ontological ambiguity of our condition, the double contingency that is the very law of man: neither made nor to-be-made, he is condemned to make himself through everything that makes him. We were "in philosophy" the way one is "in the middle class"—by divine right. The Truth belonged to us; our thinking was absolutely valid, since it could expose the errors in all other philosophies in circulation. In a world that reasoned falsely, we alone reasoned correctly. We confronted bourgeois mystifiers with history and ideologists of the proletariat with our exquisite subjectivity. We took the mystifiers apart, thanks to Marxist analysis, and at the level of ideas we felt more Marxist than the Marxists. Having dismissed both simultaneously, we remained sole masters of the philosophical terrain. Of course we "went beyond" ourselves only, and this reactive thinking could have soon become reactionary, portraying as positive truth what was in fact merely its negative virtue.

I was also able to describe, starting in 1955, the awareness that Sartre already had of this danger and his efforts to supply a remedy.[19] Today the whole world can see he has cured himself of his own "neurosis." Less well perceived is his challenge to us, which almost constrains us to do as much in our own case. Whether we sought it or not, this man has changed us. I want to try here to delineate the means by which this has occurred and what its significance has been for us.

Pure consciousnesses, cover your faces: I shall now speak of *influences*. We have undergone a series of them from this quarter.

First, the influence of the Word [*du Verbe*]. I have recalled above how in its justified equilibrium, this Word came to be the truth for us, recognizable as such by its immediate obviousness and perfect transparency. It appeared to us unsurpassable at first, because it credited us from the start with a constant power of self-surpassing. It *realized* our freedom, at the cost of casting it out into the world, to be sure, but in order thereby to make it responsible for what happens there. By virtue of this lone magical concept, "consciousness-in-situation," all our philosophical problems seemed suddenly resolved. Subjectivity, weighed down at last with its burden of having to exist, is not for that reason

19. [Jeanson wrote, for example, "La Rochefoucauld separated himself from other men with the theme: we are all false and my truth is to be aware of that fact. But Roquentin's attitude doesn't seem to differ greatly from that of the moralist: like him, Roquentin presumes to save himself, to tear himself away from the species, and ultimately to *transcend* it, solely by virtue of his lucidity." And: "Here, then, is an *ontology of ambiguity* that transforms itself into an *ethics of contradiction*. The rent in consciousness becomes in the latter a social rupture, and the original conflict with another finds its own concrete dimension through the types of humans generated by the class struggle." *Sartre par lui-même* (1955 edition), pp. 146, 162.]

subject to some objective determinism. On the contrary, the very contingency of its own reality supports it in successively "transcending" the various determinations of that reality. Meaning took on life and life took on meaning; we could *feel* ourselves existing to the point of nausea. We could "*exist* our body," assuming it in surpassing it, as Sartre showed in writing *Nausea*.

This Word seduced us by thus making itself *the idea of flesh*. The incarnation had made itself a concept, and our concepts appeared incarnated. This happened just in time, for even our "existential" philosophers were starting to take themselves for angels. If on occasion these nebulous creatures went so far as to give out a cry, it was only from an anguished soul and spiritual torment. Forsaking the metaphysical heights, Sartre proposed to us an ontology whose flights were never higher than the level of man. In passage after passage his unflagging description of ourselves brushed against our heads, creating swirls which precipitated us vertiginously into the backwash. This was because he spoke of himself, and because Contingency, *alias* the Flesh (or Facticity), was preeminently a real experience of his, a lived conflict, before it assumed sublimated form as a reflective theme in his writings. Of course our experiences differed from his. But in our eyes this was added evidence of the truth of his philosophy. *Authentic* in bringing out the meaning of what he experienced, it was also *objective* in virtue of its usefulness in deciphering our experiences. How could such potent charm fail to enchant our intellectual left-wing consciousnesses? A man had shown that by sheer digging one could draw the Universal, the human condition itself, from one's singularity. And without concessions to metaphysics, he offered us a *description* of that condition which was of unsurpassed coherence, vigor, and clarity. Obviously this was the good century. In the middle of the preceding one, Marx had constrained the theoretical history of Consciousness to become the practical consciousness of History; all that was missing for the central idea of "*praxis*" to take on meaning were, precisely, concrete consciousnesses. We had such consciousnesses; the solution was in the bag; at last man was to be able to take account of himself without thereby suppressing himself as man. Torn from its Heaven by one of us, philosophical Thought died before our eyes, allowing the birth of real thinking, a thinking in direct gear with the world and capable of yielding both the explanation and the understanding of that world. This advent, this sovereign incarnation, could not fail to usher in among us the history of man, the era of reciprocal recognition, by beginning with the revelation, within that history, of its ontological foundation in our common ambiguity.

We were still wide of the mark. And our discovery did not prevent the birth of a strange relationship between Sartre and us that would only terminate with us. Looked at from one side, a man undertook the resolution of his vital problems; looked at from the opposite side, a Sorcerer liberated us through the same means by which he had possessed us. His own attitude was neither true nor false: his undertaking was for him one human enterprise among others, hazardous and necessarily relative like the rest. Yet this enterprise was prolonged, it held out, appearing to make us more genuinely available for a true struggle while never ceasing to question itself, thereby tearing us away, thought by thought, from all the myths that haunt thinking.

The Sorcerer is the Word. His magic is in a sense merely an interminable *flight* from word to word, sentence to sentence, book to book. This flight possesses us, but if this possession liberates us, we must discover what this liberation commits us to. Here is the first sketch for an impossible portrait: Sartre is an obsessed man who palms his obsessions off on us to be rid of them, simultaneously ridding us of ourselves through the meaning he gives his obsessions in palming them off. This athlete of language employs a verbal gymnastics that makes the "me" wither away as other forms of gymnastics make the paunch wither away. But, to inveigle us into joining him in his exercises, he first had to make us admit we possessed a paunch, and he made us aware of our own fat by communicating his horror of his.

A strange fat, certainly. It was perhaps excusable if we were sometimes inept at discovering it in our own cases. For it was always elsewhere, always at odds with the idea we had of it, sometimes even clothing itself in a skinny appearance the better to mystify us. Like the Devil, its favorite ruse is persuading us that it does not exist, that we can escape it by forever striving toward that all-powerful divinity, absolute Thinness. This secretly proliferating flesh, this impalpable thought that talks inside our heads, is everything, and also anything you wish. It is being as well as nothingness. In the last analysis it is man *insofar as he is identical with what is superfluous [de trop] within himself.*

Sartre expresses this root obsession in innumerable forms. The great question for us is: "*Who* am I?" *Lucidity*, which is inherently pessimistic, answers: "I am another, I am someone possessed." We can have a good, pleasantly indulgent laugh at this for we know, don't we, precisely what we believe, namely, that lucidity is itself superfluous, that it decays consciousness by seducing it into this kind of self-interrogation. Let us greet this second lucidity happily, but without ignoring the dependence of such a superb epitome of contemporary thought on the long work of self-exteriorization to which Sartre has devoted himself for his own ends. For we willingly imagine that this work saves us too, even denying the trap ever existed. Yet we may still be entrapped, having so far triumphed only over the idea of a trap.

If Sartre raises such questions throughout his work, it is above all because he experiences the need to answer them *for himself*. He nevertheless undertakes this *before our eyes*. At no point do we abandon the task of following the current of *his* thought. Except for the extreme cases of masochism or imbecility, it follows that we feel ourselves coimplicated in his enterprise of dispossession, and, *pare passim*, more or less *possessed*. Under such conditions it is better not to hastily judge him a wicked exhibitionist who revels in fascinating us and who, more agile at game-playing than ourselves and less caught up in the questionable relationship between us he has set up, passes his time mystifying us, escaping us each time with the collaboration of our emotions. However interested we may be, we would have little chance of *understanding* his need to tear himself away from himself by addressing himself to us, if we refused to see in it, through forms that are perhaps "privileged" or exceptional, the movement of any consciousness concerned to "exist" in its own condition. Genuinely possessed, a true performer like the rest of us, Sartre plays out before others both his obsessions and his means of surmounting them or accommodating himself to them. That he does it with more or less brilliance does not make any difference. Man is, in *all* cases, *"a sorcerer for man"*;[20] and if magical powers vary individually, man's future nevertheless depends on the reciprocal recognition among us by the sorcerer that "I" am of the sorcerer that "you" are. It is a simple matter of the traffic of influences.

If one rereads *The Wall* or *Nausea* together with the descriptions in *Being and Nothingness*, leafing arbitrarily through the whole work, one constantly rediscovers the same obsession: a consciousness cast into the world, inescapably subject to the double *intrusions* of its own body and other consciousnesses.

Nausea—the absorption of the for-itself by the in-itself, the sinking of consciousness into the body—is accepted by us despite our horror of it. This troubled dizziness is a mixture of our complicity with being and our self-satisfaction. It marks the point to which we, as selves, are compromised to the core. Nausea lies *within* our freedom. It exists only insofar as we *are* our freedom, insofar as we are this contingent flesh, this "unjustifiable body" with its "base secrets," this "carnal, eternally excessive presence," this shifty and viscous consistency of being that holds our "lack of being" in fascination.[21] Nausea is existence that is *reduced to feeling itself exist*. Sartre as a child, for example, lost his "solitary truth" all at once and henceforth encountered in himself "only an astonished boredom."

> In the dark I could discern an indefinite hesitation, a light touching, pulsations, an entire living beast. . . . The mirror taught me what I had always known: that I was horribly natural.

These descriptions come from *The Words* and the last of them is followed by this short sentence: *"I have never gotten over this."*[22]

I confess this sentence troubles me. This failure to recover on the part of a man who is approaching his sixties and who nevertheless retains his grip on the world may seem a bit suspect. But why should this be suspect? A man's

20. [J.-P. Sartre, *Esquisse d'une théorie des émotions* (Paris: Hermann, 1939), p. 46; *The Emotions: Outline of a Theory*, translated by Bernard Frechtman (New York: Philosophical Library, 1948), p. 84.]

21. [*Les Mots*, pp. 75, 74; *The Words*, pp. 93, 91.]

22. [*Les Mots*, p. 89; *The Words*, pp. 109–110.]

entire life can be permeated by a firm and effective trait; may a simple obsession not also mark it equally deeply throughout its length? The answer is *no*,
assuming the question was correctly posed—which it was not. The "obsession"
in question is complex, both in origin and in development.

Since I have known Sartre with his direct manner, vitality and capacity for
work, his constant openness to others and deep-seated optimism, I have often
pondered what truth there may be in the various phantasms whose echoes his
works are always communicating to us. One day ten years ago I took it on
myself to ask him. I have given his answer elsewhere,[23] but I now believe my
question may have been too short. For, concerned as he was to provoke in us a
perpetual surpassing of our contingency, how could he go about rendering it so
horrible for us if he had not himself experienced this horror? I said then that
he was *dramatizing* his own obsessions, but this amounts to saying he enjoyed
them. Aware even then of the insufficiency of this perspective, I hastily pointed
out abstract forms of horror which so totally impregnate situations that they
become familiar and almost natural. I cited Sartre's remark on the German
occupation: "Will I be understood if I say both that it was intolerable and that
we adjusted to it quite well?"[24] The trouble is precisely that we shared
Sartre's sense that the German occupation was "intolerable" and his resaying it
made us feel it again, but the same did not hold with regard to the flesh. He
certainly made us reflect, thereby attaining his end, but in order to be able to
say it, he had to have a key to that domain which, up to that point, we lacked.
As a result, we always relied on him to also make it turn in the lock. This
key apparently still works—it served him in opening the doors of his childhood
for us. We therefore ask whether by chance his childhood itself may not have
furnished him this key. Spirits of Ali Baba, fill us with grace.

I am of course aware of his ugliness, which he occasionally speaks about to
us. Two or three thinkers, a certain number of journalists, and various rascals

23. [Before giving Sartre's answer, Jeanson first analyzed the images of bodily
viscosity, sugariness, fattiness, submergence, etc., that Sartre uses to awaken a horror
of contingency and, perhaps, a will to overcome it, a device that extends to frequently repugnant pictures of sexual intercourse; all of which indicated to Jeanson
Sartre's own "austerity in the very heart of a taste for life." *Sartre par lui-même*
(1955 edition), p. 123n. "And Sartre manages patiently to answer my question—
that is, the one asked by so many who might expect an answer by him in this book:
'When making love one has no complaints about it. . . . Except everything changes
if the act is *seen* by a third party. By putting the reader in the place of a third
party, one will therefore have the greatest chance of making him feel—with regard
to the flesh—the horror of contingency, inasmuch as he will recognize in it, in most
cases, his own adolescent reactions regarding sexual intercourse.'" Ibid. Jeanson
later notes a similar horror Sartre had described during the Nazi occupation, "a
certain way objects had of being less our own, more alien, colder, more public in a
way, as if an alien look violated the intimacy of our homes." Ibid., p. 131n., quoting from "Paris sous l'occupation," *La France libre,* published in London, no. 49
(15 November 1944), and reprinted in *Situations, III* (Paris: Gallimard, 1949), p.
23.]
24. ["Paris sous l'occupation," in *Situations, III*, p. 24.]

have either whispered this derisive "Open Sesame" in my ear or yelled it from the rooftops. That it has not allowed me to open the smallest door in my understanding of him may be due to some perversion of my own. The masculine physique on the whole has always seemed dismaying to me and I am still surprised to see women accommodating themselves to it as they do. But I must try to take account of our common experience, which seems to indicate that in the majority of cases one adjusts to it rather well. Should we not then conclude that ugliness is relative such that there will always be men (and of course women) who could be called "ugly" in comparison with their fellow humans? I agree this must follow; and I cannot deny, whatever my own appearance may be, that I would not like to be "disfigured." Yet along comes this man speaking to us quite plainly of the *"obviousness"* of *his* own ugliness. It was evident, he tells us, when he turned nine: "already my right eye was entering the twilight."[25] Describing his friend Nizan elsewhere, he furnished this interesting detail about himself: "He was cross-eyed, like me, but in the other direction, that is, pleasingly. The divergent strabismus made my face a wasteland; his . . . "[26]

I can add the following evidence: I have not known a single woman who, having met Sartre, did not later mention his charm. Admittedly, the majority of them added that one could not fairly judge this charm on the basis of mere photographs. What then? What game is he playing among us, this strange philosopher who has been in the foreground here for twenty-five years, to whom nothing has been denied (not even the Nobel Prize),[27] and who still manages to possess us by miming his phantasms, even putting on a mask of ugliness while we watch?

I do not think this is a game. We must return to the page of his autobiography that I have just cited. For the ugliness of little Jean-Paul, aged eight or nine, was a "fact" at that time only for his mother, who had the goodness, he says, to hide "the cause of her distress." "I learned of it only at age twelve, brutally."[28] This lag period between nine and twelve is confirmed at the book's end: "I shall later recount . . . when and how I served my apprenticeship to violence and discovered my ugliness. . . ."[29] There was nevertheless something already present which was not exactly either a consciousness of being ugly or a consciousness of being a body; ineffable, it was

25. [*Les Mots*, p. 85; *The Words*, p. 104.]

26. ["Paul Nizan," in *Situations, IV* (Paris: Gallimard, 1964), p. 142; "Paul Nizan," in *Situations*, translated by Benita Eisler (New York: George Braziller, 1965), p. 127.]

27. [Offered the Nobel Prize by the Swedish Academy on 22 October 1964, Sartre explained his rejection of it in a letter published in *Le Monde* on 24 October 1964; an English translation by Richard C. McCleary is given in Contat and Rybalka, *The Writings of Jean-Paul Sartre*, 1: 451–454.]

28. [*Les Mots*, p. 85; *The Words*, p. 105.]

29. [*Les Mots*, p. 210; *The Words*, p. 252. Sartre is recorded briefly discussing his ugliness in the transcript of the film *Sartre by Himself*, pp. 11–13.]

a sort of discomfort. *"I felt myself ill at ease, creepy inside my skin [mal dans ma peau]."*[30] Under Sartre's pen this ready-made expression, a banalized saying within a language that rolls on freely, recovers the essential ambiguity of its initial meaning. To feel creepy in one's skin is to fall back from transcending oneself *as* skin into the inertia of flesh. Yet, inasmuch as one falls back only as freedom in this case, one must feel creepy in one's consciousness. As Sartre has said of hunger, *the flesh is much more than flesh*, it is both our anchorage in the world, the very means to our means, and also our absolute vulnerability.

The body, the flesh, the skin, contingency, facticity: all are synonyms for the vulnerability of consciousness due to its being totally *exposed* and *in a situation*. When Sartre tells us he felt creepy in his skin at about nine as a result of discovering he was "horribly natural"; when he describes Roquentin's attacks of nausea; when, in *Saint Genet*, he puts forth an odious vision of the sexual act, we must understand that he is expressing or "rendering" our contingency in extreme or limiting forms which illuminate one-sidedly this particular aspect of consciousness. For the person who sees the sexual act without participating, that act may appear repugnant. It is because Roquentin withdraws into a solitude where no real enterprise can be embodied that he cannot hold things in their place; he feels his own existence flowing back over him and a living inertia clings to him. And it was because the young Sartre felt shame under the eyes of others and "tried to take refuge in (his) solitary truth" that, suddenly, he found in himself merely "an astonished boredom." Thus if the body itself is considered the primary fact in someone's objective history, it will nevertheless be inaccessible to him as such. For we become aware of it only through the decisive, absolutely original event which is *our encounter with other persons*.

Why then, it may be asked, did Sartre feel the need to direct our thinking to these ungraspable limits, abstractly symbolizing a phenomenon we directly experience at all times? Because, in my opinion, he was thinking from the start in accordance with the wish for freedom which is to say *in terms of influence*. He already saw that the encounter with other persons, qua original event, was our own irretrievable past, a myth in the pure state, with the result that there is nothing in us, not even our very flesh, which does not issue from it whether we like it or not. "I" is another person in body and soul, in flesh and consciousness, not only because my flesh was already there when I more or less recognized myself in it, but also, and equally fundamentally, because I could not have become myself except through others, who were also already there. When I am thinking, I do not belong to myself more intensely than when I experience in myself the life that never ceases to take place by itself, which is and is not mine. "I have a body," says man; he hastens to add "I am also possessed *by it*." But Sartre asks us to take yet a further

30. [*Les Mots*, p. 85; *The Words*, p. 105.]

step and note that we "others," we of the human type, are never possessed except by ourselves, that is, by other men like us. Freedom knows no other limitation than itself; there are only consciousnesses which can *act upon consciousnesses*.

Look at Roquentin: this "Thing" that flows back over him, that catches him "from behind" and *violates him*, is certainly existence. But when he tells of *objects* which "set about existing in one's hands," we must be on guard, for they will soon turn into *ideas* which set about existing in one's head. The *existence* which invades him, introducing itself in him without his consent, is at bottom merely *the consciousness of existing*. This is what the flesh means for him and this meaning makes itself flesh within him to the point of nausea.[31] Would his own body have appeared to him as *nature*, as *contingency*, as being "in the way" ["*de trop*"], if he had not taken from others an idea of life which life itself always challenges? How could we discover ourselves to be "unjustifiable" if the world did not constantly propose pseudojustifications to us? We are not contingent; rather, we become contingent. This meaninglessness that invades us is really a second-order meaning with which we affect ourselves when we sense the flight of that "right to existence" whose pure mirage *they* have caused to glitter before our eyes. And this new meaning, which takes possession of consciousness, is not the in-itself that consciousness *is*. It is the sense—always varying in the particular case—to which consciousness condemns itself in projecting itself into a world where it must exist its being vis-à-vis other consciousnesses. By making itself more and more reflexive, *within a relation to itself that is entirely dependent on its relation to others*, it becomes more and more *contingent* in its own eyes.

Flesh could not unilaterally *introduce itself* into consciousness. In a certain sense it is already there (consciousness is flesh), and in another it will never be (consciousness cannot contain anything). Consciousness is always beyond its own contents; it exists only by perpetually making itself *other* than itself, other than *self*. Human consciousness is indeed cannibalistic, but it eats only the ideas humans themselves create. Thus existence can be violated insofar as it is a consciousness, but only by other consciousnesses. When Roquentin owns up to being obsessed with life in its raw form—living nature—he is really speaking of "human nature." I do not believe he is trying to fool us for he has already fooled himself into believing what is both true and false, namely,

31. "Thoughts, they are more insipid still. More insipid even than flesh. They stretch themselves out so much that there's no end to them and they leave a funny taste . . . If only I could stop myself from thinking! . . . My thinking is *me* . . . At this very moment—it's hideous—if I exist, *it is because* I am horrified at existing. *I am the one* who pulls myself away from the nothingness to which I aspire; the hatred, the disgust of existing, are themselves just so many ways of *making myself* exist, of digging myself deeper into existence. The thoughts are being born behind me like a vertigo; I feel them being born behind my head . . ." *La Nausée*, (Paris: Gallimard, 1938), pp. 128–129; *Nausea*, translated by Lloyd Alexander (Norfolk, Conn.: New Directions, 1959), pp. 135–136. [Sartre's emphasis.]

that he can feel *in his body* or "somaticize" this nausea of the brain from which his consciousness suffers. But these "living things"—whose proliferation he later describes in hallucinatory terms—are disturbing precisely because the meanings they project are themselves dead. To one day find oneself with a third eye, or a tongue in the form of a centipede, would certainly be horrible. But such horrors are absurd; they substitute emotionally for the deeper horror that consciousness will be caught up in itself, clogged by the very meaning it thought to bear forth, such that one's surroundings suddenly echo this meaning like so many reflections of one's inertia and impotency.[32] The human world is a tissue of signification from which "a funny little meaning," anonymous and suspicious, comes into relief for each of us. This meaning is shifty, viscous, and compromising; it flows back over its authors and possesses them through fascination. *Our true contingency is the existence of others.* This contingency is indeed our own existence, but it is that existence as indefinitely refracted among others: " . . . I am taken from behind; I am forced from behind to think. . . . "[33]

The relation to others is therefore unsurpassable for the same reason that pure, fleshly contingency is. We are in the world both as perpetually threatened flesh and as perpetually challenged: meaning a heart failure can overcome me in an hour or I can die by inches from feeling excluded by others. This strange animal who has declared himself to be man is inherently neither good nor evil, neither true nor false, neither beautiful nor ugly; yet as a species he never stops conceiving the Good, the True, the Beautiful, and as an individual he never loses his obsession with these absences. Collectively men secrete Man, and each then finds himself intoxicated by it; if an individual tries thereby to escape the common lot, some folly worse than this evil will soon crash down upon him. We are all in the "lazaretto," the "ghetto," we are in quarantine, condemned, destined to this mutual contagion. Whatever we do or omit to do, we cannot avoid contaminating each other. The only issue is to know whether by taking on the human malady together we can succeed in bringing about the society of men. This is for Sartre the very flesh of our condition; it is the guiding direction that runs the length of his works.

You were thinking of the Plague?[34] I was also; the contrast between Camus's and Sartre's conceptions is quite striking. The former symbolizes an absolute Contingency that falls on Humanity like an evil from without (perhaps God's spitefulness over not existing); the latter describes unrelentingly all the vari-

---

32. "Or alternatively, none of that will happen, no appreciable change will occur, but one morning the people, while opening their blinds, will be surprised by a sort of frightening meaning, resting heavily upon things with an air of expectation." *La Nausée*, p. 200; *Nausea*, p. 213.

33. [*La Nausée*, p. 132; *Nausea*, pp. 138–139.]

34. [The allusion is to Albert Camus's novel *La Peste* (Paris: Gallimard, 1947): *The Plague*, translated by Stuart Gilbert (New York: Knopf, 1964).]

ties of the phenomena that manifest—through our constant affective inter-actions with others—the general infection affecting our species. On the one side there is pure Misfortune, Tragedy, and their false result: vain revolt. On the other side there is a situation created wholly by ourselves, even though it is perhaps the inverse of the one we would create were we to *recognize* that it is created by ourselves. In medical terms, for Camus the illness strikes the patient's body independently of the patient and then reverberates in his consciousness. However, since the patient is here humanity, only an extra-human medicine would be in a position to cure him.[35] For Sartre, by contrast, the illness is fully human; it is "psychosomatic"; it affects the whole of man; that is, he finds himself *implicated* by it. The Plague for Camus is Oran crushed, it is the World ravaged by a heavenly caprice. But our "condition" in the Sartrean sense would be better evoked by the metamorphosis that Kafka speaks of: an inherently ambiguous phenomenon as easily attributed to the subject's contingency as to his consciousness itself.

Who, then, has made Roquentin into this recluse who stands aside, out of the way, more or less cut off, more or less neurotic? Other Persons, of course; but with his collaboration. His dubious obsession with fleshly con-tingency rests on his avoiding intrusions of that *social* contingency which is our true incarnation. The bourgeois of Bouville are clearly hateful. Pondering them over a glass of wine or from some height overlooking their anthill suf-fices for uncovering their strangeness and delivers one from them. But one is less easily delivered of that bourgeois conception of man which a whole world, permeated by unmentionable smells, constantly inculcates in one from birth to death. Roquentin has in fact sought merely to *be* free, that is, to guarantee his freedom, to be justified, simply by taking the opposite course to their ridiculous self-assurances and empty justifications. For existence, however, freedom's being is only an inconceivable limit: no sooner does existence try to attain it than it finds itself thrown back toward that other limit, absolute contingency. Haunted by the Other and believing this can be remedied simply by being himself, Roquentin eventually makes himself before our eyes more *inhabited* by others than we could be.

All of Sartre's works testify that he has actually lived this obsession, that it lies at the heart of his philosophy, and that it has long constituted the main-spring of his various approaches. Does it continue to more or less inspire him

35. Give metaphysics a little finger and the entire man soon passes over to it. If the origin of evil is placed *elsewhere*, it becomes merely Evil, which you can't remedy—unless you rouse up its perfect adversary, Good, which also, unfortunately, can only do battle with it elsewhere. Rejecting this easy escape from the trap he set for himself, Camus's only recourse was to confound (in the dimly outlined traits of a kind of Evil Genius) what made us ill and what could cure us, according to Camus. Such is the nadir of the Absurd: a mad physician amusing himself by creating a species that is mortally impaired.

today? Or can we say that he has, for some time already, "settled his account" with it? If we accept this last hypothesis, how has his "cure" occurred? To which period of his life must we return? These questions are only specifications of our fundamental problem: that of the ways and means by which this man has been able to exercise (and perhaps still exercises) an influence on us. And since our two initial paths of influence—the body and the other—are now combined, let us see where this single road will take us.

Haunted, inhabited, stolen (from themselves), expropriated, violated, negotiated, hoodwinked, "had," falsified, maneuvered, possessed, mutilated, colonized, or bled—and always more or less cornered—these are the proper terms in which most Sartrean heroes appear to us. They complain of being false, of being double, of being created as monsters, of being "machined." As Ponge says, they do not think, *they are thought*. Someone put either cotton in their heads (that part of their bodies that others always attack) or horrible animals. Someone imparted thoughts of crabs or lobsters that reside in them forever. Let us say it: *they are rats*. So solid is their trap that they can gnaw only on themselves, which they indulge in forthwith, either each for himself or mutually.[36]

The calvary of this odd creature (the man-rat, or, I dare say, the ratman [*le ratome*]) is almost beyond conception. Scarcely born, he already feels in the way even though he suffers literally from nothing. He is nauseated by his fleshly being but also anguished by his freedom, which is a lack of being. His consciousness overpopulated by innumerable ghosts, he crumbles under the weight of his dereliction, his solitude, and his neglect. Wholly given over to himself, condemned to make himself, he may cease to bog down within himself only to find himself in thin air, the prisoner of a world that excludes him. Cast out into Evil by Good, as also into Good by Evil, false child but true bastard, as ratman he must naturally *betray*. Thus as man he will be a traitor and imposter; as rat, he will be slimy.

Such is the real deception, and it is an objective phenomenon. The fallacy in it, in us, is precisely our being *imposed* upon ourselves. I, you, he, *we* are

36. [Jeanson extends here a metaphor developed by Sartre on the basis of the slang phrase *le rat visqueux*, meaning, roughly, 'a slippery customer': "*Le rat visqueux* has not betrayed [the working class]. But the [Communist] party is sure that he would have been able to if the occasion had arisen. In brief, the word designates the following—unfortunately very widespread—category of individual in our society: the culprit who has done nothing for which he might be reproached." "Les Communistes et la paix," in *Situations, VI* (Paris: Gallimard, 1964), p. 88; first published in *Les Temps modernes*, nos. 81 (July 1952), 84–85 (October–November 1952), and 101 (April 1954); *The Communists and Peace*, translated by Martha H. Fletcher and John R. Kleinschmidt (New York: George Braziller, 1968), p. 9n. Cf. also Sartre's preface to André Gorz's *Le Traître* (Paris: Seuil, 1958), reprinted as "Des rats et des hommes," in *Situations, IV* (Paris: Gallimard, 1964); "Of Rats and Men," in *Situations*, translated by Benita Eisler (New York: George Braziller, 1965).]

cheaters who are cheated, cheaters *because* we are cheated, and each of us by all the others. Man is a rat for man, and the intensification of their ratmanlike character is the work of the ratmen themselves. Even asocial beings have a social existence.

If the ratman is double it is because he is "occupied" by other ratmen. "One and one make one," or, "I" + "one" = "I." "Hell is other people" means that, indiscreet and secret, sneakily cowering in the depths of ourselves, the elusive presence of others possesses us and ousts us, palming off on us a *me* that is not ourselves. Good luck to him who would rid himself of this presence, but "one" fears he may succeed only in identifying himself a little further, in a slightly more formidable manner, with the very strangeness he wanted to escape. A tragedy could be titled: *The Other is Always There, or The Impossible Raticide*; for we are in a trap while philosophy is at its spinning wheel. The human condition is in the form of a turnstile: in it there is a man who takes himself for a rat who takes himself for a man. Our species is a failure of creation, a caprice of God; the rat is an idea of man, who is an idea of God; and man is born with rats in his head. Man is himself a mad idea turning in the brains of man-rats.

This idea "deranges" the ratmen, of course. If the rats in your head bother you, find them some cousins: the bat "in the belfry," for example, or the bug in "bugged." "Does one ever wake up metamorphosed into a cockroach?" Sartre once asked. No, he answered immediately.[37] This is of course because we are at once both the cockroach and the "I" who refuses to be it. Rats, cockroaches, bats, crabs or black beetles, it matters little and the choice is ours; they are in any case only our hosts. Were they simply ourselves we would not be aware of them. If they obsess us, it is because we are condemned to *not be* what they make of us. True *metamorphosis* is conscious and never stops occurring; its victim feels its threat to his dying breath. It is a perpetual suspense. Since the rat in him always lies in his future, the ratman is a man on reprieve.

He is tricked to the point where his activity becomes a game consisting of relentless going and coming between himself and the Other, between what possesses him and his own consciousness of being possessed. Everything is faked in him, feelings as well as thoughts, words as well as acts. How can he know whether he really feels what he believes he feels, or really conceives what he thinks he conceives, if he cannot be certain whether it is he who is acting or the Other within himself reacting? His sole reference point is language. Again, however, the dice are loaded: words arrange themselves in his head "in virtue of habits they picked up in other heads."[38] All that re-

---

37. In an interview that appeared in *Clartés*, no. 55 (March–April 1964), pp. 41–47.
38. ["Erostrate," in *Le Mur* (Paris: Gallimard, 1939), p. 82; "Erostratus," in *Intimacy and Other Stories*, translated by Lloyd Alexander (New York: Berkley Medallion, 1956), p. 51. The passage from which Jeanson quotes is: "The very tools I used

mains are *acts*, which can also deceive, of course. But they can do so only up to the moment when the ratman discovers that on this level the world itself is manipulated. In it the best intentions materialize only at the cost of being more or less perverted; one never does what one wants and always does what one doesn't want. Even the celebrated paving stones on the road to Hell have an odd arrangement in the minds of others, and, consequently, also in one's own. The ratman is himself a living lie, a liar who can neither arrest his lying nor his consciousness of his lying and who can only chase after *his* truth.

Lucien or Roquentin, Orestes, Hugo, Mathieu, Goetz, Nekrassov or Frantz, Genet the Thief, the black who asserts his blackness, the "Jew" who becomes a Jew, Baudelaire willing his uniqueness through desertion, and twenty others besides: these fine bastards, these elite traitors, these distinguished ratmen, are all merely "lucid" consciousnesses concerned to escape contingency. Yet, they cast themselves into contingency all the more in pretending to coincide with themselves and with their freedom. Unwilling volunteers "enrolled" without their knowledge, they each play an unchosen role. Once these unfortunates notice their roles, they immediately play others, losing themselves in their new roles more effectively. This is all because they seek Salvation; they have chosen to turn to God in order to escape the Devil, Hell, and all the other ratmen that overpopulate the world.

"Man must be destroyed" says Goetz,[39] believing he has finally seen through the sinister farce into which he has wandered. He tells us: "Man dreams that he acts, but it is really God who runs things,"[40] and "I am not a man, I am nothing, there is only God; man is an optical illusion."[41] Thus the story of this notable good-for-nothing is quite simple: since the others (his fellow creatures) inhabit him despite himself, he prefers to make himself inhabited by an absolute Other in the wild hope of being freed of them, of placing himself *elsewhere* by identifying with Him. "I humble myself before all, and you, Lord, you will take me in the nets of your night and elevate me above them." *One* invades him, like Roquentin; *one* penetrates him. *But this "one" represents men like himself* who approach him "from behind" and seize him. He has

---

I felt belonged to them [to human beings]; words, for example: I would have wanted *my own* words. But those I use have dragged through I don't know how many consciousnesses; they arrange themselves of their own accord inside my head by virtue of habits they picked up in the others' heads and it is with repugnance that I use them in writing to you."]

39. [*Le Diable et le bon Dieu* (Paris: Gallimard, Livre de Poche, 1951), p. 212 (act 3, tableau 10, scene 2); *The Devil and the Good Lord,* translated by Kitty Black, in *The Devil and the Good Lord and Two Other Plays* (New York: Knopf, 1960), p. 131 (act 3, scene 10).]

40. [*Le Diable,* p. 204 (act 3, tableaux 8–9, scene 3); *The Devil,* p. 126 (act 3, scenes 8–9).]

41. [*Le Diable,* p. 214 (act 3, tableau 10, scene 2); *The Devil,* p. 132 (act 3, scene 10).]

for his part chosen to suppress himself as a man, willingly offering himself up to Anybody. ". . . man is made to destroy the man in himself and to open himself like a female to the great black body of the night."[42] This is the *all or nothing*, the Nothing for the All, the passion for Light that goes so far as to bet on Darkness, since anything ambiguously shadowy is anathema to it.

If Goetz expects God to tear him from his human condition, this God must at least exist. In what, then, lies the superiority of this great silent Existence over that indecipherable hum of talkative consciousness which he had wanted to silence? A muted clamor had haunted him, occasionally becoming clear enough for him to make out some talker and do battle with him. But he will never know the verdict of this absolute Look that transfixes and probes him. Though he was manipulated, he at least suspected as much; now he will be saved—or condemned—*in absentia*. Thus to call all these intruders God, to rename in this way all the parasitic consciousnesses that live off of his own, does not benefit Goetz one whit. He thereby succeeds only in turning a rather badly managed freedom against himself. At first this causes him bodily suffering, and I find it appropriate that it is a woman who denounces the mystification in his *nauseating* attitude:

GOETZ. The body is a mean trick.
HILDA. The body is good. The mean trick is your soul.[43]

And:

GOETZ. I shudder to touch dung with my finger tips. How can I be expected to embrace the bag of excrement itself?
HILDA. There is more ordure in your soul than in my body. The ugliness and filth of your body is in your soul.[44]

And again:

GOETZ. I wish you were an animal so I could mount you like an animal.
HILDA. How you suffer from being a man![45]

Finally:

GOETZ. Sleep wtih you under God's eyes? No. I don't care for coupling in public. (*Pause.*) But if I could just have a night dark enough to hide us from his look . . .

42. [*Le Diable*, pp. 201–202 (act 3, tableaux 8–9, scene 2); *The Devil,* p. 124 (act 3, scenes 8–9).]
43. [*Le Diable*, p. 213 (act 3, tableau 10, scene 2; *The Devil,* p. 131 (act 3, scene 10).]
44. [*Le Diable*, p. 216 (act 3, tableau 10, scene 2); *The Devil,* p. 133 (act 3, scene 10).]
45. [*Le Diable*, p. 214 (act 3, tableau 10, scene 2); *The Devil,* p. 132 (act 3, scene 10).]

HILDA. Love is that night. When people love each other they become invisible to God. [46]

God, then, is *the obsession with Others* made absolute. But in the words of a child of God (and of Capital), who is also one of our exceptional poets, "the worst is not always safe." By replacing the burden of human Looks with that of the Supreme Voyeur's Look, Goetz unwittingly puts himself in a position to discover the true meaning of his obsession. After having sought to destroy a world that excluded him, he thought of loving men, the better to dominate them, and then of annihilating "man" in his own person—flesh and consciousness—in order finally to be finished with men. These three attempts appeared to him in turn as ridiculous, as genuine failing behaviors whose succession revealed the deeper, totally distorted attitude guiding each. For, since the crowd within him, from which he sought liberation, was in his eyes only a crowd of *consciousnesses* bent on judging his own, he might as well be judged by an infinite Being as by his fellow creatures. But when consciousness plays the role of angel, the body plays the role of beast, and the internal angel soon comes to believe that he alone judges himself and that God always speaks through him. [Goetz, in retrospect:]

> I was asking myself at every moment what I might *be* in God's eyes. At present I know the answer: nothing. God does not see me, or listen to me, or know me. . . . The silence is God. The absence is God. God is the solitude of men. . . . If God exists, man is nothingness; if man exists... [47]

This decisive revelation is opposed by Heinrich, who immediately tries to reconstitute an earlier complicity of the excluded between Goetz and himself: "Goetz, have men called us traitors and bastards? Have they condemned us? If God does not exist, then there is no way to escape men." Goetz concedes this in time:

> GOETZ. Goodbye monsters, goodbye saints, goodbye pride. There are only men.
> HEINRICH. Men who will not accept you, bastard.
> GOETZ. Bah! I'll manage.[48]

Whereupon he kills Heinrich, who had wanted to kill him.

> GOETZ. The comedy of Goodness is terminated by a murder. So much the better. I shall no longer be able to reverse my course.

He then becomes capable of taking Hilda in his arms:

46. [*Le Diable*, pp. 215–216 (act 3, tableau 10, scene 2); *The Devil*, p. 133 (act 3, scene 10). Cf. above, pp. 162–163.]

47. [*Le Diable*, p. 228 (act 3, tableau 10, scene 4); *The Devil*, p. 141 (act 3, scene 10).]

48. [*Le Diable*, p. 229 (act 3, tableau 10, scene 4); *The Devil*, p. 142 (act 3, scene 10).]

GOETZ. . . . God is dead. . . . We no longer have a witness, I alone see your hair
and brow. How *real* you have become since He no longer exists.

But if he is then pleased that "the world has been struck blind" ("Alone at
last!"), he nevertheless goes to meet the armed peasants, who are by now resolved to kill him for having betrayed them when he preached love: "I need
the sight of men."[49] Having struggled *as a consciousness* against mass occupation of himself by others, Goetz-the-bastard is cornered by a solitude he can
remedy only by again becoming *a man among men*, neither Man or Rat but
simple ratman.

For the trap holds fast. Poor Goetz! One has made him play in turn the
roles of Saint and Demon (first the top side, Hero of Good, then the bottom
side, perfect Abjection). He finally realizes this and dreams merely of being
"no matter whom," of being "with everyone," wishing to feel that he is among
them, surrounded by them, totally hemmed in by them. But this too is a dream,
the dream of *being Man* by simple amalgamation within human Reality, just
as he had at first tried to identify himself with Evil, then Good, and finally
with the absolute nothingness proper to a creature of God. However, Man
does not exist. His presumed Reality is no more than a myth. The ratman
alone is real: it is and is not what it is, it does and does not do what it aims
to do (knowing this and not knowing it). Goetz wanted to be naked; instead he must put on a new outfit. Tonight they are playing peasants' war
and the only role open is that of chief.

Yet, among all Sartrean characters, it is clearly Kean who attains the highest
degree of this consciousness—which is common to all of them—of being merely
a succession of roles. An actor plays before our eyes the role of an actor who,
exasperated by constantly being someone else, brusquely casts off his role but
thereby succeeds only in *playing* the role of man. Such is *the Actor*: "an illusion
of man," "a mirage."

Kean parodying Hamlet—"An act or a gesture? That is the question."[50]—is
also Orestes concerned to tie down his freedom through a real act;[51] it is
Hugo asking whether he is a revolutionary or merely playing at being one;[52]
it is Goetz calling himself a ham and challenging his own intentions ("So

49. [*Le Diable*, p. 231 (act 3, tableau 10, scene 5); *The Devil*, p. 143 (act 3, scene
10).]

50. Other versions of the same theme are: "I am nothing . . . I play at being
what I am." "I do not truly exist, I make a semblance." "Am I myself when I act?
Is there any moment when I cease acting?" [From Sartre, *Kean*, in *Théâtre* (Paris:
Gallimard, 1962); *Kean*, translated by Kitty Black, in *The Devil and the Good
Lord and Two Other Plays*.]

51. [Sartre, *Les Mouches*, in *Théâtre* (Paris: Gallimard, 1947); *The Flies*, translated by Stuart Gilbert, in *No Exit and Three Other Plays by Jean-Paul Sartre* (New
York: Vintage, 1955).]

52. [Sartre, *Les Mains sales* (Paris: Gallimard, 1948); *Dirty Hands*, translated by
Lionel Abel, in *No Exit and Three Other Plays by Jean-Paul Sartre*.]

everything was merely lying and playacting? I have not acted; I have made gestures.");[53] it is Frantz discovering that the mere existence of the paternal Enterprise transformed all his acts into gestures in advance; it is Nekrassov realizing he is merely an "instrument" and that others have "manipulated him like a child" at the very moment he was most certain he was manipulating others;[54] and it is Genet, if you prefer: "an *actor despite himself, his rejection of the world is only a gesture.*"

And it is Sartre himself, of course.

> My truth, my character and my name were in the hands of adults. I learned to see myself through their eyes. I was a child, a monster constructed by them out of their regrets. . . . I was an imposter, . . . a false child. . . . I felt my acts changing into gestures.[55]

Had he dreamed this quasi infanticide? How then shall we explain that an imaginary crime echoed throughout his work, well before he undertook to make it expressly represent Sartre the child? "Kean died young; throw Kean to his audience. (*Laughs.*) So be quiet, murderers, you're the ones who killed him! You're the ones who seized a child in order to make him a monster!"[56] "They took a child and made a monster of him," Sartre says of Genet. "This is not a man. It is a creature of man, occupied entirely by men. They produced him, fabricated him in every detail. . . ." In a similar manner, in Bohemia, they had fabricated "very amusing and highly productive monsters." They would steal children and then "slit their lips, compress their skulls, and keep them in a box day and night to inhibit their growth."[57]

This child, mutilated to satisfy the needs of some "human" cause—let us say, roughly, for reasons of social utility—is our first inhabitant, surviving in us clandestinely. It may still survive. This "little cripple," this "deformed dwarf" is "our oldest tenant."[58]

Sartre, it will be said, was nevertheless not a true bastard like Goetz, Kean, or Genet. Even less was he a kidnapped child.

> But who is not a kidnapped child, more or less? Kidnapped from the world, from his neighbor, from himself? . . . Scarcely out of the womb, each little man

---

53. [*Le Diable*, p. 223 (act 3, tab. 10, sc. 4); *The Devil*, p. 138 (act 3, sc. 10).]

54. [Sartre, *Les Séquestrés d'Altona* (Paris: Gallimard, 1960), p. 215 (act 5, sc. 1); *The Condemned of Altona*, trans. Sylvia and George Leeson (New York: Knopf, 1961), p. 172 (act 5). Sartre, *Nekrassov* (Paris: Gallimard, 1956), p. 194 (tableau 7); *Nekrassov*, translated by Sylvia and George Leeson, in *The Devil and the Good Lord and Two Other Plays*, p. 424 (scene 7).]

55. [*Les Mots*, pp. 66–67; *The Words*, pp. 83–84.]

56. [*Kean*, in *Théâtre* (1962), p. 553 (act 4, scene 2); *Kean*, in *The Devil and the Good Lord and Two Other Plays*, p. 251 (act 4, scene 2).]

57. [*Saint Genet: comédien et martyr* (Paris: Gallimard, 1952), p. 29; *Saint Genet: Actor and Martyr*, translated by Bernard Frechtman (New York: George Braziller, 1963), p. 23.]

58. "Des rats et des hommes," in *Situations, IV*, pp. 52–54; "Of Rats and Men," in *Situations*, pp. 342–344.

is taken *for another*. . . . One takes a live brat and sews him into the skin of a dead one; he will suffocate in this senile childhood with nothing else to do but reproduce exactly his [elder's] gestures, with no hope other than to poison future childhoods after his own death. . . . Out of stolen children one eventually produces child stealers. . . . We call them parents.[59]

You think he is exaggerating? Yes, that's for sure. Parents are not necessarily these barbarians, these executioners, these ignoble sculptors of human flesh he enjoys depicting us as being. What are they for him, then? This man, who has never had cause to reproach his mother, who today still retains all his affection for her, *has not even known his father*.[60] When he pats himself on the back for this before our eyes, as if he had thereby escaped some atrocious peril, let us admit he could not have had a direct experience of this peril. If his grandfather, *without wishing to*, "made" him a writer, this double deception—a sort of second-degree cuckolding—has had truly catastrophic results. But the tonality of "rosiness" throughout his childhood—"it was Paradise"[61]— is just what inclines me to think Sartre's works paint gloomy pictures of certain phenomena only in order to illustrate a more secret horror, a sort of calm horror that was his own lot, that continues in some subtle form, and that he has for a long time doubted he could "render" with enough verisimilitude. I am well aware that words are always more or less deceiving, except for their tone, which cannot deceive. Listen to him in what follows. This is one of the greatest writers of our time, probably the greatest in various areas. While placidly telling us of his work as a writer, of his difficulties in writing, there is a sudden aside, the voice changes, an apparent incoherence arises in the text from somewhere, and there it is; it is said: *"Besides, the reader has understood that I detest my childhood and whatever has survived of it."*[62]

"I detest my childhood" and "it was Paradise": Sartre thus challenges the happiness of Jean-Paul. But, far from attributing to himself some martyred childhood, he always emphasizes that his was pleasant, easy, sometimes even exultant. Of what, then, was he complaining? I fear it was not simply of having to recognize, through this happiness, the fatal disrepute of any possible happiness. You are a little marvel, those around you never stop proclaiming. "He's *really* a little angel!" exclaims the outside world (your grandfather's guests). Everyone loves you so what could you ask for? It is pleasant to be loved; would you not be lovable? For you there will be no rights or duties,

59. ["Des rats et des hommes," in *Situations, IV*, pp. 54–55; "Of Rats and Men," in *Situations*, pp. 344–346. Jeanson has altered the order of these phrases in Sartre's text.]

60. [Sartre was one year old when his father died in 1906. After his stepfather's death, Sartre and his mother shared an apartment in Paris until her death in 1969.]

61. [*Les Mots*, p. 24; *The Words*, p. 34.]

62. *Les Mots*, p. 136; *The Words*, p. 164. Jeanson's emphasis.]

just *"a single mandate: to please."*[63] A corollary follows from this: for you there will no longer be either hate or love. "Everyone is good since everyone is happy"; but precisely because this contentment is for you the very image of life in general, you are indifferent to everyone. You make baby talk the way a dog performs tricks, you play the fool through loyalty, because that is what is expected of you in order to give pleasure. It is the poodle in you who is loved and the buffoon in you who feels happy. Is it therefore surprising if one day your happiness, your joys, and even your exultations suddenly have for you no more than the boring insipidity of "an egg without salt," or "Good without Evil," a sort of natural, contingent, indefinite life that continues to bog down in itself because of the absence of any reason for self-transcendence?

Had Jean-Paul lived only this meaninglessness, Sartre and he would probably have remained unknown to us. But he was also able to live its *inconsistency*, to be anguished over it, and then to discover the most seductive and subtly deceptive recourse against this anguish. We know how this occurred: he felt himself an actor among actors. ("I had been persuaded that we were created in order to play a comedy.")[64] Moreover, he willingly devoted himself to his histrionics—on condition of being their hero—because Literature, the religion whose high priest in his eyes was Karl [his maternal grandfather] gave those histrionics the most perfect justification.

Being fatherless, he was, in his own view, a nothing. Others inhabited him, to be sure, but in the form of "uneasiness" rather than solid assurance. He did not need to struggle against misery and hunger, which could have given a meaning to his life. All he could really do was ask himself *who* he was and suspect that he *was not*—that his fluid existence was beyond justification. Up to this point the body obviously had nothing to do with it, but it then entered the scene and became one of the principal supports of a drama that took place elsewhere. The uneasiness from which Jean-Paul suffered (" . . . I remained abstract. . . . I had no soul") remained essentially inapprehensible to him. A diffuse somatization made this abstraction barely sensible, changing his lack of soul into a sort of vague, soulful yearning. Through this polite invasion by his wish to be, through this spontaneous attempt to free himself by self-expression, the child will certainly succeed in giving his body a soul, but it will be at the cost of incarnating his anguish. "My body made itself known in a series of soft, hesitant feelings of sickness, solicited intently by the grown-ups. . . . I confused my body with my discomfort. . . ." Even though the process of identifying these two things had been highly cushioned, the result left its mark: ". . . *of the two* (body and discomfort) *I no longer knew which one was undesirable.*"[65]

63. [*Les Mots*, p. 22; *The Words*, p. 32. Jeanson's emphasis.]
64. [*Les Mots*, p. 69; *The Words*, p. 86.]
65. [*Les Mots*, p. 72; *The Words*, pp. 88–89. Jeanson's emphasis.]

He loses on both counts; perhaps because the strange violence that crops up again here is exhausted, challenged, and neutralized by its own contradictory character. Jean-Paul had earlier suffered from not being, and this in a world where others *are*, where they are *themselves*, where they are *founded*, *with respect to their being*. "I was *nothing*: an ineffaceable transparency."[66] But now he suffers from *being* this nothing, this "something": ". . . I felt myself becoming an object, a potted flower."[67] "I suddenly discovered that I counted for nothing, and I was ashamed of my presence in a well-ordered strange world."[68] He was a lack of being that complained of being too much, of being "in the way," "unjustifiable," and "superfluous" (*"bodily presence is always a surplus* [*exédentaire*]").[69] He is a useless presence among other presences that appear necessary to him because they declare themselves so and they hold authority. He is a situated freedom which cannot recognize itself, which must deny itself in advance because it is surrounded by freedoms that have chosen to be pure situations, mere prearranged positions. This is not a misfortune, it is nothing; simply a type of death that smoothly insinuates itself into the very heart of life. "A spoiled child is not unhappy. He feels bored, like a king. Like a dog. . . . Trembling minutes drop down, engulf me and forever totter on the brink of fading away. . . . These aversions are called happiness."[70]

We are free to make light of the so-called drama of this coddled brat who finds a way to consider himself a nullity and to be encumbered by it—an ironical poke in the name of all the world's starving children. Sartre himself did as much last year in a much-discussed interview following the appearance of *The Words*: "I have seen children dying of hunger. Over against a dying child, *Nausea* cannot act as a counterweight."[71] Yet let us admit that our irony would come more naturally if, on the one hand, we really did what we could for the innumerable bastards of history, these children of the Third World, these basement children, and if, on the other hand, privileged persons that we are, we could congratulate ourselves on having reached "adulthood." In any event, however different it may be from the situation of the Vietnamese children, the situation of our "developed" children seems to me no less disturbing: the former annihilates the very flesh of individuals, but the latter allows the survival of dimmed, wrecked, ravaged consciousnesses almost unavoidably turned against themselves.

66. [*Les Mots*, p. 73; *The Words*, p. 90.]
67. [*Les Mots*, p. 72; *The Words*, p. 89.]
68. [*Les Mots*, p. 70; *The Words*, p. 87.]
69. [*Les Mots*, p. 74; *The Words*, p. 91. Jeanson's emphasis.]
70. [*Les Mots*, pp. 75–76; *The Words*, pp. 93–94.]
71. Interview by Jacqueline Piatier, "Jean-Paul Sartre s'explique sur *Les Mots*," *Le Monde*, 18 April 1964; "A Long, Bitter, Sweet Madness," translated by Anthony Hartley, in *Encounter* 22, no. 6 (June 1964): 62.

I felt in the way, so I had to disappear. I was a dull blossoming-forth perpetually soliciting its own abolition. In other words, I was condemned and the sentence might be applied at any moment. I nevertheless rejected it with all my might, not because my existence was dear to me, but, on the contrary, because I did not value it: the more absurd life is, the more unacceptable is death.[72]

Sartre tells us he was this child. When I think of all the persons he tells us about, of all he has said to us about himself, of the clear lights he continues to project on our condition, our era, ourselves, I have no desire to be skeptical. To understand oneself starting with one's childhood no doubt presupposes an understanding of this childhood that starts with oneself. This dialectical tie, this two-way dependence, seems in Sartre's case to have been adequately established both by the description's internal coherence and by its realism, that is, its strict agreement with the totality of objectively recorded facts.

For all that, however, my problem has not been resolved. The more I am persuaded that Sartre was in fact Jean-Paul, the more difficulty I have conceiving how his thinking can be so close to my own, how a childhood in many respects so different from my own took, from among all possible human consciousnesses, precisely the form that could later reveal me so effectively to myself. Yet this simple testimony remains quite abstract: I may as well give up speaking of this man again if I keep parentheses around the essentials of my relationship to him. I would like to know how to say—and I believe I'll never succeed—all that I owe him. But, such as I have become, and never having ceased to take support from him in making myself, I cannot imagine the route he might take today to arrive at this self-recognition in me. Everything happens as if I was constantly using him to accentuate our basic differences; yet I feel more than ever in accord with his responses on innumerable problems that concern us. And to say it all (including the growing affection I feel for him), it seems that the more I distinguish myself from him the more I recognize him. This follows a subtle process that, with each confirmation of an actual difference, reaffirms and deepens a bizarre kinship whose most fitting designation I do not always perceive. Has Sartre become my father without my realizing it? I have reasons to doubt it. But I also know, for example, that although I have for a long time felt the need to define what I call faith vis-à-vis the Christians,[73] or that a certain taste for happiness is a central dimension of my existence, I have nevertheless had to put an effort into everything I've said, wondering what he would think if one day he read me. If this worry silenced me, or if it could not be expressed without cutting me off from him, then my freedom was clearly quite thoroughly alienated, reducing me to being a mere child of Sartre's, as these days others among us are "children of God" (of Jesus, of Mary), children of Marx, or even of

72. [Les Mots, p. 78; The Words, pp. 96–97.]
73. [See in this regard Jeanson's La Foi d'un incroyant (Paris: Seuil, 1963).]

Freud. But I believe I can say that this obvious obstacle was for me a *challenge*, a genuine *test*, and each time I broke through it (whether rightly or wrongly) I guaranteed, on the contrary, the consistency of my attitude. And if, finally, I add that I am equally concerned to maintain the maximum of coherence in my conscious activities, it will, I hope, be understood that I have given an account of my own situation in relation to Sartre only to the extent it seemed essentially the same as that of everyone who has had the courage to stay with me up to this point. We no doubt admire this man as no other, and this admiration, far from chaining us to him, seems to have had the effect of freeing us from him, for we have scarcely abstained from challenging him. I intend that also as a tribute to him. In fact, though, these challenges did not require enormous courage of me; the greatest risk is being already a bit winded in my effort to follow him to the end in his own attempt to challenge himself.

Let us go back, then, to the Jean-Paul he says he was. "There was a horrible reverse side to things; when you lost your reason you could see it. To die was to push this madness to its extreme and to be engulfed by it. I lived in terror; it was a true neurosis."[74] Things in reverse, life gone absurd, such is the appearance the world constantly threatens to take on for a child fooled by adults. They make him participate in their games without giving him— or being able to give him—the rules. The Comedy is bearable when one plays it "for real" as an established actor. But who would then consent—absent the constraint of some vital necessity—to play walk-on roles? This would amount to being an actor who is false in the eyes of actors themselves. A piece of living decor, a simple prop in the hands of those who do play, the child alienated by adults really has no part in the game, he is "out of play," he is only *played with*. Will he come to realize all this? If he does, what will be the result for him?

It is well known that children are players, like puppies and kittens. If the adults around the child play "for real" and take themselves seriously, he may content himself with carefree play in the shadow of these great consciousnesses. If, on the other hand, adults are sufficiently conscious and open about being players, all distance might disappear between the "true" and "false" comedy, between actors and mere extras. In the first case, the child will play without any problems, since childhood is made for playing. In the second, he will simply be a player who is younger than the others, playing along with them the oddest of games, consisting of never knowing which game you are playing. Things will almost certainly deteriorate in the pauses between games, when those around the child will and will not take their roles seriously, when these roles are believed in some respects but not others. Now Sartre tells

74. [*Les Mots*, p. 78; *The Words*, p. 96.]

us that if his grandparents had been genuine believers he would have been plunged into mysticism. Instead, his grandfather, a Protestant, had Jean-Paul baptized a Catholic merely out of liberalism. He did so with the approval of the boy's grandmother, who was nominally Catholic but lacked belief; "her skepticism alone kept her from being an atheist."[75] Thus the saint or the demon that Sartre might have been—had Jean-Paul been affected by different circumstances—died together at an early age. What survived was "the actor despite himself," the extra, the *maker of faces [le grimacier]*, eager to please and still overdoing it, turning himself into a laughing stock as a last resort: "I planted myself before the wardrobe mirror and made faces for a long time";[76] "I disappeared and went to make faces in front of a mirror."[77] It is clear to us that a suicide was implied each time, a veritable enterprise of self-destruction, of *self-hatred* begot, as usual, by shame.

Yet this child also wanted to live "with all his might." As we have seen, he pushed away death: *"I had been born to fill the great need I had for myself."*[78]

For this man who speaks to us, this was, I believe, the true beginning of it all, namely, *the invention of his personal God.* Our *real* origin can only be an advent, the arrival in the world of a signifying myth. Here it is the "birth" of the Son to the detriment of the Father. "I needed God and they gave him to me, I received him without understanding that I was seeking him."[79] Having in this world no right to exist that was "seriously" recognized, not feeling indispensable to anyone in particular, but also resisting with all of his being the vacuous presence to which he felt he had been reduced, how could Jean-Paul survive if not by imagining himself *indispensable to all?* Had he been a mere victim he would have chosen masochism; as a spoiled victim his only solution was sadism: *pride.* "Driven into pride, I became the Proud One."[80] He who suffers from not being taken seriously, from having no real place anywhere, and yet who does not feel concretely rejected, must raise himself to the Universal, being unable to consider himself as excrement: I accept their universal contempt of me if that signifies that they need me without yet knowing it. And since I am not allowed to recognize myself as their son without consenting to my own annihilation, I will therefore be both their father and my own. I will beget them by creating myself before their eyes, by giving myself to them. *"Being nobody's son, I was my own cause. . . . I found myself by opposing myself."*[81]

"God is dead, long live God." "Sweet Jesus," allow me to add. For this

75. [*Les Mots*, p. 81; *The Words*, p. 100.]
76. [*Les Mots*, p. 86; *The Words*, p. 106.]
77. [*Les Mots*, p. 88; *The Words*, p. 108.]
78. [*Les Mots*, p. 90; *The Words*, p. 110. Jeanson's emphasis.]
79. [*Les Mots*, p. 83; *The Words*, p. 102.]
80. [*Les Mots*, p. 90; *The Words*, p. 110.]
81. [*Les Mots*, pp. 91–92; *The Words*, p. 112.]

child, in order to save himself, ultimately proposes nothing less than to save all men together with himself: "My pride and my recklessness were such at the time that I wished either to be dead or to be needed by the whole earth."[82] Made by others, he would henceforth make himself a demiurge with respect to them. His provisional humiliation would end up appearing to them one day merely as the reverse of his redemptive function: mistrust Nothing, for it may be only an appearance of Everything. He feared the meaningless-ness of life as he feared death; he wanted to feel "mandated." By writing, by entering into Literature and renouncing himself in order to take charge of the world, he would be the Messiah, the Lord's annointed, God's elected one—no more gifted than others, yet designated for everyone's attention, offered to some universal *expectation*.

Such an insane reversal of perspective has been too thoroughly denounced by Sartre (in the cases of Goetz or Genet, for example) for us to be able to apply his condemnation of the choice of sainthood to his own childhood. Moreover, since he is careful to indicate to us that Jean-Paul himself had already condemned it[83] we must admit no masochism was involved. We should not be misled by phrases like "rejection of life," "flight into the future," and "suicide to avoid death." It is indeed a question of constructing his salvation, but in a glorious manner, and before men, not God. This will to self-annihilation is only a will to be, "to tear my life out of mere chance," to no longer exist in any place—in order to impose himself everywhere. "A parasite on humanity, my services corroded it and obliged it to constantly revive my absence."[84]

In this strange, somewhat Pascalian wager, God is invoked not as He to whom one speaks in search of a composed conscience, but as the Holy Spirit, dispenser of sacred power, and as the sum of men in the present and to come. *In relation to them*, thanks to this "inspiration," *one might ultimately be other than oneself, other than them, other than everything*. I do not be-lieve the world's literature (save, perhaps, for the New Testament) anywhere contains a more perfect description of pride and the will to power in their most essential form. To be proud is *to be "anyone" yet to be it in a manner other-than all Others*, all the while obliging them to recognize your singularity, thereby allowing you to recognize yourself in that singularity.

It is precisely on this point that this man's story refers me to my own and affects me. I also believe it allows me to understand how his story manages, from a different angle, to concern us all. Unless we have, indeed, chosen to be *victims* we will probably have to recognize ourselves in this man's pride, in the constantly proclaimed and fierce need he has to be "nobody's son," to be "the

82. [*Les Mots*, p. 138; *The Words*, p. 166.]
83. "Mysticism suits displaced persons and supernumerary children. . . . I was in danger of being a prey to saintliness. My grandfather gave me an everlasting disgust for it." "Saintliness was repugnant to me. . . . " *Les Mots*, p. 81; *The Words*, p. 100.
84. [*Les Mots*, p. 162; *The Words*, p. 195.]

son of his works," to be his own cause, to owe himself solely to himself. The key to all this is in the following short sentence: "*I became a traitor and I have remained one.*"[85] Conditioned from birth to death, betrayed by our condition, condemned never to be ourselves, we shall attain whatever worth we will have *only through betrayal*. We can be the cause of our existence only by tearing ourselves away from others and from ourselves, and we can bring about the advent of man only by tearing him away from his past, from that prehistory of the ratman that still weighs fully on our so-called history.

But we may be moving too fast. Jean-Paul, from the heights of his nine years, concentrated on his salvation and cared nought for history. Yet isn't it quite clear that, excepting starving Armenians of all kinds, true revolutionaries are precisely those who began by recognizing they must realize themselves, whatever their purposes, by their own means and despite all contingencies, "one against all" if necessary? To claim to be human in our rickety condition and in this fake world is to be unable to accept being only what others have made us and continue to make us. It is to entrust to oneself "the fine mission of being unfaithful to everything." Since everyone is a faked person, a bastard, either we resign ourselves to being *only* what we are—pure products of circumstances—or else we take on, with all the risks involved, that other part, which is completely unpredictable and which will make us fakers and traitors at each moment of our lives.

It remains to note that there are *absolute* betrayals, which cut us off from others without hope of return, and *relative* betrayals, whose success is measured only in terms of others. Betrayal may be either evasion or confrontation; flight elsewhere or flight forward. To beseech God—"Take me, I am your instrument"—is certainly to give in. It is no doubt crazy to turn toward other persons, pretending to be anyone whatever yet vowing to surpass everyone, but it is crazy in the sense that the future is the craziness of the present, or in the sense that man is the future of the ratman. It happens that you and I have already chosen between this craziness and this giving in, since I am writing this and you are reading it.

Let us recognize that our Nobel-winner-despite-himself cuts quite a figure when, at age sixty, he plunges back obstinately into the magic that enchanted his childhood. The spell was that of "the *stowaway*," lacking ticket, money, and identification, whose presence in the train must ultimately appear—in the ticket collector's own eyes—more justified than that of any of the other, paying, riders. Sartre a stowaway! I have already had occasion to note how this strange concept reveals itself, in the test of events, as unstable if not contradictory: like Goetz, let him give it up and try another "act," this impossible "somebody" [*quidam*]. Evidently not everyone can be "somebody."

I persist, despite myself, in thinking that his dream is also ours and that in

---

85. [*Les Mots*, p. 198; *The Words*, p. 238. Jeanson's emphasis.]

confronting the world we hardly have other options. Someone whispers to me: there is love; be patient, it will come. What excites me meanwhile about this man is precisely that he opted from the start for the most unpolished attitude, that this choice has been prodigiously successful (on all sorts of criteria), and that it has, for all that, not made him the "tough guy" one might imagine. What there is of tenderness in him may ultimately allow me to understand the bizarre influence he retains over us.

A man among all men, indispensable to all: "Such is pride, which is the defense plea of the wretched."[86] Of course there is misery of all sorts, but those who are truly miserable perceive death in the heart of their life as a sort of absurdity imposed from without. They must either give in to the dizziness of this absence of meaning, or choose life—and radical combat against that dizziness. For the latter, the whole question is whether this primary revolt, which is necessarily individual, will find in the situation the means for collective struggle, the drift toward a real solidarity, or whether it is condemned in advance to remaining solitary. Sartre's case is clearly in the second group: a consciousness dispossessed of itself that is nevertheless privileged. For him death was having to live his own insignificance. To the absolute forlornness of one who feels "in the way" he could only oppose another absolute, that of his own *necessity*, which must ultimately be recognized by everyone. This involves surrendering himself alive to the imaginary (sacralized literature) and confusing it with the real; yet he thereby rejects death and takes his birth into his own hands. He thus threw himself at death out of fear of death. In his rejection of living, in his flight forward and his death-denying suicide, "it was death that I sought."[87]

This relation to the Absolute at the basis of Sartre's self-begetting has several times been designated by him as a *"neurosis."* I perceive in this (across the varied circumstances differentiating each man from all others, and taking account of the global differentiation imposed between those who struggle for their life and the privileged who suffer only from a mutilation of their existence) *the initial word in every authentic moral attitude*, the very essence, and the original alienation, of the human task. Like everyone else we are absolute bastards, neither men nor rats. In addition, like all *intellectuals* in the bourgeois world, we are neither oppressors nor oppressed. The wish to avoid being an accomplice reduces us to nothingness; and, if we then presume to exist, *that wish obligates us to all*. We may well join in Sartre's irony regarding his own quests for Salvation, posthumous glory, and immortality, but we should also recognize in passing a radical urgency analogous to the starkest need to live. We may also note that this escape into the imaginary has nevertheless given birth to a man who has succeeded in recovering from that flight. Born of a creative decision, this dream, this "bitter and sweet madness," was

86. [*Les Mots*, p. 91; *The Words*, p. 111.]
87. [*Les Mots*, p. 160; *The Words*, p. 193.]

throughout the work of a consciousness, a long labor of self-transformation. A work has issued from this neurosis, a philosophy capable of informing its epoque, *in a word, a morality*. Yet it is a morality that puts us on our guard against all morality by constantly provoking us to retighten our grasp on history, to more consciously situate ourselves in history without thereby renouncing the wish to exist by ourselves.

This infernal mixture of absolute humility and absolute pride, this mad demand to regenerate oneself in an inhuman world, typify the ratman's work once he has refused either to rest content with his own sub-humanity or to resign himself to it. The need to live justifies pride, since one needs pride to fully assume the task of living. "Only travelers with tickets have the right to be modest."[88] But this pride must be shared with everyone on pain of sinking into *sadism*, "in other words, into generosity."[89] It is masochistic to accept oneself as one has been made to be (and as one never stops being made to be). To fight in solitude is to deny one's own humanity; to pretend to confer humanity on others is to deny theirs. The evidence seems to indicate that the philosopher I am speaking of, far from constructing a system and enclosing himself in it so as to escape men, has shown himself increasingly concerned to remain "miserable" by siding with all the world's miserable persons. More than anyone, he could have very soon believed himself to be "saved"; however, to that very extent he has instead wanted, more than many others, to be implicated in the human adventure. I would have some difficulty imagining that in this there was no moral attitude on his part. On the contrary, I believe I see how this choice issues from the one by which he first undertook to tear himself from non-existence. This, it seems certain to me, explains why this man has never ceased to have something to say to us.

Constrained to revolt alone in order to conquer a minimum of existence, each of us, like Sartre, finds himself more or less condemned to pride and to the wish to be "anyone whatever." This is because, like it or not, we are perfect bastards, we are *intellectuals*. "I am also one," he reminded us one day, not without a certain pride. He immediately added: ". . . intelligence is neither a gift nor a defect; it is a drama or, if you prefer, a provisional solution that most often changes into a life sentence. . . . We are so constructed that we must die or invent man. . . ."[90] All of Sartre is encapsuled here, and ourselves as well, of course.

But even as intellectuals like him, philosophizing in his wake, living to the hilt the drama he speaks of, we are nevertheless not this writer which he is. Let us draw maximum profit from his experience while avoiding, if possible,

88. [*Les Mots*, p. 91; *The Words*, p. 111.]
89. [*Les Mots*, p. 92; *The Words*, p. 112.]
90. ["Des rats et des hommes," in *Situations, IV*, pp. 62, 64–65; "Of Rats and Men," in *Situations*, pp. 352–353, 355.]

the dangers of hasty identifications. He has himself warned us against this by inviting us to consider the Writer he is as a "buffoon," an "actor," a "clown," or, more exactly, as an "imposter," a true "swindler" who is one-third Karl (Schweitzer), one-third Kean, one-third Nekrassov, with a pinch of ingenuous humility ("it is true that I am not gifted for writing"). Such would be, in sum, the recipe for the "Nobel 65."

Should my aptitude for critical examination ever find itself disqualified, I shall say so most serenely; nonetheless, in my eyes, Sartre's work is the best example one might be tempted to invoke in support of literary authenticity. It is certainly the *freest* of all and perhaps alone in attaining true self-contestation on almost all points before the readers themselves have had time to do so, while still retaining for them the marvel of creation. From this I conclude that one must stand by this work; it is to the precise extent that Sartre does not cheat that he risks becoming the worst of sorcerers in our eyes. All who have taught have had the following experience: the more you evince before your students a desire not to use sanctions, the more you address yourself to their freedom, the more, correlatively, you alienate them—by becoming, of course, more admirable in their eyes. There is no worse illusion than the feeling that one is free of the freedom of another merely because his freedom operates in full view; I decline to take myself as the only sorcerer involved simply because Sartre has revealed his magic to me. When he tells me almost everything about his origins and those of his work, I willingly admit with him that it was "a mad undertaking" to write in order that his existence might be forgiven, but I do not go so far as to be concerned, nor have I ever been, that my own existence be forgiven.

This example may suffice (many others could have been used) to illustrate the two central questions that a brief study like this must content itself with posing: 1) that of the precise modalities by which a moral experiment undertaken in full singularity has been able to make itself sufficiently universal to concern everyone, even supplying the illumination of the world and ourselves that we needed; and 2) that of the relationship between the particular flavor life has for each of us and this general orientation of the choice to exist, a relationship that indeed seems more or less common to a good number of us.

One can envision the very modest titles of the two fat volumes I would now be tempted to write concerning Sartre: Volume One: *From the History of a Morality to the Morality of History* [*la morale de l'Histoire*][91]; Volume Two: *Happiness and History*. General title: *The Problem of Sartre and Moral Philosophy*.

91. [As noted in the Translator's Introduction (p. xv, n. 34), an article with this title was published by Jeanson in 1948. A book with this title was published in 1959 by another collaborator of Sartre's on *Les Temps modernes*, André Gorz, *La Morale de l'histoire* (Paris: Editions du Seuil, 1959). It analyzes alienation and the need for revolution at a certain historical conjuncture.]

The more I scrutinize these works and absorb this philosophy, the clearer it seems that my own moral attitude conforms totally with Sartre's and yet differs in its totality. Certainly for personal reasons, but also because there is a good chance many others may share in my case, I would like to be able to grasp this contradiction more firmly. To briefly sketch the inquiry I should like to conduct on this point, I shall for a moment take up the preceding example.

A man tries to escape his own existence, which appears to him unjustifiable —in the eyes of others as well as in his own. He does so because he feels threatened in his being by the look of others. I gather from this, first, that he already has a being, and, thus, that he will ultimately need to be; secondly, since this being has been "palmed off" on him by others, he will henceforth never rest until he has given himself a being that depends only on himself. He thereby comes to grips with the ideal form, the veritable archetype, of the "bad bet," for he must obviously also pass through others in order to confirm his own autonomy. His talent for obliviousness is weak, and he quickly realized this. Moreover, rendered indifferent to God by varying sorts of religious tepidity in those around him, he is only slightly touched by the temptation to short-circuit his relations with creatures by claiming direct relations with the Creator. His remaining alternative is therefore to create himself by starting with others, supporting his being on the being others would recognize in him but decreeing in advance that his true being will always be beyond this image of him. This is to choose—if I'm not mistaken—absolute trickery, since it involves using others to feign a self-image that could remain just as inaccessible to oneself as to others. One asserts: I know what I am worth and you too will have to know it; at the same time, however, you will never know it any more than I will, for I shall always be worth something more. The only way to *be* consists in always aiming tangentially at the being one wants. Neither the sun nor death can be looked at steadily, La Rochefoucauld noted. Nor, consequently, can being itself be looked at directly, since being is the vertigo of existence, its death and its sun all at once. The shortest road from oneself to oneself is the escape route: if you do want to be yourself, continue always to be another.

This is why Sartre seems to me so aptly inspired in pointing out this theme of "flight forward" as a major characteristic of his own existence. We would gladly call it his "life style" if life were not, for him, precisely what we must *exist*, if, that is, his action and thought, including his way of writing, had not untiringly rejected all style.

Flight forward? That, among other things, is just the point. *It is the choice of the tone or "tonus" of life as against its style.* It is the constant concern never to let oneself be caught by oneself; to flee, indefinitely, the force of inertia and acquired momentum; to never be the boat that runs on its headway alone or the man who rests on his laurels, surrendering to his successes.

Style is not the man; it is the fat on our thinking; and if it sometimes makes those thoughts fascinating, the price paid is that they have themselves been fascinated, numbed, petrified, and dehumanized. Tone, on the other hand, betokens perpetually vigilant thinking that never ceases to pull away from itself and surpass itself, renewing its own impulse, increasing its speed, always giving itself more movement in order to go still further.

For that which must be can only be beyond what is, and consequently the latter can never be the foundation of the former. The real is a sticky trap that simulates the consistency of being, but it engulfs us by giving way beneath our steps the moment we place our confidence in it. The deceptive flesh of reality (whether it is our flesh, or that of language, or of history) everywhere and always threatens to suck us in once and for all.

Style, for Sartre, "is death,"[92] it is past alienation; it is also the Writer's scorn, the vengeance this "sacred monster"[93] and "furious madman" takes upon us for having been himself the victim of scorn: "behind these fulgurations hides a dead child who prefers himself to everything." Style is a man's captivity within his childhood; he tries to ensnare others in his life because he first was caught in it, having chosen to love himself in opposition to all others. It seems to me Sartre reproaches style—"that grand flourish of arrogance"[94]—above all for not being the *act* of arrogance but its empty *gesture*, a pure passion of the self. For the great problem is to remain at every moment capable of "*working loose*" *from oneself* ["*décoller*" *de soi*]. One must produce himself relentlessly to avoid being the product of contingency and of others, of that *ready-made* "being" which is already more or less *remade* and which one always becomes the moment one gives up making himself. Sartre has repeated, in various forms, that he does not believe in Progress: how indeed could he *believe* in it, having condemned himself to do it indefinitely?

March or die, the legionnaire tells himself. "Climb or topple," says Kean, who fights alone. *Speed up or break your neck* would more or less be Sartre's slogan. This signifies not the absurd frenzy to constantly go faster, but the constant wish, lived quite calmly, to never find oneself "stalling." In my view, this is *the moral wish par excellence*, at least in the formal sense, whatever its strange and difficult contents may be. What a fine Puritan or Jansenist we would have had there, had he been content to practice austerity for its own sake, the way one trains himself to jump higher or to be a better actor [*jouer la comédie*]! But it happens he preferred to put this asceticism to the service of a more fundamental need: the need to act on, to "practice," the world itself [*pratiquer le monde*]. And that is why there are so many of us—even if

92. ["Des rats et des hommes," in *Situations, IV*, p. 40; "Of Rats and Men," in *Situations*, p. 330.]
93. ["Des rats et des hommes," in *Situations, IV*, p. 46; "Of Rats and Men," in *Situations*, p. 336.]
94. ["Des rats et des hommes," in *Situations, IV*, p. 40; "Of Rats and Men," in *Situations*, pp. 330–331.]

less austere in most cases—who can recognize in his attitude the moral exigency [*l'exigence morale*] implied by all commitment.

On the basis of a singular experiment, conducted with some difficulty, this man has succeeded in proposing to us a "psychology" that delivers us from our "me," an "ontology" that is the very condemnation of the illusion of being, and, finally, a "critique of reason" that is a practical philosophy of history, inasmuch as it places itself within Marxism in order to describe the real conditions of all human enterprise. The very rigor of his wish to be is what constrained him first to give himself a personal ethics, and then to surpass it toward an ethics of history, diverting that wish away from the temptation to confuse *the human*, which is our shared need, with either one of its many individual patterns or one of its collective reifications. No doubt this same rigor permitted him to tear himself away from the illusion set up by idealist philosophers and to puzzle over the spirit of action while they were content to impute an action to spirit. To philosophize is certainly not to act. But philosophy can give itself the task of clarifying the real so as to allow human beings—in their capacity as agents of history—to ever increase their control of their own *praxis* within the real, to keep it alive and capable of surpassing its own products. The flesh of history, under the various types of the "*pratico-inert*," appears as the supreme form (not the transformation, but rather the true *incarnation*) of that "contingency" or "facticity" that Sartre first described for us in more explicitly carnal terms.

I maintained eighteen years ago, and I continue to maintain today, that Sartre's philosophy is a moral philosophy and all its virtue for us issues from this. To put it simply: from the initial, existential wish to come into being against all, this philosophy has evolved to the point where it wants to come into being among all, now conceiving man as no more than a chimera in our heads so long as we do not together undertake to invent him. Pretending to justify one's contingent existence in a personal way was indeed madness; wanting to surpass this contingency, along with all others, is realism. If it is true that morality is at once "impossible and necessary,"[95] Sartre's efforts in this domain may well be the most authentic ones undertaken thus far.

How have this realism and this madness articulated themselves in each other? How has Sartre-the-"neurotic" come to merit a "good citizenship prize"? What aided him, or constrained him, to clearly designate the radical *impossibility* of humanity as *the very condition of its possibility*, thereby reintroducing morality into the heart of history, making *praxis* the content of ethics, and charging ethics with the task of maintaining the sense of *praxis*, after rooting both ethics and *praxis* in *need*, in man's animality? These are clearly the

95. [Approximation of a key phrase in an important footnote on morality in *Saint Genet* (Fr.), p. 177; *Saint Genet* (Eng.), p. 186n. The sentences to which Jeanson alludes are quoted above, p. xv, n. 31.]

principal questions a thorough analysis would have to address. At the end of a quite summary exposition I can only indicate the two or three themes on which, in my view, such an inquiry could be fruitfully pursued.

The first theme would be the kind of objective complicity that exists between the situation of Sartre the child—that actor despite himself—and the irreducible overhang [*porte-à-faux*] of our existence from which we all suffer in various ways. For we are well aware that we must make history along with everyone else, and yet that "our" real history is constantly made in our absence. All neuroses are social, and the one described in *The Words* is no exception.[96] They invariably consist of dreaming one's life, of absolutizing it whenever one feels incapable of further living it in relativity. Perhaps such dreams best reveal all the strange relations that may be set up in different cases between our "childhood" and our "maturity." If the mature person rids himself of his childhood fear by his own means, it is because he also inherited those means from his childhood. Neurosis is reassuring; it is a response to the fear of losing oneself. But there are two ways to project oneself into the absolute so as to be assured against such ill fortune: one is to dedicate oneself forever to a passive relationship, either to the absolute of Meaning (religious attitude) or to the absolute of Meaninglessness (absurdist attitude); the other consists in laboriously undertaking some relative enterprise in the name of the Absolute. While the first attitude may be conducive to the psychoanalyst's intervention, the second leaves the subject's own chances intact.

In Sartre's case, taking this second route enhanced his chances. This double phenomenon of being possessed and dispossessed by the Other, by the "course of events," by History, this intimate self-falsification usually discovered only in adulthood, this hard irony of alterity [*l'altérité*] seems to me particularly positive in its results—for us almost as much as for Sartre—inasmuch as it constrained Sartre, starting at age nine, to confront these phenomena within that scaled-down society that is each child's family milieu. I admit having long wondered whether this pioneer and groundbreaker exaggerated the barrenness of the lands history allotted us when he called these troubles *the sickness of this century*. A certain rationalism in me resisted seeing one epoch as "privileged" in this way in relation to others; and that our epoch alone was thus favored seemed to demonstrate a rather faulty subjectivism at the level of history itself. Would not Montaigne or Zola, Saint-Just or the Communards have had grounds for making the same charge? "A century of iron," "our afflic-

96. [It is interesting to note that Sartre later made use of a notion parallel to Jeanson's "social neurosis" throughout the third volume of his three-volume work on Flaubert, *L'Idiot de la famille: Gustave Flaubert de 1821 à 1857* (Paris: Gallimard, 1971–1972). But where Flaubert's "subjective neurosis" was to be understood by Sartre as negatively influencing the "general" or "objective neurosis" of his epoch, Jeanson here understands Sartre's neurosis, or, rather, this neurosis together with Sartre's self-cure and liberation from his neurosis, as having the reverse effect on the social neurosis of Sartre's epoch.]

tions," "our midnight," are the words that come to Sartre when he is concerned to characterize *our epoch*: " 'History' presents few situations more desperate than ours. . . ."[97]

I was wrong. For some years the correctness and the positive character of such a perspective have become increasingly obvious to me. This century has indeed seen the most radical contestation ever inflicted on that eternal alibi of human beings: their "humanism." But the only thing that has been driven to despair is our way of believing in Santa Claus, of imagining that the day has arrived when man has finally been recognized—in the mirror-games played in our more advanced provinces. However much it may sadden us, this despair is healthy. Cornered and forced to own up to the present impossibility of humanity, the only exit left is for each and all of us to ground ourselves on our most exposed need, our most naked demand, on our *pride*, to put it plainly, which is to engage ourselves completely, and without the slightest guarantee, in the work of our faith.

To put this another way—and this would be the second theme of the study—true engagement in reality implies for Sartre, not the rejection of all absolutes, but rather the inversion or reversal of our inescapable relation to the Absolute. For if it is true that we are already *there*, in this world and in this history, we are there for nothing as long as we are content only to *be* there, and the same applies even if this contentment takes the form of dreams of escape. Even if I am situated as much as one could wish and engaged up to my neck, I must still engage *myself*. Were I among those who are truly starving, I would still have to choose between fighting for life or resigning myself to death. But in the name of what can we, who are hardly threatened by hunger, become true revolutionaries? And why should one want to exchange worlds if everything is relative, if there is nothing absolute in our "condition" except its inescapable ending, which is imposed on it from without?

If this neurotic has cured himself it is certainly because of his refusal to "save" himself, to flee, and because he made himself capable of refuting the false solution first offered him. But his enterprise would have remained vacuous *and uninstructive for us* if it had led merely to rejecting this solution and returning him to himself. He has said: "The absolute has departed. What remains are tasks, innumerable. . . ."[98] But from what source would these tasks draw their direction [*sens*] if not from a certain *faith* of which one could not be "cured" without cutting oneself off from others, just as one might initially cut oneself off from them by taking refuge in some *belief*? When Sartre claims to have shown the absolute the door, he must grant that he then let it reenter

97. [J.-P. Sartre, "Réponse à Albert Camus," in *Situations, IV* (Paris: Gallimard 1964), p. 110; "Reply to Albert Camus," in *Situations*, translated by Benita Eisler (New York: George Braziller, 1965), p. 90.]

98. In response to an interview question put by Jacqueline Piatier, "Jean-Paul Sartre s'explique sur *Les Mots*," *Le Monde*, 18 April 1964; "A Long, Bitter, Sweet Madness," translated by Anthony Hartley, *Encounter* 22, no. 6 (June 1964): 61.

by the window, albeit in an altered form, having subjected it to a radical *sub-version*.

The absolute is, henceforth, the human wager. It is a wager on humanity, and, for each human being, it is first of all a wager on himself. It is the choice we can make to determine ourselves through the future—by meeting the demand of a common meaning [*sens*]—and to consider the past only as the ensemble of conditions on which we must base our invention of ourselves. Either this life is nothing, or it must be everything. In being willing to lose it rather than give it over to the absurd, we install an *absolute reference* in the heart of our relative existence, a mooring, and the possibility of a meaning for all of our concrete enterprises. Such is the inescapable postulate of every attitude that would call itself human. Such is the rigorous *unconditionality* of morality; in its name all the systems—and the alienated "moralities" that are their by-products—must be surpassed in the direction of those future human beings whom morality obliges us to invent and whom so many of us are now more or less constrained to produce by the simple need to remain alive. The absolute, in this sense, is not *elsewhere*, no past stands bail in its absence, and no future could ever guarantee it. It is simply our choice to exist, to become ever more present to ourselves and to others.

"What is important in the first place," Sartre tells us, "is the liberation of man."[99] "Whatever the situation may be," he elsewhere asserted, "there is always something to be done." This is what I call *putting the absolute into the present* by wagering that human beings effectively accede to the human once—wherever they may be and whatever the cost—they undertake together to accede to it, at peril to their *lives* (or at least of their ease of living) and in order to give them *meaning*.

Prostrating oneself before the absolute or pretending to be quits with it are equally renunciations of any genuine demand. Sartre has chosen to dialecticize [*dialectiser*] his image of Man by making it depend on the inseparable realization of both himself and others; from this comes the mad optimism of this pessimist and the incredible modesty of his pride. For his morality consists in willing to make himself *capable of man*—capable of anything—and yet *defenseless*, entirely given over to everyone, with nothing in his hands or pockets. By abandoning any relation to the absolute, he would have renounced his very existence, but he supressed only his relation to God: ". . . one rids oneself of a neurosis, one does not cure oneself of oneself."[100] The "*character*" that remained comes, I am quite certain, from an original "imposture." But I also

99. [Piatier interview, *Le Monde*, 18 April 1964; *Encounter* 22 (June 1964); 62. The context is as follows: "It is necessary first that all men become men by the amelioration of their conditions of existence in order that one might elaborate a universal morality. If I start by telling them 'You shall not lie,' political action is no longer possible. What is important in the first place is the liberation of man."]

100. [*Les Mots*, p. 211; *The Words*, p. 254.]

see what he has made of it, and how the proud decision to be the product only of himself has changed into the decision to become a man among other men: "Wholly a man, made from all men, who is equal to any man and whom any man equals."[101] In the part of the world where chance has put us, it is our luck today to have a pride of this order proposed to us as a moral stance [*à titre de morale*] by a man who has been able to recognize in Marxist thought *"the unsurpassable philosophy of our time."*[102]

I know: he has also said he once wanted "to do a morality" [*une morale*] and that he was no longer considering it. But for my part, I firmly believe he still thinks of it, and it will obviously not be what he called a "writers' morality" addressed "only to the privileged few"—whose edification no longer tempts his interest at all. It will be, if I am not mistaken, the real morality of our time and, as such, will issue from both patience and impatience and will be as alien to despair as to any form of illusion, founded on work as much as on faith, playing simultaneously on the possible and the impossible, on what we are and on our refusal to be it, basing itself on the future in order to deny the past, on our demand to realize humanity in order to reject the various reifications as they come. This will be the *moral philosophy* we need in order to conceive *a veritable practice of history* [*une véritable pratique de l'histoire*]. Perhaps it will be recognized in this hasty prefiguration (which Sartre proposed seven years ago in his preface to *The Traitor*, by André Gorz):

> We are no longer beasts altogether, but neither are we men altogether. We have not yet turned to profit that frightful catastrophe that befell some representatives of the animal realm: thought. In short: we shall remain wretched mammalians for a long time to come, for this is the era of rabies, fetishes, and sudden terrors, and universality is no more than a death wish in the bosom of separation and fear. But our world has been changing in recent decades: in the very depths of hatred reciprocity shows itself; even those who take pleasure in outbidding each other on their differences must be willing to hide from themselves a fundamental identity. This new agitation, this modest but stubborn effort to communicate through the incommunicable, is not the insipid and invariably rather simple desire for an inert and already realized universal; it is rather what I shall call the movement of universalization.[103]

Finally, there is his love of life, his zest for life, his *happiness*. "I have always been happy," Sartre declared last year.[104] Unfortunately, a final spark of probity forbids me from giving an exceedingly funny quotation which conveys that

101. [*Les Mots*, p. 213; *The Words*, p. 255.]

102. [J.-P. Sartre, Preface, *Critique de la raison dialectique* (Paris: Gallimard, 1960), p. 9; *Search for a Method*, translated by Hazel E. Barnes (New York: Knopf, 1963), p. xxxiv.]

103. [Reprinted as "Des rats et des hommes," in *Situations, IV*, p. 79; "Of Rats and Men," in *Situations*, p. 369.]

104. Piatier interview, *Le Monde*, 18 April 1964; *Encounter* 22 (June 1964): 62.

this happiness—as the context of the above quotation clearly indicates—was only the happiness of writing and proceeded from his neurotic concern to justify his existence, in service to which Sartre had for thirty years "made an absolute of literature."[105] He has noted as much in *The Words*: "I used to be happy. I have changed. . . . I see clearly, I have lost my illusions. . . . For nearly ten years I have been a man who wakes up . . . and no longer knows what to do with his life."[106] Listening, the other night, to his prodigious adaptation of *The Trojan Women*, how could I fail to recognize the resonance? "Yes, I believed in happiness," or again: "A man must be mad to call himself happy before the last moment of his last day . . . . "[107]

He has changed, to be sure. But he has changed "like everyone else: inside a permanence."[108] And I doubt he has really ceased to be happy. We have seen transformations in his relation to the absolute, in his pride, and even in his recent optimism ("my most intimate phantasmagoria"). Perhaps he has merely exchanged one kind of happiness for another. But I would bet he lives today's happiness as he lived yesterday's: according to the same existential tension, the same continuing need to "work loose" from himself, to tear himself from the inertia of a present that never stops falling back into the past. Avoiding capture by the happy things in life is itself the happiness of existing, whose true taste is always for the future. "Tomorrow, they'll give free shaves."

We should be suspicious of his apparent austerity, of the daily discipline he has always imposed on himself, of the extreme regularity of his schedule: the *anti-physis* has two faces, one calm, the other less so. This diligent worker hides a strange wastrel [*flambeur*] who likes to pit his reality against his future possibilities and who never stops agitating the coals in which he burns, preferring the blaze itself to whatever it consumes. Frantz, the sequestered man of Altona, tells us "I must dope myself. . . . There were thick clouds . . . (*finger on forehead*) . . . there. I'll install a sun in there."[109] Morality and benzedrine; a choice of existence, but also, perhaps, a need to feel himself existing. Of Jacopo Robusti, "the sequestered man of Venice," Sartre tells us: "There is something of the bewildered in this taste for *forcing* [*sic*]. Robusti

105. Piatier interview, *Le Monde*, 18 April 1964; *Encounter* 22 (June 1964): 61. [For the context Jeanson refers to, see this same interview: "What I've regretted in *Nausea* is not having completely put myself at stake in it. I remained outside my hero's malady, preserved by my neurosis, which, through writing, gave me happiness."]

106. *Les Mots*, pp. 210–211; *The Words*, pp. 252–253.]

107. [Sartre, *Les Troyennes* (Paris: Gallimard, 1965), pp. 119–120 (scene 5); *The Trojan Women*, adapted by Jean-Paul Sartre, translated by Ronald Duncan (New York: Vintage Books, 1967), p. 74 (scene 5).]

108. [Piatier interview, *Le Monde*, 18 April 1964; *Encounter* 22 (June 1964): 63.]

109. [Sartre, *Les Séquestrés d'Altona* (Paris: Gallimard, 1960), pp. 103, 104 (act 3); *The Condemned of Altona*, translated by Sylvia and George Leeson (New York: Knopf, 1961), pp. 79, 81 (act 3). Jeanson has altered the order in which these sentences occur in Sartre's text.]

ran against the clock up to his death and one cannot decide whether he was searching for himself through work or fleeing himself by overexertion."[110]

As for Sartre himself, *the positively sequestered man* of an epoch whose contradictions he has chosen to assume, I can hardly imagine myself worrying, were I in his place, about what might be "lost" by continuing to blaze so well. Here, as in many other circumstances, his humor has already cautioned us against such an indiscretion since we have been able to see him solemnly ponder whether, everything considered, he was not playing "whoever loses wins."

May 1965

> What I have just written is false. True. Neither true nor false, like everything one writes about the insane, that is, about men.
>
> —Jean-Paul Sartre, *The Words*

110. ["Le Séquestré de Venise," in *Situations, IV* (Paris: Gallimard, 1964), p. 296; "The Prisoner of Venice," in *Situations*, translated by Benita Eisler (New York: George Braziller, 1965), p. 8.]

Index